# EARTH PATTERNS
## ESSAYS in LANDSCAPE ARCHAEOLOGY

# EARTH PATTERNS
## ESSAYS in LANDSCAPE ARCHAEOLOGY

*Edited by*

William M. Kelso

*and*

Rachel Most

*The glory of the garden lies
in more than meets the eye.*

Rudyard Kipling

University Press of Virginia
*Charlottesville and London*

THE UNIVERSITY PRESS OF VIRGINIA

Copyright © 1990 by the Rector and Visitors
of the University of Virginia

*First published 1990*

Library of Congress Cataloging-in-Publication Data
Earth patterns : archaeology of early American and ancient gardens and
landscapes / edited by William M. Kelso and Rachel Most.
  p.  cm.
  Revised versions of papers presented at the 1986 Conference on Land-
scape Archaeology held at the University of Virginia and Monticello,
Va., and sponsored by the Thomas Jefferson Memorial
Foundation, Inc., and the Univ. of Virginia's Dept. of Continuing
Education, Dept. of Anthropology, School of Architecture, and Dept.
of Art History.
  Includes index.
  ISBN 0-8139-1239-3
  1. Archaeology—Congresses.  2. Landscape assessment—Congresses.
3. Landscape assessment—Virginia—Congresses.  4. Garden
archaeology—Congresses.  5. Garden archaeology—Virginia—
Congresses.  6. Virginia—Antiquities—Congresses.  I. Kelso,
Willian M.  II. Most, Rachel.  III. Conference on Landscape
Archaeology (1986 : University of Virginia and Monticello, Va.)
IV. Thomas Jefferson Memorial Foundation, Inc.
CC75.7.E37  1990
930.1'028—dc20                                         89-35142
                                                           CIP

Printed in the United States of America

*To Gary Shapiro*

# CONTENTS

# PREFACE

In the mid-1980s it seemed that enough unpublished archaeological studies of cultural landscapes had been undertaken in America and the classical world to foster a "first-ever" conference on both ancient and modern landscape archaeological research. Consequently, the 1986 Conference on Landscape Archaeology was held at the University of Virginia and Thomas Jefferson's Monticello. It was sponsored by the Thomas Jefferson Memorial Foundation, Incorporated, and the University of Virginia's Department of Continuing Education, Department of Anthropology, School of Architecture, and Department of Art History. Most of the essays in this volume grew out of presentations at that meeting. Shortsighted land use and landscape preservation are, of course, critical worldwide problems today. It is our hope that learning from this volume what some of the landscape was will, in some positive measure, help determine what the landscape will become.

We would like to thank Professors Malcolm Bell, John Dobbins, Jeffrey Hantman, and Stephen Plog for their help in organizing the conference. We wish to sincerely thank the Thomas Jefferson Memorial Foundation, Incorporated, particularly Daniel P. Jordan, Director, for its support of this volume. We would like to also thank the Richard and Caroline T. Gwathmey Memorial Trust, Robin L. and David W. Munn, and the Center for Historic Preservation, Mary Washington College, for their financial support. Thanks also to the hard work of the many authors of the essays in this volume, and for their patience.

William M. Kelso and Rachel Most

# EARTH PATTERNS

## Essays in Landscape Archaeology

# PROLOGUE

# LANDSCAPES AS CULTURAL STATEMENTS

## James Deetz

At the southern tip of the African continent, one finds a little piece of England. With its squared fields, divided by hedgerows or stone walls, the resemblance to the moors of Derbyshire is no less than startling. Of course, the topography helps, rolling hills and deeper valleys here and there, but there is more to it than that, for it was not always so. The Albany district, around the frontier town of Grahamstown in the eastern Cape Province of South Africa, was settled by no less than 5,000 English immigrants in 1820. What they encountered bore little resemblance to the home they had left, and high expectations gave way to deep disillusionment. Where fifty acres might have sufficed to run a certain number of sheep in England, five times that amount was needed in this new home. Arid, hot, and covered with thick bushes of thorns, aloe, spekboom, and euphorbia, it must have seemed terribly intimidating. Yet through perseverance they prevailed and re-created the landscape they had left with remarkable precision in many parts of the district. This was not the case for all parts, however, and even now, when one moves from the cooked landscape of the 1820 settlers to the remnants of the raw bush, the contrast is spectacular. The previous landscape served well as browsing ground for the cattle of the indigenous Xhosa herders, as it does even today, but for the English settlers it could in no way suffice for the needs of their agricultural pursuits. So, in creating a landscape through making it useful to them, the settlers at the same time were making a powerful cultural statement, latently symbolic, that impresses to this day. Add to this landscape symmetrical three-over-three I houses, and one knows immediately that one is in the presence of English culture, thousands of miles from its source.

The cultural landscape is such an all-pervasive quantity that one wonders why it has not received the attention that archaeologists normally pay to other types of material culture. Of the three dimensions of archaeology (form, time, and space), the spatial dimension seems to have been approached somewhat discontinuously. Households and communities have received their share of attention, and settlement archaeology has a long tradition, but the space between houses and between communities has attracted far less attention, yet it is the very connective tissue that gives houses and communities their proper context. Gardens, fields, trees, roads, and walls all structure the environment according to the set of cultural rules of their creators.

We can guess at some of the reasons for this relative lack of attention. First, there is the implicit definition of a site, as Albert Spaulding once said, as "a place where an archaeologist digs." It follows from this not entirely tongue-in-cheek definition that archaeologists dig where there is a visible sign of human activity, and this means communities, cemeteries, ceremonial centers, butchering sites, and other such places. But to approach the landscape as a feature involves a kind of archaeology that we are simply not accustomed to. Years ago, a group of us at Plymouth invented something that we called "minimal archaeology"--digging where there was no visible evidence of past human presence. Again, we were not entirely serious, but there was more than a grain of logic in the concept. The discussion arose after we had dug a test pit well off to the side of an early seventeenth-century house site and discovered the better part of a mid-eighteenth-century salt-glaze stoneware tea saucer. That saucer got to this location through some human agency, and it left us wondering how much other material is scattered over the landscape in a thin veneer, representing activities that fall below the normal threshold of archaeological visibility. The landscape is just that from the perspective of field techniques; as William Kelso says in this volume, "*Digging* the twenty or so acres considered the most significant part of the landscape that was visible from the house could not be done in one person's lifetime." Aware of the problem, Kelso devised a set of powerful techniques that permitted the study of the landscape, but his placing of digging in italics obviously means that traditional approaches will never suffice.

A second reason for the status of landscape archaeology is related to the first; it is a question of scale. Landscapes are big. They surround us and stretch to the horizon. As such, they can be taken for granted; they lack the specific locational focus of the more usual archaeological features. It is easy to imagine a place on earth without houses but not one without a landscape, cultural or natural. It is the cultural modification of the landscape that forms the highest level of mediation between the natural and the cultural, against which all other mediating material culture is projected. So it is clearly very important to take landscape into account, as the chapters in this volume amply demonstrate.

*Landscape* is, however, a rather general, nonspecific term. For the purposes of this discussion, however, we can take the word to mean the total terrestrial context in which archaeological study is pursued and use *cultural landscape* to denote that part of the terrain which is modified according to a set of cultural plans. These terms embrace the entire range of terrain from the house lot, the smallest and the most frequently studied, through gardens and field systems to truly large units of analysis, entire regions that bear the imprint of a shared set of values. It is also important to distinguish between the archaeology of the landscape and the archaeology of behavior on a scale that transcends the strictly local--wide-ranging hunting and military engagements being appropriate examples.

Obviously, landscape modification can entail functions strictly technomic as well as those with social and ideological dimensions. But there is a danger in overly separating these types of functions, for however technomic the fields of the 1820 settlers may have been (after all, they were created in the first place to plant crops), once established, they were also a powerful, though probably passive, statement of cultural identity, to be seen and understood by others as such. The classic village-centered three-field system of the English champion country is a visible statement of an all-encompassing social order, for it is only through the use of individuals strips in shared fields that farmers can both till the soil and reside in a close, face-to-face community. If one's landholding is continuous and one resides upon it, there is no way to have closely adjacent neighbors.

Of course, there are components of the landscape that come into existence for reasons other than strictly practical and utilitarian. Decorative gardens are probably the most common examples, usually made for enjoyment outside and as a source of cut flowers for inside decoration, such gardens gave a purely social function. One can live without them, but they add a graceful note to life which enhances one's position in the social world. On occasion, however, gardens can have symbolic significance as well, as we learn from Leone and Shackel's chapter, when they are used to affirm in a more direct way the social position and power relations of and between members of the community. In a similar manner, the cultural landscapes of blacks and whites, as described in the chapter by Dell Upton, show us how buildings and landscape combine to affirm and perpetuate a set of relations between very different sectors of Virginia society in the eighteenth century.

People, then, use the landscape, shaped in a planned and ordered manner, for purposes ranging from food production through formal design of the environment to the more or less explicit statement of their position in the world. There is another kind of study that falls within the definition of landscape archaeology, but in this case, the landscape is the setting for actions played out over an extensive area. The landscape is not necessarily modified in this case, although it might be, but the archaeologist's interest is directed at material evidence that is thinly distributed but highly significant. The study of battlefields is an excellent example of this kind of research. It has long been thought that little can be learned archaeologically from battlefields, beyond the excavation of earthworks such as those at Yorktown. However, in a recent Ph.D. dissertation, Richard Fox (1988) has shown that there is much more to the study of battlefields than military architecture. By conducting a very careful, fine-grained surface survey of the site of "Custer's Last Stand" and recovering spent shell casings, bullets, and other hardware, Fox has been able to reconstruct movements in an engagement which left no surviving members of the Seventh Cavalry, although there were numerous Indian witnesses. Because shell casings bear firing marks that are unique to each weapon, it was possible to reconstruct the movement of individual troopers. Bullets in concentrations reflected areas to which heavy fire was directed. Combining these lines of evidence, spread over a one-square-mile area, Fox was able to reconstruct a version of the battle which is significantly different from that which was previously assumed. In brief, the gallant last stand that we know from tradition was instead a complete disintegration of demoralized troopers, who bunched up and lost all formation. Furthermore, shell casing analysis showed that only a small fraction had been pried from the breech, giving the lie to the commonly accepted belief that the defeat resulted partly from jamming ammunition. Perhaps most significantly, the study showed that the reports given by the Indian witnesses were far closer to the truth than people had previously assumed. Battlefield archaeology of this kind is a new area of study, and if the Little Big Horn analysis is in any way typical, it would seem that other such sites will also yield important results.

A large segment of urban archaeology also involves the landscape in a very real sense. It is by now commonly accepted by urban archaeologists that fill is an artifact in its own right. It follows that the extensive cutting and filling that characterizes the growth of modern cities is nothing less than landscape modification. The late Roger Olmsted's study of the development of San Francisco was very revealing in this respect. Tops were sliced from elevations and used to fill declivities that were sometimes as deep as 40 feet. Landfill into bays and coves is another example of such landscape modification, leading to the location of the 1849 Gold Rush fleet beneath the streets of the modern city of San Francisco. The urban landscape, then, is nothing less than the end product of large-scale manipulation of masses of fill obtained from locations near and far. Much of the fill encountered during the excavation of a portion of South Main Street in Providence, Rhode Island, was brought from

Attleboro, Massachusetts.  In such contexts, it is vitally important to determine from where the fill was obtained so that its artifactual context is not seriously misconstrued.

Gardens, landfills, and fields are all landscapes created by people who desired some specific and quite explicit end result.  It is most likely that the cultural landscape is the largest and most pervasive artifact with which we as archaeologists must deal, yet much remains to be done, and much thinking about the ways to do it must be indulged.  In many ways, this is a very positive thing, because it forces us out of the traditional 5-foot square mentality by raising new questions that must be answered through new and different field techniques and analytical methods.  It is a challenge which is both provocative and exciting in its anticipation.

The chapters in this volume constitute an important contribution to the archaeological study of the landscape and cover a wide range of subjects in time and space.  They will serve well the purpose for which they have been written, to call attention to an area of inquiry that has been largely neglected in the past.  In so doing, the study of the landscape will be given its proper place in the field of archaeology.

## References Cited

Fox, R. 1988.  Discerning history through archaeology: The Custer battle.  Ph.D. dissertation, Department of Archaeology, University of Calgary.

*I. Virginia Country Gardens and Landscapes*

# 1

# LANDSCAPE ARCHAEOLOGY AT THOMAS JEFFERSON'S MONTICELLO

## William M. Kelso

"Why are there practically no eighteenth-century paintings of the Virginia landscape?" mused the group of scholars assembled in Monticello's dome room to hear Rhys Isaac comment on his extraordinary book entitled *The Transformation of Virginia* (1982). After some floundering, the consensus answer was simply: "there was not much to paint." Insomuch as the landscape artists of the day were interested in capturing the creative accomplishments of garden and landscape designers, they must have found little of interest in what, even after almost two centuries of settlement, they saw in the Virginia countryside. Indeed, as late as the 1790s, Virginia was primarily still deep virgin forests.

> The road from Hampton to York-Town runs along through woods. The patches of cleared land are yet rare and inconsiderable. . . . the road from York-Town to Williamsburg is in many parts more agreeable. . . . [But a] long tract of woodland is here also to be passed where no cultivation is to be seen. . . . [In the] South-Mountains that Monticello is situated . . . Mr. Jefferson's house commands one of the most extensive prospects you can meet with. . . . [But the] disproportion existing between the cultivated lands and those which are still covered with forests as ancient as the globe, is at present too great. . . . the grandest and most extensive prospect is ever destitute of an embellishment requisite to render it completely beautiful. (La Rochefoucauld-Liancourt 1800:37, 44, 45, 137, 140)

Apparently in 1796 no formal landscape architecture of note existed between Hampton and the top of the Blue Ridge Mountains, at least along the land route that the duc de La Rochefoucauld-Liancourt traveled (fig. 1.1), or it seemed to this traveler, whose frame of reference was the breathtaking countryside of France. The duke predicted that when Monticello was finished, the house would deserve to be ranked with the best mansions of France and England; by the same token, one can conclude that he would have given the same high rating to Jefferson's landscape design of twenty years later.

Indeed, almost everyone would agree with La Rochefoucauld-Liancourt: Thomas Jefferson was a remarkably unique and talented man. But precisely what he accomplished that most proves his genius is the subject of much debate. Many who know the building and landscape of his Virginia mountaintop home would argue that above all else Jefferson was most exceptional as an architect and a landscape designer. Indeed, it was at Monticello in 1769 that the fledgling designer began his campaign of over one-half century to convert his little mountain into what many critics recognize as one of America's most sophisticated architectural and landscape designs. Creating that living space on a mountain was not easy;

Figure 1.1. Hampton Roads to the Blue Ridge Mountains ("A map of the inhabited part of Virginia . . .", drawn by Peter Fry and Peter Jefferson, 1751)

lack of water and access to the hilltop were constant problems, and making the sloping ground convenient for gardens, orchards, vineyards, dependent buildings, and roadways presented engineering problems of no small consequence. But bit by bit, Jefferson's years of effort to create his *ferme ornée*, or ornamental farm, left a heavy imprint on the Monticello landscape. Beginning with the leveling of the mountaintop to create the platform for the house and attached dependencies and essentially ending with the completion in 1814 of the moatlike ha-ha barrier surrounding the west lawn, Jefferson steadily made the land complement his architectural essay on the mountain.

As vital as it was to the success of his buildings, the landscape design had become only dimly visible and in some cases was completely gone by the time the Thomas Jefferson Memorial Foundation was formed in 1923 to "hold, preserve, and maintain Monticello as a national memorial." Repair and conservation of the house, basic maintenance of the landscape, and finding a way to pay the mortgage were the immediate concerns of the newly formed Monticello preservation group. For years no major restoration work was attempted on the landscape except for the creative effort of the Garden Club of Virginia to redesign the west lawn garden in 1939. But by the late 1970s the house restoration program neared completion, making it possible to focus attention on the landscape. The survival of detailed plans and notes in Jefferson's hand of the road system, roadside plantings, layout of the vegetable garden, orchards, and vineyards, and specifications for scores of ancillary buildings including a decorative garden pavilion, craft shops, slave quarters, and utilitarian outbuildings rendered the prospects of accurately redefining the lost Jeffersonian landscape at Monticello exceptionally bright. The success of the archaeological landscape research at Carter's Grove and Kingsmill plantations in Virginia and the maturing of the process of historical archaeology also strongly suggested that archaeological study could aid in the restoration efforts at Monticello, especially when conducted in concert with the unusually complete Jefferson drawings and specifications (Kelso 1984a; 1984b). Consequently, beginning in June 1979, archaeological excavations began in earnest to define Monticello's designed landscape sequentially by uncovering the remains of the roundabout road system, a ha-ha and a paling fence, a domestic, utilitarian, and industrial complex of buildings, and terraced gardens, orchards, and vineyards (Kelso and Sanford 1985) (figs. 1.2 and 1.3).

The problems attendant to archaeological work of this scale were challenging. Anyone familiar with the painfully exacting and tedious nature of the archaeological discipline would recognize that *digging* the twenty or so acres considered the most significant part of the landscape that was visible from the house could not be done in one person's lifetime. The obvious approach was to consider every possible way that relatively small test trenches could define the nature, extent, and time period of the major landscape elements without having to uncover them entirely. Fortunately, as a result of key documents, the eroded but obviously man-shaped topography, and aerial photographs taken through the years, the decision of where to test was not difficult. Also, previous experience on other early American landscape sites proved that tests made into terraces and along fence lines can be the most productive ways to redefine old designs. The redefinition of boundaries, in this case terraces and the lines of fences, in turn can reveal the overall shape of enclosed space much the same way that the foundations of buildings reveal architectural design. Where changes in the topography end and where fence lines are interrupted for gates provide key clues as to how space was divided within an enclosure. So the decision was made to hand dig tests into the various terraces, particularly the slope located below a major original axial road known as Mulberry Row, and to proceed downhill into an artificial leveled platform, then to excavate through the remnant of what was assumed to be a stone retaining wall built by Jefferson's overseer Edmund Bacon sometime between 1806 and 1809 (correspondence between Jefferson and Bacon). Additionally, machine-dug tests could be made in artifact-free areas, particularly on the south slope to reveal the remains of eroded terraces or patterned locations of disturbed soil that might suggest where the orchard trees once grew in Jefferson's experimental orchard/vineyard. After these rather confined tests, plans were made to trace the line of the fence shown to have spanned the spaces between a number of outbuildings along the upper edge of the garden at the brow of the first terrace and to open an excavation area (50 feet by 50 feet) large enough to expose any orchard tree planting holes assumed to have been spaced at 25-foot intervals. Other goals and methods included the machine removal of two modern parking lots (one of them covering a 300-foot section of Mulberry Row and the site of three servant houses) after hand testing for paving material, machine removal of the upper 8 to 10 inches of plowed soil along the assumed course of the eastern section of the first roundabout, cross trenches along the assumed course of the ha-ha ditch, and hand excavation in the yard on the north and south sides of the house. Eleven of the Mulberry Row building sites were to be studied. It is fair to say that all of these test and area excavations, a total of eight years of research, revealed either some faint clues or obvious remnants of the landscape elements suggested by Jefferson's drawing and notes or uncovered something otherwise unknown (Kelso and Sanford 1985).

Continuous trenching along the course of the garden fence shown on the 1809 survey plat uncovered lines of backfilled fence postholes detectable by observing discoloration of

Figure 1.2. Aerial view of Monticello, 1934

Figure 1.3. Aerial view of Monticello, 1988

the soil, finding concentrations of stones that once shored the posts, or locating decayed or surviving bases of the main supporting posts themselves. A major surprise in this process was to find that three and possibly four fences once spanned the same space at different times. It became a major challenge to sort out which fence line belonged to Jefferson's first garden and even beyond that, which fence line was built to protect the terraced garden of approximately 1809 to 1826, the major period of interest. The complex stratigraphy along the Mulberry Row fence line and the long period of time over which Jefferson was building and changing fences leave some question about precisely determining the nature of the garden barriers at any one time. But a relatively tight chronology could be determined by looking carefully at the dates of artifacts that happened into the backfill of postholes when the fence was erected and by determining which fence line posthole had been disturbed by another and therefore a later hole. Once the chronology was sorted out, the next goal was to locate points where the interval between posts narrowed from the usual 9- to 10-foot spacing, providing clues to gate locations. In the fence line we began to refer to as the 1809 line, none could be found. However, at a point immediately to the south of the all-weather passageway from the house, two larger postholes were found, and these were assumed to have formed a gateway. A reference to the garden gate seemed to confirm that one and only one gate indeed existed (Bear 1967:12, 87). In all, the excavation traced over 1,000 feet of the likely 1809 fence line (Kelso 1988).

Jefferson also established border beds in his platform garden below the slope along Mulberry Row (Kimball 1968:Figure 56) (fig. 1.4). Digging there revealed that a considerable amount of erosion had taken place since the "terras" (Jefferson's term for the slope) was created, filling over the border bed and preserving its outline. Along the buried border bed just below the garden gate, a line of brickbats had survived, marking the edge of the original garden layout. The alignment of bricks established a datum point with which we could begin to relate Jefferson's platform garden notes and sketches directly back to the modern lay of the land. Other key datum points emerged from removal of the plowed soil on the platform itself, namely, a central east-west change in elevation in alignment with the end of one of the buried border beds. However, a long continuous trench along the platform quickly determined that very little or nothing remained of the outline of the planting beds and walkways shown or described in Jefferson's notes. The absence of paving material in the areas where one would expect walkways

Figure 1.4. Evidence of a border bed (foreground) and terrace (right) at subsoil level on the vegetable garden platform

seemed to indicate that paths were merely of dirt or more likely of grass, as a visitor described one of them (Smith 1906:68).

Excavation uncovered two other key elements of the garden plan: the 1,000-foot-long stone retaining wall along the south edge of the platform and the foundations of a building thought to be the remains of the "temple at the center of the long walk" (Nichols 1961). The stone wall had acted as a barrier to hold the soil removed from the original slope as the leveled platform was created. Because the original slope was itself uneven, the wall varied in height to retain the garden platform fill. In some places the wall stood 11 feet high. At the higher points, the wall had to be constructed in tiers. This original tiered construction was not immediately perceptible from the archaeological evidence because much of the stone had been removed in the late nineteenth century. It was not until the entire span of the 1,000-foot-long wall ruins could be studied together that the patterns in the rubble stood out. Such a viewing was only possible from photographs, and overlapping stereo photos were taken of the wall from a consistent distance overhead (fig. 1.5). After gaining this perspective, it is clear that wherever the original stone mason had to build above chest high, he had to create a platform or tier on which to stand.

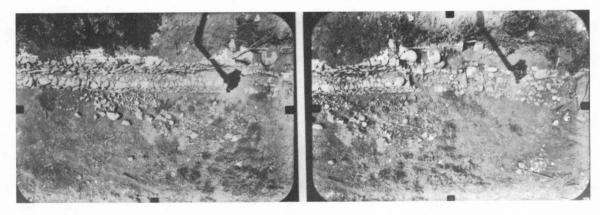

Figure 1.5. Stereo pair photographs of a section of the tiered garden wall

A stone and brick foundation uncovered at the east-west center point of the stone garden wall left little doubt that a square brick building once crowned one of the wall's highest points (fig. 1.6). Specifications in Jefferson's hand in 1811 describe a brick pavilion with a pyramidal roof and a Chinese railing to be built at the center of the long walk in the garden. Excavation uncovered brick rubble and mortar below the foundation, apparently debris scattered there by a storm which destroyed the building in the 1820s (Gray 1968:467). The archaeological evidence and Jefferson's precise specifications for the pavilion guided reconstruction of the building.

One of the most important elements of Jefferson's landscape design was his roundabout road system. Before the archaeological research, some of the road traces were still visible and in service, but other parts had disappeared from view. The roads became the focus of research efforts after the garden study, and like the examination of the wall ruins, the excavation of the roadbeds provided the initial grading required by reconstruction (fig. 1.7). Plats and maps indicated as precisely as documents can the course of the first roundabout before any digging began. Removal of a parking lot revealed a stone paving and curb and

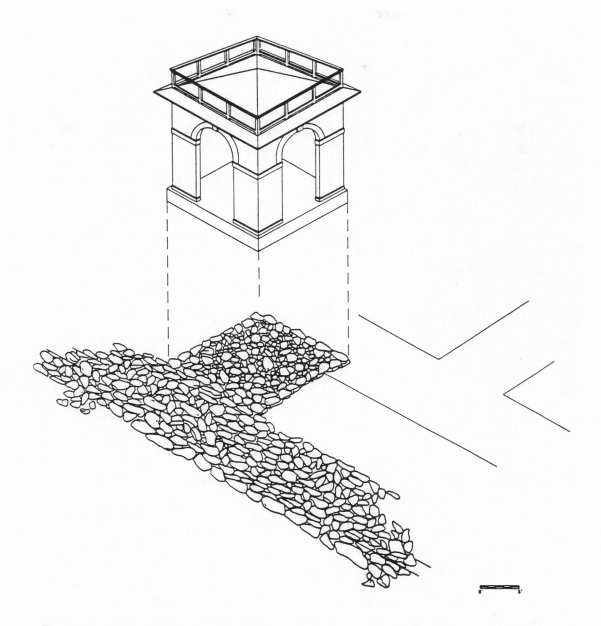

Figure 1.6. Archaeological plan of ruins of garden wall and pavilion foundation and conjectural pavilion reconstruction

what appeared to be a survey stone marked with a deep chisel cut and an X. This marker made it possible to tie Jefferson's surveys to the modern landscape; resurveys of the roadways consistently closed within 6 inches of the marked stone. However, the problem of sorting maps of what Jefferson had already constructed from his plans for the future was compounded by the fact that in certain areas the roads were likely mere traces in the dirt, leaving little or no archaeological evidence to define their course. Nonetheless, machine removal of plow zone soil did manage to locate soil stains where trees once grew beside the

Figure 1.7. Rough gravel paving, stone curbing, and apparent Jefferson-period marked survey stone

road. That effort uncovered a pattern of tree holes on 25-foot centers 18 feet apart located along the northeast course of the roundabout basically matching one of the Jefferson plans. In one area north of the house the trees roughly formed that pattern, and a series of backfilled wagon ruts seemed to exist between the tree holes. The tree stains were so visible that root cavities could be excavated. One of the excavated spaces was filled with plaster to produce a casting of the root (fig. 1.8); the documents suggested that Jefferson's roundabout trees were primarily honey locusts, which have a deep taproot not unlike the casting. A combination of the tree location pattern, the ruts, and the plans strongly suggested the path of the road.

Another archaeological feature which indirectly defined the first roundabout was the backfilled ha-ha ditch paralleling the roadway west of the house. The ditch maintained a consistent elevation, like the road, and was about 16 feet (or about one surveyor's chain length) from the road (as was recognized by Kurt Gloeckner during his survey for the possible route for the restored roundabout). The ha-ha barrier traced a 500-yard course from the north office west to a right-angle turn at the roundabout to end below the south pavilion (fig. 1.9). The discovery and relatively good visibility of the ha-ha made it possible to trace the western half of the first roundabout. The ha-ha was described in 1823 as a ditch with earth piled on each side covered with wooden rails as if a fence had fallen across it, a description not unlike a modern cattle guard (Betts 1944:533; Hooper 1823; Bacon to Jefferson, 24 Feb. 1809). However, in the area of the north office yard, fence postholes of two time periods were found at a consistent distance from the backfilled ha-ha ditch, suggesting that a fence and the ha-ha stood at the same time, defeating the purpose of a ha-ha--to protect the designed landscape without resorting to visible barriers that would interrupt the view. In fact, the overseer Bacon wrote Jefferson that if the dirt from digging the ha-ha ditch were thrown on one side only, a fence built on top of the resulting mound would require only half the wood to stand high enough to protect the planted areas inside (Bacon to Jefferson, 24 Feb. 1809). It may be that Jefferson agreed to Bacon's ditch/fence combination, which, judging from the presence of an occasional machine cut nail in the backfill, lasted until approximately 1830.

In 1783 Jefferson either planned to construct or constructed a circular road for a carriage turnaround just north of the north dependencies (Kimball 1968:fig. 34). The approximately 100-foot-diameter circular turnaround was to be lined with a fence, and along the inner circle trees were to be planted. The turnaround was to connect with a road along the east front ellipse and to tie into the first roundabout below. Considerable excavation in that area failed to find any evidence. However, to the west near the north office, the ha-ha ditch disappeared for a space of 14 feet, ample room for a carriage to pass through enroute to the west lawn. While it is clear that the 1783 plan does not show a turnaround exit at the gap point, the ha-ha construction and its related fence both seem to honor it. The significance of the apparent gate is unclear. Where were the coaches or wagons going? The obvious point of entry for the house is on the east, directly into the formal entrance hall. Visitor accounts invariably describe arrival at the east front. Perhaps the ha-ha gate was used by certain special visitors, family members, or maybe Jefferson himself to get to the west portico entrance. In any event, other than the carriage gate to the west front, archaeological evidence for a turnaround on the north side is lacking; no obvious paving material was found and no pattern of tree stains or fence lines dating to Jefferson's time appeared.

Figure 1.8. Finished root casting of a tree cavity along the first roundabout

The location of another feature, the terminus of a conduit or drainage tunnel coming from the north privy, may indirectly suggest the existence of the carriage road as well. The stone-lined tunnel ends at approximately the point where Jefferson's plan shows an upper access road entering the carriage turnaround. The tunnel was found to have silted up with clay containing a considerable amount of early to mid-nineteenth-century garbage and trash. It appears that when the drain was still open, this waste material washed out onto the hillside and probably the carriage road surface. While it may seem strange to purposely drain waste onto a road, descriptions and sketches of the late eighteenth and early nineteenth century make it clear that so-called roads in Virginia were often merely treeless corridors in the wilderness. In rainy seasons, they were nothing but mud baths. The Monticello roundabouts must have been just as informal, and it is little wonder that an engineered drainage system probably did not exist. That being the case, it is also little wonder that after the roads were no longer used, erosion and vegetation quickly erased them from view.

The privy outlet was not the only blight on the landscape. Excavations quickly proved that the north carriage turnaround area and south yard below the kitchen were once paved with domestic trash and garbage, at least from the 1770s until the late nineteenth century. There was no attempt to formalize these areas; they were the work yards below the working dependencies and therefore very much the practical side of the ornamental farm. They would have been in full view from the house and apparently stood in contradiction to the formal east and west lawns. Excavations also leave little doubt that the walk to the garden led

Figure 1.9. Overhead view of the ha-ha ditch and gate in the north stable yard

directly through the littered kitchen yard directly across another very visible eyesore: Mulberry Row, with its log servants' houses, craft buildings, and utilitarian outbuildings.

In 1796 Jefferson made a precise map of the buildings at Monticello for insurance purposes (Kimball 1968:Figure 136). On that document he located and described in detail outbuildings located along Mulberry Row, in all a total of nineteen craft buildings, storage buildings, other utilitarian structures, and servants' houses. There is no doubt from the descriptions that the structures were rather crudely built, but they were apparently "better than most [others in Virginia] but striking a contrast to the palace that stood so near" (Smith 1906:68). Excavation of ten of these buildings and the discovery of earlier, cruder ones indicate that a main street of inexpensive vernacular structures stood there (fig. 1.10). The excavations also clearly revealed that the buildings were surrounded by yards containing decades of accumulated garbage and trash--not a particularly aesthetic scene. The completion of the dependency wings of the house must have made many of the Mulberry Row buildings obsolete, and by 1809 some of the log houses on Mulberry Row were abandoned (Jefferson to Bacon, 27 Feb. 1809). It is possible that a stone house constructed in 1809 to replace a log washhouse was part of Jefferson's plan to upgrade Mulberry Row by getting rid of the wooden houses when he constructed more aesthetic replacements (James Dinsmore to Jefferson, 24 Feb. 1809). Indeed, the largest of the cabins, found to have had the most organic yard, seems to have an ending occupation date of about 1800. On the other hand, one of three of the smallest and crudest cabins continued in use as late as approximately 1820. Thus, the Mulberry Row slave quarters remained less than a positive contribution to a formal landscape scheme throughout Jefferson's lifetime.

But of more negative prominence still must have been the industrial area located at the western end of Mulberry Row. Excavations there indicate that the blacksmith's shop and attached nailery addition were mere sheds supported by posts anchored in the ground with no formal foundations. Post buildings are one of the cheapest forms of construction, and some may have had a very crude and impermanent appearance. Records and diagnostic artifacts both indicate that these buildings stood for a considerable period of time, from 1793 to possibly as late as 1819. Thus, throughout Jefferson's tenure, it can be safely concluded that the Mulberry Row buildings and yards made a jarring impact on the Monticello landscape.

Beyond the excavation of the architectural elements of the landscape (i.e., building foundations, artifacts, paving, terraces, and fence lines), several other scientific techniques were employed to find out more about historical plant materials. Soil screening in a flotation device recovered seeds from two sealed contexts in the border beds of the garden and in an ash layer found in the backfill material in a backfilled storage cellar. The border bed contained only a weed grass, but the dry-well ash, which probably came from the first kitchen fireplace, contained carbonized sorghum, watermelon, corn, peaches, and pokeberry, which may have been used to make dye. Of course, these samples were not as informative as Jefferson's detailed garden book, which lists over 400 varieties of plants and trees that he grew on the mountain (Betts 1944). Still, the recovery of the plant materials lends an unusual degree of credibility to reconstruction and recreation.

Jefferson also planned to plant a series of grass fields along the first roundabout. Soil samples were taken in that area to correlate the records with any surviving evidence of plants. The soil is now being studied for its opal phytoliths. The analysis is incomplete, but there seems to be enough of an unusual count of grass phytoliths to suggest that detailed study could prove successful. Pollen analyses gave mixed results. Pollen counts from the border bed of the garden were considered too low to be of statistical value. Pollen in the fill in the ha-ha was also relatively low but not valueless. However, the cost weighed against the chances of learning more about what was not recorded by Jefferson did not seem to make a thorough study worthwhile.

Figure 1.10. Scattered foundations of servants' houses at the southeastern end of Mulberry Row

Experiments with scientifically establishing chronology, specifically archaeomagnetic dating of burned clay, also had mixed results. Samples from the fire pit in the smokehouse/ dairy building along Mulberry Row suggested that the last fire burned there approximately 1820 ±20 years (Robert duBois, personal communication, 1982-86). This seems logical given the fact that a smokehouse was established in the house dependencies during the first decade of the nineteenth century, perhaps rendering the Mulberry Row smokehouse obsolete. But dating burned clay in an apparently fire-razed slave house at the eastern end of Mulberry Row proved unsuccessful.

Remote sensing of buried archaeological deposits also gave equally mixed results. In one case measuring soil resistivity suggested buried deposits where documents proved that a slave quarter once stood, although that technique missed similar building remains nearby. But in the last analysis, the use of soil resistivity at Monticello must remain suspect, judging from the fact that testing of the 19-foot-deep dry-well site showed no change in soil density whatsoever.  False-color aerial infrared photography failed to show worthwhile vegetation growth variation over buried archaeological features as well.  While the photos did show vivid patterns over modern septic tanks and drain fields, major Jefferson-period landscape features that subsequent excavations proved to be quite extensive were not detected before digging.

Few but significant garden-related artifacts were recovered.  Fragments of four salt-glazed stoneware bottomless pots were found in fill along the bank of the platform vegetable garden, almost certainly pieces of sea kale pots (used to keep light from plants) Jefferson ordered from Richard Randolph's pottery near Richmond in 1821 (Edmund Peyton to Jefferson, 29 March 1821).  Fragments of decorative flowerpots were also found, including a classical-inspired French earthenware vessel and a salt-glazed stoneware German *blumenkübel* (figs. 1.11 and 1.12).

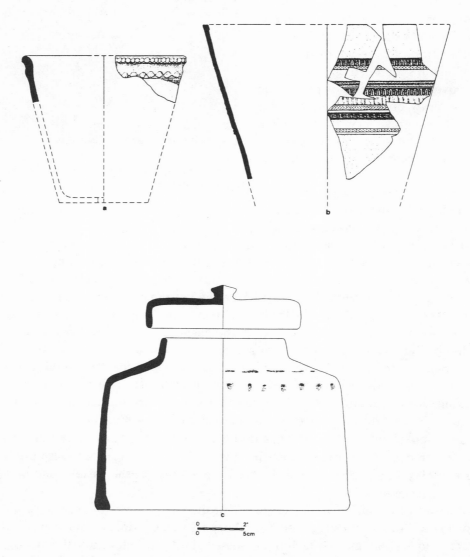

Figure 1.11.  Fragments of garden ceramics: (a) coarse earthenware, (b) terra cotta, and (c) salt-glazed stoneware sea kale pot

Figure 1.12. Fragments of an eighteenth-century spring-molded gray salt-glazed stoneware *blumenkübel*, or flowerpot, from excavations near or in the Monticello ha-ha

While all serious researchers must admit that many things about the landscape of the past are forever gone and unknowable, archaeological research in concert with historical research at Monticello was able to recapture a good measure of the elements of Jefferson's evolving landscape design. And in the process it became clear that the archaeological perspective offers a fresh interpretation of the man as well as the land. One only has to read the preamble to the Declaration of Independence to know how idealistic Thomas Jefferson could be. Yet his dreams did know bounds; his training as a farmer taught him the practicalities of life. Jefferson's pragmatic dreaming is evident in his Monticello architecture as well as his mountaintop landscape design. It is clear that the cut-and-paste design of the house blends the classical ideal with the realities of native materials and the accomplishment of craftsmanship with unskilled labor. So, too, in looking at the landscape elements and scaling them next to the plans and concepts left to us in the records, it is equally clear that while he was ever striving for the ideal ornamental farm, certain realities of time, labor, topography, and the economic, political, and social realities of Jefferson's own era forced him to accept a good deal less. For instance, as impressed as Jefferson was with the landscape designs of England and especially the open picturesque parks, he was nonetheless realistic enough to know that the oppressive heat of the Virginia climate absolutely required shade. Hence, instead of the open grass and occasional trees of the English park, Jefferson only cleared enough in his grove to create a continuous canopy of branches to fend off the oppressive Virginia summer heat. Or, while Jefferson planned four temples or pavilions along the stone garden wall, it is clear that he decided the common kitchen garden was probably the place for only one of them. And, while the ha-ha was intended to remove enough visual barriers from the landscape to suggest that all nature was indeed a garden, it apparently had a low parallel fence, with a 10-foot-high paling along the line of Mulberry Row shanties off to one side.

When considering almost anything Jefferson did, there is always the temptation to concentrate on the unique. Indeed, it almost goes without saying that the house and landscape offer much that is original. But viewed another way, they conform to many rules of their day. Jefferson deprecated all of the Georgian architecture of the Virginia of his time, yet the way his culture predisposed him to carry out much of his life kept him in his place and time. For instance, the eighteenth-century preoccupation with individualized space and architectural embellishment of rooms usually and most often seen by the public was apparently a strong influence on Jefferson's planning of the Monticello house. The same subconscious submission to the way things should be is true in Jefferson's landscape design. There Jefferson was guided, like most of his contemporaries, by a mind-set trapped in symmetry even when continually faced with the strong reality that the asymmetrical topography of the irregularly shaped Monticello site dictated what was possible. For example, it is easy to conclude that the innovative and asymmetrical *ferme ornée* concept guided his layout of the wandering roundabouts. Yet when one actually walks the land, it soon becomes obvious that for ease of transport roads had to be planned to follow relatively consistent vertical grades, which, particularly on the north side of the mountain, strike a very irregular curve at best. Elsewhere symmetry was obviously the goal; consider the bounds of the rectangular leveled lawns, the rigorous symmetry of the vegetable garden platform, the straight row of houses on the straight Mulberry Row, and the gridiron of trees and vineyard on the south slope. In fact, the garden itself is so typical that wherever leveling made it possible, the beds are laid out on near 100-foot increments, a practice followed rigidly elsewhere in colonial and early national Virginia.

Perhaps the clearest evidence of the strength of symmetry in the Monticello landscape plan is the archaeological discovery of so many landscape and architectural features located along a line which can be drawn across the mountaintop touching the western end of the dependency wings of the house (fig. 1.13). The north and south pavilions, a dry-well building, another unidentified building foundation, the termination of the ha-ha, a stone house on Mulberry Row, the termination of border beds, a drop in elevation on the garden platform, and the garden pavilion all honor that line. Using that datum as it bisects the mountain and another perpendicular to it passing through the center of the house, Jefferson may have quartered the mountain in his mind for planning purposes. The quartered plan would have included in the northwest quadrant, the grove; in the southwest quadrant, utility and industrial buildings on Mulberry Row, half the garden platform, the garden pavilion, and the orchard; in the southeast quadrant, domestic servants' quarters, the food preparation and storage dependency rooms, the other half of the garden, and the orchard with the vineyard; and to the northeast, the carriage area and a late blooming orchard (I am indebted to Douglas Sanford, past field supervisor at Monticello, for the idea that Jefferson divided Mulberry Row half to craft buildings and half to servant quarters). Recognition of this apparent design led to a closer examination of some original mountaintop plats, one of which showed

Figure 1.13. Aerial view of Monticello marked into quadrants as suggested by the alignment of archaeological features and related documents

scratched lines (a convention Jefferson often used before inking) that formed the exact quadrants suggested by the archaeology (Kimball 1968:Figure 168). Although it seems that one of the purposes of the scratched lines was to ease the calculation of acreage, it appears beyond mere chance that the lines matched what was suggested by the archaeological features on the landscape. The symmetry of four equal parts of a pie-shaped mountain could well have been Jefferson's organizing principle.

Jefferson was also typical of his time in that as much as he was concerned with the picturesque and aesthetic, he still had to tolerate the simple Mulberry Row cabins and the trash-littered side yards, all in full view from the house. Recent archaeology shows this pattern was used on other Virginia estates of the period as well (Kelso 1984a, 1984b). Apparently as long as everyone looked straight ahead from and back to the formal fronts of the houses, picturesque pleasure gardens or formal architecture met the eye. What was, in reality, going on to the left and right was so commonplace to people of the time, at least rural people, that what modern eyes consider unsightly was not noticed. Recognizing these land use patterns is perhaps the most significant contribution of landscape archaeology. Above ground, historical landscapes have evolved naturally into something quite different from their original designs, and modernization obscures signs of the past even more. But if one chooses to take a serious look beneath the emerald, overlush lawns of most historical sites, vestiges of the otherwise lost early American landscape can come to light.

# References Cited

Bear, J. A., Jr. (editor). 1967. *Jefferson at Monticello.* Charlottesville: University Press of Virginia.

Betts, E. M. 1944. *Thomas Jefferson's garden book.* Philadelphia: American Philosophical Society.

Gray, R. D. (editor). 1968. Letters of Henry D. Gilpin to his father. *Virginia Magazine of History and Biography* 76:466-468.

Hooper, W.    1823.    Description of Monticello, 20 September 1823.    Manuscript. Charlottesville: Thomas Jefferson Memorial Foundation Library.

Isaac, R. 1982. *The transformation of Virginia, 1740-1790.* Chapel Hill: University of North Carolina Press.

Kelso, W. M. 1984a. Landscape archaeology: A key to Virginia's cultivated past. In *British and American gardens in the eighteenth century: Eighteen illustrated essays on garden history,* ed. R. P. Maccubbin and P. M. Martin, pp. 159-69. Williamsburg: Colonial Williamsburg Foundation.

----. 1984b. *Kingsmill plantations, 1619-1800: Archaeology of country life in colonial Virginia.* New York: Academic Press.

----. 1988. Garden fences on Mulberry Row at Monticello. Manuscript submitted to the Restoration Committee on Archaeology. Charlottesville: Thomas Jefferson Memorial Foundation.

----, and Douglas W. Sanford. 1985. Archaeological excavations at Monticello, Albemarle County, Virginia, 1979-1985. Manuscript. Charlottesville: Thomas Jefferson Memorial Foundation.

Kimball, F. 1968. *Thomas Jefferson, architect.* Rept. New York: De Capo Press.

La Rochefoucauld-Liancourt, duc de. 1800. *Travels through the United States of North America in the years 1795, 1796 and 1797.* Volume 3. London: T. Gillet.

Nichols, F. D. 1961. *Thomas Jefferson's architectural drawings.* Charlottesville: University of Virginia Press.

Smith, M. B. 1906. *The first forty years of Washington society.* New York: C. Scribner's Sons.

## 2

# ARCHAEOLOGICAL EXCAVATIONS AT BACON'S CASTLE, SURRY COUNTY, VIRGINIA

## Nicholas Luccketti

In the sweat of they browes shalt thou eate thy bread.
>   --Charter of the Companie of Gardeners
>   of London 1605

And every of these three situations, having the fairest buildings of the house facing the garden in this manner before specified, besides the benefit of shelter it shall have from them, the buildings and rooms abutting thereon, shall have reciprocally the beautiful prospect of it, and have both sight and sent of whatsoever is excellent, and worthy to give content out from it, which is one of the greatest pleasures a garden can yeeld his Master.
>   --John Parkinson, 1629, *Paradisi*
>   *in sole Paradisus terrestris*

One of the most popular visions of seventeenth-century Virginia is that of dignified English gentlemen and their families enjoying a comfortable life in a neat house surrounded by a manicured yard carved out of a rich, hospitable new land; in essence, life in an idyllic garden. In truth, the Chesapeake garden was full of deadly serpents, and for much of the population life was a far cry from Eden. Rampant disease, dreadfully short life spans, and hostile inhabitants created a harsh disrupted world where normal behavior patterns were distorted. For example, government in early Virginia was as rugged as the environment; witness a meeting of the governor and his councillors some thirty years after the settling of Jamestown at which Governor Harvey promptly clubbed a member for verbally attacking him (Bailyn 1972). Indeed, even after nearly fifty years of colonization, the James River valley was still dangerous territory, as evidenced by a battle in 1656 near present-day Richmond where, under the command of Colonel Edward Hill of Shirley Plantation, the Charles City and Henrico County militia, along with their Indian allies, were routed by a tribe of Siouian Indians who had recently moved into the area (Morton 1960).

Surry County, on the south side of the James River just opposite Jamestown, was very much a part of that rugged and violent seventeenth-century Virginia frontier. In the late 1660s there were 280 Powhatan warriors living just outside the borders of Surry County (Morgan 1975:230). At that same time, fifty-seven-year-old Arthur Allen, a Surry County justice of the peace who signed his name with an X, ordered the cutting of trees to be used in the timber framing of his manor house that would become known as Bacon's Castle, one of only a handful of seventeenth-century Virginia brick houses.   Allen's eldest son, also named Arthur, was not available to assist his father in the construction of this magnificent brick home, for he was in his fifth or sixth year of education in England (Nicholson Manuscripts 1705).   While his father was building in Surry, there is every reason to believe that the younger Allen was studying the English countryside as well as the English textbooks, especially geometric kitchen and pleasure gardens that he saw there.   The recent archaeological discovery of the Castle's ca. 1680 garden (fig. 2.1) certainly suggests that when he returned, Allen attempted his own such formal landscape, even in the unlikely rough-and-tumble frontier days of Surry.

Figure 2.1. Aerial photograph of the garden at Bacon's Castle.  Garden buildings are outlined with white boards while postholes for an eighteenth-century fence line are shown as white dots. The scale in the center right planting bed is 30 feet.  Photo is from the southwest.

Surry was first settled in the 1620s; the plantations south of the James River were part of James City County until 1652 when Surry County was formally established.  Despite its proximity to Virginia's colonial capital, Surry remained isolated, always on the periphery of society, and consequently became poor man's territory. Historian Edmund Morgan has shown that in the third quarter of the seventeenth century, Surry may have been the poorest county in all of Virginia, having the largest percentage of one-man households and the smallest percentage of households with more than five tithables (Morgan 1975:226-29).

Arthur Allen I's holding in land and servants clearly reflects his wealth. At the time of his death in 1669 he was one of Surry County's leading citizens, possessing over 2,000 acres and eleven tithables (Kelly 1974:7). In seventeenth-century Virginia, political appointments went hand-in-hand with wealth, and during his lifetime Arthur Allen I served as vestryman, county commissioner, justice of the peace, and quorum justice (Kelly 1974:4-5).

Arthur Allen II, who later in life was known as Major Allen, returned to Surry County in 1668 and inherited the family plantation upon the death of his father the following year. Major Allen succeeded his father in admirable fashion. Whereas Arthur Allen I played a minor role in colonial affairs, his son became a leading figure in the larger political arena of seventeenth-century Virginia. After rapidly procuring several local offices, including county commissioner, county surveyor, justice of the peace, vestryman, and major in the Surry militia, Arthur Allen II advanced to one of the most esteemed positions in colonial Virginia, that of Speaker of the House of Burgesses (Kelly 1974:12-16). He was also given the lucrative job of naval officer of the Upper District of the James River (Kelly 1974:18). Arthur Allen II found time to expand the family plantation to over 8,500 acres and twenty-three tithables. It was during Major Allen's tenure that the elaborate garden was constructed at Bacon's Castle.

Bacon's Castle and Surry County have been spared many of the ravages of time and men. Not only are there many extant colonial structures in Surry, but the county records survived the Civil War, unlike most other Tidewater Virginia county records. The documentary record contains a wealth of information pertaining to Bacon's Castle. For example, there are five eighteenth-century probate inventories dating from 1711 to 1775, including two room-by-room inventories. The 1728 inventory of Arthur Allen III hints at eighteenth-century horticultural activities as it lists among the household articles "2 flower potts and 2 watring potts" (Andrews 1984:86-89). The "flower potts" were located in the garret over the hall (the third floor) and may have been for in-house use; however, the "watring potts" apparently were kept in an unnamed outbuilding. The appraisers of Arthur Allen III's estate, after recording the household goods, enumerated the livestock and then, without any break in the text, listed a number of items that seemingly were stored in a separate building. Among the planks, lumber, paint, lead, glass, and other items were the "2 watring potts" as well as an old harrow and hoes.

Unfortunately, these are the only references that may refer to a garden at Bacon's Castle. Despite the wonderfully complete Surry County records and the comparative abundance of eighteenth-century documentary information, Professor James Whittenburg's exhaustive research failed to discover any additional details regarding the garden (Whittenburg 1986). Professor Whittenburg examined the Surry County court records, probate manuscripts, travel accounts, tax records, insurance accounts, and the records of sixty-five merchants and companies mentioned in the county records, all without results.

There was, however, documentary evidence of a nineteenth-century garden. In 1935 Louis Hankins, who was born at Bacon's Castle in 1854 and lived there until 1871, described the garden to his son Richard, who then drew a sketch of the garden plan. An earlier map, more correctly a survey plat made in 1843 when Bacon's Castle was sold, depicted a 1.5-acre garden (fig. 2.2). Additional research suggested not only that the nineteenth-century garden might still be intact but also that it dated from an earlier period, which would not be

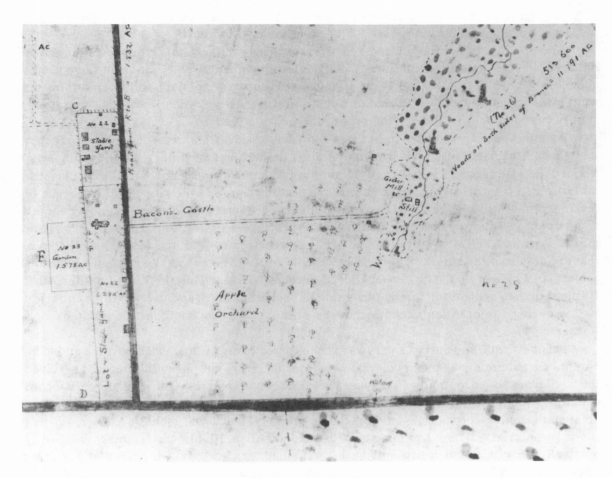

Figure 2.2. An 1843 survey plat of Bacon's Castle showing 1.5-acre garden. (Courtesy of The Association for the Preservation of Virginia Antiquities)

unexpected as gardens were typical components of colonial plantations. An infrared photograph taken of Bacon's Castle in 1974 clearly revealed a large dark rectangle in the west yard (fig. 2.3), corresponding perfectly with the garden shown on the Hankins sketch and the survey plat. Additionally, non-garden-related excavations conducted by the Virginia Research Center for Archaeology in 1982 (Luccketti 1984) recovered fragments of bell jars from mid-eighteenth-century contexts, allowing the possibility that the shadowy rectangle was part of the remains of a garden dating some 100 years earlier than that shown on the 1843 plat.

One can safely assume that there were many seventeenth-century gardens in Virginia, yet they remain strangely absent from the written record. I have reviewed 139 Surry County probate inventories spanning the years 1663 to 1715 searching for references to a garden and/or related objects. Three inventories had garden materials consisting of a flowerpot, a pruning hod, and garden "seades." A fourth, the estate of George Proctor, a prominent planter, was a rare room-by-room inventory which also listed outbuildings (Surry County Deed Book 2:199-201). It mentioned a pair of garden shears and an orchard yard. A second study was conducted on the twenty-nine seventeenth-century York County probate

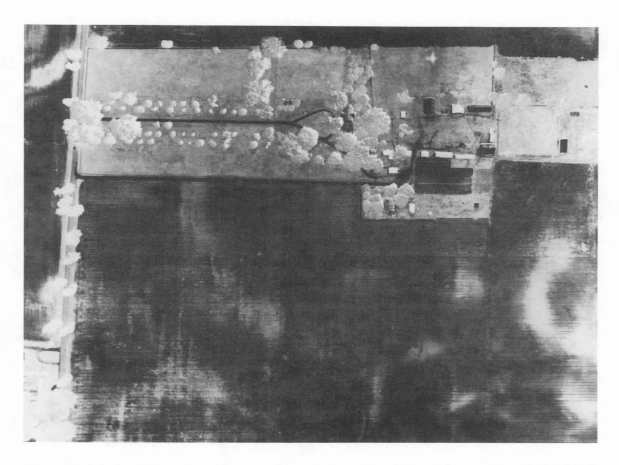

Figure 2.3. Infrared photograph revealing a large dark rectangle off the southwest corner of Bacon's Castle in the area of the documented garden. North is at the top of the photograph.

inventories that were appraised room-by-room. A similar list of garden objects (watering pots, shears, and rakes) was found in five inventories but no mention of a garden or orchard.

Stripping the overburden from the suspected Castle garden with a Gradall soon revealed the presence of a virtually intact garden plan suggested by the earlier testing (see figs. 2.1 and 2.4). After eight days of Gradall work and uncounted dump-truck loads of soil were removed from the site, a rectangular garden was exposed. Measuring 362 feet long and 192 feet wide, it more than covered the 1.5-acre garden that existed in 1843.

The garden originally consisted of eight principal planting beds arranged in two rows. The two northernmost beds were 8 feet wide (east-west) and 20 feet long (north-south). The next four beds were 74 feet wide and 98 feet long, while the two southernmost beds were 74 feet and 97 feet long. Separating the two rows of planting beds was a 12-foot-wide central path (north-south). The two internal cross paths (east-west) were 8 feet wide, and the perimeter path that surrounded the planting beds was 10 feet wide. Paralleling the perimeter path on all sides except the north end was a 6-foot-wide border bed.

The six larger planting beds were constructed of brown loam, with the soil deposited on the existing seventeenth-century surface to create a raised garden. This mounding of soil was clearly illustrated in the stratigraphy of test hole 1. Above the natural white sand subsoil was

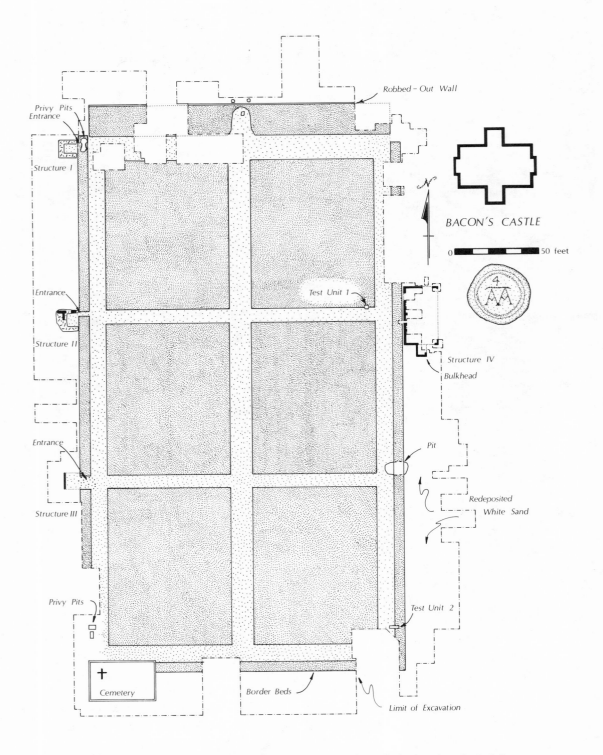

Figure 2.4. Site plan of Bacon's Castle garden excavation showing principal archaeological features

The following labels appear in the figure:

Robbed – Out Wall

Privy Pits
Entrance

Structure I

Entrance

Structure II

Entrance

Structure III

Privy Pits

Cemetery

Test Unit 1

BACON'S CASTLE

0                    50 feet

Structure IV

Bulkhead

Pit

Redeposited
White Sand

Test Unit 2

Border Beds

Limit of Excavation

a 4-inch-thick layer of dark gray/brown loam believed to be colonial topsoil. Other observations support this contention. For example, this same layer exists in undisturbed areas of the yard, particularly along the east corner of Structure IV. The layer of medium brown loam lay on top of the darker colonial topsoil. Test hole 1 also contained a surprising and significant third stratum of brick bits and chunks that was deposited between the topsoil and redeposited brown loam and likely relates to the construction of Structure IV.

In contrast to the raised construction of the six larger planting beds, the border beds and smaller northern beds were not built up but rather dug down into the subsoil. This conforms to the overall design of the garden in which the raised garden slopes gently from its highest point in the center to the original grade along the sides. Additionally, the sides of the northern beds, which are likely starting beds (Rudy J. Favretti, personal communication, 1987), that flanked the central path deviated from the rectilinear form of the rest of the garden. Here was an embellishment, as the sides had been fashioned into a bell-shaped curve (fig. 2.5). This was not the only occurrence of decorative elements used in the garden; there was also a curious hole located somewhat off-center in the path separating the two beds. This shallow hole, only 6 inches deep, with flat bottom and irregular sides may have held the base of a garden ornament.

After the brown loam for the raised beds had been mounded up, trenches for the central and cross paths were cut and then packed with sand. The paths were shaped with a turtleback contour so they, like the raised beds, would shed water. While the internal paths were man-made, the external perimeter path was undisturbed subsoil, with the limits of the path created by its position between the core planting beds and the border bed.

All eight of the planting beds showed evidence of internal planting rows, which were manifested as parallel dark lines. Difficult to see at ground level unless the planting beds were freshly scraped and the sun at a proper angle, the planting rows were very noticeable from the air and show up well in the videotape and color and black-and-white photographs taken from a helicopter. In reality, these lines may be silted-in furrows, so that the actual planting surface lies between the dark lines. The planting rows run east-west in the core beds and extend all the way to the sides of the bed, while in the smaller starter beds the rows are north-south.

During the course of excavation, several buildings were discovered in the garden. With one exception, the foundations for these structures were very shallowly seated, which, combined with later dismantling of the buildings to salvage materials, left rather slender archaeological remains to interpret. There were four areas with unmistakable evidence of structures and two more tentative locations. However, in each case, the remains, both firm and flimsy, were located at the ends of cross paths.

A U-shaped soil stain of dark brown loam with brick fragments contrasting sharply with the surrounding white sand subsoil was all that remained of Structure I (see fig. 2.4). Almost certainly, these soil stains were trenches for seating a brick foundation which supported a frame structure. When the structure was no longer used, the bricks were removed and the foundation trenches backfilled, leaving a definite, though somewhat vague, outline of an original building which measured approximately 10 feet by 12 feet. Interpretation was further complicated by the surprising absence of any hint of a fourth wall on the garden side and by the width of the robbed trenches. The back-wall trench was twice as wide as the side-wall trenches, 3 feet 6 inches versus 1 foot 9 inches, respectively.

Figure 2.5. Curved edges of starting beds. The crew member is cleaning the two in situ bricks. Note the refuse-filled hole in the central path, and that the starter-bed fill cuts through the sand path in the lower test unit. Photo is facing south.

Fortunately, there was some in situ brickwork from Structure II. It was a U-shaped building with an apparent open side next to the border bed (see fig. 2.4) similar to Structure I. Although much of Structure II had also been robbed, part of a one-and-one-half-brick-wide foundation, bonded with colonial shell mortar, survived along the north or side wall (fig. 2.6). Perpendicular to the north wall was a one-brick-wide footing, which turned strangely not from the back corner of the building but nearly 2 feet 6 inches in from the conjectured back wall line. Clearly, this was a footing for an internal screen or partition and not a wall foundation. Like Structure I, Structure II was 10 feet by 12 feet with side-wall trenches that were one half the width of the back-wall trench.

Structure III was represented solely by a remnant of a fallen brick wall (see fig. 2.4). The section, one-half brick wide and almost 10 feet long, was laid up with shell mortar. There was no evidence for side walls.

Like all the garden buildings, Structure IV was extensively robbed (see fig. 2.4). Nevertheless, there were substantial remains of the foundation because this 20-foot-by-32-

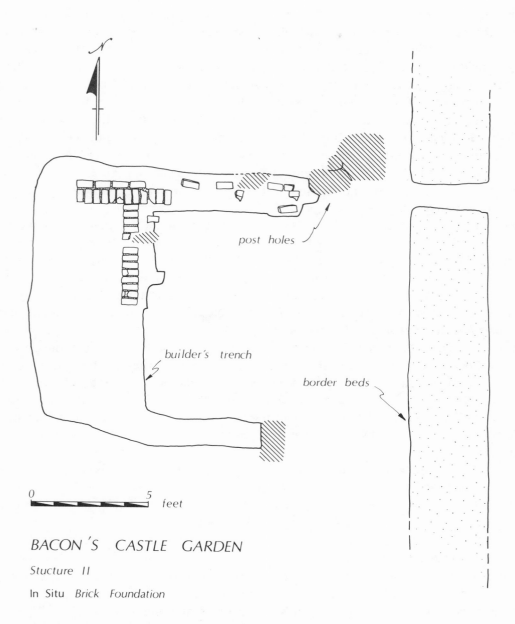

post holes

builder's trench

border beds

0       5 feet

BACON'S CASTLE GARDEN

Stucture II

In Situ Brick Foundation

Figure 2.6. Plan of Structure II

foot building had a brick-lined basement with an intact bulkhead entrance centered in the south gable. The one-and-one-half-brick-wide foundation had scored mortar joints and was whitewashed. A test square at the center of the west wall revealed racking in the wall for a partition which had been almost entirely robbed. The partition was centered on the cross path and divided the basement into two equal rooms. There was no evidence that the orange clay floor had been paved, nor was there any indication of a gable chimney. Structure IV was not left open after it was dismantled as it contained over five feet of fill, mostly white sand. There was no occupation layer on the floor, only brick and loam from the salvaging of the brick.

Two other areas of the garden had slight but suggestive evidence of additional buildings. In the southeast corner of the garden, which is obstructed by a huge pecan tree, there was a concentration of brick mixed with oyster shell, casement window glass, wine and pharmaceutical bottle glass, Chinese porcelain, and German stoneware, all dating to the late eighteenth century with the exception of the casement window glass. The 2 feet 5 inches of overlying fill consists of layers that are essentially flat, as is the spread of artifacts, indicating that this is not a pit or tree hole. Trenches cut across and beyond the artifact stratum, which was roughly 10 feet in diameter, failed to discover any structural remains. Despite the lack of architectural evidence, this artifact concentration could be argued to be the remains of a building. It is in the right place (at the end of a cross path), it is approximately the same size as the area of Structures I, II, and III, and all traces of the structure could be gone if it was as shallowly seated as Structures I, II, and III.

A second area of uncertain evidence for a garden structure or component was at the end of the cross path opposite Structure III. In the shade of the cluster of dogwood trees that grow around this spot, a large pit or tree hole was found which contained large quantities of brickbats, animal bone, and wine bottle glass dating to the late seventeenth century. Several well bricks were also found in the pit and nearby features, while surrounding layers yielded much wine bottle glass and other artifacts. It is possible that a well or cistern may be nearby or perhaps some other structure for cool storage.

Just as puzzling as the possible existence of these two structures were the form and function of Structures I, II, and III. It has been suggested that Structures I and II were really four-sided buildings and that both are coincidentally missing the wall that adjoins the garden. It is more likely that they were three-sided structures whose back faced the garden through the open side of the structure. Further, there is a clear distinction between the back wall and the side walls, as evidenced by the in situ brick in Structure II and the differing widths of the wall trenches.

It appears that Structures I and II had a footing or compartment about 2 feet 6 inches wide against the back wall. One possibility is that these features are the remains of cold frames; however, there was no substantial amount of broken glass that one would anticipate around a cold frame. The compartment could have been the catch box of a privy, but such sophisticated necessary houses are unknown on seventeenth-century plantations and again the problem of the missing wall arises.

The remains of Structure II bear strong similarity to the footprint of buildings seen frequently in depictions of medieval English gardens. These buildings, called exedras, had only three sides often, but not always, with a bench or seat along all three sides (fig. 2.7). With a bench against only the back wall, the Bacon's Castle example seems to be a close parallel to these English predecessors. This is most evident in the near identical form of construction; benches or seats for medieval exedras "were about 18 inches high and 2 feet wide, made of soil kept in position either by horizontal planks with vertical stakes or by bricks and turfed at the top" (Crisp 1924:81).

Exedras in seventeenth-century Surry County do appear to be something of an anachronism; however, there is some documentation that indicates they did indeed exist in England after the medieval period. One garden historian has written that exedras can be found in illustrations of gardens that date up to the second half of the nineteenth century (Crisp 1924:83), while three-sided structures without benches are known in seventeenth-century gardens (fig. 2.8). Also, the traveler Celia Fiennes reported that during a journey

Figure 2.7.  Exedra in an English medieval garden.  From Crisp 1924, plate CXXVI.

in 1698 she visited the estate of Sir John Astley of Patshill Park; in the garden "at the four corners are seates, shelter'd behind and on the top and sides with boards painted, on which you sit secured from the weather and looks on the water" (Morris 1949:230).  Access to Structure II was provided by a 1-foot-wide sand path through the border bed.  Using the

Figure 2.8. Three-sided garden structure dating from 1655. From Crisp 1924, plate CCLXV.

width of the entrance as a gauge for interpretation, Structure III probably had a different function because its entrance, seen as a break in the border bed, was 8 feet wide. Perhaps this building was simply an open alcove. Three-sided buildings without benches and having wide entrances are seen in gardens as late as 1655.

The entrance to Structure I is problematical because of the severe disturbance in that area from nineteenth-century privy and twentieth-century garage construction. The double-size back-wall trench, compared to its side walls, indicates that the building may have resembled Structure II.

One of the principal elements of a garden is the enclosure--wall, fence, or hedge--that protects its contents from four-legged enemies, both wild and domestic. Many sets of postholes for fence lines were found around the perimeter of the Bacon's Castle garden with at least six periods of fence lines running off the west side of the garden along the edges of the border bed. In contrast, there were only three fence lines on the south and east sides and none to the north.

Only two periods of fence lines have posts set into holes dug with a shovel rather than a posthole-digger, and from their location, neither could be an original enclosure. One of the fence lines was placed along the inside edge of the border bed; thus, it was eliminated as a candidate for the earliest one. The second hand-dug line of fence postholes had a distinctive fill which contained much brick rubble, but this line cut through the middle of the southern border bed.

Having no fence line that surrounded the entire garden, the border bed was considered as a possible enclosure if it could be shown to have been planted with a thick hedge, but no planting holes were found. Moreover, if the border bed was a barrier, the break in the bed at the south end of the central walk would have had to be closed by a gate; careful examination failed to discover any postholes for a gate. Nevertheless, hedges should still be considered as a possible enclosure outside the border bed. Hedges often enclosed later (postmedieval) gardens and would leave slender traces in the ground that could easily be lost over time (Crisp 1924:53).

Several other alternative enclosures popular in postmedieval England would result in scanty, if any, archaeological remains. One was to set posts for fence lines in a mound of dirt thrown up along a ditch. If the mound was ultimately leveled, there would be no archaeological evidence of the fence posts. Another historically ephemeral enclosure that would leave no record in the ground was known as a "dead or rough inclosure" and consisted of "drie thorne" and willow (Amherst 1896:112).

The north end of the garden seems to have been treated differently, not only in the shape of the planting beds but also in the manner of the enclosure. Along the outside or northern edge of the starter beds, there was a line of shell mortar and brick bits extending across the entire width of the planting beds. In addition, there are two whole bricks in situ in this line, indicating that a brick wall once stood at the north end. There were no other bricks under the two exposed ones; thus, the wall was shallowly seated like Structures I, II, and III. The wall may have been one and one-half bricks wide, an inference based on the width of the brick and mortar scatter. Outside the wall were two holes of uncertain purpose but suggestive location. Each hole contained a postmold; however, there were no datable artifacts in either hole.

Dating of construction of the garden is based on three sources of evidence: artifact concentrations in and beneath the garden, the relationship of Structure IV to the garden, and historical context. Taken individually, none is overpowering, but in combination they point to a date of approximately 1680 to 1690.

Research on Major Arthur Allen reveals that after the devastation wreaked by rebel forces at his plantation in 1676, he began a period of economic and political expansion; he started acquiring land, laborers, and appointments that ultimately led to his election as Speaker of the House of Burgesses in 1686. In 1675 Allen was the second largest slaveowner in Surry County; although his force declined to five tithables during the depression of the early 1680s, it rose in 1688 to ten laborers (Kelly 1974:21, 23-24). In the late 1670s and late 1680s, Major Allen was on a program of improving his position among the elite planters and had the resources to undertake an extensive project such as constructing the garden.

The garden appears to be contemporary with Structure IV, which means that the construction date of building and the garden are the same. Uniting the garden and building to the same time period is a spread of brick rubble which balloons out from the west wall of Structure IV. Because it is composed almost entirely of unmortared brick fragments, this layer is believed to be construction debris deposited both under and in the brown soil used to create the nearby raised planting bed.

In an effort to recover artifacts to date the construction of Structure IV, the builder's trench was excavated along the northeast and southwest corners, over 5 feet deep in places. Very few artifacts were recovered; only some wrought-iron nails and several fragments of wine bottle glass were found. The paucity of artifacts in itself suggests an earlier date because the later the construction, the more time passes and the greater chance of material accumulating to eventually find its way into a builder's trench. Further, the few wine bottle fragments that were identifiable were dated to between 1680 and 1710.

In the southeast corner of the garden, concentrations of artifacts were found both under and on top of the border bed (fig. 2.9). These concentrations consisted principally of wine bottle glass dating to between 1680 to 1710 along with ceramics manufactured by the Gloucester potter and Lawne's Creek potter, both of whom worked in the first two decades of the seventeenth century. Finally, while colonial material was found on the surface in all six core planting beds, each one also had late seventeenth-century artifacts including several "AA" wine bottle seals (one was recovered from one foot below the surface; see fig. 2.4).

Compared to most excavations, the amount of artifacts found in the garden was very small, and only a few were related to garden activities. Artifacts such as the several hoe blades found along the edges of the garden may have been used in other tasks such as tobacco cultivation.

The most prevalent garden objects found were fragments of bell jars or cloches, the most distinctive part being the foot rim, which was folded over for reinforcement (fig. 2.10). Used to protect tender plants and/or give crops an early start, bell jars were common in

Figure 2.9. Concentration of artifacts beneath the border bed in the southeast corner of the garden. Photo is facing west.

seventeenth-century England and Europe (Huxley 1968:259). Many fragments of variously sized bell jars were found in the garden, particularly in the beds off the southwest corner of Structure IV (which further implies that Structure IV was garden-related). Curiously, not a single glass knob handle, seen in every illustration of bell jars, was found. Other

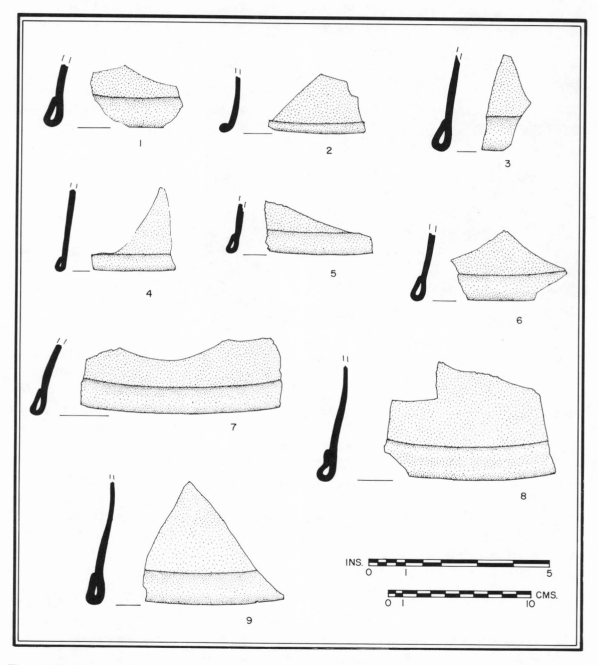

Figure 2.10. Foot rims from bell jars recovered during the garden excavation

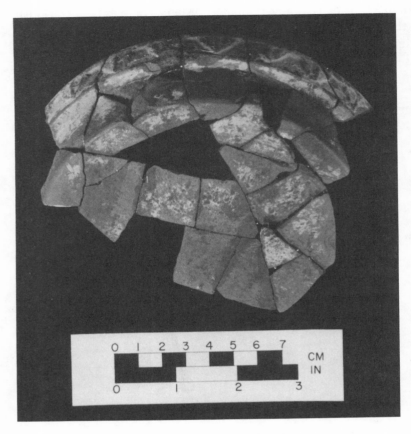

Figure 2.11.  Reconstructed coarseware flowerpot saucer found in garden

horticulturally related objects recovered from the garden include sherds of coarseware flowerpots and decorated saucer rims (fig. 2.11). These were unearthed in the northernmost planting beds along the brick wall trace.

Examination of the soils from the planting beds has focused on a fairly new method of research which can identify silica particles produced by plants known as phytoliths. Phytolith analysis has several advantages over seed and pollen analysis. First, because phytoliths are silica rather than organic like seeds and pollen, they will survive much longer and do not need particular soil conditions to prevent deterioration. Second, unlike seeds and pollen, the chances of contamination are diminished in phytolith analysis because they do not migrate (i.e., are not wind-blown). Phytolith analysis at Bacon's Castle has been set up in two phases. Initially, soil samples from various parts of the garden were examined to determine if phytoliths were present. Irwin Rovner (personal communication, 1987) has verified the presence of phytoliths. Next, a more intensive sampling of soil from planting beds will be sent for actual identification of specific plant types (each phytolith plant produces its own characteristically shaped silica particle). This sampling will be limited to the border beds and starter beds, which were taken out of use between approximately 1800 and 1820. The core planting beds continued to be used as planting surfaces until the demise of the garden in the late nineteenth century, and phytolith, seed, or pollen analysis cannot distinguish earlier or later plants in these continually used surfaces.

The study of colonial landscapes once was strictly the province of garden clubs and landscape architects interested in the horticultural reconstructions associated with historic houses. However, historians and archaeologists now recognize that the ways in which fields and forests were sculpted by our colonial ancestors have much to tell us about how our forebears viewed and settled the New World. Rhys Isaac's (1982) prize-winning book *The Transformation of Virginia* is a testament to the enhanced role of landscape study in historical research; it contains an entire chapter devoted to shapes in the landscape and the arrangement of social space. Curiously, there is only a single reference to gardens in this chapter although gardens were indispensable components of every seventeenth- and eighteenth-century quarter, farmstead, and plantation; they were essentials rather than extras.

Unfortunately, colonial gardens did not survive as well as colonial houses, nor do they produce dazzling archaeological remains; thus they have been neglected, and scholars like Isaac have little available information to work with. This situation is rapidly improving with the publication of archaeological discoveries of eighteenth-century gardens such as the ones at Carter's Grove (Kelso 1984a) and Kingsmill (Kelso 1984b) in James City County, Virginia. This material, allied with surviving garden remnants such as those at Shirley Plantation and Weyanoke plantation in adjacent Charles City County, reveals a strong Tidewater landscape pattern for waterfront plantations of the eighteenth-century elite in which a terraced garden was located directly between the riverside and the mansion.

Much of the Carter's Grove, Kingsmill, and Shirley gardens has suffered the fate of most colonial sites; they were incorporated into the neighboring fields and subsequently plowed for decades. Through sheer good fortune, the garden at Bacon's Castle was never plowed, resulting in a find of major significance because, if for no other reason, it is a virtually intact garden plan dating from the late seventeenth century.

Of course, Bacon's Castle was not the only seventeenth-century Virginia plantation that had a substantial garden. Excavations on other seventeenth-century sites of prominent planters have uncovered large rectangular areas surrounded by postholes for a fence. Almost certainly these were gardens which, if built in the medieval style of raised planting beds as was the Bacon's Castle garden but then unlike the Bacon's Castle garden assaulted by years of plowing, would leave little archaeological evidence other than the deeper posthole patterns. Interestingly, planting beds dug down into the subsoil appear later at Carter's Grove (Kelso 1984a) and also at a town garden plot dating from approximately 1715 to 1725 in nearby Williamsburg (Edwards, Derry, and Jackson 1987).

The garden at Bacon's Castle served a variety of needs: utilitarian, aesthetic and social. The presence of rows in the planting beds indicates they were used for vegetables and/or herbs rather than containing mazes, knots, and other forms of parterres, while the border bed was likely planted with ornamental plants following medieval tradition (Rudy J. Favretti, personal communication, 1987). Additional concern for a pleasing panorama is reflected by the balanced placement of the garden structures at the ends of the cross paths, the curved lines of the starter beds, and the brick-accentuated northern terminus. This combination of garden features seems to be an adaptation of a time-honored English garden plan which has been transported into the Virginia wilderness. In its skeletal form, the Bacon's Castle garden is not unlike the elaborate garden built in 1615 for the earl of Pembroke at Wilton (fig. 2.12), which had a broad central avenue, large core planting beds, and smaller border beds. Major Allen altered a traditional English plan to suit his needs in a new environment by installing a seventeenth-century pleasure garden stripped of the bulk of its ornamental features in order to produce food for the table.

The garden, with its exedras and embellishments, also marks Major Allen as a man of wealth and influence. It is clear from the archaeological research that most well-to-do seventeenth-century Virginians used architecture and objects as visible means to distinguish themselves from the lesser planters. The Bacon's Castle garden is the earliest example of the landscape employed in the same vein.

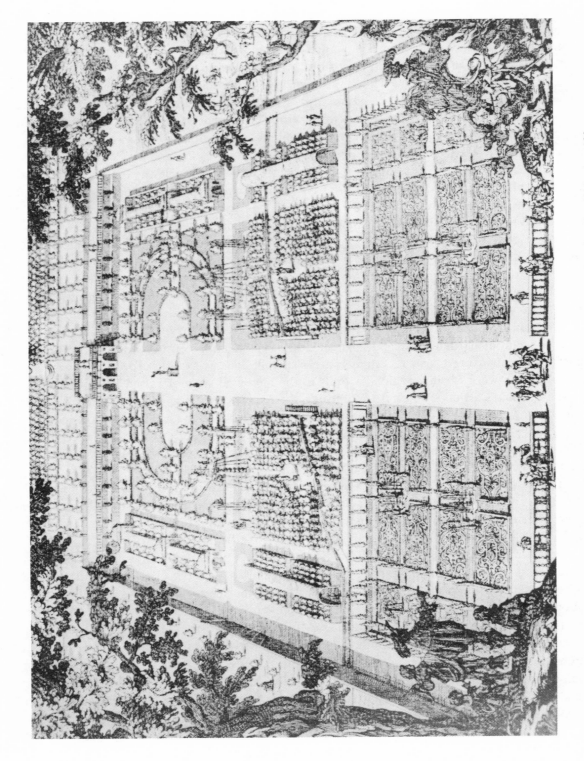

Figure 2.12. Garden at Wilton constructed in the early seventeenth century. From Batsford and Fry 1933, plate 122.

Toward the end of the seventeenth century, life was becoming less difficult in the Chesapeake. Simple survival was no longer a singular concern, and with the frontier pushed westward, there was a heightened sense of permanence. People were living longer, families were more stable, and a native born elite was emerging (Jordan 1979; Rutman and Rutman 1979; Shammas 1979). The garden at Bacon's Castle is representative of the incipient maturity of Virginia. Major Allen was one of a new generation of leaders who, unlike their fathers, was born in Virginia, and his converted pleasure garden is not only a rare intact piece of the landscape but also a sign of the times.

## Acknowledgments

Bacon's Castle, a National Historic Landmark, is one of Virginia's oldest, most significant, and most studied buildings. Architectural historians have long believed that Bacon's Castle, a nineteenth-century appellation, dated to the third quarter of the seventeenth century; this hypothesis recently was confirmed by dendrochronology, which produced a construction date of 1665. Accordingly, the Castle is Virginia's earliest surviving dwelling and likely its only standing seventeenth-century house. Measuring 45 feet 6 inches by 25 feet 2 inches, the Castle is a two-and-one-half-story brick structure with porch and stair towers, distinctive triple diagonally set chimneys, curvilinear gables, window surrounds, and a molded belt course on the front or south facade. Despite its external embellishments, the Castle conforms to the typical seventeenth-century Virginia house plan of hall-parlor with end chimneys, a fact first recognized by Cary Carson (Carson 1969:245-51). Bacon's Castle was purchased along with forty acres in 1973 by the Association for the Preservation of Virginia Antiquities (APVA). As part of its continuing program of preservation and interpretation, the APVA initiated an archaeological survey of Bacon's Castle in 1978 which was conducted by the Virginia Research Center for Archaeology, an arm of the Virginia Historic Landmarks Commission, under my supervision. In 1982 I supervised a VRCA excavation of a 10-foot-wide swath around Bacon's Castle before the installation of a waterproofing system. Next, a second archaeological survey was commissioned by the APVA in 1983 to investigate the area of a documented nineteenth-century garden. Based on the results of the VRCA garden survey, the Garden Club of Virginia agreed to fund a major excavation of the garden by the VRCA in June 1984. The excavation was assumed in July 1986 by the James River Institute for Archaeology, Inc. and continued until May 1987.

I wish to thank the Association for the Preservation of Virginia Antiquities for permission to publish the illustrations pertaining to the archaeological investigations at Bacon's Castle. I would also like to thank Dr. Kevin P. Kelly and Betty Leviner of the Colonial Williamsburg Foundation for providing me with some of the data included in this chapter.

## References Cited

Amherst, A. 1896. *A history of gardening in England.* London: Bernard Quaritch.
Andrews, S. B. (editor). 1984. *Bacon's Castle.* Richmond: Association for the Preservation of Virginia Antiquities.

Bailyn, B.  1972.  Politics and social structure in Virginia.  In *Seventeenth-century Virginia*, ed. J. M. Smith, pp. 95-96.  New York: W. W. Norton.

Batsford, H., and C. Fry.  1933.  *Homes and gardens of England*.  London: B. T. Batsford.

Carson, C.  1969.  Settlement patterns and vernacular architecture in seventeenth-century Tidewater Virginia.  M.A. thesis, Department of Early American History and Culture, University of Delaware.

Crisp, Sir Frank.  1924.  *Medieval gardens*.  London: John Lane, the Bodley Head.

Edwards, A., L. Derry, and R. Jackson.  1987.  Point of view: Archaeological excavations beyond the Peyton Randolph house.  Manuscript.  Williamsburg: Colonial Williamsburg Foundation.

Huxley, A. J.  1978.  *An illustrated history of gardening*.  New York: Paddington Press.

Isaac, R.  1982.  *The transformation of Virginia, 1740-1790*.  Chapel Hill: University of North Carolina Press.

Jordan, D. W.  1979.  Political stability and the emergence of a native elite in Maryland.  In *The Chesapeake in the seventeenth century*, ed. T. W. Tate and D. L. Ammerman, pp. 243-73.  New York: W. W. Norton.

Kelly, K. P.  1974.  The Allens of Bacon's Castle.  Manuscript.  Richmond: Association for the Preservation of Virginia Antiquities.

Kelso, W. M.  1984a.  Landscape archaeology: A key to Virginia's cultivated past.  In *British and American gardens in the eighteenth century: Eighteen illustrated essays on garden history*, ed. R. P. Maccubbin and P. M. Martin, pp. 159-69.  Williamsburg: Colonial Williamsburg Foundation.

————.  1984b.  *Kingsmill plantations, 1619-1800: Archaeology of country life in colonial Virginia*.  New York: Academic Press.

Luccketti, N. M.  1984.  Bacon's Castle archaeological project II and III: 1982 house excavation and 1983 garden survey.  Manuscript.  Richmond: Association for the Preservation of Virginia Antiquities.

Morgan, E. S.  1975.  *American slavery, American freedom*.  New York: W. W. Norton.

Morris, C. (editor).  1949.  *The journeys of Celia Fiennes*.  London: Cresset Press.

Morton, R. L.  1960.  *Colonial Virginia*.  Chapel Hill: University of North Carolina Press.

Nicholson Manuscripts.  1705.  "Pursuant to Your Excellencys command I have hereunder given a brief account of Majr. Arthur Allen of Surry" (TR21), pp. 230-31.  Manuscript.  Williamsburg: Special Collections, Colonial Williamsburg Foundation Library.

Parkinson, J.  1629.  *Paradisi in sole paradisus terrestris*.  Rept. 1975.  Norwood, N.J.: Walter J. Johnson.

Rutman, D. B., and A. H. Rutman.  1979.  "Now-wives and sons-in-law": Parental death in a seventeenth-century Virginia county.  In *The Chesapeake in the seventeenth century*, ed. T. W. Tate and D. Ammerman, pp. 153-82.  New York: W. W. Norton.

Shammas, C.  1979.  English-born and creole elites in turn-of-the-century Virginia.  In *The Chesapeake in the seventeenth century*, ed. T. W. Tate and D. L. Ammerman, pp. 274-96.  New York: W. W. Norton.

Surry County.  1671-84.  Surry County Deed Book 2, 1671-1684.  Surry County Court House, Virginia.

Whittenburg, J. P.  1986.  Looking for Bacon's Castle gardens.  Manuscript.  Richmond: Association for the Preservation of Virginia Antiquities.

# 3

# THE GARDENS AT GERMANNA, VIRGINIA

## Douglas Sanford

### Landscapes at Germanna through Time

The recent accelerating concern with past landscapes has brought together archaeologists, preservationists, landscape architects, and various scholars concerned with historic gardens. Balancing these interest groups and their respective orientations around one project represents both a challenge and a valuable opportunity. And when that project stands at the beginning stage of development, the need for an overall research design becomes immediately apparent. This chapter serves as a case study for incorporating initial archaeological and documentary investigations into plans for future research, interpretations, and preservation.

The investigations examined here centered on the landscape associated with Colonel Alexander Spotswood, the former lieutenant governor of colonial Virginia from 1710 to 1722. In the mid-1720s he located the administrative center of his vast landholdings at the plantation called Germanna, an estate situated along the Rapidan River in what is now northeastern Orange County, Virginia (fig. 3.1). Spotswood's residential complex at Germanna historically came to be known as the Enchanted Castle, an archaeological site deemed important enough to be placed on the National Historical Register. The phrase "enchanted castle" derives from an entry in William Byrd II's journal of 1732 (Byrd 1841:132). During a stay at Spotswood's home, Byrd used the term, without further explanation, to describe his host's dwelling. Byrd's cryptic phrase may refer to the visual and mental result of juxtaposing Spotwood's palatial mansion with the estate's frontier, wildernesslike environs. To date, no evidence suggests that Spotswood called his manor house the Enchanted Castle.

Before discussing the site specifics of this eighteenth-century plantation manor, a fruitful perspective can be gained from a consideration of the site's broader historical and cultural contexts. Within these contexts, the changes wrought on the surrounding landscape by past and present landowners and occupants provide one focus of attention. Finally, an additional goal of the research at Germanna includes interpreting the site and its landscape within a regional framework, that of Piedmont Virginia and its changes through time.

The name Germanna stems, on the one hand, from Spotwood's placement of German immigrants within a fortified settlement along the Rapidan River in 1714 and, on the other hand, from Spotswood's honoring of Queen Anne, then regent of England. The forty-two Germans situated within Fort Germanna comprised part of Governor Spotswood's plan for the defense of colonial Virginia's western frontier. The frontier at this time extended beyond

Figure 3.1. Aerial view of the Germanna area adjacent to the Rapidan River. View is to the northeast.

the fall line into the Piedmont zone east of the Blue Ridge Mountains. In addition to strategically placed forts, Spotswood intended to establish a buffer zone between British settlers and potentially hostile Indians to the west. Tributary Indians, those on peaceful terms with the English, composed the buffer zone and also served to funnel the fur trade to these forts and thus the colonial government (Beaudry 1980, 1985). Fort Germanna, as the northern counterpart to Fort Christanna in Brunswick County, would allow Spotswood to participate in monopolizing the local region's fur trade (Beaudry 1979).

As part of the expanding British colonial system, Fort Germanna undoubtedly altered the native Indian, or Saponi, landscape (Saponi, often spelled Sapony, was the colonial English term for several American Indian groups in the Piedmont region of Virginia). Indian occupation of the Germanna area began by at least 3000 B.P. and continued up into the 1720s and 1730s, when court records provide descriptions of Saponi resistance to European settlement, including setting the woods on fire and taking potshots at their English and German neighbors (W. Scott 1907:56). The Saponi eventually left the Germanna area, and when other tributary Indians refused to move there, the fur trade that Spotswood had envisioned failed to materialize.

The Germans established their own, if rather brief and confined, landscape within Fort Germanna, described by a visitor in 1716 as a

> town which is pallisaded with stakes stuck in the ground, and laid close the one to the other, of substance to bear out a musket shot. There is but nine families and they have nine houses built all in a line, and before every house about 20 feet from the house they have small sheds built for their hogs and hens, so that the hog stys and houses make a street. This place that is paled in is a pentagon, very regularly laid out, and in the very centre is a blockhouse made with five sides which answers to the five sides of pales or great inclosure. . . . This was intended for a retreat for the people in case they were not able to defend the pallisadoes if attacked by the Indians. They make use of this Blockhouse for divine service. (Fontaine 1972:88)

Evidence suggests that the evangelical Protestant Germans soon moved from the fort area to one more conducive to their native skills, those of mining and ironworking. In fact, Spotswood purposely brought the Germans to his lands as metalworkers rather than as occupants of a military outpost (Wayland 1956; Wust 1969).

The early inhabitants of Germanna represent dual themes that continued to characterize the area for the next two decades: frontier acculturation and rapid change. These processes involved a multiplicity of ethnic groups, including native Americans, Germans, English and Anglo-Americans, and African-Americans. And, in contrast to popular images of the colonial wilderness being settled by poor but hardy, independent pioneers who somehow became more democratic under the rigors of frontier life, the evidence at Germanna points to a more hierarchical and elite-controlled process.

For instance, Governor Spotswood not only supplied the capital and logistics to settle the Germans at Germanna but pulled the necessary political strings as well. While superficially intending the Germans to guard the colony's frontier, Spotswood cared more that they first legally settle his speculative landholdings. Next they mined previously discovered iron ore deposits and erected an ironworks on Spotswood's adjacent plantation of some 15,000 acres. Between 1718 and 1721 the ironworks eventually known as the Tubal furnace went into production (Cappon 1945). Mining and charcoaling activities associated with this large-scale operation resulted in a landscape described by William Byrd II in 1732. "Three miles farther we came to the Germanna road, where I quitted the chair and continued my journey on horseback. I rode eight miles over a stony road, and had on either side continual poisoned fields, with nothing but saplings growing on them" (Byrd 1841:132). Ever since, the maze of stunted trees, vines, and dense undergrowth characteristic of the terrain partway between Germanna and Fredericksburg has remained the Wilderness. This environment provided the setting for the 1864 Civil War battle of the same name.

A few years after effecting his frontier industrial plantation, Spotswood had workmen begin construction on his Germanna estate. Shortly thereafter, in about 1723, work commenced on his brick and stone mansion and presumably on the adjacent grounds and gardens (Wayland 1956:15). The erection of this elaborate early Georgian residence occurred in what was then an isolated region. As such, the site exemplifies an initial transference of British colonial architecture and country estate design into the Virginia Piedmont. Along with it came a slave- and tobacco-based market economy which quickly replaced a more diversified one that relied on the labor of indentured servants (Schlotterbeck 1980:11-23).

Typical of the gentry's role in this region's transition from frontier to plantation society, Spotswood promptly arranged for roads, a ferry, and a mill in the immediate vicinity of his plantation, controlling access to these critical resources. Further transforming the landscape at Germanna, Spotswood personally secured the siting of the new county seat on his estate. Westward expansion of the colony's agricultural boundary had enabled the formation of a new county in 1720, Spotsylvania, named after the governor himself. The courthouse, jail, and church complex erected in the next few years provided the basis for a villagelike community at Germanna which included artisans' shops and taverns (Miller 1985:15–35).

In keeping with models of frontier towns and settlement systems, Germanna soon developed into a focal settlement. Located at a transportation node, Germanna functioned as the nucleus for social, religious, economic, and political activities (Lewis 1977). Similarly, in line with the weighting of such models toward transition, by 1732 the county court had been moved eastward to Fredericksburg. This relocation reflected both a desire by the more densely populated portion of Spotsylvania County to avoid the inconvenience of the Germanna courthouse location and effective sociopolitical competition from Spotswood's elite status rivals. In 1734 Germanna became part of newly formed Orange County, itself a product of continued, rapid westward expansion.

Alexander Spotswood died in 1740 in Annapolis, where he was preparing to lead a military expedition to Cartagena. What happened to his estate after his death remains a mystery for archaeology and perhaps further documentary research to solve. As this chapter describes, archaeological work at the Enchanted Castle site has determined that the house burned and collapsed into its basement about 1750. By the late 1770s the estate had passed out of the hands of the Spotswood family.

From the 1780s to the 1880s the Gordon family resided upon and farmed the Germanna tract. Portions of their house, outbuildings, and roads remain visible today. The activities of the Gordons associated with these and other farm components both disrupted and encased the Spotswood house site and landscape. In itself, the Gordon estate provides a convenient comparative case study representing one hundred years of occupation. Civil War maps record some aspects of the Gordon farm and even surviving elements of the Spotwood era landscape. Military records pertaining to troop movements integral to the Chancellorsville and Wilderness campaigns indirectly note the decline of the milling and farming community of the early to mid-nineteenth century known then as Germanna Mills. The archaeological remnants of this community likely intrude upon the Fort Germanna site, one which has so far eluded archaeological efforts to pinpoint its location. Together, all of these sites, communities, and events contributed toward the formation of the Germanna area landscapes and their respective cultural contexts.

## Archaeology at Germanna

The most recent (1983–84) large-scale landscaping efforts at Germanna have taken the form of residential development. This activity instigated archaeological work beyond the limited testing in 1977 that verified the exact location of the Enchanted Castle site (Egloff 1979). Fortunately, the Virginia Research Center for Archaeology's (VRCA) salvage excavations in 1984 initiated a complicated but ultimately successful effort to preserve the site and the sixty acres immediately surrounding it. Results of the VRCA archaeological work included the delineation of the main house plan, a particularly valuable product because no descriptions, drawings, or paintings of the house are known to survive.

With overall dimensions of 120 by 240 feet, the Enchanted Castle contained three main elements (figs. 3.2 and 3.3). Typical of Georgian manor design, the main house occupied a

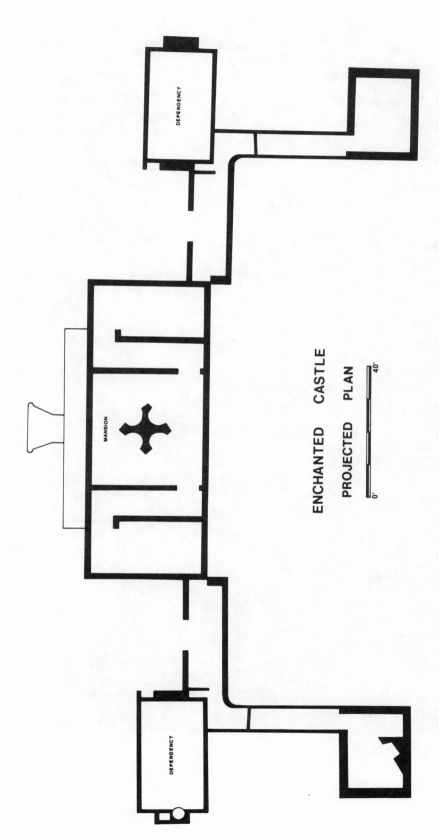

Figure 3.2. Projected plan of the Enchanted Castle based on archaeological excavations

Figure 3.3. Aerial view of the 1984 excavations of the Enchanted Castle with central portion of the house to the lower left

central position, balanced between two L-shaped dependency wings. Connecting halls, or hyphens, tied the main house together with the four buildings located in the corner and end positions of the wings. The central block measured 35 to 45 feet in width and approximately 90 feet in length. Brick and stone construction characterized both the main domestic unit and the dependencies, with the relative proportions of each material to be more fully determined by future excavation. The recovery of carved ornamental stonework from the main house may denote its relatively greater embellishment. At a distance of 180 feet south of the house, archaeologists recorded a surviving terrace. Together the house and terrace demarcate a square platform of about 240 feet on a side for the domestic complex.

Due to the site's recently attained protected status, archaeological work there fortunately switched from salvage to the formulation and implementation of an overall research and preservation design. Knowledge fundamental for that design includes an awareness of all archaeological sites and features on the property surrounding the Enchanted Castle. Thus, Historic Gordonsville, Inc., the preservation organization responsible for the site, implemented a reconnaissance survey to locate archaeological sites of all time periods within its sixty acres. Shovel test pits dug at 60-foot intervals formed the basis for the systematic survey, an intensive sampling strategy required by the densely vegetated local environment and the need to assess the date, location, size, and number of sites (fig. 3.4). Of the eighteen sites identified, at least four date to the Spotswood era, and they will aid in more completely rendering the eighteenth-century landscape. For instance, stone and brick rubble found in association with artifacts of 1725-50 likely denotes the site and/or a component of the courthouse, jail, and church complex. The other sites should correspond to some of the outbuildings, craft shops, and servant and slave quarters known from documentary research to have existed within the Germanna plantation community.

But before forming a preliminary interpretation of the Enchanted Castle and the Spotswood era landscape, their presumed designer deserves more detailed attention. In fact, a case study exists wherein Spotswood's character and his manner of architectural and garden design stand out clearly.

### Spotswood as Architect and Gardener in Colonial Williamsburg

Alexander Spotswood's stormy political career during his tenure as governor was well-recorded. Members of the Council of Virginia criticized his aristocratic and imperial style of rule and held similar opinions of the gardens he personally executed at the Governor's Mansion in Williamsburg (fig. 3.5). Spotwood's lavishing of public funds on these courtly gardens and grounds supposedly led his detractors to derisively rename it the Governor's Palace. Two of these critics, John Custis of Williamsburg and William Byrd II of Westover, were both council members and important eighteenth-century aristocratic gardeners in their own right (Martin 1982, 1984). Byrd endures as the more revealing informant about Spotswood.

Despite frequent disputes with Spotswood and his own participation in effecting the removal of Spotswood from office, Byrd retained and developed a friendship with his rival. Part of their bond rested on several mutual interests, including plantation management, ironworking, industrial slavery, and gardening. Typical of their relationship, Byrd, who in 1712 had cooperated with Spotswood in planning the orchard for the Governor's Palace, wrote John Custis in 1716 that he saw himself as a man liable to be ill-treated by a governor [Spotswood], under the notion of advancing His Majesty's interest, by which pious pretence he may heap insupportable trouble upon that officer [Byrd, who] if he should have the spirit to oppose his will and pleasure--he must either be a slave to his humor, must fawn upon him, and jump over a stick whenever he is bid, or else he must have had so much trouble loaded upon him as to make his place uneasy. In short, such a man must be either the governor's dog or his ass; neither of which stations suit in the least with my constitution. (Tinling 1977:293)

Spotswood's influence in Williamsburg extended well beyond the political realm. He furthered the townscape work of Francis Nicholson in the colonial capital, providing for vistas and scenic public areas. Architecturally, he supervised the completion of the Governor's Palace and personally designed both the Bruton Parish church of 1712-15 and the powder magazine of post-1714. An addition to the public gaol and a remodeling of the College building (now called the Wren Building at the College of William and Mary) also appear to have been his work. Like other members of the gentry, Spotswood, as a well-versed amateur architect, effectively employed classical orders and the geometrical rules of design integral to Renaissance-inspired Georgian architecture (Whiffen 1968).

With respect to gardening, Spotswood also achieved notoriety in Williamsburg. Garden historian Peter Martin terms Spotswood "one of the most forceful, ambitious, and imaginative gardeners in the colonies during the first quarter of the eighteenth century." Martin describes the Spotswood-directed grounds of the Governor's Palace as "an enormously influential garden in the history of American colonial gardening." Similar statements attach themselves to the Governor's Palace itself, considered the earliest example of Georgian architecture in colonial Virginia and the prototype for the gentry's mansions of Virginia that followed. Accordingly, the Spotswood-related mansion and gardens at the Governor's Palace served as "models of culture," symbols of civilized, elegant living, high status, and an ordered hierarchical world (Martin 1982:316). Today these models and their physical remnants symbolize for us the Georgian mind-set, the cultural model of the great planters of Virginia and of the gentry of other colonies as well (Deetz 1977; Isaac 1982).

The Spotswood gardens at the Governor's Palace, dated approximately 1710-21, represent a prime example of a large (greater than twenty acres), aristocratic estate designed according to what is usually termed the French formal, or baroque, style. Main elements included a forecourt garden between advanced flanking dependencies, orchards, a utilitarian kitchen garden, flower and fruit gardens, diamond-shaped parterres with topiary, and especially a rectangular canal located beneath three terraces of falling gardens. As expected, here architectural design dominates nature. The achieved landscape, according to the period's cultural model, presents a blend of geometry and sensory plant forms, the balance of a grand design of repetitive parts with a variety of textures and forms. Idealized nature becomes mathematically ordered within an architecture of the land which consciously projected the house design (Hadfield 1979; Hussey 1967; Thacker 1979).

The Governor's Palace also fulfilled the intent of early eighteenth-century British models for country estate design, although one adapted to a relatively urban setting. The mansion, as the center of control and perspective, offered the best vantage point both for being seen from planned vistas and for appreciating the order of the landscape plan of yards, trees, gardens, and walkways. Following the model's rules, country villas overlooked a body of water and, if located on sloping ground, incorporated falling terraces. House axes acted as lines for placing and dividing formal gardens and as bases for symmetrically orienting

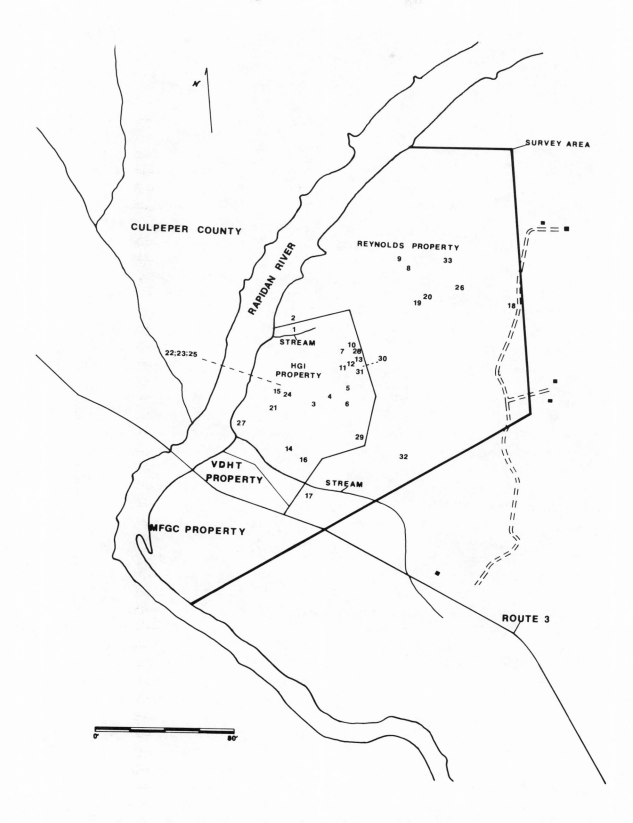

Figure 3.4. The Germanna survey area. Numbers correspond to located archaeological sites.

Figure 3.5. Aerial view of the Governor's Palace in Williamsburg and the restored gardens. (Courtesy of Colonial Williamsburg Foundation)

yards and outbuildings. In addition, yards and gardens were enclosed with fences and lined with trees (Shurcliff 1937).

Not too surprisingly, several of these landscape and architectural elements find their parallels at Germanna. The Enchanted Castle and the Governor's Palace both used advanced outbuildings or connected dependencies to frame a formal forecourt and falling terraces to establish gardens or improve vistas. This list of shared attributes could go on, and will in terms of research objectives and archaeological excavations, but the question remains, "So what?" Isn't the observed patterning one that is already known and expected? What value does another example carry? Addressing these questions involves answers framed within the diachronic and regional contexts.

## Spotswood at Germanna

From one perspective, Alexander Spotswood's move to Germanna in the early 1720s represents the transition from the relative urbanity of civilized Williamsburg in Tidewater Virginia to the wildernesslike frontier of the Piedmont. But the frontier did not force Spotswood to economize or to become more democratic. Instead, it afforded him the opportunity to construct his country villa amid a truly rural setting rather than within the confines of Williamsburg.

In line with the model of British country estates, Spotswood chose an elevated position for his house, namely, a flat but prominent ridgetop overlooking a large, gentle bend of the Rapidan River. To the north the topography quickly slopes down to a small stream feeding the river, while a gentle slope exists to the south. The house's long axis aligned east-west with the run of the ridgetop. In sum, the house visually dominated a variety of elevations and topographic features.

Together the house and its wings framed a forecourt measuring 60 by 160 feet, which, if extended to the terrace on the south side of the house, enlarges to approximately 180 by 240 feet, a ratio of two-to-three. Such mathematical relations indicate possible planning schemes or intervals used by Spotswood and may well provide keys for locating the landscape elements no longer visible above ground.

Beyond this preliminary archaeological examination, the best descriptions of the site's gardens and landscape again come from William Byrd during his extended visit in 1732. While at Germanna, Byrd recorded the topics of conversation between himself and Spotswood and his family. He also took note of daily events and his physical surroundings. Annotating Bryd's journal entries with other documentary and archaeological data provides one means of interpreting the Germanna landscape and for offering a conjectural rendering of Spotswood's estate (fig. 3.6).

Byrd began his procession through the landscape by embarking on a morning walk. "After breakfast the Colonel [Spotswood] and I left the ladies to their domestic affairs and took a turn in the garden, which has nothing beautiful but three terrace walks that fall in slopes one below another." Spotwood's terraced walks paralleled the terraces or falling gardens of the Governor's Palace both in the number and in leading down to a water landscape element. At Germanna, a small tributary stream of the Rapidan River defined this element rather than a canal.

Byrd next referred to a tree-planting scheme but in his typical satirical fashion also commented upon the passing of a public portion of the Germanna community's landscape.

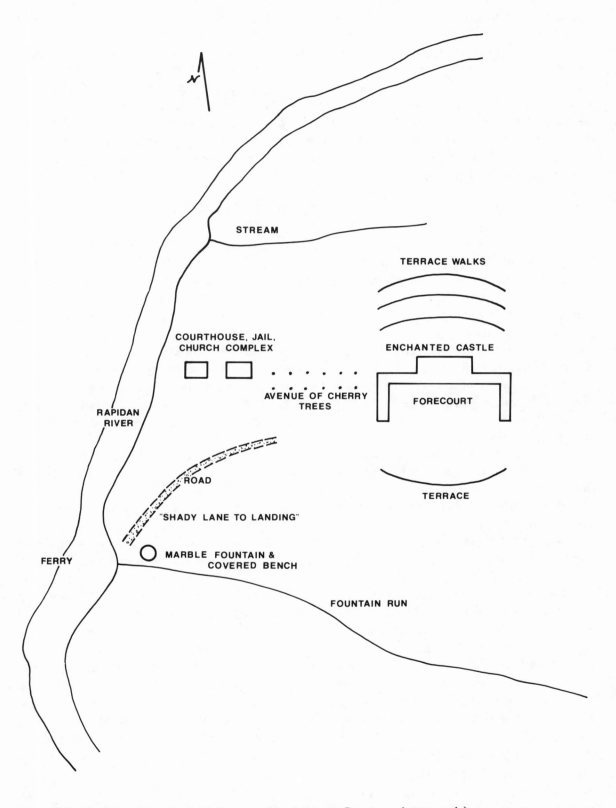

Figure 3.6. Conjectural sketch of the Spotswood landscape at Germanna (not to scale)

"There had also been a chapel [church] about a bowshot from the colonel's house, at the end of an avenue of cherry trees, but some pious people had lately burnt it down, with intent to get another built nearer to their homes." The church site once was part of the county seat complex, the location of which has been tentatively established archaeologically.

Spotswood's wife and her sister accompanied Byrd on his second landscape tour. "The afternoon was devoted to the ladies, who showed me one of their most beautiful walks. They conducted me through a shady lane to the landing." The shady lane remains visible today as a road trace along the slope down to the river and leads to the former landing for the ferry. Civil War correspondence of 1863 contains a sketch map of this area and describes an old road rising up the riverbank and passing by an old house, that of the Gordon family (R. Scott 1890:496).

Down by the river, the women introduced Byrd to a more fanciful element of the landscape when they insisted that he "drink some very fine Water that issued from a Marble Fountain, and ran incessantly. Just behind it was a cover'd Bench" (Byrd 1841:132-33). The spring that supplied the fountain still runs today at the base of the river bluff next to a permanent stream. Eighteenth-century road orders for Orange County refer to the stream as Fountain Run (Miller 1984:90).

Integrating these different types of data for interpreting past landscapes, the conjectural landscape sketch forms a significant element within the research design for future archaeology. One means for deciding on the placement of test excavations consists of imposing on the ground the possible planning schemes utilized by Spotswood. For example, the 240-by-360-foot rectangular area containing the terraced walks, the main house site, and the terraced area to the south would have incorporated logical segments based on proportional increments of these overall distances. Formal and symmetrical parterres presumably occupied the forecourt area, balanced to either side of a central north-south axis line or walkway. Projecting a line from the approximated house entrance on the mansion's north side (based on archaeological evidence) implies that a stepped walkway or ramp once ran perpendicular to the terraced walks. Corners and other prominent locations of the main house and dependency buildings should mark former terminal points for fences enclosing yards and perhaps additional gardens to either side of the house.

Excavations in the immediate future will focus on the house itself and its immediate environs and should locate the predicted fences, their gates, and related walkways. Such work forms the initial and critical step in more fully delineating past gardens, grounds, and yards. Aiding in this research and that concerned with the greater landscape beyond the main house are intended physical studies of soil chemistry, botanical remains, and remote survey techniques such as infrared photography.

Evidence for Germanna's greater landscape requires that archaeologists define this topic so as to encompass areas beyond the immediate house and gardens. For instance, the fountain and shady lane visited by Byrd denote a consciously and aesthetically manipulated landscape of a larger scale. This evidence takes on increased importance when viewed in tandem with an awareness of Spotswood's broad intellectual interests and his stay in England from 1724 to 1730, a period when the formal French garden design was giving way to elements of the pictorial, naturalized English landscape garden popular from the mid to late eighteenth century onward. Spotswood may have introduced a different and new landscape design for the further reaches of his estate. His continual contact with William Byrd may have also contributed to this notion of a semiformal landscape contrasting with the more rigid design at the Enchanted Castle.  According to Peter Martin, Byrd redesigned his gardens at Westover in the late 1720s according to the "then-emerging English naturalized or pictorial style" (Martin 1983).  Although the possibility that Spotswood adopted the same innovations remains tenuous at present, it marks another factor for archaeological consideration.

But the point remains, "So what?"  Can archaeology at Germanna do no more than identify an early example of Georgian architecture and landscape design on the Piedmont frontier?  Obviously archaeology can go beyond such mere stylistic and chronological fine-tuning, namely, by interpreting architecture and landscapes from the perspective of a broader social history and a contextual framework which includes diverse, changing cultures. For example, just as Spotwood's academically designed mansion contrasted with the vernacular architecture of the other plantation residents, so did his elite landscape contradict and encompass a variety of less grand but more common gardens and grounds.  The hired artisans, indentured servants, and black slaves of Germanna represent more sites but also more cultural perspectives that figured into the process wherein a multiplicity of landscapes were created and occupied.  The archaeology of the Enchanted Castle site and the greater landscape at Germanna will gain additional significance because it entails the more complete definition of this range of social or community landscapes through time.

## References Cited

Beaudry, M. C.  1979.  Excavations at Fort Christanna, Brunswick County, Virginia: The 1979 season.  Manuscript.  Richmond: Virginia Research Center for Archaeology.

----.  1980.  Fort Christanna: Frontier trading post of the Virginia Indian Company. Manuscript.  Richmond: Virginia Research Center for Archaeology.

----.  1985.  Colonizing the Virginia frontier: Fort Christanna and Governor Spotswood's Indian policy.  In *Comparative studies in the archaeology of colonialism*, ed. S. L. Dyson, pp. 130-52.  British Archaeological Reports 233.  Oxford.

Byrd, W.  1841.  *The Westover manuscripts: Containing the history of the dividing line betwixt Virginia and North Carolina; a journey to the land of Eden, A.D. 1733; and a progress to the mines.*  Petersburg: Edmund and Julian C. Ruffin.

Cappon, L. J. (editor).  1945.  *Iron works at Tuball: Terms and conditions for their lease as stated by Alexander Spotswood on the 20th day of July 1739.*  By Alexander Spotswood. Roanoke: Stone Printing and Manufacturing Company.

Deetz, J.  1977.  *In small things forgotten.*  New York: Doubleday.

Egloff, K.  1979.  Spotswood's Enchanted Castle, 440R3, Orange County.  Manuscript. Richmond: Virginia Research Center for Archaeology.

Fontaine, J.  1972.  *The Journal of John Fontaine, an Irish Huguenot son in Spain and Virginia, 1710-1719.*  Ed. E. P. Alexander.  Williamsburg: Colonial Williamsburg Foundation.

Hadfield, M.  1979.  *History of British gardening.*  2d ed. London: John Murray Publishers.

Hussey, C.  1967.  *English gardens and landscapes, 1700-1750.*  London: Country Life.

Isaac, R.  1982.  *The transformation of Virginia, 1740-1790.*  Chapel Hill: University of North Carolina Press.

Lewis, K. E. 1977. Sampling the archeological frontier: Regional models and component analysis. In *Research strategies in historical archeology*, ed. S. South, pp. 151-201. New York: Academic Press.

Martin, P. 1982. "Promised fruites of well ordered towns": Gardens in early eighteenth-century Williamsburg. *Journal of Garden History* 2(4):309-24.

----. 1983. Williamsburg: The role of the garden in "making a town." *Studies in Eighteenth-Century Culture* 12:187-204.

----. 1984. "Long and assiduous endeavors": Gardening in early eighteenth-century Virginia. In *British and American gardening in the eighteenth century: Eighteen illustrated essays on garden history*, ed. R. P. Macubbin and P. Martin, pp. 107-29. Williamsburg: Colonial Williamsburg Foundation.

Miller, A. B. 1984. *Orange County road orders, 1734-1749.* Charlottesville: Virginia Highway and Transportation Council.

----. 1985. References to the Germanna site in the records of Essex, Spotsylvania, and Orange counties, Virginia. Manuscript. Charlottesville: School of Architecture, University of Virginia.

Shlotterbeck, J. T. 1980. Plantation and farm: Social and economic change in Orange and Greene counties, Virginia, 1716-1860. Ph.D. dissertation, Department of History, Johns Hopkins University.

Scott, R. N. (editor). 1890. *The war of the rebellion: A compilation of the official records of the Union and Confederate armies.* Washington, D.C.: Government Printing Office.

Scott, W. W. 1907. *A history of Orange County.* Richmond.

Shurcliff, A. A. 1937. The gardens of the governor's palace, Williamsburg, Virginia. *Landscape Architecture* 27(2):55-96.

Thacker, C. 1979. *The history of gardens.* Berkeley: University of California Press.

Tinling, M. (editor). 1977. *The correspondence of the three William Byrds of Westover, Virginia, 1684-1776.* Vol. 1. Charlottesville: University Press of Virginia.

Wayland, J. W. 1956. *Germanna: Outpost of adventure, 1714-1956.* Staunton, Va.: McClure Printing Company.

Whiffen, M. 1968. *The public buildings of Williamsburg, colonial capital.* 2d ed. Williamsburg: Colonial Williamsburg.

Wust, K. G. 1969. *The Virginia Germans.* Charlottesville: University Press of Virginia.

# 4

# ROBERT "KING" CARTER AND THE LANDSCAPE OF TIDEWATER VIRGINIA IN THE EIGHTEENTH CENTURY

## Carter L. Hudgins

Recent archaeological and historical studies of eighteenth-century Virginia have drawn attention to the stark economic and cultural differences that separated the colony's wealthiest planters and its middling and poorer residents (Carr and Walsh 1980; Kelso 1984; Menard, Harris, and Carr 1974). It is not surprising that studies of probate inventories and surviving eighteenth-century dwellings reveal that wealthy planters owned more than their poorer neighbors. But these studies of Virginia's colonial material culture also have revealed how and why the nature and character of life in Virginia in the seventeenth century was markedly different from the eighteenth century. More and more, questions about the relationship between wealth and cultural expressions are emerging as a very effective way of understanding not only the day-in, day-out ordinary role assigned to material things but how things shaped social and political relationships and provided meaning and context for everyday life.

The study of landscapes is emerging as an important component of this effort. Enough research has been completed to suggest that during the first decades of the eighteenth century, the colony's once-unified culture, a set of ideas and assumptions that had arrived in Virginia early in the seventeenth century and had their origins in rural England, was joined by a new and distinct set of cultural premises. This newer set of ideas emanated from London and other European metropolitan centers and became, in Virginia, the province of the colony's wealthiest planters and their friends and clients. One result of the arrival of what can be called a patrician culture was that new notions about the character of houses and gardens shaped the colony's landscape. Analysis of these changes can define not only how the colony's landscape changed but why and can be instructive of the tensions that animated relations between the colony's social and racial groups. Until the beginning of the eighteenth century, a remarkable sameness characterized Virginia's landscape, but by about 1730, there were many landscapes, some made for and by the wealthy and others for and by those who were not. These landscapes, old and new, reflected the ideas that colonists held about what they thought was and was not necessary for life in Virginia. These ideas were changing as the seventeenth century ended and the eighteenth century began, and as old gave way to new, Virginians often took their bearings from material things--from houses and fields, from yards and table settings. They did so because in their world houses and fields, and the folks who lived in and tended them, were read as tangible evidence of success and failure, of ties to friends and the community, and of membership in the local social network or a wider social net, or both or neither. Virginians looked for proof in material things, but sometimes they did not find it. One good record through which to encounter the mental world of eighteenth-century Virginia and how colonists read evidence is a case which came before the justices of Lancaster County at the beginning of the eighteenth century.

In May 1712 John Tully, a planter of modest means and accomplishments who lived in Lancaster County, brought a complaint to the county's justices against his neighbor Robert Scofield. Tully charged that Scofield was a "person of lewd life and conversation and a common disturber of the peace," and complained that Scofield, despite strong warnings, had done more than pay an occasional obnoxious visit to his plantation. When he came home on the afternoon of the "12th of April last," Tully told the justices, he had discovered Scofield "in bed with his wife in his house, John's own house, and the door shut and bolted." It would seem that the implications of Tully's accusation were clear enough, just as were Scofield's intentions, but the justices had difficulty making a decision. The justices asked for and heard further testimony from both men, and then, no doubt to Tully's great surprise, dismissed the case "for as much as there was no evidence" (Lancaster County, Virginia, Order Book 8).

The cuckolding of John Tully reveals several things about the mind of early eighteenth-century Virginia. The case suggests something about the literalness of proof in the eighteenth century. And it also suggests that the planters of Virginia's Tidewater read and understood the fields and fences and houses and churches that populated their landscape as indications, as proof, of much more than that men, women, and children lived, worked, and worshiped in them. One of the best places to get a clear picture of the economic distances that separated rich and poor in the colony and how that distance shaped Virginia's eighteenth-century landscape is Corotoman plantation in Lancaster County--the seat of Virginia's wealthiest colonial planter, Robert Carter (Hudgins 1982) (fig. 4.1).

Just where the Rappahannock River broadens before it flows into Chesapeake Bay, on a peninsula wedged between the Corotoman River and smaller Carter's Creek, there is the site of an ancient plantation. Already old by Virginia standards when it enjoyed its heyday during the first decades of the eighteenth century, this plantation, called Corotoman by its owner and the planters who lived near it, was between 1690 and 1732 the home of Robert Carter, a planter renowned for his haughtiness and his wealth and who was, for both reasons, called "King." When Robert Carter inherited Corotoman after his half brother John's death in 1699, the plantation was already extensive and prosperous. Robert reaped the benefits of his father and brother's prodigious labors and thus began his career as a planter with a considerable head start. Not many planters began life with as many advantages and privileges, and not many achieved as much as Carter. By the time he died, his plantation empire stretched from the Tidewater to the foothills of the Appalachians through more than a dozen Virginia counties. A labor force which numbered hundreds of black men, women, and children and dozens of English servants worked in his fields. And together, Carter's land and his laborers produced a fortune and economic power that only a few men in eighteenth-century North America could match (*Gentleman's Magazine*; Wright 1940).

Robert Carter and his prickly personality have long been a staple of historical accounts of Virginia in the eighteenth century. For just as long, Corotoman has been a tempting target for an archaeological investigation. The reasons for this are several. First, Carter's extraordinary wealth and political accomplishments suggested that Corotoman would be a rich site. Since the 1930s archaeologists had thought that the site would, when excavated, yield artifacts impressive in both number and in quantity. Second, the dwelling Carter constructed in the 1720s burned, tragically, during the winter of 1729. Carter did not rebuild

Figure 4.1. "A map of the inhabited part of Virginia . . ." (drawn by Joshua Fry and Peter Jefferson, 1751), showing the site of Corotoman in Lancaster County, Virginia, on the northern shore of the Rappahannock River

his mansion. Old and infirm, he spent the last three years of his life living next door to the ruins of his mansion in a house constructed at the end of the seventeenth century. Robert Carter's brick mansion at Corotoman became, in essence, an archaeological time capsule on that winter night. Its excavation would, archaeologists thought, provide a clearly focused image of life there during the first decades of the eighteenth century. Third, and most promising, Corotoman reached its zenith during the important economic, cultural, and social changes that transformed Virginia between 1680 and 1740.

While archaeologists working in Virginia have conducted a good deal of research on sites that date from the eighteenth century and in recent years have worked extensively on sites dating from the first three quarters of the seventeenth century, no project had studied how the rise of a native-born elite in Virginia affected the character of everyday life in the colony.  Corotoman, where Robert Carter eventually filled the same county and provincial positions of political prestige and authority his immigrant father had, was an ideal site at which to investigate how accumulated wealth and political power affected the colony's landscape.

Between 1977 and 1980, excavations at the heart of the plantation focused on two domestic sites.  One was the ruins of a small story-and-a-half timber house constructed late in the seventeenth century.  The second was a later and larger brick mansion which was, for a short interval, the plantation's principal residence (fig. 4.2).  Excavation of these two dwellings provided important information about changing architectural preferences at the plantation (Hudgins 1982).  And these two dwellings and their yards led to a wider study of the cultural landscape of Lancaster County between 1680 and 1740 and what Robert Carter referred to as the "necessary calls of humanity and decency" (Robert Carter Letterbook, 1728-31).

Figure 4.2.  The excavated foundation of Robert "King" Carter's mansion at Corotoman.  (Courtesy of Virginia Division of Historic Landmarks)

Recent studies of the material culture of the seventeenth- and eighteenth-century Chesapeake have drawn attention to contrasts between what Lorena Walsh and Lois Green Carr have called the stark sufficiency of the seventeenth century and the relative comforts and occasional splendors of the eighteenth century (Carr and Walsh 1980).  Perhaps nowhere in the Tidewater are these differences more apparent than at Corotoman.  Life there was centered around a rather modest timber structure and, later, a brick dwelling until the 1720s when Robert Carter constructed his imposing brick mansion, a house which had few rivals in size and very few rivals in architectural pretension. In size and plan, Carter's mansion was nearly identical to the so-called Wren Building at the College of William and Mary in Williamsburg. Carter's large new brick mansion was also in many ways like a country house which Christopher Wren designed for an English client (fig. 4.3). Like other large country houses constructed in England during the late seventeenth and eighteenth centuries, Wren's house bore the significant imprint of Renaissance ideals and motifs.

The rejection of traditional timber framing and wooden clapboards and the enthusiastic embracing of classical architectural form and style at Corotoman in the second quarter of the

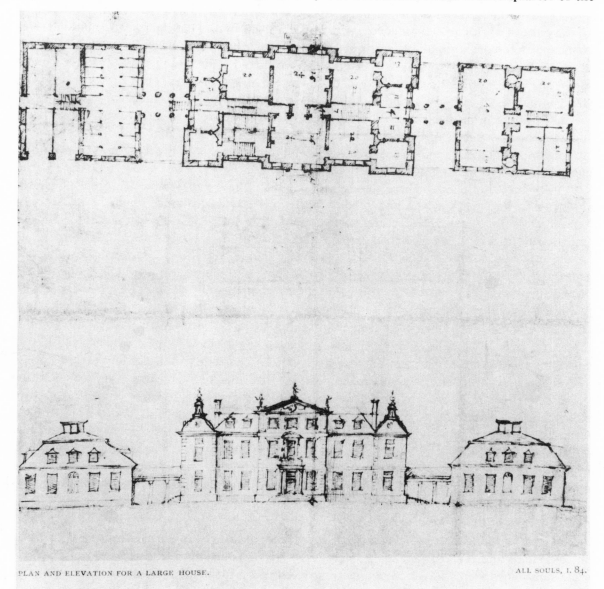

PLAN AND ELEVATION FOR A LARGE HOUSE.                                    ALL SOULS, I. 84.

Figure 4.3. Design for a "large house" by Christopher Wren. (Courtesy of All Souls College, from the Wren Society, vol. 12, plate 14, 1935, Oxford University Press)

eighteenth century was paralleled at dozens of other plantations in the Virginia Tidewater. This shift in architectural preference is indicative that the broadly shared cultural tradition which had guided the colony since the first decades of the seventeenth century was, at the plantations of the colony's persons of distinction, being joined by a new set of cultural assumptions.

At Corotoman and elsewhere a new distinct patrician culture emerged while the life-styles and everyday routines of the colony's middling and poorer colonists changed little. This is, of course, not a new notion. The complex and profound reorientation of building and buying activity in the colony has been referred to as the arrival of the Georgian mind-set by James Deetz (1977). Much has been said and written by archaeologists recently about Deetz's paradigm, but however much it is criticized, it is widely accepted as a sufficient explanation for the pattern of things that archaeologists find in the ground. That the transformation from vernacular to Georgian took place is not in doubt. What has yet to be explained in any kind of satisfying way, however, is why the change occurred. By asking why Virginia's once homogeneous traditional culture diverged into two distinct cultures, each of which had its own characteristic patterns in house building, garden tending, and landscape taming, it is possible to determine what the colonists defined and understood as the "necessary calls of humanity and decency" as well as the political and cultural tensions and intentions that were broadcast in swatches of yard and garden, in fields and houses, and in any other aspect of the shaped landscapes of eighteenth-century Virginia.

Virginia's eighteenth-century landscapes are not without their irony. The great mansions of Virginia, and the gardens and tended landscapes that surrounded them, were truly a remarkable cultural and architectural achievement. It is not without reason that these houses and their furnishings and gardens have long been accepted, without critical questioning, as an appropriate symbol of Virginia's so-called Golden Age. Yet however fitting the Tidewater's mansions are as a symbol for the success of the elite, they are also symbolic of the decline of the economic and political fortunes of almost everybody else. While wealthy planters scattered brick mansions throughout the Tidewater, they reaped fortunes with the labor of unfree black men and women; lifelong tenancy became a greater and greater likelihood for many of the colony's free whites, and the chances that men who arrived in the colony as indentured servants might rise to modest affluence dwindled (Menard 1977).

Since approximately 1978, archaeological, architectural and historical research has made it possible to reconstruct a vivid picture of Virginia's eighteenth-century landscape. If we have come to understand anything at all about Virginia's landscape, it is that during Robert Carter's lifetime, it was one of sharp contrasts. When Robert Carter rode out to inspect his outlying quarters, a task he performed less and less often after gout became his companion in middle age, he passed through a mélange of fields and forests. Carter rode on roads that meandered along the spines of the necks and peninsulas punctuating most sections of the Tidewater and were laid out and maintained by county surveyors of highways according to the consensus of the freeholders of the district through which they passed (fig. 4.4). The road system that resulted was not elegant, but it worked. Most roads turned frequently as they skirted fields and then turned again to resume their original route, and at nearly every turn were small hoed fields in which young tobacco and corn plants competed for space with the stumps of recently cut trees (fig. 4.5). In other fields, grown tired in the planter's parlance, and resting for some future use, small pine and oak and locust saplings struggled to overcome the clutch of vines and brambles. Often a road entered forests that had not yet fallen to ax

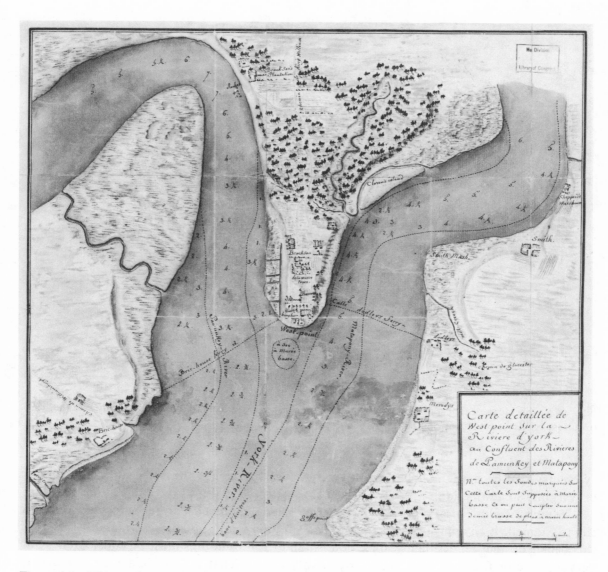

Figure 4.4. Eighteenth-century roads meandered along the spines of the Tidewater's low ridges, connecting scattered plantations. (Map, ca. 1781, Rochambeau Collection, no. 54, LC-M, courtesy of Map Division, Library of Congress)

and hoe and in which cows, pigs, and, occasionally, horses roamed and foraged. Carter occasionally had to dismount and open gates that marked the end of one man's property and the beginning of another's, and when he did, he complained about the inconvenience but he never questioned the assumptions that had created this higgledy-piggledy agricultural landscape.

Clergyman John Clayton and other European visitors were puzzled by Virginia's curious agricultural landscape, and they sometimes made suggestions they thought would make land use in the colony neater (Berkeley and Berkeley 1965). They never succeeded. The rough mix of fields and forests, largely untamed and generally untouched and unmarked by the

Figure 4.5. In Tidewater fields, new plants competed with stumps. Watercolor by Benjamin Henry Latrobe, 1798. (Courtesy of Maryland Historical Society, Baltimore)

symmetry that became the hallmark of gentry houses, remained the dominant characteristic of Virginia's countryside.

Stumpy fields, briary growth in old fields, and untamed forest, nature subdued or slightly tamed, is an appropriate metaphor for Virginia's cultural landscape, and it is against this backdrop that tended landscapes, houses, and farm buildings must be considered. One very important fact has been made irrefutably clear. That is, Virginia was in the first decades of the eighteenth century, as it had been in the seventeenth century and as it remained until recently, a land of small wooden houses. Upton's research in the counties that lay to the south of the James River and the work of other students of the colony's seventeenth- and eighteenth-century buildings make it clear that most houses were seldom larger than a room or two (Upton 1980). In Lancaster County, for example, one- and two-room houses account for nearly 60 percent of inventories that listed possessions room by room. These room-by-room inventories represent less than 10 percent of all the county's inventories from the period 1680 to 1740 and indicate that perhaps less than 5 percent of all households occupied houses larger than two rooms. The early eighteenth-century landscape was dominated by small houses. It is also apparent that most houses served their owners or tenants for many years. In Virginia, as in Maryland, it could typically be said that a planter's house "Tho' 'twas made of wood/Had many springs and summers stood" (Cook 1969:592).

Virginians were, in short, content with modest houses. Some of the space that many travelers assumed was missing from Virginia houses was contained in separate structures to which many household routines had been relegated. The hodgepodge of dairies, smokehouses, quarters, and sheds that bunched around even modest planters' houses were there to house activities conducted by slaves. Erecting separate buildings for each activity not only kept them apart, it also kept the slaves who did them from entering the more private dwelling space of the plantation's master and his family (Dauphine 1934:113; Neiman 1978).

One of the best descriptions of how a plantation dwelling was supported by its outbuildings comes from an entry in William Byrd's secret diary. The winter of 1712 was not noticeably colder than the winters that had preceded it, but it was a winter of unusually heavy snowfalls. On the morning after a night of steady snow, Byrd discovered that he and his family were as close to being snowbound as anybody ever is in Virginia. More than a foot of snow was heaped on the ground, and to get his household operating that morning, Byrd ordered his slaves to clear paths between his dwelling and the separate structures that, lumped together, formed his house. Paths in the snow soon connected Byrd's dwelling, the building where he slept and ate, with his kitchen, his library, his office, and other structures (Wright and Tinling 1941:323).

Byrd's snow trails, an ephemeral artifact of winter, marked links to rooms that in other parts of the English world might lie under one roof but in Virginia were in different buildings. At Westover and elsewhere, then, the cluster of buildings that formed what we should think of as a single house often fooled travelers, one of whom, in trying to sort out his impressions of the colony, reported that "when you come to the house of a person of some means, you think you are entering a fairly large village" (Dauphine 1934:120).

Corotoman was such a place. By the end of the seventeenth century when Robert Carter inherited Corotoman, the plantation boasted more than a dozen buildings at its home quarter. And all but one of these buildings, a new dwelling house, were made of wood. Corotoman, like Virginia, was a place where small wooden houses dominated the landscape and where brick houses were uncommon. To be sure, brick houses, when there were any, stood out markedly. Even in Annapolis, a town Governor Francis Nicholson goaded into becoming a respectable urban place, brick houses made "a great show among a parsell of wooden houses" (Kammen 1963:372). The same contrast was apparent at Corotoman and throughout the Tidewater.

As remarkable as the contrast between small wooden houses and large brick houses was in the late seventeenth century, the contrast became starker during the eighteenth. When, for example, Robert Carter built his new brick mansion at Corotoman, a dwelling which was nearly the size of the so-called Wren Building at the College in Williamsburg and shared many architectural traits with it, he built a house which contained more than eight times the floor space of the house in which he spent his childhood. Robert Carter's new mansion was bigger, it was bolder, and it shared little with the older timber houses that surrounded it. Brick and big and tall and symmetrical and bedecked with classically inspired architectural details, it was not like anything in Lancaster County while it stood. Quite rapidly, then, Robert Carter increased the distance that separated him from his Lancaster County neighbors, and when he made other improvements to the yards around his mansion he made those distinctions even starker.

Not very much is known about the gardens that once existed at Corotoman. Carter did hire an English gardener shortly after he moved into his mansion, and he ordered this gardener to bring the yards around the mansion into closer accord with the architectural rhythms of the mansion. But the nature of the garden's plan, as well as the gardener's day-to-day routine, remain unknown (Robert Carter's Diary).

It is known, however, that Carter's notion about how a lawn should look clashed with ideas about how a yard should be maintained. Robert Carter's labor force was dispersed widely through his quarters. There was a home quarter near his mansion, and it was the scene one day of a clash between two notions about yard maintenance. On a tour of this quarter, Carter embroiled himself in a noisy quarrel with the women of the quarter when Carter objected to the way they kept their yards. It was the womens' custom to sweep the ground around their houses and the paths that connected their houses and garden plots, but this was a habit that Carter did not understand and remained one he did not attempt to fathom. He objected to it strenuously, but he seems not to have changed the minds of any of the women at the quarter, who continued to sweep their yards in accordance with a custom that was older than Corotoman. The irony of slave yards swept bare of grass lying in the shadow of a house surrounded by a lawn grassed and maintained by a gardener is worth savoring (Robert Carter's Diary).

The landscape of early eighteenth-century Virginia was a landscape of sharp contrasts and ironic juxtapositions. It came to be that way because the Virginia gentry came to need and rely on the symbolic power of material things to legitimize their social and political positions. Reading the symbolic value of signs on the cultural landscape was a much-practiced skill. When Hugh Jones wrote that Virginians were "more inclined to read men by business and conversation than to dive into books" (1956:81), he clearly meant to draw attention to the careful reading Virginians gave to achievement, status, and performance and to point out that his countrymen understood one another more for what they did than for what they thought.

What does all this have to do with the landscape of early eighteenth-century Virginia? Little, aside from the fact that if we are to understand the clues Virginians took from the landscape, we must first understand something about how they thought. It is necessary to remember, for example, that William Byrd and his planter friends were happiest when they were treated with "great courtesy" and with "abundance of respect" or when they could report that "everybody respected me like a King" (Wright and Tinling 1941:409). The winning of respect, from superiors and inferiors, was the goal of the gentry's actions and was, in some respects, a special kind of currency in which the gentry traded. Respect, or esteem, was earned in a number of ways. For Robert Carter, respect was something he gained if his crops did well. He once concluded that he had "lived at a very little purpose if I cannot get as much for my tobacco as other men" (Wright 1940b:96). There were, of course, other ways to gain and earn respect; the gentry's intense competition on race tracks and dance floors and dinner tables is well known. William Byrd counted kisses, both from the ladies and from Governor Spotswood, and confided to his diary once that the governor had given him "a kiss more than other people" (Wright and Tinling 1958:400). Robert Carter kept track of how much he spent on public entertainments and crowed often that nobody spent more.

There were, of course, threats aplenty to a planter's esteem. The potential sources of trouble were as plentiful as Job's afflictions, and it is sufficient here simply to mention that threats to authority and to esteem were not taken lightly. Robert Carter's response to a group of striking miners was to remind them that "we are your masters" (Carter 1731). But even that direct approach did not win complete approval. While seated in Marrot's Tavern one evening after sitting all day at the General Court, Carter and a companion were surprised when a disgruntled freeholder "cast a brick from the street into the room." The brick "narrowly missed" and made a point about respect that Carter did not soon forget (Wright and Tinling 1941:429).

It is necessary to indulge in this sort of review of the most salient characteristics of the gentry and the aspirations that lay behind them because the gentry landscape was shaped by and for the aspirations and anxieties that the Tidewater's great men carried with them. Few aspects of the cultural landscape of Virginia were not changed in some way by the gentry's embracing of the patrician culture. How they did that, and how in the process they changed their definition of what was necessary and what was sufficient, is revealed in the cultural landscape that Robert Carter knew as a young boy and as an old man.

## References Cited

Berkeley, E., and D. S. Berkeley (editors). 1965. *The Reverend John Clayton, a parson with a specific mind: His scientific writings and other related papers.* Charlottesville: University Press of Virginia.

Carr, L. G., and L. S. Walsh. 1980. Inventories and the analysis of wealth and consumption patterns in St. Mary's County, Maryland, 1658-1777. *Historical Methods* 13:81-104.

Carter, R. 1722-28. Robert Carter's diary. Charlottesville: University of Virginia Library.

----. 1731. Robert Carter letterbook, 1728-31. Charlottesville: University of Virginia Library.

Cook, E. 1969. The sot weed factor. In *Colonial American writing*, ed. R. H. Pearce, pp. 588-608. New York: Holt, Rinehart and Winston.

Dauphine, D. de. 1934. *A Huguenot exile in Virginia, or voyages of a Frenchman exiled for his religion with a description of Virginia and Maryland.* Ed. G. Chinard. New York: Press of the Pioneers.

Deetz, J. 1977. *In small things forgotten: The archaeology of early American life.* New York: Doubleday.

*Gentleman's Magazine.* 1732. Robert Carter's obituary. 2:1082.

Hudgins, C. L. 1982. Archaeology in the "King's" realm: Excavations at Robert Carter's Corotoman. Manuscript. Yorktown: Virginia Research Center for Archaeology.

Jones, H. 1956. *The present state of Virginia.* Ed. R. L. Morton. Chapel Hill: University of North Carolina Press.

Kammen, M. G. (editor). 1963. A letter from the Reverend Mr. Hugh Jones to the Reverend Dr. Benjamin Woodroffe, F.R.S., concerning several observables in Maryland. *Journal of Southern History* 29:362-72.

Kelso, W. M. 1984. *Kingsmill plantations, 1619-1800: Archaeology of country life in colonial Virginia.* New York: Academic Press.

Lancaster County. 1730. Order Book 8, 1729-1743. Richmond: Virginia State Library.

Menard, R. R. 1977. From servants to slaves: The transformation of the Chesapeake labor system. *Southern Studies: An Interdisciplinary Journal of the South: Special Issue on Colonial Slavery* 16:355-90.

----, P. M. G. Harris, and L. G. Carr. 1974. Opportunity and inequality: The distribution of wealth on the lower western shore of Maryland, 1638-1705. *Maryland Historical Magazine* 69:169-84.

Neiman, F. D. 1978. Domestic architecture at the Clifts plantation: The social context of early Virginia building. *Northern Neck of Virginia Historical Magazine* 28:2096-3128.

Upton, D. 1980. Early vernacular architecture in southeastern Virginia. Ph.D. dissertation, Department of Anthropology, Brown University.

Wright, L. B. 1970. *The first gentlemen of Virginia: Intellectual qualities of the early colonial ruling class*. Charlottesville: University Press of Virginia.

----. (editor). 1940. *Letters of Robert Carter, 1720-1727: The commercial interests of a Virginia gentleman*. San Marino, California: Huntington Library.

----, and M. Tinling (editors). 1941. *The secret diary of William Byrd of Westover, 1709-1711*. Richmond: Dietz Press.

----, and ----. (editors). 1958. *The London diary and other writings*. New York: Oxford.

# 5

# IMAGINING THE EARLY VIRGINIA LANDSCAPE

## Dell Upton

Simple descriptions of past landscapes can be deceptive. They suggest a fixed character and, more importantly, a fixed experience of the landscape by every observer. Yet this is never the case. A complete account of a historical landscape must therefore take into account its evanescent qualities and the differences in the ways it was experienced. Admittedly, this is much more difficult than to create an inventory of specific features. As with any interesting history we must start with what we know and proceed gingerly to what we think we understand. In this spirit, I will use an analysis of the physical landscape to explore mental ones.

The landscape of the wealthiest Virginians has been extensively described, if not particularly well understood. At the top of the architectural scale were the Corotomans and Monticellos, the great brick mansions of the cream of local society. Aubrey Land's calculations suggest that these may represent the houses of the top .5 percent to 3 percent of Chesapeake society (Land 1965). Three qualities seem to set them apart from other Virginia houses. They were built of brick, always an exceptional building material in Virginia; its use in any house is a sign of considerable wealth. They were two-story houses in a colony where one and one-half stories was the rule, and they were two rooms deep when one-room-deep houses were standard. Finally, their blocklike, symmetrical, hip-roofed form and much of their architectural decoration (although traditionally interpreted as references to high-style European ideas) mark these large houses as products of the international popular culture that transformed all of Euro-American material culture in the eighteenth century (Upton 1988).

The great houses demand to be considered as one element of the larger gentry landscape. It is misleading to set the mansions apart from the smaller two- or three-room gentry houses often erroneously labeled yeoman houses. The latter were sometimes built of brick and showed the influence of the popular-culture ideas that shaped the great houses (fig. 5.1). Spatially, large and small planters' dwellings, together with the churches and courthouses that constituted the public portions of the gentry landscape, were organized according to the same principles.

Although more slave houses than poor white farmers' houses survive, there is plenty of evidence to suggest that the two should be set apart from the mansions and prosperous planters' houses. The houses of both slaves and poor whites were spatially and structurally similar. After all, from a certain viewpoint slaves were simply one group of poor people in Virginia. In contrast to the gentry houses, the houses of slaves and small planters were

Figure 5.1.  Britt house (ca. 1790), Southhampton County, Virginia

ordinarily wooden buildings, as often as not post-built or, in the case of slaves, constructed of logs.  They were one room deep and one or two rooms long, and could be extraordinarily small.  The original portion of Perkinsons, a surviving small planter's house in Chesterfield County, is 12 feet by 14 feet, and there were others smaller that have now disappeared (fig. 5.2).  Extant slave houses tend to be about 18 feet square (324 square feet), but the documentary evidence shows that these were among the largest eighteenth-century slave dwellings. Houses as small as 12 feet by 8 feet (96 square feet) can be identified in the records.  Among all surveyed and documented buildings, the median was 232 square feet and the mean 218 square feet.  Among documentary examples only, the median was 192 square feet and the mean 233 square feet (Upton 1982a:25-34).

Thus, a thorough understanding of the early Virginia scene requires concurrent analysis of both the gentry world and the overlapping lower-class sphere, for gentry, poor whites, and slaves often shared the same physical structures but constructed very different mental landscapes from them.  In the white planter's landscape, houses, churches, courthouses, and other public structures, as well as the roads and ways that linked them, were conceived as an articulated spatial network.  In the landscape of the poorest white planters and, preeminently, of slaves, the same structures, along with slave quarters, woods, fields, and informal gathering

Figure 5.2. Perkinsons (late eighteenth century), Chesterfield County, Virginia. The small wing at the right is the original house; the larger wing in the foreground was built at the beginning of the nineteenth century.

places, appeared as a ragged patchwork of free and controlled spaces, one that was neither systematic nor particularly coherent.

The static landscape of the slaves and ordinary planters was a traditional one. At its core were long-standing ideas about workers' space and workers' prerogatives that were shared by whites and blacks. The living and working spaces of farm laborers traditionally were incorporated within the English farmhouse. By the third quarter of the seventeenth century, even before slaves took over agricultural labor, Virginia's planters had removed the workers to separate buildings. They remained closely associated, however (Carson 1978; Neiman 1986; Upton 1982b). Surviving domestic complexes show that slaves' houses and slaves' work spaces were located adjacent to one another and sometimes shared the same buildings. For example, at Howard's Neck, a nineteenth-century complex in Goochland County, a village down the hill from the main domestic buildings contains shops and farm structures, a building reputed to be the overseer's house, and a row of slave houses, two built of log and one of frame, and all altered in postbellum times.

This was the slaves' territory. They worked in the farm buildings, and their dominion over the space and their tools was acknowledged, often through the levying of customary fines and fees to the slaves against those who trespassed on them. The eighteenth-century Westmoreland County tutor Philip Fithian paid a forfeit for intruding on the baker's domain and another for touching the plowlines. He attended slaves' cockfights at Nomini Hall's stables, but objected to his pupil Harry Carter spending time "either in the kitchen, or at the Blacksmiths, or Carpenters Shop" (Fithian 1957:37, 88, 201).

The slaves' houses, too, were under their control. Between the widely set buildings they tended gardens, raised poultry, and kept their numerous pet dogs. In spare moments they made small objects to furnish otherwise spartan dwellings. The standing quarters give evidence of improvised shelving, and documents record stools and small boxes, as well as homemade musical instruments. These were all obtained outside normal channels, which provided meager supplies of blankets and iron cooking pots as the only standard furnishings (Upton 1982a; Vlach 1987).

Slaves asserted their rights to their territory, and some had locks for their doors to enforce their claims. One of Landon Carter's slaves locked Carter out to avoid punishment and declared his refusal to be treated harshly on his own ground, even by his master (Upton 1982a:45-46).

Outside the quarters, there were other places that the slaves might command. Although the planter might own a vast tract, his effective control was often limited to the immediate environs of his house. Even that was not assured. Landon Carter wrote bitterly of the "knife triflers" who insisted on carving up the posts of the arcade connecting his house and his kitchen (Carter 1965:100). Thus, slaves had room to maneuver. Those whose duties required them to stay in the house often had small holes and boxes in which they could store personal possessions. The woods and waterways were theirs as well, as Isaac (1982:53, 328-36), Kulikoff (1978:248), and Vlach (1978:101-2) have demonstrated. Those who wished to avoid work or punishment sometimes hid in the nearby woods, often for weeks at a time, coming and going to the quarters for food and other necessities without being found. Similarly, slaves who were skilled watermen were able to slip away to visit loved ones and to return of their own accord weeks later.

The theme of the slave's landscape, then, was control. Those areas effectively beyond the master's reach, whether they were ceded on traditional grounds, such as the quarters and shops, or whether they were seized by slaves, as in the case of the woods and the waterways, could be considered the slaves'. The directions slaves gave to inquiring travelers suggest that bondsmen did imagine the landscape in this manner.[1] According to the exasperated travelers, the landscape was presented as an unrelated collection of barriers or pitfalls with no relation to any other part of the landscape; neutral points were simply forgotten. The subject was missing: there was no sense that perception of the landscape might change as an observer moved through it. The architect Benjamin Henry Latrobe, for example, found it necessary in getting directions from a slave "to make minute enquiry after all the byeroads and turnings which I am to avoid. By this mode of enquiry I in general astonish my directors by discoveries of difficulties they never thought of before. This was the case with my old negroe" (Latrobe 1977:137-141). This kind of landscape, instead of being a network through which the observer moves, is a series of spots where customary social relationships are in effect, where control and possession are present, and where they are not. The evidence suggests that small white planters looked at it the same way. The traveler Thomas Anburey noted that the local "tells you to keep the right hand path, then you'll come to an old field, you are to cross that, and then you'll come to a fence of such a one's plantation, then keep that fence, and you'll come to a road that has three forks . . . then you'll come to a creek, after you cross that creek, you must turn to the left, and then you'll come to a tobacco house . . . and then you'll come to Mr. such a one's ordinary" (Anburey 1923:196-97).

These directions exasperated men like Latrobe and Anburey, because they represented an alien and, to them, irrational mode of thought. These outsiders shared another way of seeing the landscape with the great and minor gentry. The gentry landscape was radically different in underlying conception from the ordinary landscape. Theirs was the dynamic, flexible, continuous landscape that I call articulated.

The gentry landscape was experienced dynamically; its meanings could not be comprehended at a glance. The observer was required to move through space and piece together many partial signals. It was a landscape in which the parts were related sequentially in space and time. Take the Anglican parish churches, for example. On the whole, these were relatively plain buildings. Any decoration was carefully applied with a clear intention: to cue movement through the building and to suggest how one ought to interpret the experience. The parishioner approached the church to find a walled yard with an elaborate gate (fig. 5.3). In the yard, the parishioners gathered to talk business or simply to socialize. At the appropriate hour, they moved into the building through doorways that, after the early eighteenth century, were embellished with pediments (fig. 5.4). The pediments over the gate and the doorway were traditional signs of honor that at the simplest level signified the importance of the place. Yet they also marked a transition from one state to another: from the undifferentiated community outside the walls, to the informally sorted community inside the walls, and in turn to the officially sorted community inside the church. Once inside, parishioners found themselves seated according to a rank determined, not without frequent objections, by the parish elite. Seating was distributed along axial aisles. Dignity was indicated by location in the church and by size and elaboration of the seating. Traditionally, the best not only had the biggest seats but those near the east, or altar, end. According to Philip Fithian, the parish's leading gentlemen often waited outside until the service was well along, then entered en masse, making a conspicuous parade down the stone-flagged aisles to find their seats near the front (Fithian 1957:137). A simple principle of arrangements determined importance: the farther from the west entrance, the better. As the eighteenth century progressed, however, another criterion was added: gentlemen now wished their pews to be above everyone else's, where they would see, but not be seen by, those whose lives they dominated. The pews near the east end were now the second best; those in hanging pews (private galleries) were now preferred (Upton 1986).

In other words, the congregation encountered a series of barriers or markers. As each one was passed, a new order was created. The place of each person in the procession varied, as did the degree to which he or she participated in it. Some people arrived inconspicuously on foot, others grandly on horses or in carriages. Some could sit almost anywhere they chose, the guests of their neighbors, while many were confined to a couple of unassigned public pews at the rear. Most entered through the west door, but a few could come in through the south door and reach their pews more directly. Those who were given private galleries were often granted private entrances and stairways and even windows to go with them.

The principles of hierarchy and movement, as well as the use of height and distance as physical indicators of status, organized other elements of the gentry landscape, courthouses,

Figure 5.3. Blandford Church (1734-37; 1752-70), Petersburg, Virginia. The churchyard wall dates from the second construction period.

for example. From undifferentiated public space, one passed into a walled courthouse yard, sometimes through an intermediate arcaded portico, and into the courtroom. A bar separated the congregation from the litigants, and the litigants from justices and jury. The justices sat on a raised bench, arranged by rank, with the senior justice at the center, often under a pediment of his own. An apse often served subtly to differentiate rank, moving the senior justice slightly farther away than his colleagues. The bars served to filter out those who moved along the axis, and the justices could sometimes circumvent it altogether through a separate door near their end of the courthouse (Lounsbury 1987a, 1987b; Upton 1986:205-6).

Articulation characterized the landscape of the great houses with which we began. One of the most complete examples is Mount Airy in Richmond County. The siting and architectural decoration at Mount Airy were manipulated carefully to make use of the principles of procession through distance and elevation to distinguish among users of the complex and to impress upon them John Tayloe's centrality in Mount Airy's microcosm. Eighteenth-century visitors approached the house along a circuitous route skirting a sunken park, which served to emphasize the loftiness of Mount Airy's terraces (fig. 5.5). The first

Figure 5.4. St. John's Church (ca. 1731-34), King William County, Virginia, Virginia. The pediment over the north door was added in the mid-eighteenth century.

Figure 5.5. Mount Airy (ca. 1760), Richmond County, Virginia. View is from the park. One of the quadrants and wings is visible at the left.

terrace was the stopping place for the lowest order of outsiders. Urns and steps called the visitor's attention to a second, low terrace to be crossed on the way to the house. The towering quality of the main building was exaggerated by the close set wings on either side, an old architectural device. (Originally the wings were freestanding, but the connecting quadrants were added early in Mount Airy's history.) After crossing the terrace and climbing the steps, the visitor encountered an open loggia, another barrier in his or her progress to the central saloon or, for the most favored, the dining room, the sanctum sanctorum of Virginia sociability (Reid 1967:62). This route placed a series of barriers in the caller's path, barriers emphasized by architectural devices (fig. 5.6). Each barrier successfully passed augmented the outsider's sense of worth and at the same time set it off against the greater importance of the host. As at church or at court, some people might circumvent this path; the processional route was not for everyone. Members of the family could enter the house directly into the east end through an appropriately elaborate doorway. A more discreet doorway marked a separate entrance to the dining room for the slaves who served it. For the resident of Mount Airy, the dining room was the heart of the family's domain. For the outsider, it was the goal of a status-affirming procession. To the slave, it was perhaps the most controlled space in the landscape.

The fashionable architectural language of Mount Airy must not obscure fashion's service of Virginian aims. Smaller gentry houses lacked the formalized unity of Mount Airy, but they were intended to be experienced in the same manner. The small houses are primary;

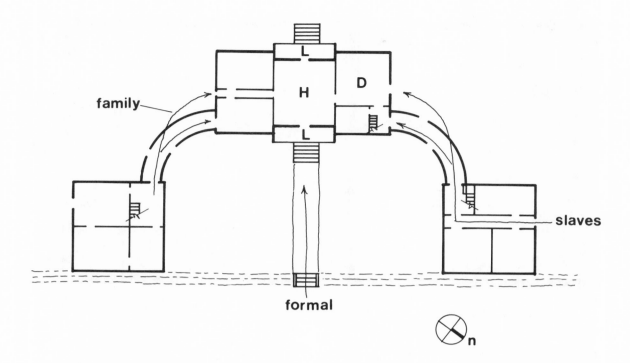

Figure 5.6. Mount Airy. Schematic plan showing formal, family, and slave routes to the dining room (D).

they established the themes that Mount Airy developed. Small gentry houses preceded the mansions in scattering household functions among a main house and a series of domestic outbuildings (Upton 1982b). In the smallest houses, the domestic outbuildings were usually set beside or behind the main house, but they sometimes were used to define a ceremonial route for the visitor, and the main house was raised up on its storage cellar above all the other buildings. The visitor thus passed through the outbuildings, up to the front door, and entered directly into the hall, or main room, the most decorated space of the house. In some examples, the stair was moved from its customary position on the wall between the hall and the chamber to the far corner adjacent to the fireplace (fig. 5.7). The concentration of architectural decoration in mantel, stair, and sometimes cupboard created an appropriate visual termination of the visitor's journey (Upton 1986:209-13). A house of this sort had fewer social barriers than Mount Airy. There were no terraces or loggias to shield the occupants from visitors. Yet the principles of organization of space were there. These small gentry houses served the same social purposes in the same ways as churches, courthouses, and great plantation houses, and it is this which ties them to the landscape of the mansions and separates them from the poor planters' and slaves' territory.

Of course, dynamic landscapes antedate eighteenth-century Virginia by many centuries. Our period departs from earlier ones in incorporating a new sense of time in the landscape. It was a purely internal time, in which contingent events were linked only by an individual consciousness which blended each moment into those before and after it. In this kind of time, relationships among events constantly shift according to the position of the observer; there are no fixed bench marks against which to measure them. As Tayloe's visitors moved

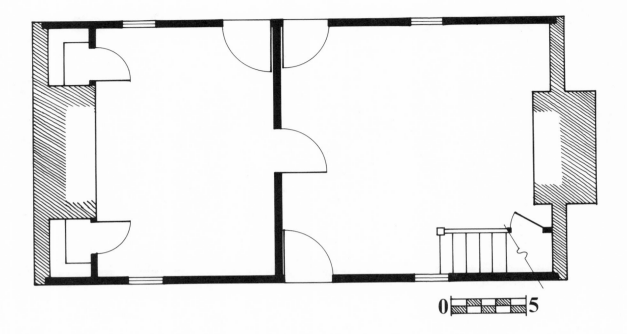

Figure 5.7. Britt house plan

through Mount Airy, the awareness of where they had been gave significance to where they were. Virginians shared this conception of time with other Euro-Americans; it grew in part out of investigations of the physical universe. Those inquiries replaced the fixed hierarchies of an older worldview with a shifting network of relationships. The American scientist David Rittenhouse's orrery can stand as an emblem of this new idea of the world (Boorstin 1948:13). A mechanical model of the solar system in which the planets moved about the sun when a crank was turned, Rittenhouse's orrery attempted to account for the evanescent character of planetary relations. It denied that a single image could sum up the solar system.

The recognition of evanescence and change led Euro-Americans to an understanding of the articulated character of their world. They saw that the network of relations that bound both the natural and social worlds was flexible and could be manipulated from many points within it. Evidence of the new viewpoint can be found everywhere in the eighteenth century. Objects which once had only one state, or at best two, now had several; their appearance, use, and contents could change from moment to moment. For example, furniture could be opened or closed, its contents distributed among a variety of separately accessible compartments of varying sizes and shapes, its parts adjusted to fit the individual user (figs. 5.8 and 5.9). More important, eighteenth-century designers attempted to depict the evanescent qualities of these new objects. They were represented in several separate states simultaneously; all the ways one might want them to be could be seen at once. The *Nude Descending a Staircase* had an ancestor in the chairs and cabinets illustrated in books like Thomas Chippendale's (figs. 5.9 and 5.10). In Virginia, the manipulability of a landscape broken into many small, related, but carefully distinguished parts is evident in everything from household goods to fence types and field patterns. It is pointless to ask what these new spaces and subdivisions were

N.º CXX.

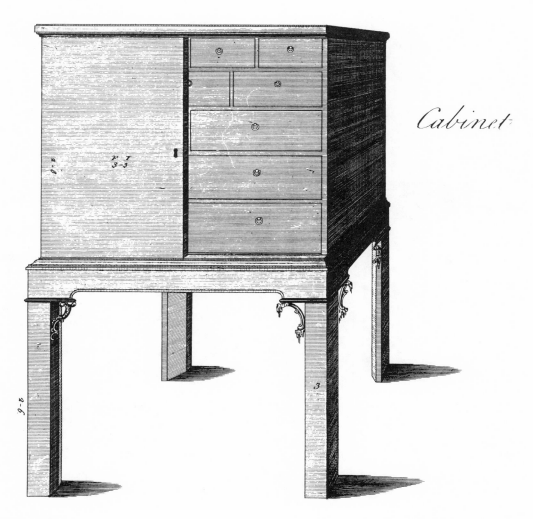

*Cabinet*

T. Chippendale inv. et del.                    Pub. according to Act of Parliam. 1753.

Figure 5.8. Multistate furniture. Cabinet designed by Thomas Chippendale, with drawers of various sizes and shapes, capable of being adapted to the user's changing demands. Chippendale attempted to represent the fluidity of the form by showing it both open and closed. From Thomas Chippendale, *The Gentleman and Cabinet-Maker's Director*, 3d ed. (London 1762), plate CXX.

for--they could be for anything you wanted them to be, and that could change from moment to moment.

Elite Virginians reveled in these discoveries, but there were more serious implications for them as well. No fixed image could embody the dynamic character of local society as Virginia's gentry perceived it. Only in moving through the related settings of church, courthouse, and greater and lesser plantation houses could Virginia be understood.

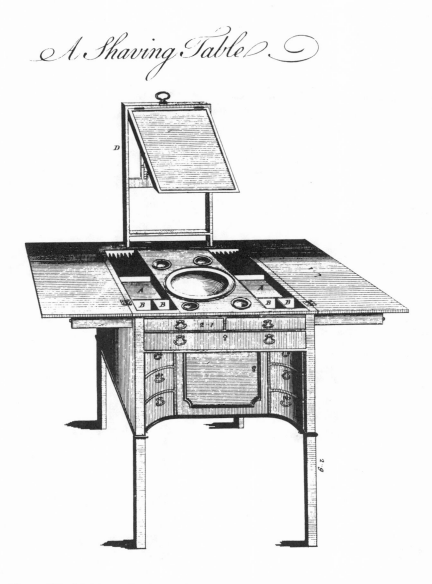

*A Shaving Table*

Nº LIV.

Figure 5.9. Multistate furniture. Shaving table adjustable to meet the demands of the individual user. From Chippendale, *The Gentleman and Cabinet-Maker's Director*, plate LIV.

Decoration served to assert that all were complementary aspects of the same world (Upton 1986:101-62).

The gentry began to enjoy the articulated landscape aesthetically. They placed their houses where they could be seen and at the same time liked to site them where they could survey the landscape around them. Philip Fithian caught the spirit when he wrote that he "love[d] to walk on these high Hills where I can see the Tops of tall Trees lower than my Feet, at not half a miles Distance--where I can have a long View of many Miles & see on the Summits of the Hills Clusters of Savin Trees, through these often a little Farm-House, or Quarter for Negroes" (Fithian 1957:178).

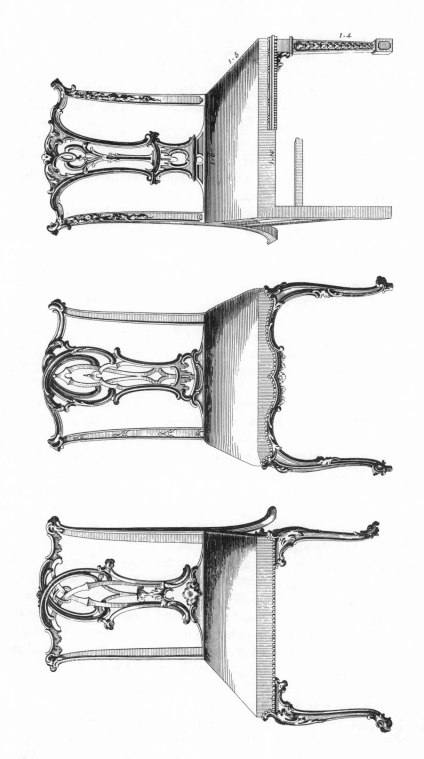

Chairs.

T. Chippendale. inv. et del.     Hemerick Sculp.

Figure 5.10. Depiction of all possible forms of an object in one view. From Chippendale, *The Gentleman and Cabinet-Maker's Director*, plate CXX.

At the same time, Virginians realized that the hierarchical social relationships implied in their landscapes were not immutable. No one need accept a subordinate place. The scramble for private pews, the construction of a setting like Mount Airy's, represented each planter's striving to manipulate the network to place himself at the center. The centripetal impulses present but controlled within the articulated landscape now broke loose.

Monticello was the climax. Situated on the flank of its little mountain, Monticello, like Mount Airy, was approached indirectly along a route which concealed the house until one was very near. While Monticello could not be seen, its builder commanded the prospect of a vast territory around it. The Blue Ridge Mountains, the lowlands, and other planters' houses all were part of a prospect Isaac Weld thought stretched forty miles in each direction (Weld 1799:119). Although the ground rose behind Monticello, potentially dominating the house, it, too, was made to serve the master. Gardens, vineyards, and orchards embellished Monticello's hillside and picturesque garden walks were threaded through it. Jefferson originally intended to scatter striking pavilions about the grounds that could be seen to advantage from his house, and to place the grandest one of all on Montalto.

The entire landscape of Piedmont Virginia was thus focused on Thomas Jefferson. The furnishings were in the same spirit. The house was filled with such things as a revolving desk, dumbwaiters, a two-faced clock, a device to open doors in unison. Here was the articulated landscape in its most optimistic and its most egocentric form; the natural and human worlds were refashioned to converge on a single individual at its center. The landscape devices used were the same as those found in the pre-Revolutionary church, courthouse, and plantation. Height and distance were there, but on a grander scale than any attempted before the Revolution.

The critical difference was that changes only implied in the late pre-Revolutionary landscape were realized at Monticello. Jefferson in his aerie, like the gentleman in his hanging pew, could see and not be seen. The complementary, dynamic quality of the older landscape was gone. Everything at Monticello was made to be absorbed from a single point of view by the central actor. The dome, which might have served a dynamic scheme, creating a processional goal by focusing the surrounding landscape and offering a vantage point for its occupants, is at the rear of the house. At Monticello, dynamism was drained from the articulated landscape.

The appeal of this more loosely articulated landscape was that one's neighbor could do the same thing; the web of hills, farms, and valleys could be made to focus on Jefferson's neighbor as well as, and at the same time as, on Jefferson himself. There was no need even to acknowledge the existence of others. How different from the slave's landscape, with its constant awareness of the power and presence of others, and how different even from the earlier processional landscape, which also depended on a consciousness of relationships.

The articulated landscape of the wealthy and the static mental landscape of the poor were separate worlds that occupied the same physical spaces. Little about this physical landscape was unique to Virginia, but the imagined landscape interpretations grew out of the specific experiences of each group in Virginia.

The sense of empowerment manifested in the articulated landscape was the product of both the Virginia elite's familiarity with the early Euro-American intellectual world and their social power in the Old Dominion. In the first instance, historical research, scientific inquiry, and political and philosophical discourse all contributed to a growing Euro-American confidence in the ability of humans to know the essence of their world as a system; if to know it, to understand it; if to understand it, to improve it for their own benefit. This sense of power was particularly resonant for Virginia's gentry, who gave it a peculiarly local cast. Travelers in eighteenth-century Virginia repeatedly stressed the sense of absolute and unquestionable power that slavery gave the elite (Upton 1986:167). If Enlightenment intellect offered slaveholders the abstract image of the world as a flexible network that could be manipulated by the informed, Virginia's social system invited them to give the network physical existence.

For the powerless--for the poor white planter and especially for the slave--no such confidence was warranted. Subject to the overbearing demeanor and irascible conduct of their social betters, barely scratching a living from the soil or allowed only a fraction of the fruits of their labors, they had little reason to imagine such a useful world. They searched instead for the holes in the net.

## Notes

1. Throughout this passage, I use the word *slaves* and not *blacks*, because the slaves' way of seeing arose from the power relationship of slavery rather than from ethnicity.

## References Cited

Anburey, T. 1923. *Travels through the interior parts of America, 1798.* Boston: Houghton, Mifflin.

Boorstin, D. 1948. *The lost world of Thomas Jefferson.* Boston: Beacon Press.

Carson, C. 1978. Doing history with material culture. In *Material culture and the study of American life*, ed. I. M. G. Quimby, pp. 41-64. New York: W. W. Norton.

Carter, L. 1965. *The diary of Colonel Landon Carter of Sabine Hall, 1772-1778.* Ed. Jack P. Greene. Charlottesville: University Press of Virginia.

Fithian, P. 1957. *Journal and letters of Philip Vickers Fithian, 1773-1774: A plantation tutor of the Old Dominion.* Ed. H. D. Farish. Rept. Charlottesville: University Press of Virginia.

Isaac, R. 1982. *The transformation of Virginia, 1740-1790.* Chapel Hill: University of North Carolina Press.

Kulikoff, A. 1978. The origins of Afro-American society in Tidewater Virginia and Maryland, 1700-1790. *William and Mary Quarterly* 35(3):248.

Land, A. C. 1965. Economic base and social structure: The northern Chesapeake in the eighteenth century. *Journal of Economic History* 24:639-54.

Latrobe, B. H. 1977. *The Virginia journals of Benjamin Henry Latrobe, 1795-1798.* Ed. E. C. Carter II and A. Polites. New Haven: Yale University Press.

Lounsbury, C. 1987a. The early courthouses of Virginia. *Colonial Williamsburg Interpreter* 8(1):5-6.

----. 1987b. "An elegant and commodious building": William Buckland and the design of the Prince William County courthouse. *Journal of the Society of Architectural Historians* 46:228-40.

Neiman, F. D. 1986. Domestic architecture at the Clifts plantation: The social context of early Virginia building. In *Common places: Readings in American vernacular architecture*, ed. D. Upton and J. M. Vlach, pp. 292–314. Athens: University of Georgia Press.

Reid, J. 1967. The religion of the Bible and religion of KW County compared. *Transactions of the American Philosophical Society* 57(1).

Upton, D. 1982a. Slave housing in eighteenth-century Virginia: A report to the Department of Social and Cultural History, National Museum of American History, Smithsonian Institution. Manuscript. Washington, D.C.: Smithsonian Institution.

----. 1982b. The origins of Chesapeake building. In *Three centuries of Maryland architecture*, pp. 44–57. Annapolis: Maryland Historical Trust.

----. 1986. *Holy things and profane: Anglican parish churches in colonial Virginia.* New York: Architectural History Foundation and Cambridge: MIT Press.

----. 1988. New views of the Virginia landscape. *Virginia Magazine of History and Biography* 96(4):403–70.

Vlach, J. M. 1978. *The Afro-American tradition in decorative arts.* Cleveland: Cleveland Museum of Art.

----. 1987. Afro-American domestic artifacts in eighteenth-century Virginia. *Material Culture* 19(1):3–24.

Weld, I. 1799. *Travels through the states of North America . . . during the years 1795, 1796, and 1797.* London: John Stockdale.

*II. Early American Urban Landscapes*

# 6

# THE SEVENTEENTH-CENTURY LANDSCAPE OF SAN LUIS DE TALIMALI: THREE SCALES OF ANALYSIS

## Gary Shapiro and James J. Miller

In 1633 Franciscan priests arrived in north Florida to convert the Apalachee Indians to Christianity. They had the blessings of the Spanish crown because Apalachee was the most fertile and populous province in Florida. If Apalachee could be brought under Spanish control, its abundant produce could provide much-needed sustenance for the Spanish colony at St. Augustine.

In March 1984 the Florida Department of State launched an intensive archaeological and historical investigation of San Luis de Talimali, the seventeenth-century capital of Spanish missions to the Apalachee (fig. 6.1). The site had been purchased by the state of Florida for development as a public archaeological and historic park. Our immediate research goal was to determine, in the broadest sense, the location and distribution of archaeological remains over the entire 20-hectare tract. From there, our research design developed into an investigation of the mission era town plan. This has been accomplished by integrating historical documentary research and archaeological field studies. Translation of contemporary Spanish religious and administrative reports (Hann 1987, 1988) revealed all of the town's major public features, and these have now been confirmed archaeologically. The current phase of research focuses on a detailed investigation of domestic life in the mission village.

At the outset, we recognized that San Luis did not exist in a vacuum. It was a town whose character was closely linked to large-scale political, demographic, economic, religious, and environmental forces. Many of these variables were related intimately to the regional landscape of Apalachee and the local setting of San Luis itself. A research strategy that dictates investigation at various scales was adopted, and that is the way the landscape archaeology of San Luis is presented here. In the broadest sense, the landscape geography of Florida's seventeenth-century missions can be understood first with reference to the preexisting Indian settlement pattern and then in terms of Spanish interests. First it is necessary to take a broad-scale look at southeastern Indians.

At the time of European contact, most southeastern Indians were horticulturalists who located their settlements near productive soils. In most of the Southeast this meant that villages were located in bottomlands of silt-bearing rivers, whose relic levees were fertile and easy to till (cf. Smith 1978). Accordingly, rivers were at the heart of most southeastern polities, but the situation was quite the opposite in north Florida. Because Florida rivers emanate from tannic swamps and springs, rather than large drainage basins, they do not carry the loads of silt needed to produce and fertilize natural levees. Swampy Florida bottomlands

Figure 6.1. Artist's conception of San Luis based on historical research and broad-scale archaeological testing. The view is from the north-northeast.

are among the worst microenvironments for growing crops, and the best soils are found, instead, in the uplands between river valleys. One result is that for many north Florida groups, rivers were at the boundaries rather than the centers of political regions. This was the case for the Utina, Potano, Yustega, and Apalachee (fig. 6.2).

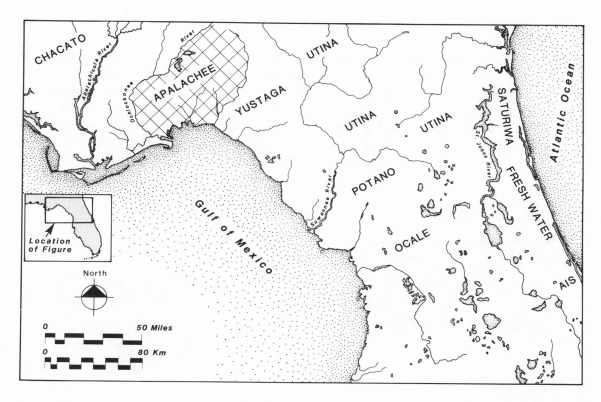

Figure 6.2. Locations of Apalachee and neighboring Indian groups in the early seventeenth century

From the time of de Soto's 1539 visit until 1704, Apalachee was bounded by the Aucilla and Ochlockonee rivers. This 30-mile-wide territory may have held a population of 30,000 in 1528, but its population was closer to 10,000 throughout the 1633-to-1704 mission era (Hann 1988).

Apalachee was famous among Florida's Indians as a wealthy province. Spanish explorers Narváez in 1528 and de Soto in 1539 traveled there in haste with hopes of finding gold. In fact, Apalachee's wealth was in its produce. The province included some of the best corn-growing lands in Florida, and this was the magnet that eventually attracted Spanish interests a century after de Soto passed through.

St. Augustine had been founded on the Atlantic coast in 1565 to protect Spanish territorial claims and shipping lanes. Its location was strategically sound, but poor soils in the area precluded self-sufficiency. St. Augustine depended on imported supplies and crops grown by Indians. By establishing missions among nearby Indians, the Spaniards hoped to gain their allegiance and simultaneously to fulfill their spiritual, economic, and political goals.

Florida's earliest missions were concentrated on the Atlantic coast and inland near St. Augustine. By the mid-seventeenth century, epidemics, harsh treatment, and native unrest had greatly diminished the ability of the nearby Timucua Indians to provide food for St. Augustine. But to the west, leaders of the populous and fertile Apalachee province began asking for missionaries early in the seventeenth century. A formal mission effort was launched in 1633 with the hope that food from Apalachee could help support St. Augustine. Apalachee produce was to power the settlement that protected the gold and silver on which

Spain depended for its economic survival. In this way Apalachee became integrated within a world economy.

Apalachee included fourteen principal missions and more than forty satellite villages in 1675. One of the most interesting features of Apalachee's regional landscape is the Cody Scarp, a topographic break which separates the fertile red clay hills on the north from the sandy coastal plain to the south (fig. 6.3). Most of the nine known mission sites were located directly on the scarp, where the highlands are nearest the streams that were navigable by canoe to the coast (fig. 6.4). This setting was especially important to the Spaniards, whose interests dictated that agricultural produce find its way easily to the coast for shipment to St. Augustine.

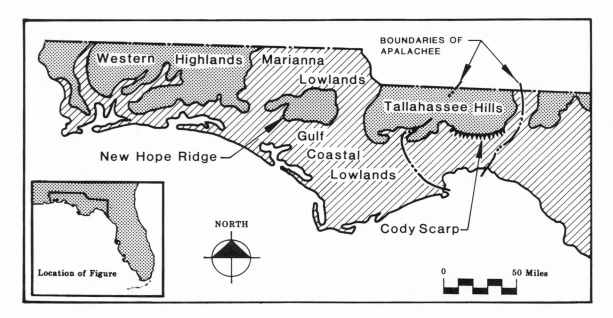

Figure 6.3. Physiographic regions of northwest Florida

## San Luis

San Luis was the largest Apalachee village and was the Spanish capital of the province from at least 1656 until 1704. Together with its two dozen satellite villages, San Luis in 1675 held a population of 1,400 Apalachee, about one dozen Spanish soldiers, a Franciscan priest, and nine Spanish families. But only a few years later, Apalachee began to experience the first slave raids by the British-allied Indians that would eventually bring the province to ruin. In 1704, after devastating attacks by British and Creek Indian forces, the Spaniards themselves burned San Luis and evacuated the province, an event which heralded the end of a once vibrant Indian-Hispanic culture that was unique to La Florida.

San Luis's local setting is typical of most Apalachee mission sites that have been located to date (Jones and Shapiro 1987). It occupies a broad, flat hilltop, with at least one steep side or ravine in which springs are located (fig. 6.5). This combination of high elevation, rich soils, and a reliable water source are aspects of the landscape that made San Luis a favored location for human settlement for at least 10,000 years. During the seventeenth century, this

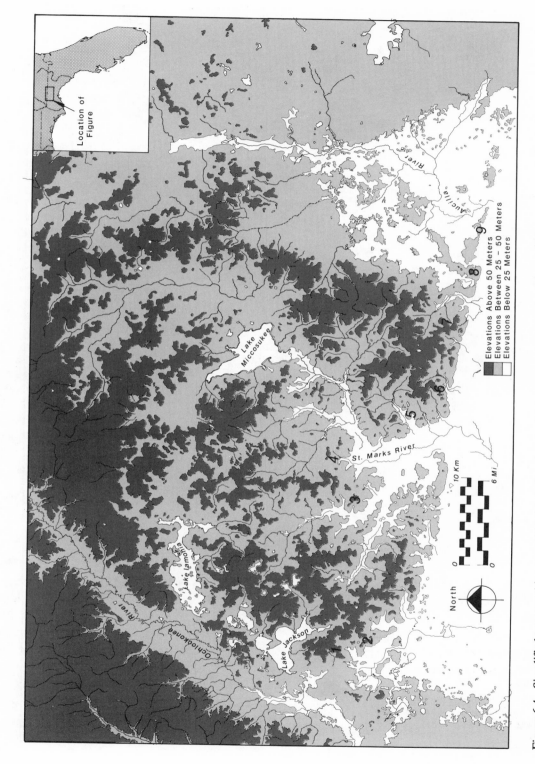

Figure 6.4. Simplified topographic map of Apalachee's uplands with locations of nine known mission sites. San Luis is no. 4.

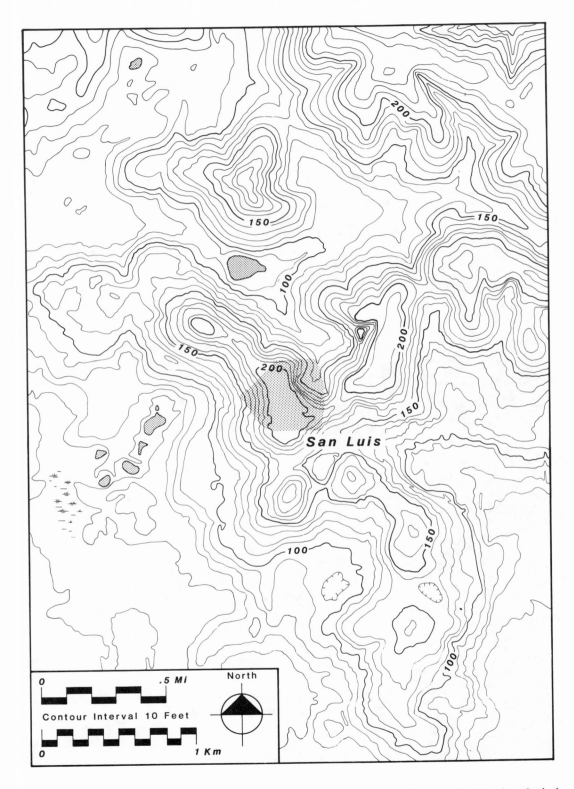

Figure 6.5. Topographic setting of San Luis. Shading indicates boundaries of the San Luis Archaeological and Historic Site managed by the Florida Department of State.

hilltop and most of the surrounding landscape would have been treeless, affording a commanding view in most directions.

With the exception of the fort location, partially excavated during the 1940s and 1950s, most features of the settlement were known only through brief mention in historic documents (Griffin 1951). In addition to the fort, San Luis included a church, cemetery, and *convento* (the priest's house). There was a substantial village, at least one town plaza, and a large Indian council house. Several additional structures or activity areas are also mentioned briefly, including a public granary, a forge, and an area in which grain was milled. While these features are known to have existed, only the fort location was known with certainty when the project began in March 1984.

The first step was to conduct broad-scale surveys as a foundation for intensive research in specific portions of the site (Shapiro 1987). Through a program of detailed topographic mapping, systematic auger survey, electronic remote sensing, and judgmentally placed test pits, we hoped (1) to locate distinct portions of the settlement known from documents, (2) to determine whether there was evidence for formal structure in the town plan, and (3) to determine whether residential areas appeared segregated according to ethnic or socioeconomic affiliations of the residents.

Thirty thousand elevations were recorded at 2-meter intervals across the site. This level of detail was selected with the hope that surface contours would indicate locations of collapsed seventeenth-century structures or other features such as roads, streets, or a plaza. A computer was employed to produce topographic maps from the 30,000 readings. Several conventional contour maps were drawn, but three-dimensional images of site topography were even more useful for interpretations. In figure 6.6, the fort location appears in the foreground as a low rise, but the most intriguing feature is a large circular depression, approximately 125 meters in diameter, surrounded by a low ridge of earth. This feature has been labeled the great circle. Artifact distributions and excavations leave little doubt that, as originally suspected, this feature is the seventeenth-century town plaza.

Another notable topographic feature is a flat platform located on the southeast end of the great circle. It measures about 40 meters in diameter and is surrounded by depressions that we suspected were borrow pits. Excavations in 1986 confirmed this platform as the location of San Luis's enormous Indian council house.

All the topographic maps show traces of roads, most of which probably postdate the seventeenth century, but the deep depression on the northwest (based on evidence from aerial photographs) may be part of the seventeenth-century mission trail. Finally, the mound on the north edge of the great circle is built up of soil excavated in 1938 for the basement of a mansion which still stands on the site.

While the topographic survey was underway, subsurface testing was started. Auger tests, 20 centimeters in diameter, were excavated every 10 meters with a gasoline-powered soil auger. Data from these 1,436 tests were used to produce a series of computer-generated maps that show artifact distributions and densities (Shapiro 1987).

Some of these data are illustrated in figure 6.7. Artifacts from the 1,436 auger tests were weighed and counted. These data were combined in various categories, such as aboriginal pottery, Spanish pottery, nails, and glass, then plotted by computer as contour maps of artifact distribution by weight or count. The shaded area shows the 5-gram contour for total pottery. The area marked by diagonal lines is the 5-gram contour for burned clay. Many mission-period buildings had clay walls or prepared clay floors, and the burned clay

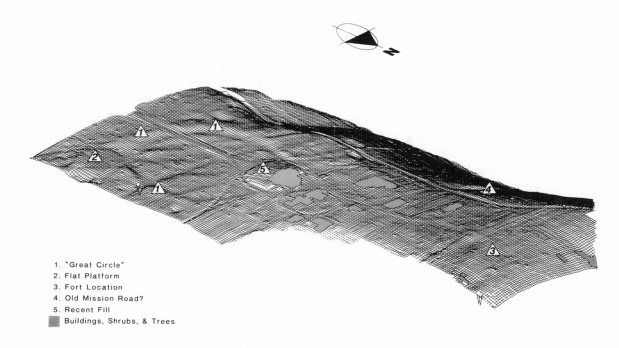

1. "Great Circle"
2. Flat Platform
3. Fort Location
4. Old Mission Road?
5. Recent Fill
▓ Buildings, Shrubs, & Trees

Figure 6.6. Site topography viewed from the northeast: (1) great circle surrounding the plaza, (2) Apalachee council house, (3) fort location, (4) seventeenth-century (?) road, and (5) modern fill from cellar of adjacent house

distribution provides evidence for architectural features. The wedge-shaped symbols are wrought-iron nails or spikes.

Taken together, historic accounts, topographic maps, and artifact distribution maps suggested locations for several known features of the settlement. These locations are discussed in the following paragraphs.

The location of the fort was known from nineteenth-century accounts and from earlier excavations (Griffin 1951). Here, the fort is indicated by a slight rise in the ground surface and by concentrations of burned clay (architectural debris) and pottery.

Pottery is abundant to the immediate southwest of the fort, but neither wrought-iron nails nor burned clay was recovered. This is probably an area which saw a great deal of activity but held no substantial structures. It is not surprising to find that, for defensive purposes, an area so near the fort would have been free of substantial structures, but this does not explain the abundance of pottery there. Given its advantageous topographic setting, on a high, flat part of the San Luis hill, it is unlikely that this area was a refuse dump. As a working hypothesis, this pattern may represent a marketplace or some other type of open activity area.

Near the center of the site, a roughly rectangular concentration of pottery coincides with the largest contiguous distribution of burned clay. Eleven of the twenty-six wrought-iron nail fragments recovered from auger tests were found in this area. Nails were a relatively precious commodity in Apalachee (Boyd 1951:23), and an abundance of nails here suggests a well-constructed building. These characteristics, together with the location at one end of the suspected town plaza and a relatively high frequency of Spanish ceramics, suggested this was the site of the church complex at San Luis. This interpretation was confirmed in 1987.

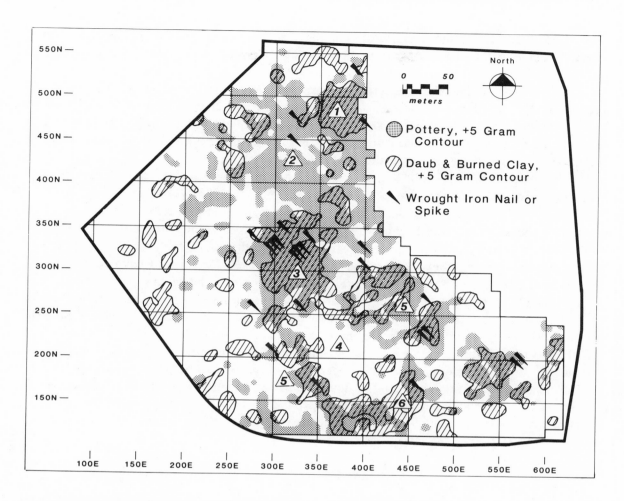

Figure 6.7. Distributions of pottery, burned clay, and wrought nails recovered from auger tests: (1) fort location, (2) open activity area, (3) church, (4) plaza, (5) village, and (6) Apalachee council house

Immediately south of the church location, absence of artifacts or daub in a rectangular area suggests a town plaza bordered by houses. This area is surrounded by a low earthen embankment. Seventy-five years after San Luis was abandoned, William Bartram observed Creek Indian towns whose plazas (chunk yards) were surrounded by a low bank of earth (Van Doren 1955).

At the southeast end of the probable plaza is the flat area surrounded by a series of depressions that may be borrow pits. Auger tests and a 2-meter test excavation showed that this flat platform, perhaps of artificial construction, supported a substantial structure. Documents mention a large Indian council house in which dances were held, visitors were housed, and decisions were made. Such structures were supposedly large enough to accommodate 2,000 to 3,000 people and were usually located adjacent to a plaza (Andrews and Andrews 1981:65–68; Swanton 1970:76; Wenhold 1936:13). Because this platform is situated on the plaza and directly opposite the suspected church location, it seemed likely to be the council house location. This was confirmed in the spring of 1986.

A gridded town is suggested by alignments of pottery and burned clay, especially on the northeast side of the plaza. Pottery and burned clay alignments are oriented approximately 45 degrees west of north.

In addition to the above interpretations, the auger survey provided clues to socio-economic aspects of the settlement plan, indicated by the uneven distribution of Spanish pottery in the suspected village. In the village area, most of the imported Spanish pottery was found on the east side of the plaza, suggesting that the residents there were wealthier or more Hispanicized than those living on the west side of the plaza.

The auger survey was followed up with eleven 2-meter test pits to recover larger artifact samples from each interpretive area, and by November 1986 we were able to create a speculative image of the way San Luis may have looked (see fig. 6.1). A view from the north-northeast was chosen because it would place the fort in the foreground; this was the only feature whose location was certain in 1984. Southwest of the fort the hypothetical marketplace is shown. Beyond it is the church complex, which would have contained the cemetery, a kitchen, and the *convento*. The church is on one end of the plaza, opposite the council house. Finally, data on domestic life at the missions are so poor that it is not known whether houses were round or square. Because of the disparity in the distribution of Spanish pottery on either side of the plaza, we chose to portray houses on the east as square and those on the west as circular, because circular floor plans are known from the few nonmission Apalachee sites excavated to date. It is hoped that future excavations in the village will begin to fill the gaps in our understanding of domestic life at the missions. The ravine is shown in figure 6.1 as a wooded area because no testing had been done there and trees were a convenient way to mask our ignorance. The area almost certainly would have been cleared of trees.

## Reading the Landscape of San Luis

The historical landscape at San Luis, as it is beginning to take shape as a result of archaeological and historical studies, represents in the most direct sense a reconstruction of natural and cultural features--an assemblage of houses, public buildings, streets, a plaza, as well as fields, forest, and agricultural plots. Determining the nature and location of such landscape components has been the subject of much of the research at San Luis so far. Indeed, to understand the physical landscape of this seventeenth-century mission town is to know a great deal about the daily life of the people who lived there. Failure to understand the town plan as a first step in the study is to lack a context for interpretation of the archaeological results.

There is an abstract landscape of San Luis as well, a mental image of what a settlement should look like to those who made decisions regarding its development. There is no doubt that San Luis was a planned town. There is a strong suggestion of a grid of streets separating regularly spaced houses surrounding the central plaza. The principal native and Spanish public structures faced each other across the plaza, and the fort occupied the strategic hilltop location with ready access to a permanent water source.

To learn the meaning of a historical landscape, to "read" it, it is necessary to separate the natural and human factors and to understand their relationship. In this sense landscape may be viewed as a dynamic record of interactions between people and the environment--dynamic in that the process of environmental change is a continuous and long-term interplay between natural events and human events. Each has the potential of leaving some record or evidence on the landscape, and each has the potential of modifying, confusing, or destroying evidence of previous events. Landscape is a complicated accumulation of effects and is open to interpretation once the chronology of causes can be determined.

At San Luis the natural landscape offered an appealing combination of factors for human settlement. The site is located on a high, well-drained, commanding hilltop composed of fertile soils, richly vegetated, and providing a reliable source of clean water. Climax vegetation in the Tallahassee Red Clay Hills is longleaf pine forest, a fire-maintained association characterized by an open understory, a grassy ground cover, and tall, straight pines as the dominant species. Hardwood forests dominate where drainage is poorer or where fire has been infrequent. Historical documents suggest that the hilltop was unoccupied when the Spanish established the community, for the chief of the principal village of Anhaica offered to move his village there in 1656 (Hann 1988). It is likely that the hilltop was vegetated, if not in longleaf pine forest, then at least in second growth.

The town plan of San Luis is now recognized not only to be quite deliberate in its design but also to be consistent with other mission sites in the province in size, orientation, and location of the principal buildings (Jones and Shapiro 1987). It is clear that design of major towns followed explicit models like the "Royal Ordinances concerning the Laying Out of New Towns" (Nuttall 1922), but there is no documentary evidence of such models for the design of small mission centers. Whether the design for a mission town was on paper or simply general knowledge, it is clear that while the basic pattern was European, there were significant Indian elements in the plan. At San Luis the plaza is round, yet the surrounding buildings appear to be laid out on a grid. Orientations of the principal buildings and the apparent rows of houses are consistent. At the northwest end of the plaza is situated the church complex consisting of the chapel, the *convento*, and the cemetery, whose arrangement and burial pattern are clearly European but whose population is mainly Indian. At the southeast end of the plaza sat the principal Indian public structure, the council house, a round building large enough to accommodate 2,000 to 3,000 people. Historical accounts document the importance of the council house as a locus of traditional Indian cultural practices, along with the repeated attempts of the friars to control such pagan activities.

By 1675, about a generation after the village of Anhaica moved to join the Spaniards at San Luis, the town is recorded as having a population of 1,400 natives within its jurisdiction. During the same period it is estimated that the Indian population of the entire province was around 10,000 (compared to its precontact level of 30,000 or more). The regional landscape of the province on the clay hills above the sandy coastal plain was organized in a series of districts, each with a principal village having a permanent church. Additional dispersed villages, known as satellites, were associated with each of the fourteen or so main villages in the province. The principal mission sites are between one and two leagues (2.5 to 5 miles) apart along the several branches of the Spanish trail, and where information is available, the average number of satellite villages within a district is around three (Hann 1988).

Surrounding the towns and villages would have been extensive cleared fields, mainly on hilltops and shallow slopes with red clay soils. These would have been either in cultivation or in second growth, as the soils appear to have become exhausted after about twenty years of production. Dispersed among the lands devoted to corn production were probably small farmsteads of a few households. Intensive site surveys in the region indicate that this was the prehistoric agricultural pattern; because Indians conducted virtually all of the farming activities during the mission period, whether for subsistence or export, it is not likely that the rural landscape was much different. Both north and south of the Cody Scarp it is recorded that Spanish cattle ranches existed; in fact, there is mention of several conflicts arising from destruction of crops by free-ranging cattle, as well as a complaint that cattle in the sandy coastal plain were eating acorns that had traditionally been reserved for the use of an Indian chief.

The settlement hierarchy may be extended one more level to place San Luis in the perspective of the territory of La Florida. While the Apalachee province was an important source of labor and produce to support the St. Augustine colony, it was not the only province with a mission chain. Missions extended northward along the Georgia coast among the Sea Islands in the Guale province, and the Spanish Trail between St. Augustine and Apalachee traversed the mission chain of the Timucua province. In all of the provinces, Spanish friars, soldiers, and officials were under the control of their superiors in St. Augustine. Some ninety leagues from San Luis, St. Augustine was the seat of the Florida territory. During the entire Spanish occupation, St. Augustine failed to establish its self-sufficiency, relying instead on the yearly *situado*, or subsidy, from Mexico, supplemented by corn and cattle from the missionized provinces. Around the time of the destruction of the missions in the first decade of the 1700s, St. Augustine's population was under 1,000; by 1706 its influence extended little distance beyond its walled perimeter (Deagan 1983).

The pioneering studies of Jackson (Jackson 1951-68; Zube 1970), Hoskins (1955), and Watts (1957) demonstrated the value of landscape as a historical record. And more recently Stilgoe (1982) has documented the nature and meaning of the changing American vernacular landscape before the Civil War. Cronon's influential *Changes in the Land* (1983) and subsequent work has clearly established the field of ecological history in the United States, using the New England landscape between 1600 and 1800 as an example. For our discussion of Spanish Florida in the seventeenth century, and particularly San Luis, we have used landscape as an organizing principle, as a point of view which can accommodate a wide range of historical and archaeological facts. Our example is more complex than some, as our historical landscape has had to be reconstructed through excavation and interpretation of documents. Nonetheless, discovering the buried landscape of this frontier colonial town has indicated the usefulness of landscape as artifact, as analytical tool, and as a means of understanding the relations between people and their environment three centuries ago.

## Acknowledgments

We wish to thank the Bureau of Archaeological Research of the Florida Department of State for permission to reprint the illustrations from Gary Shapiro, Archaeology at San Luis: Broad-scale testing, 1984-1985, *Florida Archaeology* 3 (Tallahassee, 1987).

References Cited

Andrews, E. W., and C. M. Andrews (editors). 1981. *Jonathan Dickinson's journal.* Port Salerno, Fla.: Florida Classics Library.

Boyd, M. F. 1951. Fort San Luis: Documents describing the tragic end of the mission era. In *Here they once stood*, by M. F. Boyd, H. G. Smith, and J. W. Griffin, pp. 1-104. Gainesville: University of Florida Press.

Cronon, W. 1983. *Changes in the land: Indians, colonists, and the ecology of New England.* New York: Hill and Wang.

Deagan, K. A. 1983. *Spanish St. Augustine: Archaeology of a Creole community.* New York: Academic Press.

Griffin, J. W. 1951. Excavations at the site of San Luis. In *Here they once stood*, by M. F. Boyd, H. G. Smith, and J. W. Griffin, pp. 139-62. Gainesville: University of Florida Press.

Hann, J. H. 1987. Spanish translations. *Florida Archaeology* 2. Tallahassee: Florida Bureau of Archaeological Research.

----. 1988. *Apalachee: The land between the rivers.* Gainesville: University Presses of Florida.

Hoskins, W. G. 1955. *The making of the English landscape.* London: Hodder and Stoughton.

Jackson, J. B. (editor). 1951-68. *Landscape.* Vols. 1-17. Santa Fe.

Jones, B. C., and G. Shapiro. 1987. Nine missions sites in Apalachee. Paper presented at the annual meeting of the Society for Historical Archaeology, Savannah.

Nuttall, Z. 1922. Royal ordinances concerning the laying out of new towns. *Hispanic-American Historical Review* 5:249-54.

Shapiro, G. 1987. Archaeology at San Luis: Broad-scale testing, 1984-1985. *Florida Archaeology* 3. Tallahassee: Florida Bureau of Archaeological Research.

Smith, B. D. 1978. Variation in Mississippian settlement patterns. In *Mississippian settlement patterns*, ed. B. D. Smith, pp. 479-503. New York: Academic Press.

Stilgoe, J. R. 1982. *Common landscapes of America, 1580-1845.* New Haven: Yale University Press.

Swanton, J. R. 1970. *Early history of the Creek Indians and their neighbors.* Washington, D.C.: Smithsonian Institution.

Van Doren, M. (editor). 1955. *Travels of William Bartram.* New York: Dover Press.

Watts, M. T. 1957. *Reading the landscape: An adventure in ecology.* New York: Macmillan.

Wenhold, L. L. (translator and transcriber). 1936. A seventeenth-century letter of Gabrial Diaz Vara Calderón, bishop of Cuba, describing the Indians and Indian missions of Florida. *Smithsonian Miscellaneous Collections* 113. Washington, D.C.: Smithsonian Institution.

Zube, E. H. 1970. (editor). *Landscapes: Selected writings of J. B. Jackson.* Amherst: University of Massachusetts Press.

## 7

# RECENT EVIDENCE OF EIGHTEENTH-CENTURY GARDENING IN WILLIAMSBURG, VIRGINIA

## Marley R. Brown and Patricia M. Samford

Some years ago, James Deetz argued in an important but still unpublished paper that historical archaeology's strength lies in the contribution that it can make to reconstructing the folk cultural traditions of the recent past--traditions that escaped documentation in conventional historical sources (Deetz 1980). He was suggesting that archaeologists should lead to this strength rather than compete with historians and other scholars in the analysis of those subjects for which material evidence is at best rarely more than window dressing for the more compelling and comprehensive evidence of the written record. While this advice may seem obvious, many archaeologists still labor to show the relevance of excavated data to questions that are now and will continue to be more convincingly answered by social and economic historians.

### Gardening as Folk Tradition

One important premise of this chapter is that the advice Deetz has given should be heeded when turning to the general subject of landscape archaeology and, more specifically, to the topic of town and country gardens as discussed in most of the chapters in this volume. It is fair to say that much of what can be called garden archaeology has been concerned with delineating the physical appearance of the gardens of the elite, which were created by men who often did leave behind some form of written evidence of their work, whether in the form of correspondence, journals, or actual sketches and plans. Such research is especially important in aiding the restoration and interpretive efforts of those organizations which manage these properties, but there is no question that the interests of these relatively few men and their involvement in pleasure or ornamental gardening clearly distinguished them from the great majority of their contemporaries.

It seems, then, that archaeology's real value rests with the opportunity it affords to explore the vernacular landscape, to identify an important dimension of the folk tradition that informed the practice of gardening undertaken by most people during the colonial period. After all, this was a time when professional gardeners were scarce and when the knowledge of what and how to plant came with the experience of actually doing it, an accommodation, through trial and error, of the instructions contained in how-to guides written for use in England. There is no evidence to suggest that such guides were widely distributed among the general population in the colonial Tidewater, although they clearly did influence the leading gardeners of the day; again, the latter were members of a small group of well-educated elite whose libraries contained such treatises and whose correspondence often attests to their close connections with prominent gardening authorities in England (e.g., Colonel John Custis's letters to Peter Collinson in Swem 1957).

As for the much larger group that Peter Martin labels the anonymous multitude of gardeners in his recent book on Virginia gardening (Martin, in press), these folk kept essentially practical (kitchen) gardens and did not leave behind plans of their work, write letters about it, or otherwise record what they were doing. Martin states:

> In this late eighteenth-century world of Williamsburg plants, and their propagation, it is astonishing that no American book had yet been published, as a type of supplement to Miller's *Dictionary*, to help gardeners tend their gardens and grow their plants. Doubtless hand-written "Calendars" were circulated, or gardeners kept their own notes taken from their own experiences or from Miller year after year, but a considerable degree of uncertainty and inconsistency must have resulted, especially as Miller did not write chiefly for American colonial gardeners. (Martin, in press)

Knowledge of what and how to plant appears to have been disseminated mainly through word of mouth and by on-site experimentation and demonstration, as gardeners made their own compromises in adapting English plants to the distinctly non-English climate of the Tidewater. Interestingly enough, within Williamsburg, this multitude of anonymous gardeners included among its members many substantial gentlemen as well as craftsmen, artisans, tavern keepers, and the rest of the town's ordinary citizens.

At least for Williamsburg, it is not until the third quarter of the eighteenth century that documentary evidence, in the form of John Randolph's garden treatise (Randolph 1924) and Judge Joseph Prentis's garden calendar (Webb-Prentis Papers, n.d.), reveals some of the results of several decades of experimentation in cultivation. Randolph's work, thought to have been written between 1760 and 1770, represents a notable achievement, namely, the adaptation of the system described in Philip Miller's *The Gardener's Dictionary* (1735) to the Virginia environment. Prentis's *Monthly Kalendar*, written between 1775 and 1779, accomplishes the same kind of adaptation. These sources report directly upon what had been learned in Virginia, through trial and error, by the third quarter of the eighteenth century.

Archaeological excavation is beginning to shed some light on the gardening activities of Williamsburg residents in the years before the Revolution. The intention in reviewing some of this evidence here is not to draw any profound conclusions about the gardens of Williamsburg, in terms of their layout, precedents for their design, or planting schemes, or to wax eloquent about their symbolic or ideological import. Rather, this chapter focuses on the kinds of information that archaeological research might reasonably be expected to provide about vernacular gardens as evidenced by the physical remains of activity guided by the early eighteenth-century folk gardening tradition of Tidewater Virginia. This tradition begins to be articulated in writing toward the end of the century but for most of this period is preserved only by those archaeological features that cut into subsoil.

## An Archaeological View of Williamsburg Gardening

In his recent review of the role of Williamsburg in defining the Colonial Revival garden, Charles Hosmer draws attention to the fact that the restored gardens there and elsewhere were not really intended to be historically accurate. He observes that:

the primary goal was to produce a "frame" for attractive views of the past. The plantings were rarely historically accurate revivals of eighteenth- and nineteenth-century landscapes. Trained in twentieth-century concepts of design, landscape architects became artists who helped to perpetuate the idea that the life of the past was always blissfully harmonious. There was a conscious refusal to accept the conclusions of research reports that implied colonial gardens had been simple, functional, and even somewhat bare. . . . The research efforts that supported garden restorations should have been carried out by professional archaeologists along with the landscape architects, but in most cases trained archaeologists were only able to provide minimal data about walls, outbuild-ings, paths, and watercourses. They did not have the right training to interpret postholes and fragments of fences or tools that appeared in their trenches. (Hosmer 1985:53)

In some ways, Hosmer's statement is too kind. At Williamsburg, garden restoration could not benefit even from trained archaeologists; instead, it had to make do with information provided by laborers working under the supervision of an architectural draftsman. The design process was controlled by one very persuasive and opinionated landscape architect by the name of Arthur Shurtleff (later Shurcliff) who, according to one prominent resident of the town, had "boxwood on the brain" (Hosmer 1985:61).

It is not our intention to denigrate the legacy of one of the most prominent landscape architects of this century or to belabor the obvious--that Williamsburg's gardens are much more a creation of his depression-era vision of America's colonial landscape than they are an accurate re-creation of town gardens in Virginia's colonial capital. Instead, this chapter pursues Hosmer's observation about the role that properly executed archaeological excavation should play in research on gardens by addressing the following question: what have new techniques of excavation, focused on the problem of reconstructing the spatial organization of behavior on Williamsburg's residential and commercial properties, revealed about the vernacular gardens of the town?

During the last five years, excavation has uncovered features that are clearly related to gardening activity during the first half of the eighteenth century. Many of these sites were not known to be locations of renowned or well-documented gardens. In the past few years, it has also been possible to explore sites where two of Williamsburg's most notable late eighteenth-century gardeners resided, namely, the properties of John Randolph, Jr., the attributed author of *A Treatise on Gardening* (Randolph 1924), and of Judge Joseph Prentis, author of an unpublished garden calendar and garden book.

At all of these sites, especially those of John Randolph and Joseph Prentis, the use of careful block excavation to reveal the overall plan of gardens, kitchen or ornamental, was thwarted by the fact that subsequent use of the properties during the last two centuries had obliterated much of what must have been there, a problem of preservation not uncommon in intensively used urban spaces. Instead, what has been observed is a variety of features in amongst outbuilding foundations, walkways, and fences that are likely the tangible expres-sions of vernacular gardening activities, especially during the first half of the century.

The sites in question, taken in order of the dates they were excavated, represent three substantial eighteenth-century urban plantations, those of Sir John and Peyton Randolph, Peyton's brother John, and Judge Joseph Prentis, as well as one lot in the commercial core of Williamsburg, in which property ownership and use of properties changed frequently during the course of the eighteenth century. This latter site, on Duke of Gloucester Street near the Capitol, was used as a tavern for most of the first half of the eighteenth century and as a rental property for most of the second half.

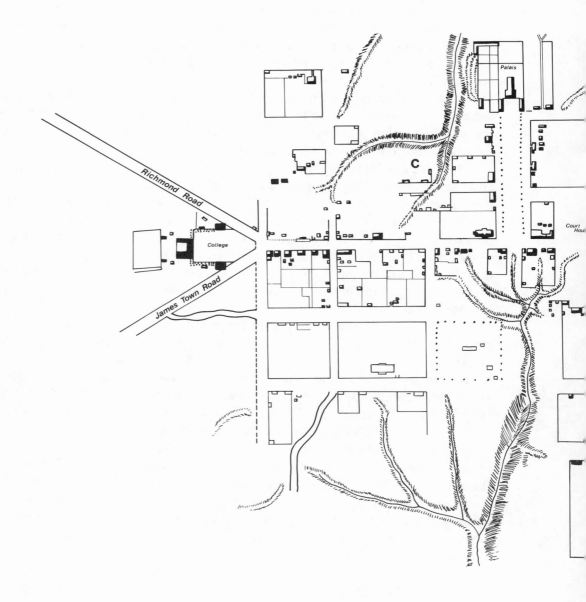

Figure 7.1. The Frenchman's Map (1782) of Williamsburg, showing the residences of (A) Peyton Randolph, (B) John Randolph, Jr., and (C) Judge Joseph Prentis and (D) Shields Tavern. (Tracing of original in Swem Library, College of William and Mary)

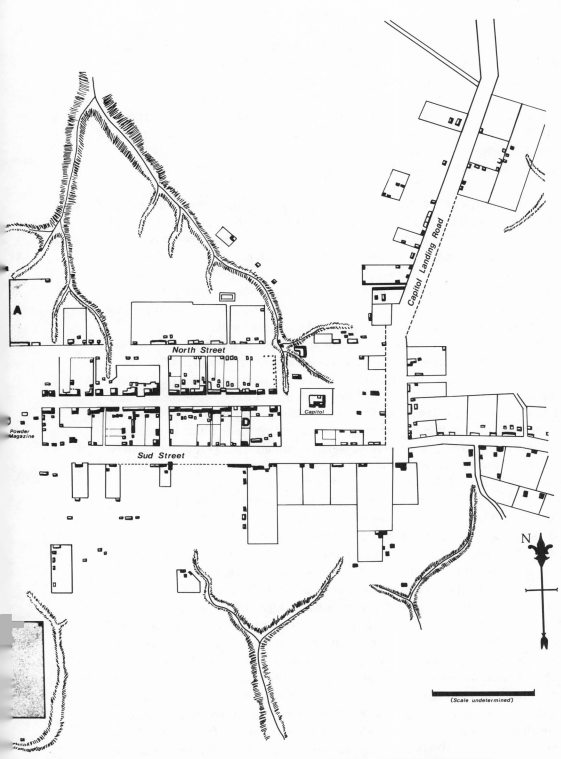

The location of each of these different sites is illustrated on the Frenchman's Map (1782), a plan of Williamsburg drawn by a French cartographer who was likely studying billeting possibilities for French troops late in the Revolutionary War (fig. 7.1). Gardens on two of the properties, the peripheral plantations of John Randolph, Jr., and Joseph Prentis, at Tazewell Hall and Green Hill respectively, should illustrate the merging of formal, ornamental gardens with more expansive gardens emulating the English landscape school of the later eighteenth century, while gardening on the Peyton Randolph and Shield's Tavern sites would be expected to be primarily utilitarian, being set in the midst of active backyard areas.

The first notable encounter with unrecorded, vernacular gardening came in the course of excavating the Peyton Randolph backyard in search of more and better information about the location and function of supporting outbuildings. Because the area had previously been examined through archaeological cross-trenching and a plan had been drawn of obvious foundations, it was decided to abandon the historical archaeologists' typical excavation grid of 10-foot-square units in favor of broad expanses of block excavation, in which horizontal control was kept by piece plotting and artifact recovery in 2.5-foot squares, a technique that is now used consistently when reexamining properties in the historic area.

As horizontal exposure progressed on this site, an interesting soil pattern was observed in one area. Even through the midsummer drought, a rectangular area measuring 20 feet by 13 feet remained moist and dark while the remainder of the site parched and dried. Here, subsequent excavation revealed a pair of features filled with a rich dark brown loam, most certainly early eighteenth-century garden beds, the first to be revealed in Williamsburg and the earliest such features known for this region (fig. 7.2). Planting beds I and II measured 20 feet by 8 feet and 20 feet by 4 feet, respectively, were separated by a 1-foot-wide alley, and cut .75 feet to 1.5 feet into sterile yellow clay. Further work on the site revealed two more features, again in a pair, oriented north-south rather than east-west, larger (32 feet by 12 feet and 29 feet by 8 feet) and of a slightly later date than those first identified on the site.

There were other important differences between the two pairs of beds, most notably in the materials used as linings. In the early beds, large animal bone and wine bottle bases were used primarily (fig. 7.3), with some large ceramic sherds, while the later beds were lined with some bone but mostly with oyster shell. An examination of eighteenth-century garden manuals indicates that it is reasonable to assume that most planting beds in kitchen gardens of this period (circa 1715-45) were raised above ground. Why, then, were these beds excavated deeply into subsoil, and what was the purpose of the lining? It seemed a logical answer could be found in establishing what was being planted in these beds. The fill of the four beds was wet-screened through window mesh, and voluminous soil samples were taken to permit seed, pollen, and parasitological analyses. A large sample of seeds was recovered from these beds, and among those present in two of the beds were several remains that may represent asparagus (they were too poorly preserved to determine definitively the presence of the exterior dimple that is the distinguishing attribute of *Asparagus officinalis*). Other seeds recovered from the beds most likely reflected colonization and subsequent secondary succession or, for that matter, could have been introduced in the composted soil used as the growing medium.

From this evidence, a tentative conclusion was drawn that these were special planting beds, in the sense that they were trenched into the clay substratum rather than raised, and were most likely used for growing asparagus. In his discussion of asparagus, John Randolph stressed that "the principal thing to be regarded with these plants, is the bed in which they are to be placed. . . . Nothing more is necessary than to make your beds perfectly rich and light, that the head may not be obstructed in its growth upwards. Two feet of mould and dung is depth sufficient for any plant" (Randolph 1924:4).

Some months later, background research on Judge Joseph Prentis's garden showed that, at least by the end of the eighteenth century, gardeners had standardized what may have been an experimental method fifty years earlier. In his calendar Prentis wrote for March: "After a Rain plant out Cucumber Seed. Set out asparagus as follows. Dig a trench as wide as you intend your Beds to be, and two feet deep, lay a layer of Oyster Shells, six Inches, then lay on six Inches of Horse Dung, and as much Mould, continue so to do, till the Bed is done. Take your Roots raised from Seed, and set them out in Rows, a foot Wide let there be a space of about a foot between each Row" (Webb-Prentis Papers, n.d.).

The physical character of the planting beds found in the backyard of the Peyton Randolph house closely matches the description of asparagus beds contained in the advice of both John Randolph and Judge Prentis, who were writing some fifty and sixty years later. The only departure from their recommendations is in the kind of paving material, with the early beds making use of wine bottle and bone rather than oyster shell. English garden journals make no reference to paving of

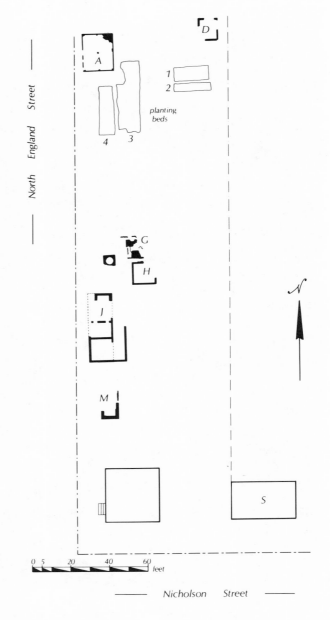

Figure 7.2. Plan of the four planting beds revealed through archaeological excavation on the Peyton Randolph site. (Map by Natalie Larson, courtesy of Colonial Williamsburg Foundation)

any kind. This may have been an experiment to see what worked best as drainage material in the water-retaining clay soil of the Tidewater, an accommodation not necessary in England. With these beds trenched deeply into the clay to allow room for the growth of the asparagus shoots, drainage may have been doubly important, because one of the advantages of raised beds is that they drain well.

Figure 7.3. Planting beds I and II, fully excavated, showing the paving of wine bottle glass and animal bone. (Photograph by Andrew Edwards, courtesy of Colonial Williamsburg Foundation)

The discovery of the evidence of early eighteenth-century kitchen gardening at the Peyton Randolph site suggested that further excavation would likely uncover more such features, as well as those related to other aspects of vernacular gardening. To aid in the identification of these physical remains when they were encountered, members of the staff undertook an examination of those few sources available that captured in writing what was customary procedure during most of the colonial period. Except for John Randolph's treatise, these calendars were private documents, left unpublished among the personal papers of individuals who obviously enjoyed gardening and reflecting upon it. For Williamsburg proper, besides the writing of Randolph and Prentis, there is a garden journal belonging to Joseph Hornsby, once a resident of Williamsburg, who described gardening in Kentucky at the turn of the nineteenth century (Hornsby 1798). Hornsby is known to have gardened at several sites in Williamsburg, most notably the Peyton Randolph property, which he bought from Peyton's widow in 1783 and where he lived there until his departure for Kentucky in 1797.

These sources were mined for information about the physical character of planting and gardening behavior in much the same way prehistorians use the method of ethnographic reduction and analogy to aid their interpretation of the archaeological record (Bennett 1984). From this research, it is possible to identify the main types of garden or, more exactly, gardening-related features and the kinds of plants with which they would have been associated. By virtue of the interests of the keepers of garden calendars in the late eighteenth century, this information relates almost exclusively to the successful keeping of a kitchen garden. Tables 7.1-7.3 chart the instructions given in various seventeenth-, eighteenth-, and nineteenth-century English and American garden manuals for the planting of asparagus, artichokes, and cauliflower, respectively.

In view of the discovery of the asparagus beds at the Peyton Randolph site, one of the major concerns of this analysis was to determine the nature of bed construction, in order to anticipate the kinds of beds that might have made an imprint in the subsoil. Most cultivating beds and hotbeds of the eighteenth century seem to have been raised and supported by wooden planks or brick (fig. 7.4). The instructions are often quite specific as to the width (generally 3 to 5 feet) and spacing (generally 1 to 2.5 feet) of beds, the accommodations that allow for weeding and harvesting, but depth into the ground is rarely specified. When it is, it is usually no more than six to eight inches, the depth of the spade, or "to the clay." Save for Prentis's instructions for asparagus, no mention is made of paving or drainage materials.

Given the preponderance of references to raised beds, it is understandable why so few planting beds have been identified through excavation on Williamsburg lots. Raised beds were easy to remove later by simply shoveling them away, and they would have left behind no trace in the subsoil. The intensity of activity on these properties, culminating in the extensive landscape restoration activities of the Colonial Williamsburg Foundation commencing in the late 1920s, has obliterated most of this kind of evidence.

But excavated beds do survive; in addition to those found behind the Peyton Randolph house, they have been recovered at the Shield's Tavern, in part of John Randolph's large garden at Tazewell Hall, and in what was almost surely Judge Prentis's garden square next to the east chimney where his garden book indicates he planted vegetables (including asparagus) between 1784 and 1788. Where remains of excavated beds are encountered, furthermore, it may be assumed that other components of a kitchen garden once were present, notably the much more ephemeral raised beds, as well as planting trenches, individual planting holes, and rows of garden stakes within raised beds that, like asparagus beds, leave their mark in the ground.

Examples of these other planting features have been encountered at Williamsburg sites, most notably trenches and stake holes. Trenches were recommended by both Prentis and John Randolph for growing a number of plants, including onions, horseradish, and celery, as well as for the preservation of certain vegetables over the winter. These trenches were filled with the harvested vegetables, some horse dung, and either sawdust or straw to protect the vegetables from freezing. The excavation of trenches was especially important for the

Table 7.1.  Planting references for artichokes

| Author | Year | Reference | Size | Depth of fill | Spacing | Comments |
|--------|------|-----------|------|---------------|---------|----------|
| Bailey | 1717 | | | Dug very deep | | Mix with good dung |
| La Quintinie | 1717 | Beds | 4' wide | 1/2' deep | 1' path between beds | Filled with mould |
| Miller | 1735 | Beds | | | Rows 5' apart | Very rotten dung |
| Anonymous | 1744 | Rows | | 2' deep | Rows 4' apart | Dig it a double spit; mix with rotten dung |
| Justice | 1759 | Rows | | Trench ground | Rows 4' apart | Old well-rotted dung |
| Randolph | 1760/70 | Hills | | 2' deep | Hills 4' apart | Use sheep dung and ashes yearly |
| Stevenson | 1766 | Beds | 4' wide | 2' deep | 1' path between beds | Requires dung yearly |
| Prentis | 1784 | Beds | | | | |
| Gardiner | 1804 | Rows | | | Rows 4' apart | Dig in plenty of rotten dung |
| M'Mahon | 1820 | Beds | | One good spade deep | | Good quantity of rotten dung |
| Bridgeman | 1853 | Beds | | One good spade deep | Rows 5' apart | Lay on good quantity of rotten dung |
| Cobbett | 1856 | Rows | | | Rows 6' apart | Litter for cold protection |

Table 7.2. Planting references for cauliflower

| Author | Year | Reference | Size | Depth of fill | Spacing | Comments |
|---|---|---|---|---|---|---|
| Worlidge | 1688 | Hotbed | | | | Rich manure |
| Bailey | 1717 | Hotbed | | | | Raise in hot bed in spring |
| Langley | 1728 | Hotbed | | | | Use frames or bell glass to protect from cold |
| Bradley | 1731 | Hotbed | | | | Use glass bells in the winter |
| Miller | 1735 | Bed | 2.5' | | 3' between rows | Rotten dung 6" or 1', use bell glass in winter |
| Anonymous | 1744 | Bed | 3' wide | | 3' between rows | Rotten dung, use bell glasses and mats to protect from cold |
| Justice | 1759 | Hotbed | | | | Use frame or glasses |
| Randolph | 1760/70 | Trench | 1.5' wide | Quite down to the clay | Plants 5' apart | Rich light soil, long dung |
| Prentis | 1784 | Trench | 18" wide | Of sufficient depth | | Rotten dung, sawdust to protect from cold |
| Prentis | 1784 | Bed | 2.5' wide | Spade deep | 2' apart | Rich, light soil |
| Squibb | 1787 | Bed | 3' wide | | | Good, rotten dung |
| Gardiner | 1804 | Trench | 18" wide | Dug to clay | Plants 5' apart | Earth mixed with long dung |
| M'Mahon | 1820 | Bed | 3' wide | One good spade deep | Alleys 1' wide | Ground to be well-manured with well-rotted dung |
| Cobbett | 1856 | Hotbed | | | | Use long dung around hot-bed frame for additional cold protection |

Table 7.3. Planting references for asparagus

| Author | Year | Size of Bed | Depth of fill | Spacing of Beds | Comments |
|---|---|---|---|---|---|
| Abercrombie | 1791 | | | 1/2' deep | Dung 1 yard high, then 6-7" earth on top of dung, raise one end of bed 5-6" |
| Miller | 1735 | 4' wide | 2.4' apart | | Good rich earth, rotten dung 1/2' deep |
| Anonymous | 1744 | Length and width of frames | Good spit[a] deep | 2.5' apart | Good quantity of well-rotted dung; beds of hot dung mixed with straw and coal ashes 3" thick for a winter crop |
| Bradley | 1731 | 4' wide | | 2' alleys | 6-8" of horse dung, well-rotted |
| Justice | 1759 | 5' wide | 2 spadings & 1 shovel | 1.5' alleys | Cover bed in November with well-rotted dung |
| Randolph | 1760/70 | 4' wide | 2' mould & dung | | |
| Miller | 1735 | Width of frame | | | Winter crop; 3" new horse dung, then 6" earth, cover with a frame |
| Prentis | 1784 | 2' deep | | | Cover beds with horse dung |
| Cobbett | 1856 | 4' wide | 2' 9" deep | | Raised beds will aid in weeding; place manure in bottom of bed |
| Bailey | 1717 | 4' wide | 2' deep | | Fresh horse dung, 4-5 fingers |
| Langley | 1728 | 4' wide | 2 spit & 2 crums[a] | 2.5' apart | Well-rotted horse dung |
| Squibb | 1787 | 3' wide | Dug to a good depth | 20" apart | Large quantity of rotten dung |

| | | | | | |
|---|---|---|---|---|---|
| M'Mahon | 1820 | 4.5' wide | 2 spades deep | 2' alleys | Large supply of rotten or other good dung laid thereon several inches thick |
| La Quintinie | 1717 | 3-4' broad | | | Raise beds in areas that are poorly drained |
| Stevenson | 1766 | 3' wide | | 2' path | For a hotbed use 3' of horse dung covered by 5" of earth |
| Gardiner | 1804 | 4.5' wide | 12-16" | 2' alleys | Bury plenty of rotten dung in beds |
| Bridgeman | 1853 | 4' wide | Trenched 2 spades | 2.5' alleys | Well-rotted dung buried deep 12-15" deep |

[a] The *Oxford English Dictionary* defines a spit as "such a depth of earth as is pierced by the full length of a spade-blade" and crum as "loose and crumbled earth."

Figure 7.4. Raised garden beds supported by wooden boards and stakes shown in an early eighteenth-century garden manual. From Louis Liger, *The Retir'd Gard'ner* (London: Gentil, 1706).

successful cultivation and preservation of cauliflower. Prentis recommended: "Plant out your Colliflowers as follows. Prepare your Ground as for a Hot Bed, then dig a trench Spade Deep, and two feet and a half Wide, make holes at convenient distances, set five Plants in each hole, put your Glasses on, raise them on the South Side, when it is warm" (Webb-Prentis Papers, n.d.). In the fall, the gardener should "dig a trench eighteen Inches Wide and of a sufficient depth, put in Rotten Dung, then lay your Plants with their Heads to the Sun. Cover them with Mould up to their Leaves. Add to this a coat of Saw Dust--When apprehensive of Frost, cover them with Straw" (Webb-Prentis Papers, n.d.). For preservation, Randolph told the gardener to "put them in the ground, in a hole dug about two feet below the surface, well sheltered by straw or thatching, as near one another as you please" (Randolph 1924:12).

Advice such as this must have resulted from years of experimenting with the growing of this plant and others, particularly in the difficult seasons of the Tidewater, which experienced more extreme weather conditions than did the mother country. There was clearly no one standard way of doing things; rather, individuals like Prentis, Hornsby, and Randolph, and no doubt others whose identities will never be known, were actively engaged in trial and error that surely brought many failures for every success. Prentis's garden book gives testimony of his experimentation in his chimney garden immediately to the east of his house, where, in addition to planting beds, evidence of planting trenches was observed.

More elaborate experimentation was seen at the site of what became John Randolph's large formal garden during the period 1762-75. In an examination of what remained of the garden area closest to the house on the west side, several trenches were revealed, as well as an unusual circular pattern of stake holes. These features and the fact that they stratigraphically predate the construction of the house most likely attest to Randolph's use of this area as an experimental garden before he formally received title to the land upon his mother's death sometime toward the end of the 1750s. It is thought that he wrote his treatise shortly thereafter (i.e., sometime between 1760 and 1770). The profiles of the trenches illustrated in figure 7.5 are of slightly different sizes and shapes, perhaps relating to the kinds of plants with which Randolph was experimenting.

Some of the recent evidence regarding the physical remains of vegetable cultivation in Williamsburg over a period of nearly one hundred years indicates that the overall plan of kitchen gardens will be most difficult to reconstruct from archaeological excavation alone. In fact, it is not really possible even to identify these expressions of a vernacular or folk gardening tradition without turning to the few written sources that articulate this tradition toward the end of the eighteenth century. Without physical remains marking the overall plan of raised beds in relationship to excavated beds and to other planting features such as trenches and holes that also left behind some signature in the ground, as well as to those like rows and hills that did not, only the written sources can provide glimpses of the overall spatial organization of these vernacular gardens. For example, in his garden diary Joseph Hornsby (1798) described his planting in such a way that it is possible to plot the position of the beds in relation to one another. There may be other such detailed diaries that can be reasonably used, by extension and analogy, to create such comprehensive planting schemes.

Some later garden plans drawn from memory also help in this process; for Williamsburg proper, these are Luty Blow's sketch of a Sussex County garden based on her great-grandfather Benjamin Waller's garden behind his Francis Street house and the plan drawn by Kate Blankenship of the Wythe House garden between 1837 and 1844 (fig. 7.6). These later glimpses are especially tantalizing, showing as they do the position of vegetable and fruit in relationship to trees, ornamental shrubs, and herbaceous borders, as well as capturing the character of overall garden design. While they are helpful for the actual treatment of the yards at these two properties, they are too late to be of use in reconstructing the plans of early eighteenth-century utilitarian gardens of the kind found on most Williamsburg lots; that is, gardens created by the actions of ordinary citizens, working within a folk gardening tradition.

These vernacular gardens are the ones that the Colonial Williamsburg Foundation would like to portray more accurately. While there are several notable gardens whose stature as monuments to the Colonial Revival vision argue for their preservation, there are many more small and less visible gardens which are now recognized as too formal for the backyard work spaces where they have been planted. Already, as part of Colonial Williamsburg's new interpretation at the Benjamin Powell House, its garden has been greatly simplified, losing ground to Powell's lumberyard and storage shed. It can be hoped, too, that the garden behind Shields Tavern, charming in its symmetrical simplicity but baseless in fact, can be replaced with a landscape plan incorporating the fence lines and walkways contemporary with the Shields Tavern period (circa 1745-50), and the kitchen garden area that was revealed by the presence of the planting beds.

In the next few years, research in the archaeology department at Colonial Williamsburg will continue to emphasize recovering as much information as possible about the ordinary

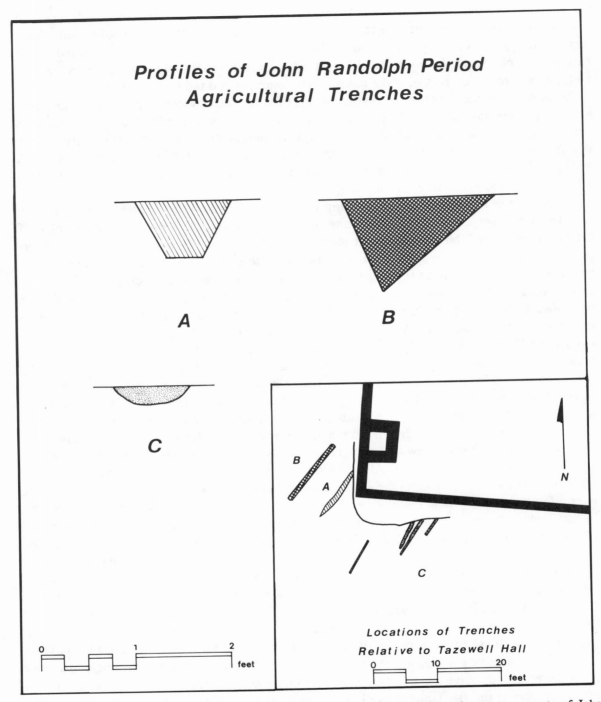

Figure 7.5. The varying profiles of agricultural trenches located on the eighteenth-century property of John Randolph, Jr., suggest experimentation with different gardening methods. (Drawing by Virgina C. Brown, courtesy of Colonial Williamsburg Foundation)

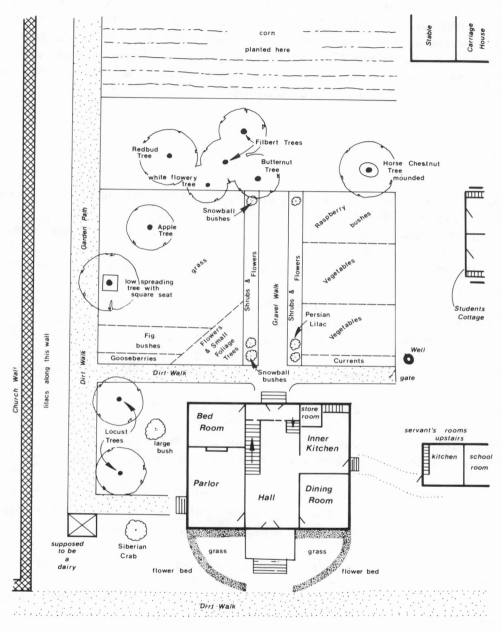

corn
planted here

Stable

Carriage House

Filbert Trees

Redbud Tree

white flowery tree

Butternut Tree

Horse Chestnut Tree mounded

Snowball bushes

Raspberry bushes

Apple Tree

Garden Path

grass

Shrubs & Flowers

Gravel Walk

Shrubs & Flowers

Vegetables

low spreading tree with square seat

Persian Lilac

Vegetables

Students Cottage

Fig bushes

Flowers & Small Foliage Trees

Well

Gooseberries

Dirt Walk

Snowball bushes

Currents

gate

Dirt Walk

Locust Trees

large bush

Bed Room

store room

Inner Kitchen

servant's rooms upstairs

kitchen

school room

Parlor

Hall

Dining Room

Church Wall

lilacs along this wall

supposed to be a dairy

Siberian Crab

grass

grass

flower bed

flower bed

Dirt Walk

Street

### George Wythe Garden

adapted from plan drawn from memory
by
Kate M. Blankenship
circa 1837-44

Figure 7.6. Adaptation of the George Wythe House garden in Williamsburg, drawn from memory by Kate M. Blankenship in the nineteenth century. (Courtesy of Colonial Williamsburg Foundation)

gardens of the town and their placement in and among the outbuildings, walkways, and fences of individual lots. Evidence will be sought from both the ground and from contemporary garden diaries, journals, and calendars. This study will seek to unravel the grammar of the vernacular code that guided Williamsburg's anonymous multitude of gardeners during the colonial period, leaving the grand formal gardens of a precious few to stand as beautiful reminders of one era's perception of the colonial past.

## References Cited

Abercrombie, J.  1791.  *Every man his own gardener.*  London: Printed for J. F. and C. Rivington, T. Longman, and B. Law.

Anonymous.  1744.  *Adam's luxury and Eve's cookery, or the kitchen-garden display'd in two parts.*  London: Printed for R. Dodsley.

Bailey, N.  1717.  *Dictionarium rusticum, urbanicum, and botanicum.*  London: Printed for J. Nicholson.

Bennett, A. E.  1984.  A treatise on gardening by a citizen of Virginia:  Three sources of documentation for physical remains of eighteenth-century Williamsburg gardens.  Paper presented at the annual meeting of the Society for Historical Archaeology, Williamsburg, Virginia.

Bradley, R.  1731.  *New improvements for planting and gardening.*  6th ed.  London: Printed for J. Knapton and J. Knapton.

Bridgeman, T.  1853.  *The young gardener's assistant.*  New York: For sale by the author.

Cobbett, W.  1856.  *The American gardener.*  New York: C. M. Saxton and Company.

Deetz, J.  1980.  Historical archaeology, anthropology, and folklife studies.  Paper presented at the annual meeting of the Society for Historical Archaeology, Albuquerque, New Mexico.

Frenchman's Map.  1782.  Plan de la ville et environs de Williamsburg en Virginie, 1782.  Williamsburg: Special Collections, Earl Gregg Swem Library, College of William and Mary.

Gardiner, J., and D. Hepburn.  1804.  *The American gardener.*  Washington, D.C.: Printed by Samuel H. Smith.

Hornsby, J.  1798.  Diary of gardening and planting, 1798.  Manuscript.  Williamsburg: Colonial Williamsburg Foundation.

Hosmer, C. B. Jr.  1985.  The Colonial Revival in the public eye:  Williamsburg and early garden restoration.  In *The Colonial Revival in America*, ed. A. Axelrod, pp. 52-70.  New York: W. W. Norton.

Justice, J.  1759.  *The Scots gardiners director.*  Edinburgh: Printed for A. Donaldson.

Langley, B.  1728.  *New principles of gardening.*  London: A. Betteswoth and J. Batley.

La Quintinie, J. de.  1717.  *The complete gard'ner: or, Directions for cultivating and right ordering of fruit-gardens and kitchen-gardens.*  London: Printed for A. Bell and W. Bell, abridged by George London and Henry Wise.

M'Mahon, B.  1820.  *The American gardener's calendar: Adapted to the climate and seasons of the United States.*  Philadelphia: T. P. M'Mahon.

Martin, P.  In press.  *From Jamestown to Jefferson: The world of Virginia gardening.*  Williamsburg: Colonial Williamsburg Foundation.

Miller, P. 1735. *The gardeners dictionary: Containing the methods of cultivating and improving the kitchen, fruit and flower gardens, as also the physick garden, wilderness, conservatory and vineyard.* Vols. 1-3. London: Printed for the author and sold by C. Rivington.

Randolph, J., Jr. 1924. *A treatise on gardening by a citizen of Virginia.* Ed. M. F. Warner. Rept. from *The American garden of John Gardiner and David Hepburn.* 3d ed. Richmond: Appeals Press.

Squibb, R. 1787. *The gardener's calendar for South-Carolina, Georgia, and North-Carolina.* Charleston: Printed by Samuel Wright and Company for R. Squibb.

Stevenson, Rev. Mr. H. 1766. *The gentleman gardener.* London: Printed for J. Hinton.

Swem, E. G. 1957. *Brothers of the spade: Correspondence of Peter Collinson of London and of John Custis of Williamsburg, Virginia, 1734-1736.* Barre, Mass.: Barre Gazette.

Webb-Prentis Papers. N.d. Charlottesville: Manuscripts Department, University of Virginia Library.

White, G. 1975. *Garden kalendaar, 1751-1771.* London: Scolar Press.

Worlidge, J. 1688. *The gardener's monthly directors.* Rept. 1980. Edinburgh: Clark Constable.

# 8

# GARDEN ARCHAEOLOGY IN OLD SALEM

## Michael Hammond

This chapter is not about excavated results but rather one of potential. This potential is unique in that within an urban context, there are undisturbed archaeological remains from a late 1700s planned religious community. Concomitant with that uniqueness are rather bountiful archival data. Both resources allow for the cross-checking of the accuracy of interpretation. The Moravians kept very careful records of all aspects of community life, which have been preserved in the archives of the Moravian Church and in the files of Old Salem, Inc. This plethora of archival material consists of town plans, estate inventories, diaries, store receipts, craftsmens' inventories, decorative arts, and the complete minutes of the biweekly meetings of both the Elders Conference and the Aufseher Collegium. Consequently, the Salem archival material offers a unique opportunity both to generate and to test hypotheses in conjunction with archaeological resources.

Old Salem is a restored community in the piedmont region of North Carolina. It was founded in 1766 by the *Unitas Fratum*, more commonly called the Brethren or the Moravians after the region in Europe where they originated. The Moravians trace their origin to the martyr John Huss, who was burned at the stake on 6 July 1415, primarily because of his statements about reforming the papacy (see Fries et al. 1922-69; Hamilton and Hamilton 1983). The Moravians spent considerable time underground fleeing from persecution; it was not until 1722 that they began to reassert themselves as a religious sect. At that time, Count Nicholas Zinzendorf of Saxony became their spiritual and financial benefactor and allowed the Moravians to settle on his estate. By 1734 the Brethren had received a land grant which allowed them to settle in Savannah, Georgia. Caught there in the battleground between the English Carolinas and Spanish Florida, they fled the South moving north to settle primarily in Pennsylvania. Another northern refuge for them was one of the estates of Charles Carroll of Carrollton who, because of religious persecution that his grandfather had felt as a Catholic in England, allowed them to rent land at the rate of one rose per year (Fries et al. 1922-69).

In 1740 the Moravians acquired land in Pennsylvania and started to develop settlements which they called Bethlehem, Nazareth, and Lititz (Gollin 1967). They flourished there for several years, and then, desirous of expansion, they began to look for new lands. Their industrious reputation made it easy for them to get permission to establish colonies in other places. One such place was in North Carolina where Lord Granville in 1753 deeded 98,985 acres (154.6 square miles) to the Brethren. The area was called Wachovia after Count Zinzendorf's estate, Der Wachau, in Saxony. The land was purchased by the Moravians as nineteen separate parcels, thereby insuring that if they ran into financial difficulties, they would not have to forfeit the entire parcel back to Granville (see Thorpe 1982).

The first settlement that they established was Bethabara, known as the House of Passage (fig. 8.1). As the name implies, Bethabara was conceived from the beginning as a temporary town. The Moravians already had plans to construct a main congregational town, to be called Salem, about six miles from Bethabara. In 1766 the first trees were felled in Salem and construction of some of the dwellings began. In later years, major buildings such as the Single Brothers' House (1769), the Gemein House (1771), and the Single Sisters' House (1786) were constructed. Some sixty-six of the original buildings still stand within the eighty-four acres of the restored community.

Salem was to be a community with all members sharing in the work and all sharing in the rewards. The sacred and secular aspects of life within the community were overseen by two governing bodies. The Elders Conference was charged with overseeing the spiritual affairs of the congregation. The Aufseher Collegium, or supervising board, cared for the material and financial aspects of the community. These two bodies developed and enforced the rules and regulations of the community. They even established regulations pertaining to plant material surrounding a house.

The documentary evidence for the first town, Bethabara, is as equally rich as that of Salem. A 1766 map in the Archives of the Moravian Church in America, Southern Province, shows the general location of Bethabara within its environmental setting, including some of the major garden features. Depicted on the map are the *Gemein Gartten*, or community garden, as well as the bottom garden alongside Johanna Creek and a summerhouse located on an island in the creek. Another map done the same year by the surveyor Philip Christian Gottlieb Reuter indicates where some of the gardens were located in Bethabara (see Hinman 1986). After Salem was constructed, Bethabara remained, albeit with diminished population and importance.

In order to adequately test archaeological methodology and its results, an accurate archival representation of the area to be excavated would be ideal. One such example for Bethabara would be the 1759 map of the upland garden which shows the individual plot layouts for the entire one-half-acre garden (fig. 8.2). The marginal notes to the map indicate where various species of plants were located. These help to understand both the kinds of crops that the Moravians were growing and their concepts of how to organize a garden. This latter consideration is a unique feature of the information available about the Moravians. While probable plant lists can be compiled from store account books that record purchases of seeds, it is rare that locations of the plants within such a small area can be pinpointed. In addition, the area of garden space utilized for various species can also be calculated. Questions regarding spatial relationships of cultivated species can also be entertained. Were certain plants cultivated in close proximity to one another for their mutual benefits? Section 8 (top center plot of the map) was planted only with seeds that were brought from Germany. Why is this section given special attention? Is it an attempt to establish a seedbed? Was it used to supplement the local plants with some of those from the mother country? An important methodological question is whether such spatial information can be recovered archaeologically. The upland garden with its precise documentary description could serve as a control to refine some recovery methods and analysis methodology.

The Hortus Medicus, Bethabara's medicinal herb garden, is depicted in a 1761 drawing (fig. 8.3). Again, a description of the plants grown in the plots as well as a scale to calculate

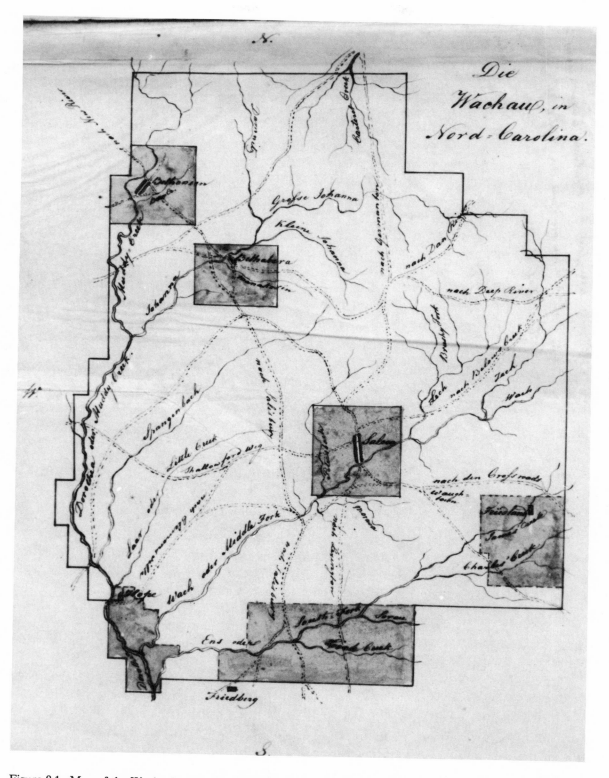

Figure 8.1. Map of the Wachovia tract showing the location of Salem and Bethabara. (Courtesy of the Moravian Archives, Herrnhut, East Germany)

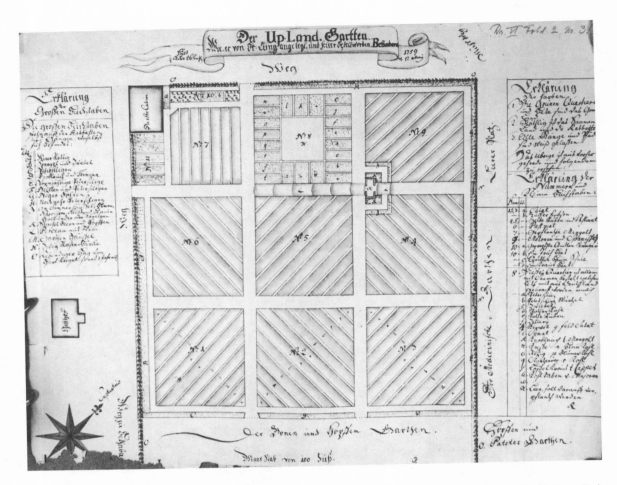

Figure 8.2.  The upland garden, Bethabara, North Carolina.  (Courtesy of the Moravian Archives, Bethlehem, Pa.)

areal extent is provided on the map.  The Moravian records provide extensive information about disease variables and their methods of curing those diseases.  Can a correlation be found between the amount of space devoted to each plant and the illness that it aided in curing?  Is there a correlation between the amount of space and the population of the town?  What is the full range of medicinal herbs that were being cultivated?  What percentage of them were indigenous to the Old World or the New?  The information in the drawing provides an excellent starting point to explore these and other questions.

The permanent town of Salem was located almost in the exact center of the acreage that the Moravians purchased.  The 1766 map of the Wachovia tract (see fig. 8.1) depicts its location within the tract, as well as that of Bethabara and some of the other towns that were formed.  Along with maps, numerous drawings and paintings provide ideas about land use within the community.  A painting entitled *A View of Salem in North Carolina, 1787* by Lugwig Gottfried von Redeken shows the town from the southeast.  In the foreground are split-rail snake fences that have plants growing on them--one has been identified as a grapevine.  More importantly, the painting provides us with information about town planning and agricultural techniques.  The garden area of the Single Brothers' House is seen in the

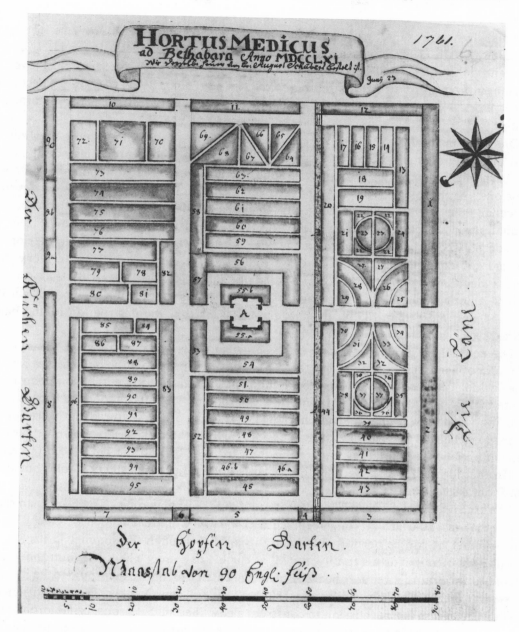

Figure 8.3.  The Hortus Medicus, Bethabara.  (Reproduced by permission of the Moravian Archives, Winston-Salem, N.C.)

painting.  Other drawings indicate that at a later time, in the 1840s, the formality of the Bethabara gardens was not preserved in Salem.  The drawings that were required of all students at the female academy founded in 1772 also recorded the flora of Salem.  One of a hyacinth by Christiana Kramasch, dated 1815, is exact in its rendition of a botanical specimen.

Archaeologically, little research has been focused specifically on the gardens of Old Salem.  The archaeology program in Salem has been in existence for only about two and a half years. However, other archaeologists have done work with the Moravians in the past, e.g., Stanley South (1972) at Bethabara and Old Salem, Gary Wheeler Stone (1972) in Old Salem, and John Clauser (1978) in both of the towns. Within Old Salem, however, the archaeology program is still in its infancy, functioning primarily as part of the restoration process. Work with gardens is being done tangentially to that required for the restoration of buildings.

One such example is the recent excavation of the Dr. Samuel Benjamin Vierling barn so that the building could be reconstructed. A late 1860s photograph indicated the location of the barn but, like most archival photographs, did not provide information about all of the dimensions. Archaeology provided those answers. One archaeological surprise was a stone-lined cellar hole at the northeast corner of the barn straddling what would have been the continuation of the eastern wall of the barn. The dimensions of the pit are 7.5 feet on a north-south direction and 4.3 feet for its maximum east-west direction on the interior. The excavated contents included pottery (redware, creamware, and pearlware), an ivory thread waxer, a deciduous molar with a gold-foil filling, an ivory toothbrush, lead toys, and tumblers, among other things. The dates of these artifacts range from about 1804 until the late 1890s, and more than likely, they represent trash from the destruction of the barn in the late 1890s.

The contents of the cellar hole gave no clues as to its original function. It is possible that fodder of some sort was placed in the cellar hole, dumped from the outside and retrieved on the inside. The fodder may have been mangolds (*Beta vulgaris*); the Moravian records indicate that this plant was being grown for cattle fodder. "A cellar under the barn is useful, for storing vegetables for cattle" (Beecher 1841:44). Some of the features that were found in the yard area behind the barn provided support for this theory. A series of postholes were located at about 5-foot intervals separating the yard area behind the barn from the lot next door. In that lot, there was a parallel line of large holes adjacent to the postholes but slightly offset from each other.

The archival information about the lot provided the explanation. The Moravian records indicate that in 1804 Dr. Vierling received a cow from a patient in lieu of cash. He then asked "whether he can be permitted to keep this animal through the summer in his lot, since he needs a lot of milk for his family as well as for his patients. The Collegium thought that we could grant him this request because of the necessity of the cow, provided he never lets the cow run free" (Aufseher Collegium 1804). That fall, on October 23, he petitioned the Aufseher Collegium for permission to construct a cow shed on his property. In order to keep the cow fresh, he needed a calf. Add to this a horse for his buggy, some pigs and chickens, and one has a busy barnyard. The offsetting holes, which were about 1.5 feet in diameter and about 2 feet deep, were perhaps dug to plant shrubbery so that Vierling's neighbor did not have to look at the menagerie next door.

The second season of excavations (1986) revealed that there was a wagon road leading to the cellar hole and that it was bordered by cedar trees, whose stumps were recovered archaeologically. On the downslope side of the road a large surface deposit of trash was located. Among the most prevalent artifacts recovered were small flowerpots about three inches in height, which a horticulturalist will explain are for starting plants. Who did these pots belong to? One person associated with the Vierling house after the doctor's death in 1817 was Louis David von Schweinitz, the administrator of Wachovia from 1812 until 1821 (Bynum 1975). Von Schweinitz is also known as the father of American mycology. During his stay in Salem, he collected plant specimens and wrote "Flora Salemitana," the manuscript of which, along with personal papers, is in the Manuscripts Collection of the Academy of Natural Sciences of Philadelphia. There are thousands of pressed examples in his herbarium. During his tenure as administrator he was joined on many of his collecting trips by two other Moravian ministers interested in botany, Samuel Kramasch, the father of Christiana who drew the hyacinth in 1815, and Christian Frederick Denke. Kramasch prepared two descriptions of the flora of Salem that are in the Moravian Archives. Denke, however, is the key person in this story for he too lived in the Vierling house. His was a short stay while his house was being constructed; he may well have been starting plants to put in its ambitious gardens. In a letter to von Schweinitz in 1833, he stated: "When my Pilgrim's rest in the Western Liberties, with ornamental gardens, waterworks, the greenhouse, etc., is complete it will be a true paradise. As you know, the house was constructed 25 feet back to accommodate a garden in front of it" (Denke to von Schweinitz, 13 June 1833).

Archaeological work on the Denke lot has been confined to searching for the outbuildings that Old Salem wishes to reconstruct. There are, however, some tantalizing views of its gardens. An 1832 painting done by Maria Denke, his wife, shows the house being constructed. Other drawings show backyard garden plots and the backyard divided as Denke described it in his letter: "My lot is . . . 95 foot front and 300 deep . . . so we will have a culinary garden and pasture for cow and horse" (Denke to von Schweinitz, 13 June 1833).

Perhaps the most interesting view is that portrayed in an 1850s watercolor (fig. 8.4). The Denke lot is on the right. The space utilization is that of a work area close to the house, followed by gardens with an orchard in the very back. One of the fruit trees depicted must be a Buckingham apple, for Salem's newspaper of 16 September 1836 reported: "Beat this who can! We were presented with a mammoth apple of the Buckingham kind grown on the plantation of the Rev. C. F. Denke, of this neighborhood measuring 15 1/2 inches in circumference and weighing 19 ounces" (*Weekly Chronicle and Farmers Register* 1836).

Archaeology does not take place only in the ground. A cabinet located in the botany department at Salem College, originally the Female Academy of the Moravians, contained some important herbarium materials. The herbarium of Miss Emma Lehman, who taught at the academy from 1864 until 1915, forms the bulk of the collection. Although her academic specialty was English, she was truly the Renaissance woman. Her notes describe objects as diverse as stone tools seen on her trips to the Egyptian desert to relics at La Chapelle aux Saints containing fragments of the true cross, a nail from the cross, and the crown of thorns. She also made careful drawings of all botanical specimens that she observed (Siewers Room, Gramley Library, Salem College). Her files also contain photographs of some of the backyards of Salem, one being next to the Vierling backyard (fig. 8.5). The terraced gardens had elaborate wooden steps leading down the slope of the hill; at the bottom was a lily pond containing *Victoria regia*. Her notes indicate that the photograph was taken in 1889 and that it is little Lettie Gilner weighing 65 pounds sitting on the pad. Obviously by 1889 the experimental botanists in Salem were reaching out to the world for exotic ornamental plant specimens. Miss Lehman collected and pressed many specimens, giving the exact location from where the specimen was taken and the date of the pressing. Many of these are designated as having come from the environs of Salem.

There is just one other person who needs to be introduced, and that is Maria Denke, the wife of Christian Fredrick Denke. She taught botany at the college for close to fifty years. If Emma Lehman was the Renaissance woman of Salem, Maria Denke was the first

Figure 8.4.  An 1850s view of Salem, artist unknown.  (Courtesy of Historic
Old Salem, Winston-Salem, N.C.)

liberated woman.  When her husband died in 1838, she left Salem and went as a governess
on a two-year trip to Paris.  She was always being reprimanded by the governing body of
the school for staying out overnight to attend political meetings.  But one thoughtful
contribution she made to the college helps us understand the botany of Salem; it is the
donated collection of her husband's herbarium.

The herbarium is rather complete.  It contains specimens that are identified, in German
script (fig. 8.6), as occurring locally and those that were imported.  While there are a wide
range of ornamentals such as *Dicentra formosa*, of particular interest are the narcissi, which
include *Narcissus odorns*, collected by Denke in 1829 in Salem with his notes indicating that
the native habitat for the species was from France to Spain; *N. jonquilla*, collected in 1829

Figure 8.5. An 1889 photograph of the Steiner lot and *Victoria regia*. (Courtesy of Historic Old Salem, Winston-Salem, N.C.)

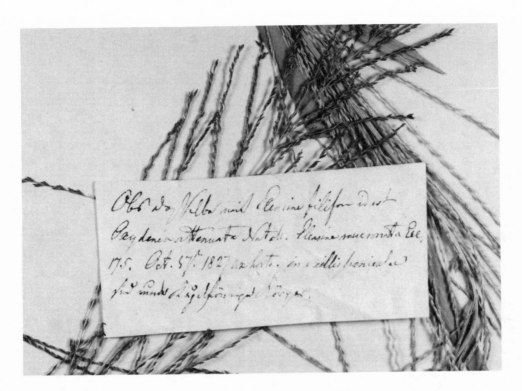

Figure 8.6. Material from the Christian Frederick Denke Herbarium. (Photograph from the Botany Department, Salem College, courtesy of Historic Old Salem, Winston-Salem, N.C.)

in Salem with notes indicating a native habitat of China and Japan; and *N. pseudo narcissus*, again collected in 1829 in Salem with notes indicating the original native habitat was from Sweden to Austria. These are representative plants of Salem from the 1820s before cross-pollination and its resultant hybridization, and they are extremely valuable resources. They tell us that Denke was involved in world markets for ornamental plants.

The archival evidence indicates that many plants have been imported into the natural landscape of Salem. The Denke lot, combined with specimens from the herbarium, has the potential to test thoroughly the methodology of palynology and phytolith analysis. Samples could be taken from the 1829 specimens and used as a control for comparisons with those samples recovered archaeologically. This unique repository of specimens should allow us to understand thoroughly the horticulture of the early 1820s.

From a barnyard with flowerpots to personalities and their herbariums, the richness of Salem's archival materials combined with the archaeological potential of various sites will allow the testing of numerous mutual concerns. It is an excellent location to test the effectiveness of opal phytolith analysis with ornamental and herbal plants. More importantly, however, it will allow researchers to define that illusive interface between archival and archaeological data.

References Cited

Aufseher Collegium Notes. 1804. Translation on file at Old Salem, Inc., Winston-Salem, N.C.

Beecher, C. E. 1841. *A treatise on domestic economy.* Boston: Marsh, Capen, Lyon, and Webb.

Bynum, F. A. 1975. Father of American mycology. In *The three forks of Muddy Creek*, vol. 2, ed. F. Griffin, pp. 41-50. Winston-Salem: Old Salem, Inc.

Clauser, J. W., Jr. 1978. The excavation of the Bethabara kiln: An analysis of nineteenth-century potting techniques. Master's thesis, Department of Anthropology, University of Florida.

Fries, A. L., K. G. Hamilton, D. L. Rights, and M. J. Smith (editors). 1922-69. *Records of the Moravians in North Carolina.* 11 vols. Raleigh: Department of Archives and History.

Gollin, G. L. 1967. *Moravians in two worlds: A study of changing communities.* New York: Columbia University Press.

Hamilton, J. T., and K. G. Hamilton. 1983. *History of the Moravian Church: The renewed Unitas Fratum, 1722-1957.* Bethlehem: Interprovincial Board of Christian Education, Moravian Church in America.

Hinman, W. 1986. Philip Christian Gottlieb Reuter: First surveyor of Wachovia. Master's thesis, Department of History, Wake Forest University.

South, S. 1972. Discovery in Wachovia. Manuscript. Winston-Salem: Old Salem, Inc.

Stone, G. W. 1972. Excavations at the fifth house. In Discovery in Wachovia, by S. South, pp. 208-58. Manuscript. Winston-Salem: Old Salem, Inc.

Thorpe, D. P. 1982. Moravian colonization of Wachovia, 1753-1772. Ph.D. dissertation, Department of History, Johns Hopkins University.

**9**

# MOUNT CLARE: AN INTERDISCIPLINARY APPROACH TO THE RESTORATION OF A GEORGIAN LANDSCAPE

## Carmen A. Weber, Elizabeth Anderson Comer, Louise E. Akerson, and Gary Norman

In the eighteenth century Charles Carroll, known as the Barrister, owned a plantation called Mount Clare outside the small port town of Baltimore, Maryland (fig. 9.1). Today in urban Baltimore at Mount Clare, an interdisciplinary study of the landscape involving archaeology, historical research, and architecturally based landscape analysis attempts to understand the practical and pleasurable aspects of the Carrolls' Georgian landscape (fig 9.2). Archaeo-botanical techniques such as flotation and pollen analysis have been important additions to historical research into the Carrolls' eighteenth-century plants. Archaeology has also revealed significant information on soil stratigraphy and patterning.

Figure 9.1. Mount Clare with reconstructed forecourt wall. (Photograph © Aaron Levin 1987)

Figure 9.2. Aerial view of Mount Clare and the orchard excavations. (Courtesy of Baltimore Center for Urban Archaeology)

The Mount Clare Plantation Restoration Project, essentially an effort to reconstruct a past lifeway of the mid-eighteenth century, was approached from three different perspectives: anthropological, scientific, and historical. The anthropological approach examines the Mount Clare landscape within the framework of technological, social, and ideological human behavior patterns. An anthropological perspective guided the study of Mount Clare's evolving landscape as it was shaped by the practical technology of growing plants in the Chesapeake and by English landscape styles. The second approach drew more on the hard sciences, utilizing quantitative and qualitative analyses of soils recovered during excavations. The third approach focused on traditional methods in historical archaeology, casting excavation method and theory within the context of historical records.

Of paramount importance to the Mount Clare study were four paintings dating from the eighteenth century through early nineteenth century, three of them painted by Charles Willson Peale. Most significant was Peale's 1775 rendering of Mount Clare and its gardens (fig. 9.3), and the depiction of the first terrace in Margaret Carroll's portrait was also useful (fig. 9.4), as was the view of the forecourt shown in the Barrister's portrait. Of immediate archaeological interest was the illustration of an orchard to the southwest of the mansion. Excavation of the orchard was expected to provide information on the planting pattern of fruit trees. Tree stains were assumed to be located equal distances apart; the placement of these features within the orchard area would determine the planting pattern. Thus, the orchard area became the initial focus of archaeological excavation, including soil flotation and floral analysis, pollen analysis, and soil chemical analysis.

Figure 9.3. Mount Clare, garden front, south side, painting by Charles Willson Peale, 1775. The orchard is on the extreme left side. (Courtesy of The National Society of the Colonial Dames of America in the State of Maryland, Mount Clare Collection)

Along with excavation, other types of data collection were planned and initiated. Surface reconnaissance of the excavation site began with the examination of infrared aerial photographs. These photographs, along with the results of other excavations, such as the Eleutherian Mills garden site (Wilkinson n.d.), pointed to the need to consider crop marks when looking for potential tree stains and other features. Although geophysical techniques were considered, it was decided that they could more profitably be applied to other aspects of the garden excavation.

Another aspect of surface reconnaissance was a survey of existing vegetation. Numerous extant trees in the vicinity of the orchard were identified and cored for dating purposes. Many of these ornamental trees, laid out along curved brick walkways running perpendicular to the slope on which the house rests, dated to the late nineteenth century. No trees were identified as eighteenth-century specimens.

Examination of the available historical documentation started with orders that the Barrister had placed to England for fruit trees. His letterbooks contain copies of orders he placed with his English merchant, William Anderson, between 1755 and 1769. In addition

Figure 9.4. Margaret Tilghman Carroll (1742-1817), portrait by Charles Willson Peale, 1770-71, altered by Peale in 1778. (Courtesy of The National Society of the Colonial Dames of America in the State of Maryland, Mount Clare Collection)

to these letterbooks, a major portion of the Barrister's library is housed at Mount Clare, and it contains two English garden books, Phillip Miller's *The Gardener's Dictionary* (1759) and Thomas Hale's *The Compleat Body of Husbandry* (1758). The Barrister also ordered from England John Hill's *The Gardener's Kalendar* (1758). These were examined for botanical information on the known varieties of Carroll's fruit trees. Examples of other regional orchards were sought in a survey of other plantations' notices in the *Maryland Gazette* for the years 1755 to 1765 (Duvall 1985).

As the months progressed, the data were combined to give a more complete view of eighteenth-century Mount Clare. The technological sphere, entailing orchard planting and management in the eighteenth century, was examined in a variety of ways. Research in the Barrister's and other eighteenth-century gardening books brought to light techniques for orchard maintenance specific to the English climate. This same information could not be profitably examined in American gardening books as those located dated after 1780. Some clues as to colonial understanding of the American climate were learned from shipping instructions sent by the Barrister to England. For example, according to the Barrister "the Pears should be grafted on Quince stocks or they will not last long here" (quoted in Trostel 1980:57). Knowledge about orchard technology recorded in account books, diaries, and correspondence throughout the colonial Chesapeake has been compiled in an excellent secondary source by Pryor (1983), and it represents a sphere of knowledge available to the Barrister through family and social contacts. Additional information on orchards gathered from the *Maryland Gazette* (Duvall 1985) through printed notices of land sales often included what could be considered brief descriptions of typical orchards of the immediate region in the Barrister's time, such as

> To be SOLD, by the Subscriber, for Bills of Exchange, Sterling Cash, or Current Money, A Tract of Land, lying near Seneca in Frederick County, containing 408 Acres, a choice Place for raising Stock, and very good Land for Grain or Tobacco; about 40 acres of which is clear'd, some Meadow clear'd, and a great Plenty of Meadow Ground to clear, some good Houses thereon, and a fine young Apple-Orchard, and a Number of Cherry and Peach Trees. (*Maryland Gazette*, 16 August 1759; cited in Duvall 1985:25)

The views of landscape architect Patricia O'Donnell (personal communication, 1985) on the cultivation of fruit trees in the climate, soil, and situation of the Mount Clare orchard provided further data. Topographic examination of the orchard hillside indicated it was extremely uneven in its current configuration. Its uneven topography would have been unfavorable for an orchard, as sunlight and water would not have been equally distributed among the fruit trees. A gently sloping hillside, with a southwestern exposure as recommended by Thomas Hale in *The Compleat Body of Husbandry* (1758), would have been optimal for orchard growth. Although the exposure was correct for an orchard, the degree of slope and unevenness were not. Examination of an 1896 topographic map of the grounds indicated that some of the cuts into the hillside were related to access for late nineteenth-century park buildings.

These observations corresponded with the results of the ongoing archaeological excavation. Numerous tree stains were located, but artifact analysis of feature content indicated that many of these features had artifacts dating to the eighteenth and nineteenth centuries. Closer examination of one tree stain provided evidence of replanting, where a small planting hole with more recent artifacts intruded into a larger planting hole. It was noted that replanting would not necessarily be detected when the new planting hole was larger than the earlier planting hole. Of the twenty-one tree planting stains located in the orchard area, none could be identified as from the eighteenth century through artifact analysis of their content (Norman 1985a, 1985b, 1985c).

However, when Gradall trenches were excavated in the orchard, the removal and addition of soil to the hillside was confirmed. This disturbance removed most of the eighteenth-century ground surface and with it, most of the eighteenth-century remains of the orchard.  One small area around a large elm tree, dated by coring at 160 years old, appeared to be relatively undisturbed by landscaping activities.  In this area, four small tree planting stains were identified as eighteenth century through their size, relative depth compared to other stains, and artifact content.  These four stains represent a possible planting pattern of 28 feet between trees in rows 30 feet apart (Norman 1985).

Further research into the potential source of the extensive disturbance of the eighteenth-century ground surface at Mount Clare located the annual reports of the Baltimore Board of Park Commissioners (1891-1917).  These reports chronicle extensive changes made to enhance the appearance of Mount Clare in a city park setting.  This project included the removal of many worthless trees and the planting of hundreds of trees and shrubs, along with the regulation of terraces and excavation for roadways, noted in the 1896 topographic map.  Profile elevations from the Gradall trenches and elevations near the house were used to produce a landscape plan to reconstruct the hillside slope as it appears in the 1775 Peale landscape painting.

The patterning of the orchard, in 28-foot-by-30-foot intervals, was more difficult to interpret.  Miller (1759) recommended that trees in a close orchard be no less than 40 feet apart.  Hale (1758) recommended rows 30 yards apart, with the trees in each row 20 yards apart; if these distances were in feet, not yards, they would be close to the distances found.  One possible interpretation of this seemingly small, tightly planted orchard is that it was planted before the Barrister's use of the site for a permanent country residence.  The Barrister's father lived at the site in the 1730s through early 1750s only occasionally, and he may have planted an orchard as a source of food, drink, and/or animal fodder (Norman 1985).  However, the Barrister's orders to England indicate he did have numerous fruit trees sent to Mount Clare.  These orders included varieties of trees not noted elsewhere in the Chesapeake (Pryor 1983) and thus indicate his interest in experimentation.  This experimentation could have carried over to the placement of trees within the orchard.

It is the orchard placement relative to the house and remaining grounds that represents the ideological sphere of interpretation.  On first inspection, the siting of the Mount Clare orchard appears to deviate from the normal preoccupation with Georgian symmetry so often seen at the root of the Georgian mind-set (Deetz 1977; Isaac 1982).  For example, the eastern border of the orchard is located at an angle which appears to disrupt any appearance of a balanced overall plan.  This angle is not parallel or perpendicular to the house, as at the Paca Garden in Annapolis (Leone 1984) and Burwell's Kingsmill plantation in Virginia (Kelso 1984), but runs along the slope diagonally toward the garden in front of the house (fig. 9.5).

Further examination of the topography immediately surrounding the house suggested perspective, not necessarily symmetry, was an overriding consideration of the Barrister in the placement of the orchard.  The importance of perspective and rules of mathematics for eighteenth-century garden designers has been studied in other Chesapeake gardens (Leone 1984; Paca-Steele and Wright 1987).  At Mount Clare, the orchard and other elements of the landscape were interrelated to produce a particular visual effect.  Thus, study of the terraces of the falling garden is necessary to understanding the orchard placement.

When the first three terraces of the falling garden in front of the house are closely examined on the map, they appear to become smaller as they descend.  The edge of these terraces creates a diagonal line similar to the orchard border.  The device of perspective is used in other Chesapeake gardens with diagonal lines.  At Mulberry Fields, for example,

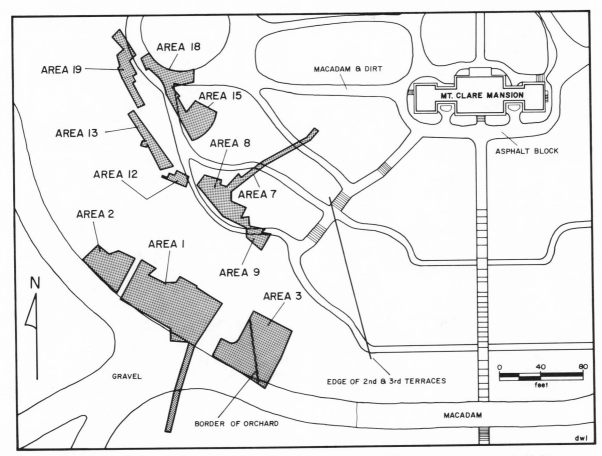

Figure 9.5. Mount Clare orchard area, illustrating the orchard border and edge of second and third terraces. (Drawn by Donald W. Linebaugh)

constructed around 1755 on the Potomac River near St. Mary's City, the trees are planted along diagonal lines between the house and the river. These two lines of trees are four times farther apart at the river than by the house. This perspective creates an optical illusion, making the river appear closer than it actually is (fig. 9.6). This perspective can also operate in the reverse, when the house is looked at from the river (fig. 9.7). The river was a key element in the landscape at Mount Clare. John Adams in 1777 noted in his diary that from the Annapolis road "you have a full view of the elegant, splendid Seat of Mr. Carroll Barrister. It is a large and elegant House. It stands fronting looking down the River, into the Harbour. It is one Mile from the Water" (quoted in Trostel 1980:48). From the house, diagonal lines formed by the terraced garden would make the garden appear farther away and thus larger than it actually was. The diagonal formed by the orchard border would also focus attention on the river, located about a mile from the house (Weber 1986).

The illusion was not lost on Mary Ambler, who in 1770 commented in her diary that "the house . . . stands upon a very High Hill & has a fine View of Petapsico River. You Step out of the Door into the Bowlg Green from which the Garden Falls & when You stand on the Top of it there is such a Uniformity of each side that the whole Plantn seems to be laid out like a Garden" (quoted in Trostel 1980:48).

Figure 9.6. View of the river from Mulberry Fields. (Drawn by Muriel Kirkpatrick)

Figure 9.7. View of Mulberry Fields from the River. (Drawn by Muriel Kirkpatrick)

Planting the orchard along the diagonal would have created an irregular plan as the rows descend along the slope of the hillside. Regularity appears to have been not as important as the overall visual effect; indeed, Miller (1759) stated that regular rows were not necessary in an orchard. Therefore, the orchard reconstruction plan utilized splayed diagonal rows of trees, placing 200 historic varieties of apple, pear, peach, quince, plum, and cherry trees over a 4.7-acre area.

Soil analysis was another part of the Mount Clare excavation that provided additional data. Soil was collected throughout both survey and excavation phases for chemical, flotation, phytolith, and pollen analyses. The phytolith samples were taken to supplement the pollen and floral studies; however, these samples have not yet been analyzed.

Initially, eleven flotation samples from what appeared to be eighteenth-century garden features (i.e., deposits intruding into subsoil, some sealed with a layer of oyster shell, containing eighteenth-century artifacts and/or oyster shell, charcoal, and fish remains) were sent to ethnobotanist Dr. Cheryl Holt (Analytical Services for Archaeology) for identification and analysis along with samples from the bowling green, forecourt area, house ventilation tunnel, orangery, and second terrace in the falling garden (Holt 1984a, 1984b, 1985, 1986). Floral analysis identified the remains of elderberry, oak, black cherry, hackberry, buckthorn, dogwood, mulberry, and pear, defining the wide range of fruit and ornamental trees that were cultivated at the Carroll estate. The identification of pot herb specimens greatly enhanced understanding of the subsistence system as well as medicinal practices common to the eighteenth century. In addition, a range of plants utilized for their greens and seed were suggested by seeds recovered from the site area. Purslane, pennyroyal, dock, wood sorrel, mustard, dandelion, pokeweed, knotweed, yarrow, Saint John's-wort, pigweed, and chicory are all likely to have been cultivated in the gardens and probably were important dietary as well as medicinal plants to the Carrolls. Wild fruit seeds such as strawberry and blackberry suggest the utilization of native plants in the Carroll garden as well. The recovery of clover, vetch, rye, meadow grass, fescue, crabgrass, and alfalfa suggests that the Carrolls utilized ground covers for animal foraging, to discourage other weeds, and to enrich the soil. Many of these varieties appear in the Barrister's orders to England; he ordered enough seed to plant eight acres of meadow (Charles Carroll, Barrister, Letterbook, 2 April 1765). The presence of weed seeds within the recovered assemblage indicates an untended habitat such as would be expected around buildings and cultivated fields. The recovery of ornamental plant seeds provided data on the composition and variety of the Carroll flower gardens. Delphinium, foxglove, aster, amaranth, buttercup (bachelor's button), bedstraw, sweet pea, Solomon's seal, as well as Jimsonweed seeds, all plants common to eighteenth-century gardens, were recovered, suggesting they were most likely components of the Carrolls' falling garden.

Soil samples taken from these planting features were also subjected to chemical analysis to see if eighteenth-century soil conditions could be defined or if a pattern or relationship between features could be discerned. This analysis was conducted in the Baltimore Center for Urban Archaeology laboratory using a LaMotte soil-testing kit. The soil was tested for pH, potassium, and phosphorus. Phosphorus and potassium are chemical elements required by plants in macroquantities and are essential for healthy plant growth. It was hypothesized that in order to grow healthy apple, pear, and peach trees, phosphorus levels would need to be low and potassium levels would need to be medium to low. These elements, however, cannot be assimilated by plants unless the soil pH is between pH 5.0 and pH 6.9, or slightly acidic (*The LaMotte Soil Handbook* 1978). In the orchard, phosphorus levels for tree stains were in the low to medium range and for planting holes/postholes in the medium to high range. Potassium levels for the eighteenth-century tree stains and planting holes/postholes were medium to high; and pH levels ranged from pH 4.0 to pH 8.0. Chemical analysis of the soil in the features sent to Dr. Holt indicated that the phosphorus levels for those features were low, medium, and high. The levels should be low. The medium and high levels were probably not acceptable for healthy fruit trees. The potassium levels were all high, which is also probably not acceptable for healthy fruit trees. The pH levels ranged from pH 6.0 to pH 8.0, slightly acidic to slightly alkaline. This soil was probably not suitable for healthy fruit trees, and testing for phosphorus and potassium was abandoned.

However, testing soil for pH revealed an interesting phenomenon. It was observed that nearly all the planting holes/postholes in excavation area 3 were neutral or slightly alkaline. Excavation area 3, characterized by a maze of 100 roughly circular features, was interpreted as a planting area, located between the falling garden and the orchard (fig. 9.8). Further analysis of this area indicated four of the circular features, nos. 78, 79, 94, and 95, appeared to be perpendicular to the western edge of the planting area, and they were exactly 6 feet apart. It was also apparent that four other features, nos. 54, 72, 96, and 98, paralleled the western edge, and the distance between feature nos. 96 and 98 was 9 feet. These features therefore exhibited a planting pattern of 6 feet by 9 feet (fig. 9.9).

A closer examination of the 1775 Peale landscape painting indicated that this planting area could represent a vineyard (see fig. 9.3). A review of the Barrister's copy of *The Gardening Dictionary* (Miller 1759) revealed a recommendation for planting a vineyard in a southeast to northwest alignment and in rows of 6 feet by 10 feet. The alignment of features was southeast to northwest. A 6-foot-by-9-foot grid was placed over the entire area, and each feature near the intersections was examined. Only those features containing eighteenth-century artifacts and/or shell, charcoal, and brick were retained. Features containing coal were eliminated because of the proximity of a twentieth-century greenhouse utilizing coal. The location of numerous features at or near the intersections displayed a convincing planting pattern. Other features could represent stakes because Miller recommended staking of grapevines at various times of the year.

Three out of the initial eleven flotation samples came from excavation area 3. Those three samples contained edible greens, flowers, weeds, grasses, and clover, but the most exciting seed specimens recovered were the pear (*Pyrous* sp.) and two varieties of clover (*Medicigo hispida* and *Trifolium*). The Barrister ordered pear trees, and both types of clover were recommended by Phillip Miller (1759). Information on seed varieties found in all the planting pattern features was needed to complete the analysis. Additionally, an explanation for the good seed preservation and a possible correlation between this preservation and the pH of the soil were sought. Therefore, an additional eight samples from area 3 were analyzed. Seed recovery could not be statistically related to soil pH but was somewhat random in nature. Seed recovery also was not directly related to the planting hole/posthole contexts. No new information regarding fruit tree specimens was discovered; however, fruit tree specimens (pear) were found only in the orchard/vineyard area and nowhere else on the site. The recovery of flaxseed gave more insight into possible domestic activities and enhanced the assessment of the range of plants cultivated by the Barrister.

Unfortunately, no grape pips were recovered, so that there is no direct evidence for a vineyard in excavation area 3. However, investigation into historical sources indicated that vineyards were not uncommon in the eighteenth-century Chesapeake. A land sale notice in

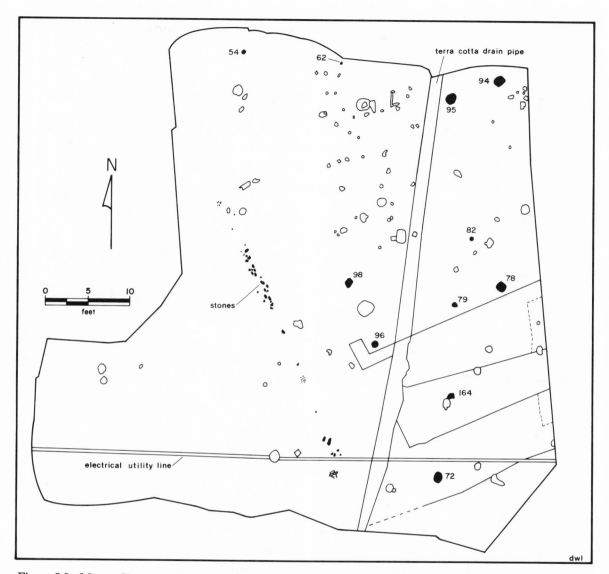

Figure 9.8. Mount Clare orchard, area 3, plan view. (Drawn by Donald W. Linebaugh)

the *Maryland Gazette*, dated 2 February 1758, mentions a vineyard. Another notice dated 5 November 1761 describes a property purchased from "the late Col. Tasker," containing "the late Governor Bladen's Vineyard." (Duvall 1985:38–39). This last notice is particularly interesting in light of the social relationship between these individuals and the Barrister. Governor Bladen was Colonel Benjamin Tasker's father-in-law, and Colonel Tasker was an elderly business associate of the Barrister. Thus, it seems likely the Barrister would have known of this vineyard. As the notice suggests, Governor Bladen's vineyard had a reputation beyond just the immediate family. Additionally, a distant cousin of the Barrister's, Charles Carroll of Carrollton, had a vineyard at his country estate (Pryor 1984). Reexamination of the Peale landscape painting indicated no other area suggestive of a vineyard (see fig. 9.3). The historical research indicating older and contemporary vineyards and the correspondence

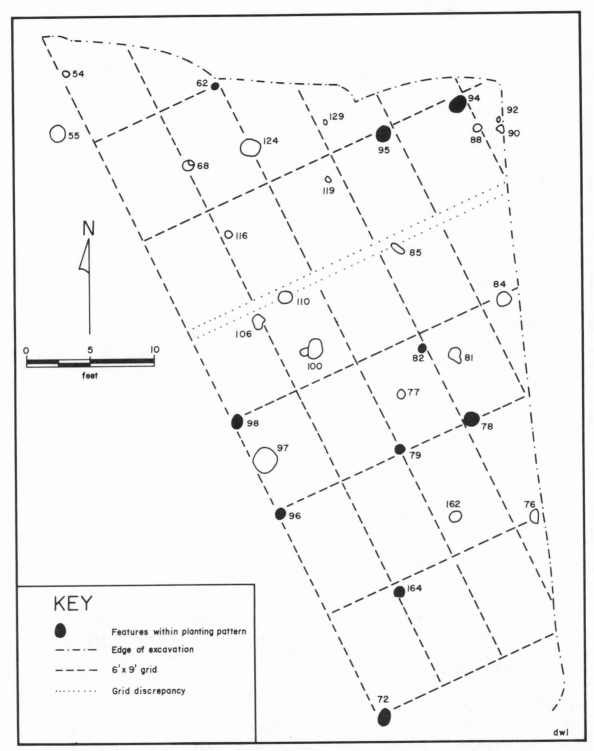

Figure 9.9. Mount Clare orchard, area 3, planting pattern. (Drawn by Donald W. Linebaugh)

between the alignment and patterning of the planting features and Miller's (1759) directions make the interpretation and reconstruction of this area as a vineyard reasonable. In this instance, soil testing of excavated areas contributed information that could not have been discovered using any other means, thus strengthening the final restoration interpretation.

A third approach utilized at Mount Clare involved the use of archaeological excavation, documentary research, and examination of extant historic gardens. Archaeological investigations were conducted in 1985 in an effort to locate and identify remains of the bowling green. Because a 1770 diary description of Mount Clare locates the bowling green between the house and falling garden, excavation was concentrated on the first terrace directly in front of the main house. The primary goal of the excavation was to determine the location and configuration of the bowling green so that it could be more accurately reconstructed during the planned restoration of the first terrace.

Hand excavation of over 1,000 square feet of the first terrace did not provide evidence of the bowling green. Our research strategies had been based on the assumption that the remains of a ditch, bank, hedge, or other boundary would emerge as excavation proceeded in that area. No such boundary remains were found, and we returned to the documentary sources. The annual reports of the Baltimore Board of Park Commissioners (1891-1917) revealed that the city landscaped and regulated the terraces around the mansion in the early 1890s, but the exact magnitude of that work was not recorded. Colonel Scharf, the chronicler of Baltimore history, observed about Mount Clare in 1874 that "this old mansion, which yet survives, is a graphic monument of the past time. One may fancy its amplitude and grave dignity of exterior, with the old lions carved in stone that stood rampant on the pillars of the gateway, and there was a fine terrace overlooking the town. It has been but a few years since these disappeared" (Scharf 1874:50). It was not clear whether the terrace had disappeared, the lions had disappeared, or both. From this reference and the changes reported by the Board of Park Commissioners, it appears neglect of the gardens and grounds, beginning with the mid-nineteenth-century abandonment of the property by the Carroll family, contributed to the dilapidation of the old terraces to such an extent that they required total reconstruction.

A review of eighteenth-century English literature pertinent to bowling greens produced useful information about the nature and perceived function of these grass plots. John Abercrombie (1778), a gardener and botanist in the late eighteenth century, defined a bowling green as "a spacious level grass plat in pleasure grounds, designed both for ornament, and the recreation of bowling in summer." He also stated that a bowling green was usually planted near the house, next to the back or side, where it could also serve as a lawn. He recommended that the green should not be less than one acre in size, if space permitted, and should be bordered with plantings of flowers and shrubs.

The first terrace, where the bowling green was said to have been located, is scarcely one-third of an acre in size. If the Barrister had wanted to utilize as much of this space as possible, he may have ignored Abercrombie's recommendation of a border around the green. It appears from the documents that the well-meaning park commissioners destroyed most of the evidence of pre-1890s garden features on the first terrace.

Employing a strategy of tracing the development of the terrace, two trenches were excavated with a Gradall on the first terrace. They began about 20 feet from the front of the house and extended across the entire terrace. A layer of soil found in both trenches at approximately the same elevation appears to have been earlier ground surface (fig. 9.10, part B). This surface outlines a smaller, lower terrace which occurs up to 3 feet below the current

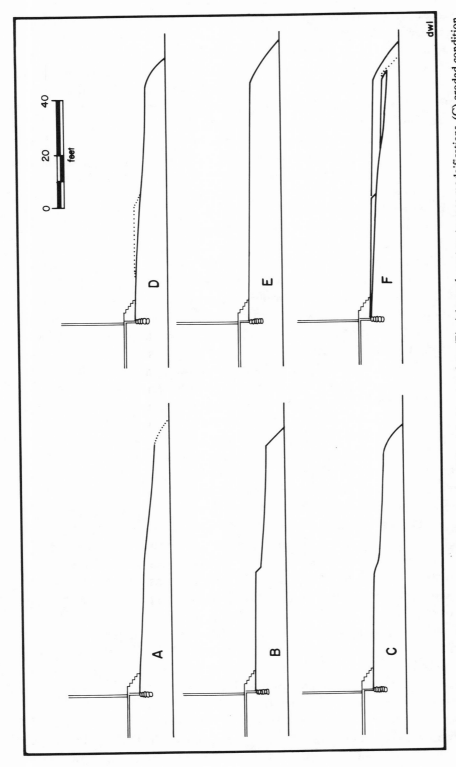

Figure 9.10. Conjectural elevations for the first terrace: (A) original land surface, (B) eighteenth-century terrace modeifications, (C) eroded condition by 1890, (D) bowling green terrace removal by grading in 1891 and 1892, (E) restored twentieth-century terrace configuartion, and (F) comparative overlay. (Drawn by Donald W. Linebaugh)

terrace surface, weathered at its southern edge. If interpreted as the remainder of an eighteenth-century terrace, its 4 percent slope from the house could have been designed for drainage and the weathered southern edge could be explained by natural erosion processes (fig. 9.10, part C). The comments of Scharf and the park commissioners' reports support the theory of erosion. Further neglect of the lawns and grounds by the German Schutzen Society during their tenure from 1870 to 1890 could have caused erosion that eradicated any clear-cut terrace pattern on the south side of the mansion. If this was the case, then the park commissioners may have attempted to reconstruct the terraces based on the eroded and undecipherable remains of the original terraces (fig. 9.10, part E).

In both trenches, the original terrace level disappears at distances of 45 feet and 48 feet from the house. The profiles reveal no apparent reason for these levels not to continue northward toward the main house. Nevertheless, they terminate at approximately the same distance from the house at approximately the same elevation, suggesting that this level may have been removed closer to the house. The profiles indicate that this removal must have occurred before or during the 1890s phase of terrace reconstruction because uninterrupted layers of early twentieth-century fill seal the areas in question.

Again, closer examination of the 1775 Peale landscape painting suggests that a small terrace may have held the bowling green (see fig. 9.3). The west edge of this terrace appears to be parallel to the west wall of the office wing. Presumably the east edge would have paralleled the east wall of the kitchen wing, giving the terrace a length of about 108 feet. Based on the stratigraphic evidence of the trenches and a conjectured length for the slope of the terrace edge of 2 to 2.5 feet, the width of the small terrace would be no more than 43 feet.

If the bowling green was constructed as a small, elevated platform or terrace of earth, the profiles could be explained by the later grading of the southern edge of that terrace or removal of it entirely. The use of a small terrace as a bowling green is not without precedent. Sabine Hall on the Rappahannock River in Virginia, the eighteenth-century home of Landon Carter, maintained a bowling green on its first terrace with only a slight drop of about 3 feet to the second terrace (Wellford, personal communication, 1986; also see Rasmussen 1980).

In seeking to understand this apparent unusual size for a bowling green, Miller's *The Gardener's Dictionary* was examined. The changing function and perception of a bowling green in the eighteenth century can be chronicled through the varying instructions for creating one that Miller gave in the various editions of his dictionary (Rasmussen 1980). The term *bowling green* does not appear in the Barrister's edition of Miller (1759). Instead, bowling greens are discussed in the section on parterres, which Miller defined as a level division of one, best located in front of a house, facing generally to the south. Many types of parterres are discussed; however, Miller stated that the plain parterres are the most beautiful in England because of excellent turf. The Barrister's bowling green would have been considered a plain parterre. Miller indicated that the breadth of the parterre should take its dimensions from the front of the house and that "a parterre should not be less than twice as long as it is broad; twice and a half is accounted a very good proportion" (Miller 1759).

If the Barrister based the size of his bowling green parterre on the front of the house, the Peale landscape suggests that he included the office wing and probably the kitchen wing in these calculations. Dividing the length of 108 feet (the distance between the outer walls of the two wings) by Miller's recommendation of 2.5 feet to procure a measure for the optimum width of the parterre, the measure obtained is within 1 foot of 43 feet, coinciding very well with the width suggested by the stratigraphic evidence.

If a small terrace was used for the bowling green and the hypothesized erosion occurred, then by the time of the 1891 terrace reconstruction, the bowling green may have resembled nothing more than a high spot on a large terrace. Grading down part or all of what was once the smaller terrace would not have been questioned (see fig. 9.9, part D).

These examples of archaeological investigation of the orchard, vineyard, and bowling green at Mount Clare demonstrate the need for more than one source of data for creating a plausible interpretation of the past. By meshing together archaeological excavation and analytical techniques, historic documentary evidence and research, and architectural landscape reconnaissance, a more complete and accurate interpretation and restoration of the landscape were developed. For example, although infrared photography located only nineteenth-century features, knowledge of these features was of critical importance in recovering the earlier landscape. Other special techniques, such as pollen analysis, soil analysis for phosphorous, potassium, and pH, and seed identification from flotation samples of eighteenth-century garden deposits, contributed to the interpretation in varying degrees. Of these, comparative pH levels and seed identifications were most useful; pH levels may have enhanced seed recovery rates. Although these seeds were not charred and there is controversy over the length of time uncharred seeds can survive in the ground (Yentsch et al. 1987), the seed samples from Mount Clare do contain plant remains that appear to be eighteenth century in origin.

At Mount Clare the Carrolls combined the existing topography--a commanding hill--with practical garden concerns--terracing for plant growth--to produce a visual expression of their position among the wealthy elite of Chesapeake society. In the 1770s they rented out their town house and garden in Annapolis in order to reside year-round at Mount Clare. During that same period, Baltimore achieved greater prominence as an urban center. This prominence eventually led to the growth of the city to include the former plantation of Mount Clare. Our interdisciplinary investigations will continue to explore the complex eighteenth-century landscape of Mount Clare.

## Acknowledgments

We would like to thank former Baltimore Mayor William Donald Schaefer; the City of Baltimore Department of Recreation and Parks, especially Chris Delaporte; the National Society of Colonial Dames in the State of Maryland, and the Archaeology, Horticulture and Architecture Committee, particularly Mrs. Mary Imboden, for all their support of archaeology at Mount Clare. We would also like to thank Anne Yentsch for her comments on this paper.

## References Cited

Abercrombie, J. 1778. *The universal gardener and botanist, or A general dictionary of gardening and botany.* London: G. Robinson.

Carroll, Charles. 1755-69. Letterbook. Manuscript no. 208. Baltimore: Maryland Historical Society.

Deetz, J. 1977. *In small things forgotten.* New York: Anchor Press.

Duvall, V. 1985. Mount Clare: On gardens and equipment. Manuscript. Baltimore: Baltimore Center for Urban Archaeology.

Hale, T., Esq. 1758. *The compleat body of husbandry.* London: T. Osborne.

Hill, J. 1758. *The gardener's new kalendar.* London: T. Osborne.

Holt, C. 1984a. Floral analysis: Mount Clare garden terraces. Manuscript. Baltimore: Baltimore Center for Urban Archaeology.

----. 1984b. Floral and faunal analysis: Mount Clare orangery. Manuscript. Baltimore: Baltimore Center for Urban Archaeology.

----. 1985. Mount Clare orchard floral analysis. Manuscript. Baltimore: Baltimore Center for Urban Archaeology.

----. 1986. Mount Clare bowling green and forecourt floral analysis. Manuscript. Baltimore: Baltimore Center for Urban Archaeology.

Isaac, R. 1982. *The transformation of Virginia, 1740-1790.* Chapel Hill: University of North Carolina Press.

Kelso, W. M. 1984. *Kingsmill plantations, 1619-1800: Archaeology of country life in colonial Virginia.* New York: Academic Press.

LaMotte Chemical Products Company. 1978. *The LaMotte soil handbook.* Chestertown, Md.: LaMotte Chemical Products Company.

Leone, M. 1984. Interpreting ideology in historical archaeology: Using the rules of perspective in the William Paca Garden in Annapolis, Maryland. In *Ideology, power, and prehistory,* ed. D. Miller and C. Tilley, pp. 25-36. London: Cambridge University Press.

Miller, P. 1759. *The gardener's dictionary.* 7th ed. London: John Rivington. Copy in Mount Clare Library.

Norman, J. G. 1985a. Restoration archaeology report: Archaeological investigations in the forecourt at Mount Clare Mansion, Baltimore, Maryland. Manuscript. Baltimore: Baltimore Center for Urban Archaeology.

----. 1985b. Restoration archaeology report: Archaeological investigations on the first terrace, Mount Clare Mansion, Baltimore, Maryland. Manuscript. Baltimore: Baltimore Center for Urban Archaeology.

----. 1985c. Restoration archaeology report: The Mount Clare orchard/vineyard excavation. Manuscript. Baltimore: Baltimore Center for Urban Archaeology.

Paca-Steele, B., and St. C. Wright. 1987. The mathematics of an eighteenth-century wilderness garden. *Journal of Garden History* 6(4):299-320.

Pryor, E. 1983. *Orchard fruits in the colonial Chesapeake.* National Colonial Farm, Research Report No. 14. Accokeek, Md.: Accokeek Foundation, Inc.

----. 1984. *"Heaven's favorite gift": Viticulture in colonial Maryland.* National Colonial Farm Research Report No. 23. Accokeek, Md.: The Accokeek Foundation, Inc.

Public Park Commission. 1891-1917. *Annual Report.* Baltimore: Board of Commissioners.

Rasmussen, W. M. 1980. Sabine Hall: A classical villa in Virginia. Ph.D. dissertation, Department of Architecture, University of Delaware.

Scharf, Colonel J. T. 1874. *The chronicles of Baltimore: Being a complete history of Baltimore town and Baltimore city for the earliest period to the present time.* Baltimore: Turnbull Brothers.

Trostel, M. F. 1980. *Mount Clare: Being an account of the seat built by Charles Carroll, Barrister, upon his lands at Patapsco.* Baltimore: National Society of Colonial Dames of America in the State of Maryland.

Weber, C. A. 1986. Mount Clare: The Georgian landscape, 1750–1780. Paper presented at the Mid-Atlantic Archaeological Conference, Rehoboth Beach, Del.

Wilkinson, N. B. N.d. Archaeological report on the Eleutherian Mills garden site. Manuscript. Baltimore: Baltimore Center for Urban Archaeology.

Yentsch, A., N. F. Miller, B. Paca, and D. Piperno. 1987. Archaeologically defining the earlier garden landscapes at Morven: Preliminary results. *Northeast Historical Archaeology* 16:1–29.

# 10

# PLANE AND SOLID GEOMETRY IN COLONIAL GARDENS IN ANNAPOLIS, MARYLAND

## Mark P. Leone and Paul A. Shackel

"Archaeology in Annapolis" is a ten-year exploration of the archaeological remains in the Historic District of Maryland's capital. Studies to determine the possibilities for historical archaeology were undertaken by St. Clair Wright and Henry Wright (1958), and testing was done from the late 1950s onward. Later, South (1967) worked on the William Paca House and its adjacent courtyards for Historic Annapolis, Inc. Extensive work was directed at recovering the William Paca Garden from 1967 to the present (Contract Archaeology 1967-68; Little 1967, 1968; Orr and Orr 1975; Powell 1966; Yentsch 1982). In 1981 Historic Annapolis, Inc. and the University of Maryland began a project which is intended to view the entire historic core of Annapolis, an area of about one-third of a square mile with 2,000 standing buildings in it, as an anthropological unit. Because this project considers the city as a unit, and because so much of the archaeology of the eighteenth century is intact, it was inevitable that the space connecting the buildings also attracted interest.

This chapter describes some of the research that has been performed on the formal landscapes or connecting spaces that survive in the city. These gardens, together with the city's formal and elaborate street plan, combined to make Annapolis an orderly, attractive, and much admired city in the later eighteenth century (Land 1969). The aim here is not to describe the whole city or all the effects of urban landscape planning; rather, the subject is the kinds of precision used to create a comprehensive, formal landscape. Eventually the city should be studied as a whole in order to show the principles behind its design that likely provide the continuity which exists within its evolution. But here the purpose is to show that the system of plane geometry which characterizes the Paca Garden was used on other gardens and that the plane geometry was coordinated with principles of solid geometry in order to create landscapes with the properties of volumes.

The period from 1760 to 1780 saw the building of about one dozen large and elaborate houses in Annapolis, most of which survive. The houses were predominantly brick and range from those professionally designed and decorated like the Hammond-Harwood and Chase-Lloyd houses to the equally impressive but less famous Brice, Paca, Ridout, and Carroll houses. Some of the houses have five parts (main block, hyphens, and wings), and some have a very large three-story main block. They are city houses, bigger and more elaborate than their contemporary peers at Williamsburg, and they compose an impressive expression of wealth concentrated in this port city/capital from 1760 to 1780.

No surviving record explains explicitly how these houses were situated throughout the city, but each great house was given a special setting when it was built. The design and intentions of these settings are the concern here. Before considering the formal landscapes created for the houses, it is important to contemplate the city's plan as a whole. That plan is sixty-five years older than any of the great houses; it not only helped to determine their locations but also in all likelihood helped to determine the idea of a landscaped setting.

Annapolis, first known as Anne Arundel Town, was settled in the 1650s as a tiny tobacco port and had the most casual of plans, so far as it can be reconstructed (Baker 1983) (fig. 10.1). It was a town of little importance where land was probably not very valuable. The Catholic Calverts, Lords Proprietor, were displaced in 1689, and an Anglican royal governor was installed. In 1694 Sir Francis Nicholson, an educated administrator, moved the colony's capital from St. Mary's City in heavily Catholic southern Maryland to the more Protestant area of Annapolis. He took the existing incomplete grid of Annapolis and superimposed over it two circles with a series of streets radiating out from the circles (fig. 10.2). The two sunbursts were either imperfectly designed or incompletely executed because they had to be fitted to articulate with what remained of the earlier grid. Because the circles were on high spots and held the state house and Anglican church, the radiating streets acted to create vistas to and from the centers of established authority as well as to carry traffic.

Nicholson's plan for Annapolis is often and accurately called baroque (Ramirez 1975; Reps 1972). The major attribute of this kind of city plan, different from all the later grids used for virtually every other American city, is that space is considered a volume in which the management of sight is an important component. Baroque city planning often involved the positioning of social hierarchies and their enhancement by visual devices that could demonstrate how large, grand, or omnipresent they were (Bacon 1968:98-137). Streets in a baroque design are planned to be akin to tunnels or funnels, not two-dimensional traffic plans. They are to direct sight. Nicholson's pattern still exists, largely intact, in Annapolis, and its visual properties are still apparent and operate to enhance objects of authority.

The theory of planning behind Nicholson's effort was derived from Salviati, Fontana, Wren, and the group of Renaissance and baroque architects who created the rules for perspective and the devices for creating the illusions that objects appear to be what they are not: bigger, smaller, higher, lower, nearer, farther, three-dimensional when they were flat, or interior when they were exterior (Bacon 1968:101, 109, 112, 159). These were all conscious, known, and published rules or principles. Nicholson designed not just Annapolis but also Williamsburg a little later when he was the royal governor of Virginia. Even though Williamsburg was laid out on a grid, Nicholson's plans for the two capitals makes it virtually certain that he referred to a body of literature on urban design with which many were familiar. That literature included directions for building and situating houses, urban institutions, and country estates as well as cities (Gibbs 1729, 1732; Langley 1750; Swan 1745, 1757). And it is to those buildings in Annapolis in the last third of the eighteenth century that the same body of literature, or its intellectual descendants, was applied sixty-five years after the city plan was laid out.

An enormous amount of material on gardens and house design in colonial America has been produced by architectural and landscape historians (Davis 1947; Hopkins 1963; Isham 1928; Maccubbin and Martin 1984; Shurtleff 1967; Upton 1984, 1986; Whitehead 1931a, 1931b). There is an equally large literature on the historical archaeology of city houses, country estates, and plantations. But there is only a small body of literature in historical

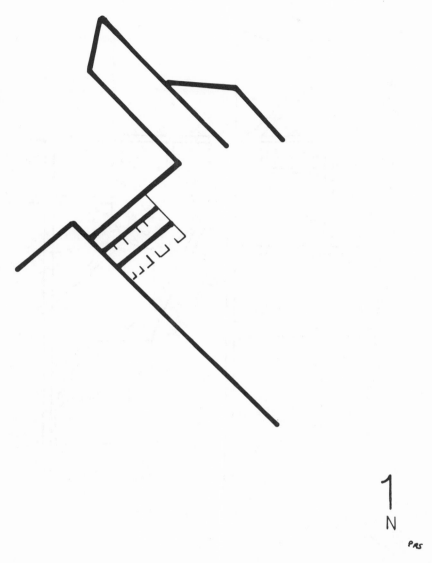

Figure 10.1.  A reconstruction of Anne Arundel Town in 1683.  From Baker 1983:17

archaeology on landscape as a whole (Kelso 1984; Little 1967, 1968; Orr and Orr 1975; Powell 1966; South 1967).  Historical archaeology is just beginning to analyze formal (i.e., planned) landscapes.  Because the best work, like that of Hunt (1986), on these large areas has been in the history of landscape gardening, it has been important to take those treatments and add an anthropological program for our own work.

   In Annapolis we have made two moves in order to accomplish this.  We have utilized the analysis of plane geometry of the William Paca Garden by Barbara Paca, who has done extensive work on American and English gardens (Paca-Steele and Wright 1987), and applied it to other gardens; and second, we have asked why the geometry was used when it was.  Most of the Paca Garden's detail and all of its general dimensions were established archaeologically in the 1960s; thus, Barbara Paca worked from a base of valid information.  The two-acre

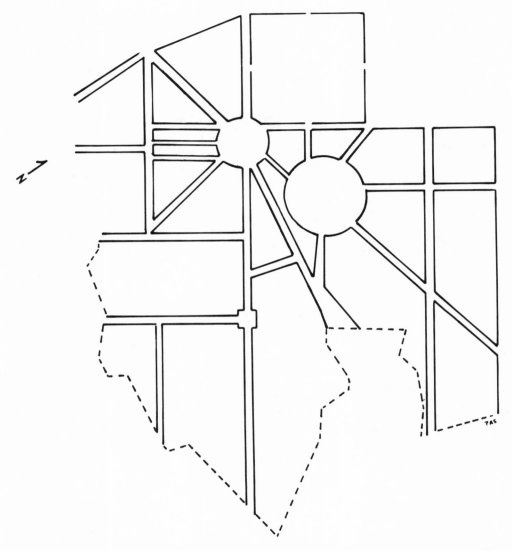

Figure 10.2. Governor Francis Nicholson's plan of Annapolis, 1694-95, as recorded by James Stoddard in 1718. (Original plan on file, Maryland Hall of Records, Annapolis)

garden contains four slopes (called falls or descents) and five terraces (also called flats), for a total drop of 16.5 feet. Its features include paths, outbuildings, a pond, terraces of varying widths, and a pavilion/focal point. Also key is the garden's general relationship to Paca's house (fig. 10.3).

Barbara Paca's analysis found a set of geometrical relationships which characterize the house and garden dimensions. The original Paca property is two adjacent squares, each 198 feet on a side. These are the original dimensions of the town lots and precede William Paca's ownership, probably dating from Nicholson's layout of the city in 1694-95. Sitting on the edge of these two squares is Paca's house. The floor plan of the main block of the five-part house is two 3-4-5 right triangles, or a right rectangle measuring 36 by 48 feet. The house

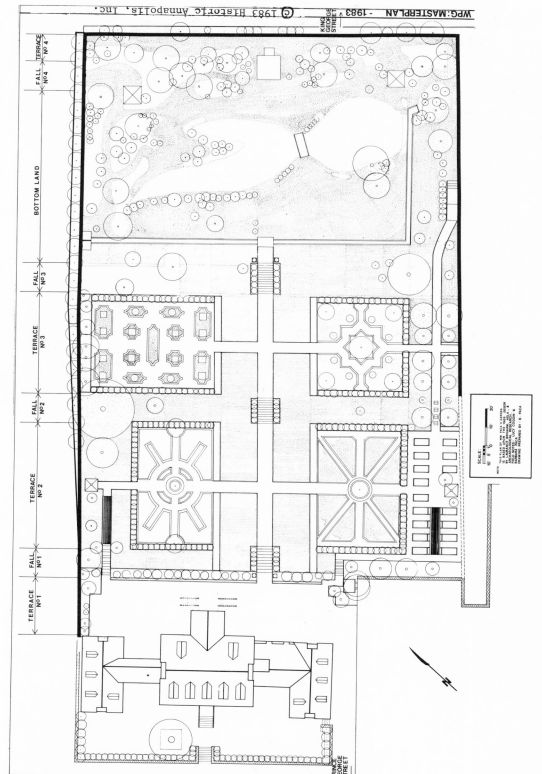

WPG:MASTERPLAN - 1983

KING GEORGE STREET

TERRACE N° 4

FALL N° 4

BOTTOM LAND

FALL N° 3

TERRACE N° 3

FALL N° 2

TERRACE N° 2

FALL N° 1

TERRACE N° 1

SCALE:
10'  5  10'  20'

NOTE: THIS PLAN OF WM PACA'S GARDEN
IS BASED UPON THE 1965 DESIGN
BY LAURENCE BRIGHAM, ASLA &
ARCHAEOLOGICAL RESEARCH &
FIELD NOTES BY LUCY COGGIN &
BARBARA PACA.
DRAWING PREPARED BY B. PACA

PRINCE GEORGE STREET

Figure 10.3.  Plan view of the William Paca Garden, ca. 1765.  (Drawn by Barbara Paca for Historic Annapolis, Inc. from the reconstruction)

sits centered on a surrounding terrace which is also two 3-4-5 right triangles, or a right rectangle measuring 99 by 132 feet. A quarter of this house-terrace, 49.5 by 66 feet, forms the unit of measure for the garden. When multiplied and stretched over the garden, this rectangle forms a grid with twenty-four equal units. The lines of this grid account for most of the major features in the garden, including the edges of major terraces, the central axis, the location of the major outbuildings, and even some major plantings.

Barbara Paca's work raises two questions. First, does such plane geometry characterize other Annapolis gardens, and second, why was such a system used when it was? Archaeology in Annapolis has mapped three other largely intact eighteenth-century gardens in or near the city. Topographic maps of the Ridout house (1763) and garden were made by Joseph W. Hopkins (1984); of the Charles Carroll of Carrollton house (ca. 1720 and ca. 1770) and garden (ca. 1770) by Billy Ray Roulette and Eileen Williams (figs. 10.4 and 10.5); and Tulip Hill (1750) and its larger garden by Eileen Williams, Michele Feutz, and Robert Fernandez. These three gardens are two acres, four acres, and six acres, respectively. The analysis reported here is devoted only to the details of the Carroll garden.

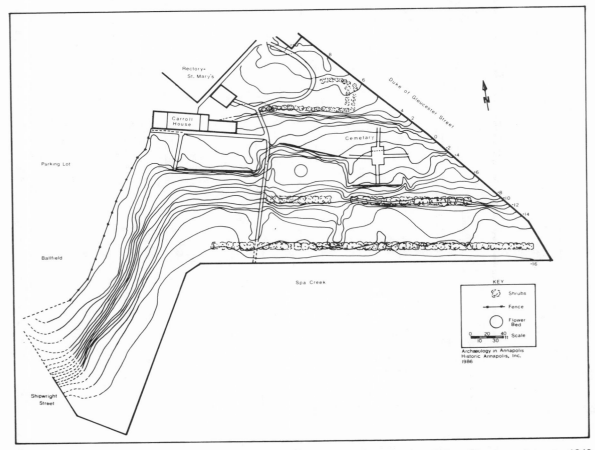

Figure 10.4. Topographic map of the Charles Carroll of Carrollton garden, 1771. Cemetery dates to 1948. (Surveyed by Billy Ray Roulette and Eileen Williams, 1986)

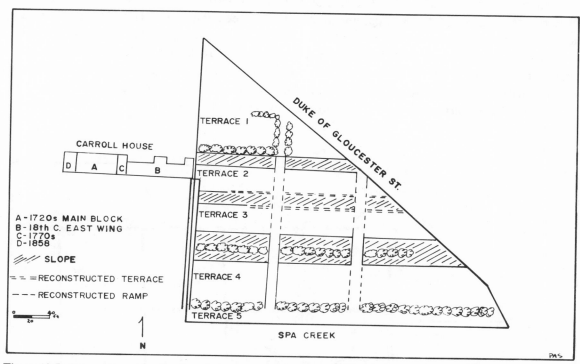

Figure 10.5. Schematic reconstruction of the Charles Carroll of Carrollton garden with terraces 1 to 5, which drop a total of 25 feet to Spa Creek. The Carroll house is shown with its construction phases from the 1720s to the 1850s.

Barbara Paca's exercise in plane geometry was applied to the Charles Carroll of Carrollton garden in detail by Paul Shackel. The garden is in the city and sits on a natural slope within a plat that is roughly triangular. The garden is laid out in five terraces and four slopes (see fig. 10.5). Numbered 1 through 5, the first terrace is farthest from the water, and the fifth is adjacent to the waterfront. Terraces 2 and 3 have been modified recently by the current owners of the Carroll property, the Roman Catholic Redemptorist Community. Part of terrace 3 was raised to the height of terrace 2 for use as a cemetery in 1948. Ground-penetrating radar (Bevan 1987) determined the location of the original terrace, represented by a double-dotted line in the schematic reconstruction of the garden in figure 10.5. The garden is bordered by 400 feet of waterfront, by almost 500 feet of one of the city's main streets, and by a third leg of 320 feet, which includes the eastern end of the Carroll house itself, first built by the 1720s and then greatly enlarged about 1770; thus, the house wall borders the triangle's shortest side. In following the direction started by Barbara Paca's work (1987), Shackel experimented with the measurements of the house and garden and discovered that Charles Carroll of Carrollton used virtually the same principles of plane geometry that William Paca employed. Shackel found that Charles Carroll, who was trained in surveying techniques in England (Carroll 1764), employed three strategies: (1) to overlay a grid on the garden which was a multiple of the basic length of the house (45 feet); (2) to manipulate a basic geometric figure, the 3-4-5 right rectangle; and (3) to control the depth of the garden and the angle of the falls. These three strategies appear to mark all the prominent features in the garden including its use of perspective distance.

Carroll used multiples of the length of the early Carroll house to design the widths of the terraces, lengths of the ramps, and distances between the ramps (fig. 10.6). The first pattern to emerge is the use of a 90-foot grid, which, when extended over the garden, marks the edges of terraces 1, 3, and 4 (fig. 10.6:J-K, L-M, N-O). Edges of terraces 1 and 3 are marked by slopes, while the end of terrace 4 is marked by boxwoods. Marking a grid line with terraces was a common technique in eighteenth-century garden design and occurred in the William Paca Garden as well (Paca-Steele and Wright 1987:317).

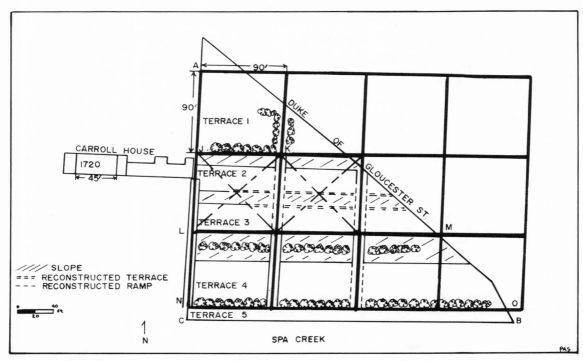

Figure 10.6. Net of squares 90 feet on a side over the Charles Carroll of Carrollton garden based on doubling the 45-foot length of the original 1720s Carroll house. The grid marks the edges of several terraces and each of the three ramps.

Shackel found the distance between each of the garden's three ramps to be 90 feet. The western boundary of the garden (fig. 10.6:A-C) is parallel to and includes the eastern end of the Carroll house and is a ramp which extends from the water at least to the east wing. Ninety feet to the west of the first ramp is the most prominent ramp in the garden, which falls on the grid line, is 180 feet long, and is a multiple of 45. The ramp begins at the upper edge of terrace 2 at its midpoint (fig. 10.6:K). This edge is also on the line of the north front of the Carroll house. Also falling on the 90-foot grid line are the faint traces of a third ramp. In fact, it was through this geometric exercise that we discovered this particular ramp, which had all but disappeared from surface view and became clear to us only after verifying it on an aerial photograph.

Plane geometry made it possible to describe the major features in Carroll's garden and to draw tentative conclusions as to how the garden articulated with the Carroll house. The next step was to consider the use of triangles, particularly 3-4-5 right triangles, and the Palladian idea of a square and a third, which is two adjacent 3-4-5 right triangles.

The whole garden fits within a nearly perfect 3-4-5 right triangle (fig. 10.6:A-B-C), a geometric figure often used in the eighteenth century (Paca-Steele and Wright 1987:299). Its hypotenuse measures 490 feet. This line runs along one of the city's main streets, Duke of Gloucester Street, laid out by Nicholson. Spa Creek, the body of water at the base of the garden, forms the second edge of the garden and measures 400 feet. The third leg measures about 320 feet. Thus, the garden as a whole falls just short of being a 3-4-5 triangle. The imprecision is likely a product of preexisting features like the street and the 1720 house, rather than Carroll's understanding of geometry.

Terrace 1, the highest terrace in the garden, was planned by Carroll as a triangle formed by extending a line parallel to the eastern edge of the Carroll house (fig. 10.7:A'-A), then by using the edge of the topmost terrace (fig. 10.7:A'-A"), and third, by including Duke of Gloucester Street (fig. 10.7:A-A"). Respectively, these measurements are 120 feet, 160 feet, and 200 feet, or a 3-4-5 right triangle. This is the only 3-4-5 right triangle within the garden itself.

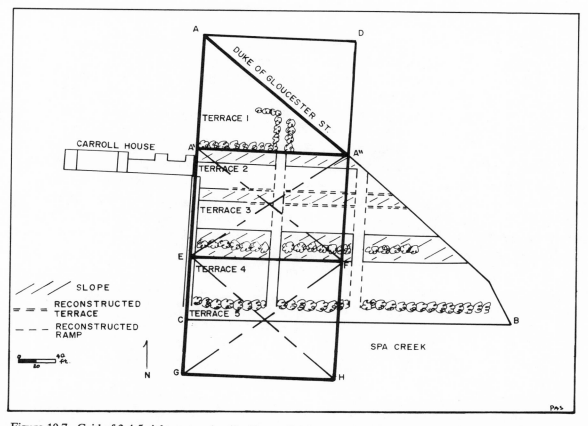

Figure 10.7. Grid of 3-4-5 right rectangles (2 adjacent 3-4-5 right triangles) over the Charles Carroll of Carrollton garden. The long side of the rectangles and hypotenuses mark several terrace edges.

The right triangle is part of a larger right rectangle (fig. 10.7:A-A'-A"-D) that is divided by the hypotenuse (A-A"), thus creating two 3-4-5 right triangles. The width of this figure is always a multiple of three, and the length is a multiple of four. Palladio calls the rectangle a "square-and-a-third" (Paca-Steele and Wright 1987:307). At present the function of terrace 1 and how it articulated with the rest of the garden are uncertain; for example, it is not clear whether it was a continuation of the main formal garden or served as a wilderness garden.

The 3-4-5 rectangle (fig. 10.7:A-A'-A"-D), with the sides of 120 feet and 160 feet, when multiplied over the garden, was used to place some major features in the garden. When a grid of 3-4-5 rectangles is laid out over the garden, some terrace edges fall on the grid lines (see fig. 10.7). Not only is the edge of terrace 1 marked by the longer side of a 3-4-5 rectangle (fig. 10.7:A'-A"), but the same is true for one edge of terrace 4 (fig. 10.7:E-F). The rectangle (fig. 10.7:E-F-G-H) imposed over the fourth and fifth terraces extends into Spa Creek and determines major features in the lower garden. If diagonals are drawn within the rectangle E-F-G-H, their points of intersection, or the midpoint of their widths, mark the southernmost boundary of the garden. The land below the waterfront boxwoods has been extended several feet by the construction of a new bulkhead in the 1980s, covering the old seawall constructed by Carroll around 1770. There probably was a 10-foot-wide terrace at the water, below terrace 4, with a 1- to 2-foot drop in elevation. This was the fifth terrace designed by Carroll, ending at the water's edge where the diagonals intersect.

The general argument here is that baroque gardens are exercises in solid as well as in plane geometry. The measurements that indicate how volumes were built start with extending the use of the proportions 3-4-5. In the Carroll garden, terrace 2 is 30 feet wide, terrace 3 is 40 feet wide, and terrace 4 is 50 feet wide. Carroll used yet one more constant. The existing topography indicates that the total drop in elevation of the garden from terrace 1 to terrace 5 is just about 25 feet. This elevation probably was measured by an eighteenth-century surveyor's unit, the perch, which is a subdivision of a Gunter's chain. A chain is equal to 66 feet, and a perch is one-fourth of this measurement, or 16.5 feet. The elevation of the garden is thus 1.5 perches. Further, the angles of the slopes between terraces 1 and 2 and terraces 2 and 3 are determined by the drop in elevation and the need to conform to the 90-foot grid. The edge of terrace 2 was determined by drawing diagonals in the grid imposed over terraces 2 and 3, and the diagonals' intersection marks this location. Terraces 2 and 3 measure 30 feet and 40 feet wide, respectively; thus, the total distance of the two slopes within the plane must equal 20 feet in order to conform to the 90-foot grid. Thus, it becomes clear that the horizontal ratios, when combined with vertical controls, act together to produce a systematically constructed volume.

Falling gardens, a type of landscape favored by designers in Europe and England, accompany great city houses in Annapolis and country estates or plantations along Chesapeake Bay from the last third of the eighteenth century. They are situated on mounts or rises, or on the edge of a rise with a slope on one side and often with a plane on the other (Langley 1726; Miller 1733). Convention called for gardens on each side, or front, of the house. The flat side often had a geometrically ordered set of planting beds in simple rectilinear or curvilinear design.

The sloping sides of Annapolis and associated country gardens are either open-ended views to Chesapeake Bay or a river, or aim to a focal point in the city. While it is now quite clear from Barbara Paca's work and our verification of it in the Carroll garden that these sloping gardens were planned out on paper using plane geometry and were explicit in their use of grids, it appears to be just as clear that the gardens were thought of as three-dimensional spaces. The use of the perch, an eighteenth-century unit of measure, in the Paca and Carroll gardens demonstrates that total depth was to be measured precisely and that slope was determined by the ratio between terrace widths and total drop of the garden.

Based on the conventional understanding of Renaissance and baroque design, Leone has elsewhere developed descriptions of the Paca and Ridout gardens as volumes constructed to manage views (1984, 1987, 1988). Views from these city houses act upon the eye so as to make nearby objects appear to be more distant than they actually are in measurable space. The devices built into the landscape accomplished this in Annapolis.

By making the widths of descending terraces narrower as the Paca and Ridout gardens sloped downward, the builders created the appearance that anything at the bottom of the garden, such as water, a pavilion, or statuary, was farther from the viewer at the head of the garden than was actually the case. The same effect could be sustained if the edges of descending hedges, paths, or planting beds were not parallel but converged slightly in order to enhance the fact that parallel lines appear to converge. By making the lines slant toward each other, they created the illusion that an object at the focal point was farther away than it really was.

The terraces that form the view in the William Paca Garden are roughly 60 feet and 45 feet wide from top to bottom. The main terraces in the Ridout garden are 44 feet and 35 feet wide from top to bottom. Each ends in a wide bottom plane. Any evidence for converging sight lines in the Paca Garden is gone, but trapezoidal beds, which may be original or modern duplications, exist in the Ridout garden and aid in creating the impression that the vista and the space are longer and bigger than they actually are.

The Paca Garden was completely enclosed by a high wall. The surroundings of the Ridout garden are unclear, although its chief vista may have been open to the Annapolis harbor. Charles Carroll's garden had hundreds of feet of waterfront and overlooked Spa Creek, then known as Carroll's Creek, which is hundreds of feet wide and had plentiful river and harbor traffic. Carroll had an unlimited, open-ended view or vista, whereas Paca and possibly Ridout had limited short vistas with which to work. Paca had an urban problem and Carroll a rural problem. Both were conventional settings with conventional solutions.

Carroll reversed the widths of the terraces, so they are, from top to bottom, 30 feet, 40 feet, and 50 feet wide. Carroll's drop is 50 percent greater than those of Paca and Ridout (i.e., 25 feet versus 16.5 feet). Carroll's terraces start narrow and widen. This produces two effects still visible today. The lesser effect is to pull objects on the creek closer and make them appear less distant. The more pronounced effect, however, is to make his house on the mount appear to be higher and thus considerably grander than it is in fact. This enhancement occurs at the garden's waterfront, one of the principal entry points in the seventeenth, eighteenth, and nineteenth centuries.

All these observations can be summed up by seeing that first, a garden was built using dimensions taken from the house; second, the garden was therefore a space whose dimensions were precisely proportional to the house; third, the garden, like the house, was a volume or set of volumes; and fourth, the two related harmoniously to each other by being multiples or fractions of the same dimensions (Lockwood 1934:5-7). These manipulations were conventional, not extraordinary, and probably can be found widely once the rest of the formulas are derived and applied to a sample of surviving gardens.

The last question remaining is why these rules for proportions and their attendant visual effects were employed in Annapolis only from the 1760s on when they were available at least sixty years earlier. This question has been addressed at length (Leone 1984, 1987, 1988); although that response should be regarded as hypothetical, it deserves the following summary. Renaissance and baroque planning and execution of space and decorations featured the appearance of illusion; things were not what they appeared to be. Historians of art, the theater, gardens, and intellectual developments have all been concerned with the drama, make-believe, play with light, dimensionality, and juxtaposition of unnatural forms that are characteristic of the baroque arts. Braudel (1979:489-493) and Bacon (1968:98-137) have noted that baroque play on illusion was often associated with regimes interested in bolstering their authority, influence, and power. Monuments, vistas, institutions, and allusions to glorious pasts, noble ancestors, and divine beginnings were all available to expand, prop up, or create power. Such effects could be created with great skill through illusion, which expressed itself as mastery of the natural rules of proportion, optics, astronomy, horticulture, hydraulics, or a dozen other areas (Bennett 1985; Porter 1985).

All the Annapolis gardens feature the same kind of careful use of a natural system, planned out with skill and executed with great care, which has the effect of creating a visual illusion. Because the era in which these gardens were built was short but turbulent--the 1760s and 1770s, or two decades--the question arises whether there is a reason for their construction then, beyond the understandable love of gardening most people have. The great houses were built during this relatively brief time, and they feature architectural illusions (Saunders 1986) with their rooflines and pediments, false windows and niches; perhaps the illusions in their landscapes derive from the same impulse.

Equally apt for explaining the illusions built in Tidewater Maryland is Rhys Isaac's (1982) explanation of developments in Tidewater Virginia. Men and women of agrarian and merchant wealth, isolated from the slave and poorer white classes, as well as from England by the home country's mercantilist policies, sought to bolster their eroding social and political positions by ostentation and elaborate etiquette, which they embedded in learned discourse and demonstration of the laws of nature. Men and women of the Enlightenment whose economic, social, and political situations were being threatened, but who possessed land and capital wealth, attempted to hold themselves up and apart by using the political theories of the day, namely baroque concepts of hierarchy, design, and the natural order.

The houses and the landscapes of the Maryland and Virginia Tidewater featured wealthy individuals who wished for themselves more power than they had. They strove for personal independence as one of the highest attainable characteristics of life. They also were not independent in any way, and they all knew Parliament was intruding on them more and more. It appears to us that before the Tidewater planters, gentry and merchants initiated, justified, and led the American fight for independence, they attempted to use an older notion, the baroque justification for hierarchy, which was an appeal to the hierarchical order of nature, to achieve the same end. The gardens explicitly show off the owners' ability to create illusions by managing natural phenomena and law. The use of nature's order, under control, produced statements in houses, views, and landscapes that provided seemingly independent evidence as to who knew nature well enough to master it.

This technique was not to last long. The crisis it was meant to hide was resolved by violence and revolution. But the technique and its theory were powerful enough in some cases to convince people in the colonies that those who could rule nature were sound enough to rule the new nation which they were to argue was a natural creation or order.

## Acknowledgments

We are indebted to the Redemptorist Community for access to their property in Annapolis, and to Dr. Robert Worden for his scholarly help on the Carroll family. We are grateful to St. Clair Wright, Barbara Paca, Barbara Little, Etta Saunders, and Julie Ernstein for comments that improved and clarified sections of this chapter. Although Historic Annapolis, Inc., a nonprofit preservation and educational organization, has provided funding for and shared its research findings with Archaeology in Annapolis, our opinions and theories do not necessarily reflect the views of Historic Annapolis, Inc.

Historic Annapolis, Inc. (194 Prince George Street, Annapolis, Maryland 20401) would be pleased to locate archaeologists who worked on the William Paca Garden during its reconstruction.

## References Cited

Bacon, E. N. 1968. *Design of cities.* New York: Viking Press.

Baker, N. 1983. Annapolis, Maryland, 1695-1730. In Annapolis and Anne Arundel County, Maryland: A study of urban development in a tobacco economy, 1649-1776. Ed. Lorena S. Walsh. NEH Grant Number RS 20199-81-1955. Manuscript. Annapolis: Historic Annapolis, Inc.

Bennett, J. 1985. The scientific context. In *Science and profit in eighteenth-century London*, pp. 5-9. London: Whipple Museum of the History of Science.

Bevan, B. W. 1987. A geophysical survey at the Carroll house. Prepared for Historic Annapolis, Inc. and the Charles Carroll of Carrollton 250th Anniversary Committee. Annapolis: Historic Annapolis, Inc.

Braudel, F. 1979. *The wheels of commerce: Civilization and capitalism, fifteenth to eighteenth century*, Vol. 2. New York: Harper and Row.

Carroll, C., of Carrollton. 1764. Letters to Charles Carroll of Annapolis, 21 March, 26 July. Baltimore: Maryland Historical Society.

Contract Archaeology. 1967-68. The Paca House gardens. Drawings on file. Annapolis: William Paca Garden Visitors' Center, Historic Annapolis, Inc.

Davis, D. 1947. *Annapolis houses, 1700-1775.* New York: Cornwall Press.

Gibbs, J. 1729. *A book of architectures.* Rept. 1968. New York: Benjamin Bloom.

————. 1732. Rules of drawing. Rept. 1968. Hants, England: Gregg International Publishing.

Hopkins, H. P. 1963. *Colonial houses of Annapolis, Maryland, and their architectural details.* Baltimore: Schneidereith and Sons.

Hopkins, J. W., III. 1984. A map of the Ridout garden, Annapolis, Maryland. Manuscript. Annapolis: Historic Annapolis, Inc.

Hunt, J. D. 1986. *Garden and grove.* Princeton, N.J.: Princeton University Press.

Isaac, R. 1982. *The transformation of Virginia, 1740-1790.* Chapel Hill: University of North Carolina Press.

Isham, N. M. 1928. *Early American houses: The seventeenth century.* Rept. 1968. Watkins Glen, N.Y.: American Life Foundation.

Kelso, W. M. 1984. Landscape archaeology: A key to Virginia's cultivated past. In *British and American gardens in the eighteenth century: Eighteen illustrated essays on garden history*, ed. R. P. Maccubbin and P. M. Martin, pp. 159-69. Williamsburg: Colonial Williamsburg Foundation.

Land, A. (editor). 1969. *Letters from America by William Eddis*. Cambridge: Harvard University Press.

Langley, B. 1726. *New principles of gardening*. London: Bettsworth and Batley.

----. 1750. *The city and country builder's and workman's treasury of designs*. Rept. 1967. New York: Benjamin Blom.

Leone, M. P. 1984. Interpreting ideology in historical archaeology: Using the rules of perspective in the William Paca Garden in Annapolis, Maryland. In *Ideology, power and prehistory*, ed. D. Miller and C. Tilley, pp. 25-36. London: Cambridge University Press.

----. 1987. Rule by ostentation: The relationship between space and sight in eighteenth-century landscape architecture in the Chesapeake region of Maryland. In *Method and theory for activity area research*, ed. S. Kent, pp. 605-32. New York: Columbia University Press.

----. 1988. The Georgian order as the order of merchant capitalism in Annapolis, Maryland. In *The recovery of meaning: Historical archaeology in the Eastern United States*, ed. M. P. Leone and P. B. Potter, Jr., pp. 235-61. Washington, D.C.: Smithsonian Institution Press.

Little, J. G., II. 1967-68. Archaeological research on Paca Garden, 8 November 1967, 24 May 1968. Letters. Annapolis: William Paca Garden Visitors' Center, Historic Annapolis, Inc.

Lockwood, A. B. 1934. *Gardens of colony and state: Gardens and gardeners of the American colonies and of the Republic before 1840*. 2 vols. New York: Charles Scribner and Sons.

Maccubbin, R. P., and P. Martin (editors). 1984. *British and American gardens in the eighteenth century: Eighteen illustrated essays on garden history*. Williamsburg: Colonial Williamsburg Foundation.

Miller, P. 1733. *The gardener's dictionary*. London: Printed for the author.

Orr, K. G., and R. G. Orr. 1975. The archaeological situations at the William Paca Garden, Annapolis, Maryland: The spring house and the presumed pavilion house site. Manuscript. Annapolis: William Paca Garden Visitors' Center, Historic Annapolis, Inc.

Paca-Steele, B., and St. C. Wright. 1987. The mathematics of an eighteenth-century wilderness garden. *Journal of Garden History* 6(4):299-320.

Porter, R. 1985. The economic context. In *Science and profit in eighteenth-century London*, pp. 1-4. London: Whipple Museum of the History of Science.

Powell, B. B. 1966. Archaeological investigation of the Paca House garden, Annapolis, Maryland. Manuscript. Annapolis: William Paca Garden Visitors' Center, Historic Annapolis, Inc.

Ramirez, C. W. 1975. *Urban history for preservation planning: The Annapolis experience*. Ann Arbor: University Microfilms.

Reps, J. W. 1972. *Tidewater towns: City planning in colonial Virginia and Maryland*. Williamsburg: Colonial Williamsburg Foundation.

Saunders, E. 1986. Patterns in the architecture of eighteenth-century Annapolis: The acceptance of the Georgian mindset. Manuscript. College Park: Department of Anthropology, University of Maryland.

Shurtleff, H. R. 1967. *The log cabin myth: A study of the early dwelling of the English colonists in North America.* Cambridge: Harvard University Press.

South, S. 1967. Russellborough: Two royal governor's mansions at Brunswick town. *North Carolina Historical Review* 44:360-72.

Swan, A. 1745. *The British architect.* Rept. 1967. New York: De Capo Press.

----. 1757. *Design in architecture.* Vols. 1 and 2. Rept. 1972. Hants, England: Gregg International Publishing.

Upton, D. 1984. Pattern books and professionalism. *Winterthur Portfolio* 19(2/3):2-49.

----. 1986. Vernacular domestic architecture in eighteenth-century Virginia. In *Common places: Readings in American vernacular architecture*, ed. D. Upton and J. M. Vlach, pp. 315-35. Athens: University of Georgia Press.

Whitehead, R. F. 1931a. The Brice house, Annapolis, Maryland. *White Pine Series of Architecture Monographs* 15(6):153-56.

----. 1931b. The Mathias Hammond House, Annapolis, Maryland. *White Pine Series of Architecture Monographs* 15(4):97-100.

Wright, H. 1958. Excavation notes from the Shiplap house. Manuscript. Annapolis: Historic Annapolis, Inc.

Yentsch, A. E. 1982. Spring house at Paca Garden, 16 March 1982. Letter. Annapolis: William Paca Garden Visitors' Center, Historic Annapolis, Inc.

# 11

# THE CALVERT ORANGERY IN ANNAPOLIS, MARYLAND: A HORTICULTURAL SYMBOL OF POWER AND PRESTIGE IN AN EARLY EIGHTEENTH-CENTURY COMMUNITY

## Anne Yentsch

At the juncture where anthropology and history meet there is a dearth of theory available to the historical archaeologist who wishes to present his or her findings within a humanistic ethnographic framework. One must turn to other fields and other writers to enter into a dialogue with the past. These fields may include classical archaeology, philosophy, studies of ancient technology, and even Latin literature. Such was the case when archaeological excavation at the Calvert site in Annapolis, Maryland, brought to light a puzzling brick feature: the remains of a dry-air heating system built using a device first developed by the Romans and known as a hypocaust.

To make sense of the hypocaust involved understanding its relationship to orangeries, the symbolic meaning of orange trees and other exotic plants, the role of gardens in display, and delineating a culture-nature dichotomy in Anglo-American society in which elements of the natural world were turned into symbols of power and prestige. Hence this chapter draws not only on archaeological data but also on the writings of seventeenth-century horticulturalists like John Evelyn and eighteenth-century botanists such as Richard Bradley and Philip Miller, and on the interpretive epistemologies of contemporary anthropologists and social scientists, especially Raymond Firth (1973), Clifford Geertz (1983), Marshall Sahlins (1981), and Charles Taylor (1987). Working outward from a central core of archaeological data on a single feature--the hypocaust--to a consideration of the symbolic elements in horticultural activity, ethnographic information from other sources is interwoven into the analysis. This, in turn, creates a context in which the presence of a hypocaust in an early eighteenth-century Chesapeake town is comprehensible.

In each society there are mechanisms whereby families and households convey to others information on the power and prestige the family possesses. The Calvert family used the domain of horticulture to do this. They built an orangery containing a modified Roman heating system and filled it with rare, exotic, or difficult-to-grow plants, and they maintained an elaborately landscaped town lot. Through their control of the natural world, the Calvert family visually expressed the fact that they had access to scarce resources and the ability to protect, conserve, or use them at their will. In doing so, they utilized a symbolic system which gave different meaning to plants and horticultural activities than the system based on an industrial view of the environment that took its place. The latter, not the former, is incorporated into our own worldview and guides current perceptions of gardens and their accoutrements.

E. P. Thompson has written that class is self-defined by any given people in any given time. If class is defined by people as they live their own history, then with changes in the definition, there are also "changes in what man is, such that he has to be understood in different terms" (Thompson 1966:11). This is simply another way of saying that definitions of hierarchy are culturally relative. The problem that the historical archaeologist often encounters is that he or she is studying his or her own past. It is difficult to recognize that as recently as 250 years ago, the people of our past were people of a different culture which followed another logic, or way of organizing the world, than what we use and hence expect to find when studying the everyday lives of our ancestors. Speaking from experience, it was initially difficult to ascertain any order in the buildings or space at the Calvert site that made sense if one accepted the premise that the Calverts were a politically powerful and wealthy household who would have left a tangible mark of their elite life-style in the things they owned or used that entered the archaeological record. Speaking from experience, it is also now easy to say that this difficulty arose because the symbolic forms of material culture that they used to express their position in the social hierarchy were not the expected ones. As Durkheim might say, the historical past does not exist for people except as it is thought. The real world does not necessarily exist as an individual perceives it to exist, because his observations of it are dependent to a large extent on the way material phenomena are cognitively organized by his culture. This means the world may not exist in the way we think it does, nor did it necessarily exist in the way past peoples described it in oral tradition or in historical documents when speaking or writing of their own culture (Sahlins 1981).

Because archaeological data are unintentionally informative, they provide information on how people actually lived. If as people live their lives they define their own status, then archaeology should tell much about the real-life markers of social hierarchy. That is, it should if we work from the data outward and pay attention to the ambiguities that are puzzling as a site is excavated and analyzed. The measure of a successful interpretation is the degree to which it clarifies a structural coherence or order that, when its pattern is delineated, makes sense of what was once ambiguous (Taylor 1987:33). As I looked at the ethnographic information in other sources, reinterpreted the archaeological information on the Calverts' house and carefully landscaped yard, and cast the Calvert site against the background of the town's landscape, the site and its artifacts gradually became something that I understood. This holistic approach suggests dimensions of the earlier world and of the colonial experience not recoverable through a strictly materialist or processual study of the archaeological record of Annapolis.

## Background

As codirectors of Archaeology in Annapolis, Richard J. Dent, Mark P. Leone, and I were given responsibility by Historic Annapolis, Inc. for interpreting sites in the city. In 1981 we created a research design for studying the effects of social hierarchy on the archaeological remains of eighteenth-century communities. First, on the basis of information in historical documents, Nancy Baker (Research Director at Historic Annapolis, Inc.) delineated the socioeconomic position of Annapolis families. Our archaeological strategy was then to excavate sites occupied by households from varying levels of the social ladder, to assess the customary status markers in their assemblages, and to test for correspondence between the two data sets. We expected to find a more complex pattern of symbolic delineation than the direct, amplified representation of status seen in early hierarchical societies. There was a beguiling simplicity to the strategy, but it overlooked both the complexity of the social process wherein objects became signs of rank and the wide variety of objects that were of symbolic use in designating status. It did not account for a complicated symbolic inversion wherein elite men took nature as symbolic of power, collapsing customary boundaries between the domain of culture and nature to claim control of processes perceived as both natural and mysterious.

From the onset of work at the Calvert site (fig. 11.1), the field crew recovered types of ceramics and glassware that were among the more luxurious and expensive tablewares of the period. Furthermore, they recovered these in large quantities. The building was once the home of two royal governors, one a younger son of Lord Baltimore, and it seemed only reasonable that there would be archaeological evidence of their occupation of it. Architectural elaboration was the usual way of designating status in the New World. However, the architectural evidence suggested a simple home with little elaboration in its building fabric. The contents of the home as listed in two probate inventories, dated 1731 and 1734, were not simple and stand in contrast to the architecture of the building. Renovations of ca. 1727 enlarged the building, but not unusually so. This seeming contradiction may be explained by the fact that neither of the two sons of Lord Baltimore who first lived in the house expected to remain in Maryland, while Governor Charles Calvert, who was a resident of the province, lived in it for less than a decade before he died.

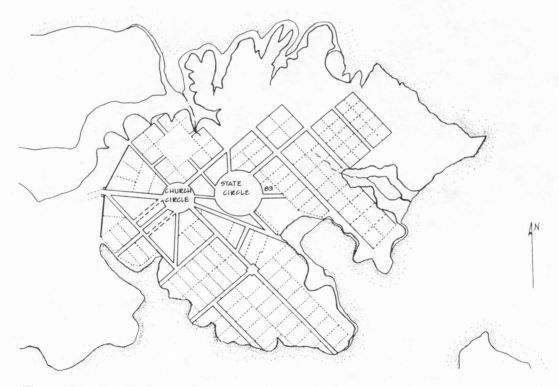

Figure 11.1. Lot 83, the location of the Calvert site, is shown on the Nicholson town plan superimposed on a 1784 French military map of Annapolis. (Drawn by Hanna McKee)

## The Hypocaust Feature

### The Identification of the Feature as a Hypocaust

During the first few weeks of excavation, archaeologists uncovered one corner of the south exterior brick wall of the hypocaust demolished ca. 1765. It lay only 2 to 3 inches below the surface of the crawl space beneath the ca. 1765 south addition to the Calvert dwelling (fig. 11.2). Despite its proximity to the surface, it was eight months before the outline was fully delineated. The rubble-filled deposit that lay immediately above it and almost sealed it was an incredibly rich one. There was excellent preservation of all types of organic and inorganic materials in the dry, powdery soil protected from weathering for more than 200 years by the house wall and floorboards. Taking out this deposit and waiting for the addition to be shored and stabilized were time-consuming processes.

Figure 11.2. Interior wing of the Calvert house as excavation began. (Photograph courtesy of Celia Pearson)

Before the installation of shoring, information was obtained on the feature when testing three 2-foot-square units where supports were to be placed. One of these units came down inside the feature, revealing an earth floor whose dramatic wine-red color suggested that the interior of the structure had been subjected to extremely high temperatures that altered the color of the local subsoil. We also knew that we were working on a vaulted structure. What type of building could it have been?

Two different types of outbuildings known to exist in early American towns were possibilities. A kiln, the first possibility, was discarded immediately because there was no evidence of pottery-making equipment or debris in the levels above or adjacent to the outbuilding. A bake oven, the second possibility, at first seemed more likely, for Historic Annapolis, Inc. had documentary evidence in its data bank that large quantities of dry biscuits had been baked somewhere in Annapolis and supplied to the American forces during the Revolution. Because little evidence of the baked materials would have been left behind, it seemed reasonable that the feature might be the remains of such an oven. Yet none of the exposed brick walls accorded with known plans for either commercial or domestic baking ovens.

By late November 1982 the building was shored, and Historic Annapolis, Inc. had raised enough money for work to begin anew. In early December all the walls were exposed, and we could see the footprint of a strangely shaped building (fig. 11.3). It was 10 feet square and 1.5 feet deep. Its south wall, 1.5 feet thick, was of sufficient width to support a large superstructure; its other walls varied from 8 inches to 14 inches thick. The interior consisted of a snaking barrel vault 2.5 feet wide. An apse-shaped ashbox was attached at the southeast corner, and a narrow brick runway, with an upward sloping floor, angled off to the north, gaining in elevation as it went until it passed through another building wall 5 feet farther north (fig. 11.4).

Figure 11.3. Interior wing of the Calvert house after excavation of the hypocaust. (Photograph by Marion Warren for Historic Annapolis, Inc.)

**EAST WALL OF MAIN BUILDING c.1727** ↓

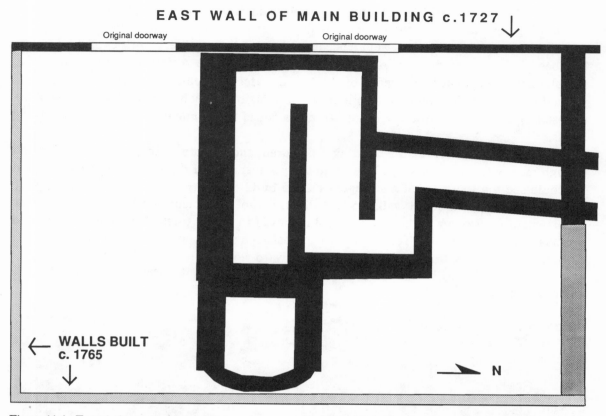

Figure 11.4. Foundation outline of the Calvert hypocaust (built ca. 1730) found within the ca. 1765 crawl space of the south addition. Walls shown in light gray are associated with the later addition; those shown in black or drak gray existed in tandem with the orangery. (Based on a field drawing by F. D. Langenheim)

No one knew what the building was until a visiting archaeologist familiar with classical sites in Britain and the Continent recognized its form. When Henry T. Wright identified the foundation as the base of a hypocaust, everyone breathed a sign of relief. St. Clair Wright of Historic Annapolis, Inc. was delighted, as she realized that this feature meant the Calverts had possessed an orangery. Others argued that the dry-air heating system had been used to heat a bathhouse, but for many reasons this argument was finally set aside (Yentsch 1988).

Why would a governor of Maryland in the early eighteenth century build an orangery? Did an orangery possess cultural qualities that gave it a cachet above other commonly described luxuries such as Chinese porcelain, fragile wine glasses, bottles with coats-of-arms, and silver spoons? The latter items were also possessed by the Calvert household and found their way into its archaeological record, but then similar artifacts were also routinely found at other sites associated with wealthy families in the Chesapeake. The quality of its artifacts did not set the Calvert household apart from others in the region, and if one looked at their faunal remains, they had more commensal animals than zooarchaeologists normally report at urban sites; although ranges elsewhere on the site were low, in the hypocaust area commensal taxa constituted 25 percent of the faunal assemblage (Reitz 1988). It did not seem reasonable to associate a high frequency of rats with a high-status site. Further, in terms of its architecture, the Calverts' Annapolis home was a simpler building than one would expect given the quality of the artifacts and the social position of the family. St. Clair Wright believed it was the orangery that denoted the family's status.

Placing the Archaeological Feature in a Historical Context

The historical study began at a basic level: understanding how a hypocaust functioned within an orangery and learning how orangeries were used. Research told us the technical function of orangeries: they were conservatories--protected, sheltered places where men placed tender, exotic plants to survive the winter. In 1731 Philip Miller provided a list of such plants, including "Plants of the hottest Parts of the East and West-Indies," that might be raised in an orangery (table 11.1). While the practice of warming tender plants to keep them alive was documented by Columella in the first century B.C. and observed in the archaeological record of Pompeii, the first recorded use of a heated room for conserving plants after the Dark Ages appears in a 1635 Italian garden book (Senesis, quoted in Van den Muijzenberg 1980). Conservatories were closely related to the development of botanical gardens in the 1500s. As Renaissance thought spread throughout Europe, the horticultural practice of expressing the depth of one's botanical knowledge and skill by growing and maintaining stocks of rare or difficult plants diffused with other Renaissance ideas, reaching France, Holland, and then England in the seventeenth century.

The better orangeries were provided with stoves beneath their floors (i.e., hypocausts) to heat the interior space where the plants resided. Lesser orangeries were heated with charcoal fires contained in metal pots or wheelbarrows. In the late seventeenth century, La Quintinie noted that if a gentleman had a minimal conservatory, he should cake the back wall with a thick layer of dry dung and hold it in place with wooden lathes. Acknowledging that dung was "not so sightly & sweet, a retreat for rats and mice," the French horticulturalist still insisted it was far better to have rats and mice in the conservatory than to lose an orange tree to the "deadly and pernicious" frost (1693:22). Although there is ample archaeological evidence that the Calvert household had its share of rats and mice (and perhaps more than its share) (Reitz 1988), there is also archaeological evidence that the Calverts altered their firebox to improve its heating capacity by adding two rows of dry-laid, unmortared brick to the passageway between the ashbox and the main heating chamber after construction. Henry T. Wright (personal communication, 1988) notes that similar alterations have been made to Japanese pottery kilns to raise temperatures within their chambers.

The technology on which these dry-air heating systems were based was developed originally by Sergius Orata in approximately 80 B.C. for use in aquaculture, specifically the artificial cultivation of oysters and fish (Forbes 1958:41). Adapted for use in heating baths, the technology was also used to heat country villas, city houses, large meeting rooms, public buildings, and even portions of the church of St. Caecilia in Rome (Forbes 1958). Six were found at Vavai (Bievelet 1950), and other examples were excavated at Pompeii (Overbeck 1884), Herculaneum (Winckelmann 1762), Saalburg (Jacobi 1897), in Africa (Boeswillwald 1897), in Switzerland (Jecklin and Coaz 1923), Germany, France, and in Great Britain where they were first described in the Calverts' own lifetime--in 1733--and in recent times by Rook (1978), Brodribb (1979), and Noël-Hume (1956).

The primary innovation that distinguishes the Calvert hypocaust from its Roman prototypes is the channeling of hot, dry air through enclosed, vaulted brick ducts. Although Roman hypocausts have been excavated in Britain, they are primarily of columnar or radial

Table 11.1.  "The Most Tender Exotick Trees and Plants" recommended by Philip Miller (1731:ST) as suitable for growing in a conservatory

| | |
|---|---|
| Acajoou or Cashew | Fig Tree, the Arched Indian |
| Allegator Pear | Flower-fence of Barbados |
| Allspice or Pimento | Fustick Tree |
| Arrow Root | Ginger |
| Bananas | Guajacum |
| Bastard Cedar of Barbados | Logwood |
| Bastard Locust of Barbados | Macaw Tree |
| Bully Tree | Mamee Tree |
| Button Wood of Barbados | Mancinel Tree |
| Cabbage Tree | Mimosa or Sensitive Plants |
| Cocoa Tree | Nickar Tree or bonduc |
| Calibash Tree | Palm trees of several sorts |
| Cassada | Papaw Tree |
| Cassia Fistula | Plantane Tree |
| Cedar Tree of Barbados | Plum Tree of Jamaica |
| Cherry Tree of Barbado | Sapotilla Tree |
| Cocoa-nut Tree | Sope Berry Tree |
| Cortex Winteranus | Sowre Sop |
| Custard Apple | Sugar Apple |
| Date Tree | Sweet Sop |
| Dumb Cane | Tamarind Tree |
| Fiddle Wood | Tulip Flower or White-wood |

form.  It is unclear when and where the innovation seen at Annapolis occurred.  Forbes (1958) states that small masonry vaults were observed at Linz in Tyrol but provides no date.  Volckamer (1714) first illustrated enclosed ducts beneath conservatory floors, supposedly drawn from Bohemian sources, but experts agree that other botanists knew about them at an earlier date.  There was an orangery (of unspecified age) at the family home of Lord Baltimore in England upon which the Annapolis example may have been based.  Evidence of its existence is provided in an account of the discovery of the Calvert Papers (now at the Maryland Historical Society) discovered in England among the litter and rubbish of an old conservatory (i.e., orangery) in the late nineteenth century (Cox 1973:312).  It is also intriguing that Governor Benedict Leonard Calvert studied with the noted British antiquarian Thomas Hearne at Oxford and made extensive tours of ancient Roman sites in England, France, and Italy.

According to Agricola (1719:57), stoves were best placed in the ground and stoked from outside.  There are similarities between his preference and those of John Evelyn (1664); both are also similar to the type of stove used for the House of Diomed at Pompeii and illustrated in Forbes (1958:38).  The hypocaust in Annapolis is similar to an illustration in Philip Miller's

*Gardener's Dictionary* of 1731. Against its east wall was a small shed containing the furnace or stove; at the Calvert site, this was placed in the ground as Agricola recommended.

Very little is known about the Calvert orangery building above the level of its hypocaust. Almost all architectural evidence of the building on its immediate north side was destroyed either by construction of an early twentieth-century cellar or by the foundation pit dug in the 1970s that caused a partial collapse of the building. It is obvious that orangeries of the Calvert era (fig. 11.5) did not possess the visual impact of later versions with their immense facades of glass. The Calvert orangery might or might not have been one of the tomblike buildings Nichol described as characteristic of seventeenth- and early eighteenth-century conservatories (1812:86). Because the importance of light (as opposed to the quality of air) was not fully recognized by early horticulturalists, many conservatories were dark despite the fact they had more windows than ordinary rooms. The Calvert orangery was better oriented to the sun than many of its English counterparts. The archbishop of Canterbury unwisely placed his so that his church hid the sun from the building until 11:00 A.M. on short winter days (Gibson 1796).

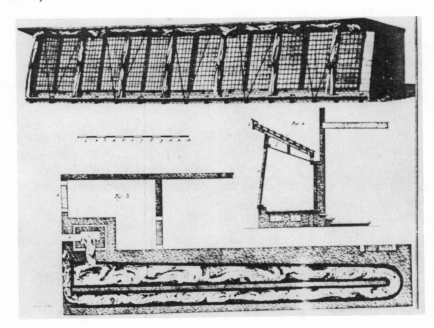

Figure 11.5. A mid-eighteenth-century conservatory showing the hypocaust beneath. (From de Groot 1752: vol. 3, figs. 1-3)

Architectural investigations showed there were two doorways in the section of the main house adjacent to the orangery. One, set at a slightly lower level than floor joist pockets in the west house wall adjacent to the feature, was located south of the structure and opened directly to a terraced sideyard extending toward the harbor and containing planting beds lined at their base with broken bottles for drainage. The other door opened directly into the orangery over the hypocaust. This is in line with Bradley's advice to have an interior door open into the conservatory so that no cool air would enter the orangery without being softened by the warmth of a fire (Bradley 1724).

Loudon (1825:310) wrote of seventeenth-century orangeries as "chambers distinguished by more glass windows in front than usual in dwelling rooms." La Quintinie (1693) specified a southern exposure instead of an eastern one to admit as much light as possible, to be facilitated by large windows up to 6 feet wide extending from floor to ceiling. He specified chambers no deeper than 10 feet by 40 feet so that light could penetrate fully and advised a north wall of good brick and mortar. Henry Van Oosten (1703) believed that the better orangeries had other buildings, a dry hill, or stand of tall trees on the north side. The builder of the Calvert orangery followed this advice, for it adjoined or shared the thick south wall of the north wing and was only 10 feet deep.

Descriptions of contemporaneous orangeries of English lords suggest that the Calvert orangery was a small building of wood and brick, perhaps 12 feet tall with 3-foot-high and 5-foot-wide arched windows facing south toward East Street. Two small postholes and a rotted sill beam are evidence of the wooden elements; the south brick wall was located 2 feet north of these in almost precisely the position recommended by Miller (1737) for placement of the first flue. The structure perhaps accorded well with La Quintinie's 1693 suggestions for orangeries and with those in Van Oosten (1703) who instructed: "Doors must be so wide that orange trees may be easily carried in and out. Windows must be large and high, reaching quite to the ceiling from the breast work which is commonly 3 feet high. The breadth of windows must be 5 or 6 feet that when you open them in winter, when the sun shines brightly . . . the sun may shine on them all at once. . . . Walls must be good and without least hollowness . . . . Those are best that have on the north side some other building" (Van Oosten 1703:253-74).

The enthusiasm for botany shown by educated, intelligent English gentlemen scientists "spilled over into the fields of mathematics, meteorology, antiquarianism, experimental philosophy, and invention" (Wright 1934:54). To govern a New World province or common-wealth well also required intelligence and education. Knowledge of agriculture was necessary, for daily life depended upon the successful growth of plants and succor of livestock. The seventeenth-century gardens at Pennsbury Manor are evidence of William Penn's botanical knowledge, as are the books owned by Governor William Nicholson in 1695 (Nicholson 1655-1738). These included La Quintinie's *Compleat Gardener* (1693), John Evelyn's *Sylva* (1664), Worlidge's *Systema Agriculturae* (1669), Meager's *The English Gardener* (1670), and Cook's *Manner of Raising, Ordering, and Improving Forest and Fruit Trees* (1676). The evidence that the Calvert men who served as governors of Maryland also participated in this circle of activities can be seen in the orangery they built at State Circle ca. 1730 and in the broken bell jars and glazed flowerpots their gardeners left behind.

Precisely what the Calvert household grew in the building may never be known, although phytolith analysis is being done on some of the soil samples. The site's botanical remains contained no orange or lemon seeds (Miller 1988), nor can any floral remains be documented to the height of agricultural activity at the site. Instead, the fruit and nut seeds, from a range of plants commonly cultivated in early eighteenth-century communities, entered the archaeological record either as the feature was demolished (ca. 1765) or during repairs and renovations ca. 1785 and ca. 1820. These plants included edible nuts (almonds, American chestnuts, hazel, hickory, pecan, and walnut), fruits (apricots, cherries, olives, papaw, peach, and plum), and other foodstuffs (corn, grape, melon, peanut, pumpkin/squash, and watermelon). Still, plants did prove to be an important element in perceiving how the structure represented by the feature fit into the scheme of things in eighteenth-century

Annapolis. Further, what was important about the plants was not their role in the foodways system but their pivotal placement in the symbolic language associated with plants.

## The Ethnographic Context of an Orangery

### The Extraordinary Value of Orange Trees

World exploration and commercial trade with distant countries from ca. 1081 into the early modern era increased the interest in the cultivation of exotic plants. The circle of eastern Mediterranean trade brought the orange from China via Persia to north Italian gardens in Venice and Genoa. Italians gave it religious symbolism by associating it with the Virgin Mary and the tree of knowledge (Levi 1977). Royalty had always maintained extensive gardens, but the 1500s also saw the growth of botanical gardens at other secular and religious institutions in Italy (Hix 1974). These gardens were more than places to raise plants for food and medicine; they were also encyclopedias of living plants, exotic and rare (i.e., curiosities), that required skilled observation, record keeping, an awareness of the environment, botanical knowledge, extensive labor, and monetary resources to maintain. As compilations of living plants they required specialized accoutrements for tropical species not adapted to cooler climates. A heated winter room was an indisputable asset, and it is not surprising that the ancient technology described in surviving manuscripts was revived, for the botanists were thoroughly familiar with Latin.

Some introduced plants, like the tulip in Holland, captured people's imaginations and became favored for reasons fanciful and real. Switzer (1724) touted peaches because they cooled the stomach, dissipated thick blood, and quenched the heat of the human liver. Instead of an apple a day, he encouraged "lovers of health" to eat peaches every morning. Van Oosten preferred orange trees; in his opinion "in all the compass of gardening, there is not a plant or tree that affords such extensive and lasting pleasure" (1703:241). At the height of their popularity in the seventeenth and early eighteenth centuries, 169 different kinds of orange trees were grown in Europe and England. The virtues of orange trees were extolled in botanical literature, and their cultural value is easily seen in the praise. Oliver de Serres (1607) wrote evocatively of orange trees, finding it difficult to express adequately the beauty of these precious plants with their dazzling and colorful foliage and fruit. Among the benefits of the fruit was a fragrance which delicately perfumed enclosed rooms at a time when strong odors were considered potentially malevolent.

The monetary value of such trees was correspondingly high. John Tradescent (whose son, John, Jr., collected plants in Virginia) purchased eight pots of grafted orange trees in Paris in 1611 for ten shillings each at a time when an earthen pan might cost a threepence or sixpence, a gardener's day rate was only one and a half shillings, a mirror would be a shilling, and Bibles were appraised at three shillings (Plymouth Colony Probate Records, vol. 1, 1621-1640). In 1649 Queen Henrietta Maria's orangery building was valued at £55.13.4, but her forty-two large orange trees were appraised at £420 pounds, while her lemon tree with its big fruit was worth £18 pounds. Such fruit trees were scarce resources, and only families with wealth and access to international trade networks could afford them. Herein lies an important clue to the significance of oranges and orange trees.

Although the best orangery in England at Beddington Gardens produced 10,000 oranges in 1690 (Black 1983; Lemon 1962), oranges were not grown as money-making ventures.

Neither florists nor merchants grew them. Instead, the trees became the focus of activity for gentlemen with interests in medicine and botany, such as John Evelyn, or the possessions of the elite. It took skill and money to build a good greenhouse; a bad one could only be torn down and rebuilt again (Nichol 1812). Glass was expensive, and not until its price dropped in the mid-eighteenth century did true greenhouses appear. No one without servants could maintain an orangery; the need for skilled gardeners is noted in most discussions of the care and cultivation of orange trees. Unskilled boys did not have the talent to water the worthy plants listed in table 11.1. Charles Carroll of Baltimore sought a man over the age of thirty to care for his plants (Michael F. Trostel to J. M. P. Wright, 15 May 1980).

In seeking the meaning of the Calvert hypocaust, this chapter has considered orangeries in technical and economic terms. One can readily see in the evocative descriptions of orange trees that they were perceived as special plants. Despite their expense, the connection between status and oranges has only been suggested. If, as Charles Taylor writes, "interpretation aims to bring to light an underlying coherence" (Taylor 1987:33), making sense of something that is cloudy and unclear, then the task of interpreting the orangery at the Calvert site is still incomplete. Why was an orangery a status marker? To understand this relationship requires establishing a connection between oranges and orange trees and a perception of power as expressed in man's control of rare and mysterious trees.

## The Symbolism of Orangeries and Orange Trees

To understand how objects work as status markers, one must analyze artifacts as symbols. Status markers are always embedded in symbolic systems of meaning. A symbol is an object or action which represents another entity by virtue of an assigned conceptual relation between them (Firth 1973). Because the relationship is assigned, symbolic meanings of artifacts remain elusive unless documented through ethnographic sources, used as one would use an anthropological informant, or unless documented through well-reasoned analogies.

With respect to the hypocaust and its orangery, there is excellent ethnographic information in the texts written by seventeenth- and eighteenth-century men. This information has been used in a companion article (Yentsch 1989) which analyzes a change in the landscape elements of the Calverts' town lot and their use of space throughout the eighteenth century. The article demonstrates how the Calverts placed themselves at the visual center of political power in the province of Maryland. It is built on Clifford Geertz's statement that "at the political center of any complexly organized society, there is both a governing elite and a set of symbolic forms expressing the fact that it is in truth governing" (1983:124). Geertz notes that the symbolic forms "mark the center as center" and tie those associated with them to the way the world is organized (1983:124).

Pragmatically, the hypocaust that now lies beneath a glass floor at the Calvert Hotel worked once as a stove to heat the orangery when nights were cold and water turned to ice in earthen mugs (see James 1712). It was an apparatus derived from antiquity, a bit of ancient technology which provided a connection through association between the Calverts who ruled the province of Maryland and the Romans who ruled the Old World. Control of it gave the Calvert household control over nature, something no one else in Maryland had accomplished by 1730.

Seventeenth- and eighteenth-century men and women lived with nature as part of their daily lives. Scientific observation and classification as the modern world knows them were not in existence. Thus, for orangeries the technical requirements, including heat and light, which are well understood in today's world, were not fully comprehended in the culture; hence, they were perceived as mysterious. The importance of agriculture as nature ordered by man was simultaneously central and deeply embedded in the logic or knowledge of the way the world was built.

Wild and domestic animals were conceived of as relatives of man; the kingly elephant or lion stood at the point in the chain of life where man and animal were joined; the lowly oyster of Chesapeake Bay was situated at the border between animal and plant life. In beehives, wonderfully organized bees served to "teach the art of order to a peopled kingdom" (Tillyard 1943:80). People belonged where God had put them. The natural world served as symbol of and metaphor for the human world. Human lives followed a diurnal pattern and possessed seasonal rhythms. There were very few people whose lives were not touched in some way by agricultural activities and the countryside penetrated into city life.

Among people for whom agricultural pursuits are closely woven into the fabric of daily life, gardens and gardeners assume a significance unknown in our entrenched industrial society. Fifteenth-century Italian nobility boasted of their green thumbs as markers of their knowledge of and interest in horticulture. In the preindustrial world, getting the day's daily food was the day's daily work for men and women (Firth 1973). The Greek and Latin authors read by literate people expressed this focus on nature, for they often wrote of ways to enhance and protect food resources. Columella provided advice for cold foggy days and frosty nights: "In the spring-time, see that you have heaps of chaff and straw placed among the rows in the vineyard. When you shall see the cold contrary to which is usual in that season of the year, set all the heaps of chaff and straw on fire" (*De arboricus*, 1745 translation, chap. 13, p. 587). Bradley (1725) indicated that since Roman times, Italians had known of the use of "hot beds on wheels" as containers for growing fruits and vegetables. Continuity in agricultural practice was reinforced through such reading material, which formed an accessible body of knowledge for gentlemen farmers in the Chesapeake (Isaac 1987).

By 1682 Jean de La Quintinie, gardener to France's Louis XIV, was famous because he could procure early and out-of-season fruits and vegetables for the king: fresh asparagus in December, lettuce in January, strawberries and peas in April, figs and melons in June (Van den Muijzenberg 1980). In other words, La Quintinie had learned to order nature in its seasons by forcing plants contrary to nature; therein lay his power and his fascination for Englishmen. To do so, he used the ancient technology of dry-air heating.

There was available to La Quintinie and to other educated men of his time a whole body of knowledge concerning the natural world. Yet the way in which this information was presented and the way in which early horticulturalists interpreted it was organized by a nonmodern logic. Texts offered readers, at the same level of importance, anatomical descriptions of animals and plants that included anatomy, methods of raising, growing, or capturing, allegorical uses, modes of reproduction, habitat, legendary dwelling places, food preferences, medicinal uses, and recipes for human consumption. This information was intermingled in compendia until 1738 when Linnaeus brought scientific order to biological taxonomy by stripping extraneous material from the basic descriptions (Foucault 1973). This modernization, however, took place after the Calvert orangery and represents a worldview unfamiliar to the Calvert family.

What the Calverts knew was that oranges were a fruit occasionally eaten; their cultivation in northern Europe was a mysterious art practiced by kings, nobles, and influential men. The orange leaves, the blossoms, the ripe fruit, and even the peel had medicinal qualities. An ounce of orange flowers dropped in a half pin of brandy and placed in the sun for a fortnight yielded a tincture good for colds and distemper. Placing the leaves on a bruise healed it, and thankfully, powdered peel warmed any stomach that might have been overly cooled by peaches. Each with its own beauty, the trees also possessed a free sweetness "like unto that of a horse chestnut or lime tree" (Van Oosten 1703:274). Their very fragrance refreshed and recreated the spirit. Orange trees with their beauty, elegance, and the air they created provided an extra fillip to daily life which could not be purchased in the marketplace. Ships brought the fruit to market ports where the fruit was common and known to all. The trees were "strange and rare" (Rea 1676:14).

## Conclusion

An orange tree was a beautiful, precious, strange, and rare plant whose very fragrance brought health and refreshed a man. Its nurture was not without difficulty. Johannes Volckamer of Nuremberg reported that a woman's touch could destroy an orange tree (McPhee 1978). In his *Neurenbergische Hesperiden*, he described how women could cause whole trees to die.

> Many will derive this as something foolish, and I myself should not have believed it had not it caused the undoing of some of my most valuable trees. Once, in winter, I noticed a woman of my gardener's household seated upon a beautiful orange tree in full bloom. The next day, the tree started drying up from the top downwards, and so rapid was the progress of the disease that in the course of a few days it had infected every single branch, causing all the leaves to wilt and die.
> (McPhee 1978:74-75)

Originally they were grown by the gods, and over time emperors and kings learned how to cultivate them (McPhee 1978). During the Renaissance, noblemen, rich members of the gentry, and learned medical men and botanists also acquired this skill. Orangeries were the delight of kings, nobles, and gentlemanly scientists. The trees became a quintessential seventeenth-century symbol of male power and prestige.

From their concern with oranges and orange trees as part of their interest in nature and horticulture, the enthusiasm of these men spilled over into other domains only then beginning to emerge as intellectual disciplines in their own right: mathematics, meteorology, antiquarianism, experimental philosophy, and invention. These men were among the small number of privileged people, wealthy and powerful, who governed, administered and directed England and its colonies. When they constructed their orangery at Annapolis, the Calverts laid claim to a metaphorical kinship with these rulers, intellectuals, philosophers, and scientists.

When viewed in terms of such symbolism, the Calvert orangery is an extremely revealing artifact. Its location and surrounding gardens served as symbols of regal power in Annapolis based on principles of medieval thought: association through contiguity and the linking concepts of correspondence, analogy, and resemblance (Foucault 1973). The trees were carefully arranged in an orangery each fall and sheltered while the world outside grew cold (fig. 11.6). Common turnips were left in the ground. Therein lay one division of the plant world. Inside, however, the arrangement of orange trees and other plants was also highly structured. Ideally, greater trees were placed on pedestals; lesser trees and shrubs were used for ornament. Vases graced the interior entranceway. The plant world thus served as metaphor of social hierarchy.

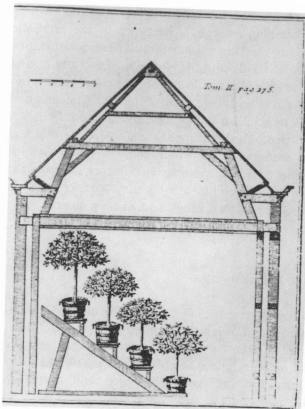

Figure 11.6. Hierarchical arrangement of plants, as suggested by La Quintinie and other early horticulturists, shown within a French conservatory. From de Groot 1752: vol. 2, p. 275.

Power needs display and ornament. The presence of the orangery at the Calvert house on State Circle set it apart from the homes of other men in the Chesapeake. Orangeries were distinct rarities in the New World. The Calvert orangery was rare and ornamental. It served the needs of politically powerful men by displaying their mastery over nature, by denoting that the center of power in the town was indeed the center, and by providing a visual reminder of the way society was structured and the world was organized (Geertz 1983). Given the classificatory schema of the seventeenth- and early eighteenth-century culture, the Calvert orangery was an unexcelled horticultural symbol of power.

As relatives of Lord Baltimore, the Calvert men who resided in early eighteenth-century Annapolis when the orangery was built were among the members of British society entitled to material luxuries. But the eighteenth century also saw the emergence of a consumer society where material aspirations were not limited to birth alone (McKendrick et al. 1982). Other upwardly mobile households in Annapolis, including Governor Sharpe's (ca. 1740 to 1760) and Dr. Alexander Hamilton's (ca. 1747 to 1780), sought to express their social rank with the construction of conservatories, just as did wealthy men living in the cities of Baltimore and Philadelphia, on plantations at Wye Island, and along the James River. George Washington built an orangery at Mount Vernon based on plans an aide obtained in Maryland. The more recent orangeries, however, were built by men in a later time when oranges had ceased to be mysterious. While they built structures they labeled as orangeries, the buildings functioned differently. Orange trees were revalued in the mid-eighteenth century. The symbolism of the trees themselves was lost. The more talented botanists, like Peter Collinson, devoted their energy to orchids; the preferred fruit became the pineapple, more exotic than the orange and without claim to the mythological heritage rooted in classical antiquity.

A world where men could tolerate rats and mice so that their orange trees might survive at night seems strange indeed. A world in which a woman could lean against the limb of an orange tree and cause it to shrivel and die is almost beyond credibility. Yet such beliefs were the world of the early eighteenth century, and in these beliefs is encoded the structure of the culture.

As one begins to learn about events in such a world, the symbolic forms through which its social world is displayed and articulated begin to emerge. The terms of the symbolic forms and the way men defined them in their daily lives are neither familiar nor comfortable. Yet it is clear that for a relative of Lord Baltimore, resident in the New World and attempting to govern with Baltimore's needs in mind, it was indeed sensible and appropriate, even if not monetarily prudent, to build an orangery and fill it with rare plants, common flowers, and useful herbs. In doing so, he left an indelible imprint on the archaeological record.

Such is an interpretive analysis of the archaeological feature at the Calvert site that was identified as a hypocaust. The interpretive framework on which the analysis was built permitted the archaeologist to penetrate an earlier symbolic system. This in turn gave insight into the social behavior and the worldview of men in eighteenth-century Annapolis. It is no accident that this took place at a juncture where anthropology and history meet.

## Acknowledgments

The archaeological research was supported in part by grant RRO-20600-83 from the National Endowment for the Humanities, by funds from the Maryland Commission for the Preservation of the Capital City, the Maryland Council for the Humanities, the Maryland Heritage Commission, the Society for the Preservation of Maryland Antiquities, the Colonial Dames (Chapter 1), the Annapolis Institute, Historic Inns of Annapolis, Inc., and the city's preservation agency, Historic Annapolis, Inc.

The research on orangeries was undertaken at the Botanical Gardens of Cambridge University, Cambridge, England, while I was teaching in the Cambridge Summer Program of the College of William and Mary. The work could not have been done without the kind and generous assistance provided by Clive King, Archivist of the Library at the Botanical Gardens. Neither would this chapter have been written without the encouragement and support of Mrs. J. M. P. Wright and Henry T. Wright. Comments and information provided by Anne Webster-Smith, Henry T. Wright, and Barbara Paca are integrated into this version of the chapter. Originally presented at the 45th Conference on Early American History, The Colonial Experience: Eighteenth-Century Maryland, held in Baltimore on 13 September 1984, the first version was revised with support, in part, from National Endowment for the Humanities Grant RO-21482-87. This is a condensed version of the information in Calvert Interim Report No. 9.

## References Cited

Agricola, G. A. 1719. *The artificial gardener; being a discovery of a new invention for the sudden growth of all sorts of trees and plants.* Trans. from the High Dutch. London.
----. 1721. *The philosophical treatise of husbandry and gardening.* Trans. Richard Bradley. London.
Bievelet, H. 1950. L'exploration archéologique de Bavai: Notes sur les hypocaustes de Bavai. *L'Antiquité Classique* 19:82-92.

Black, V. 1983. Beddington: "The best Orangery in England." *Journal of Garden History* 3(2):113-20.

Boeswillwald, E. 1897. *Timgard, une cité africaine.* Paris: Publié par les soines de la Commission du Nord de l'Afrique et accompagné de plans et desoins exécutes par le Service des Monuments Historiques de l'Algérie.

Bradley, R. 1718. Cambridge herbarium lectures. Manuscript. Cambridge: Botanical Library, Cambridge University.

----. 1724. *New improvements of plants and gardening.* London: W. Mears.

----. 1725. *A survey of ancient husbandry and gardening . . . collected from Cato, Varro, Columella, Virgil, and others, the most eminent writers among the Greeks, and Romans: Wherein many of the most difficult passages in those authors are explained.* London: B. Motte.

Brodribb, G. 1979. A survey of tile from the Russian bath house at Beauport Park, Battle, E. Sussex. *Britannia* 10:139-58.

Columella, L. J. M. 1745. *Of husbandry in twelve books and his book concerning trees [De arboricus].* London: A. Miller.

Commelyn, J. 1683. *The Belgick or Netherlandish Hesperides. That is, the management, ordering, and the use of the limon and orange trees.* Made English by G. V. N. London (from the Dutch of Commelin). London: J. Holford.

Cook, M. 1676. *The manner of raising, ordering, and improving forest and fruit trees.* London: Peter Parker.

Cox, R. J. 1973. A history of the Calvert Papers, Ms. 174*. *Maryland Historical Magazine* 68:309-22.

de Groot, M. 1752. *Les agaremens de la campagne.* Paris.

de Serres, O. 1607. *Le théâtre d'agriculture et messages des champs.* Trans. by N. Goffe.

Evelyn, J. 1664. *Sylva, or a Discourse of forest-trees . . . to which is annexed Pomona, or an appendix concerning fruit-trees & etc.* London: Martyn and Allestryby.

----. 1693. A treatise of orange trees. In *The complete gard'ner; or directions for cultivating . . . fruit gardens and kitchen gardens by Jean de La Quintinie.* Made English by John Evelyn. London: Gillyflower and Partridge.

Faris, J. J. 1932. *Old gardens in and about Philadelphia.* Indianapolis: Bobbs-Merrill.

Forbes, R. J. 1958. *Studies in ancient technology.* Vol. 6. Leiden: E. J. Brill.

Firth, R. 1973. *Symbols: Public and private.* Ithaca: Cornell University Press.

Foucault, M. 1973. *The order of things: An archaeology of the human sciences.* New York: Random House.

Geertz, C. 1983. *Local knowledge: Further essays on interpretive anthropology.* New York: Basic Books.

Gibson, J. 1796. A short account of several gardens near London, with remarks on some particulars wherein they excel, or are deficient, upon a view of them in December 1691. *Archaeologia* 12:181-192.

Hix, J. 1974. *The glass house.* Cambridge: MIT Press.

Isaac, R. 1982. *The transformation of Virginia, 1740-1790.* Chapel Hill: University of North Carolina Press.

Jacobi, L.    1897.    *Das Römerkastell Saalburgei Hombaerg vor der Hohe*.    Nach den Ergebnissen der Ausgrabungen und mit Benutzung der hinterlassenen Aufzeichnungen des Konigl. Konservators Obsersten A. von Cohausen.  2 vols.  Homberg: Reichs-Limes-Kommission.

James, J.  1712.  (translator).  *Theory and practice of gardening done from the French original.*  [La Theorie et la practique du jardinage, by A. J. Dezallier d'Argenville.]  London: G. James.

Jecklin, F., and C. Coaz.  1923.  Fund einer römischen Heizanlage im Welsch Dörfli (Chur.).  *Anzieger fure Scheweizerische Altertumskunde* 25:78-82.

La Quintinie, J. de.  1693.  *A treatise on the culture of the orange tree.*  Trans. John Evelyn.  London: Matthew Gillyflower.

Lemon, K.  1962.  *The covered garden.*  London: Museum Press.

Levi, M. d'Ancona.  1977.  *The garden of the renaissance: Botanical symbolism in Italian painting.*  Firenze: Leo S. Olschky Editore.

Loudon, J. C.  1825.  *An encyclopedia of gardening.*  London: Longham, Brown, Green, and Longmans.

McKendrick, N., J. Brewer, and J. H. Plumb.  1982.  *The birth of a consumer society: The commercialization of the eighteenth century.*  Bloomington: Indiana University Press.

McPhee, J.  1978.  *Oranges.*  New York: Farrar, Straus, and Giroux.

Martin, P.  1893.  Long and assiduous endeavors: Gardening in early eighteenth century Virginia.  *Eighteenth-Century Life* 8(2).

Meager, L.  1670.  *The English gardener, & c.*  London: J. Dawks for M. Wotton.

Miller, N. F.  1987.  *The Calvert site, Annapolis, Maryland: Seed remains.*  Calvert Interim Report No. 7.  Annapolis: Historic Annapolis, Inc.

Miller, P.  1724.  *The gardener's and florist's dictionary, or a complete system of horticulture.*  London: Folio.

----.  1731.  *The gardener's dictionary.*  London: Folio.

Nichol, W.  1812.  *The planter's kalender.*  Ed. and completed by E. Sang.  Edinburgh.

Nicholson, W.  1655-1738.  Catalogue of my books taken May 30, 1695.  Typescript prepared by Rev. Pearson.  Nicholson Papers.  London: Society for the Propagation of the Gospel.

Noël-Hume, I.  1956.  *A Roman bath-building in Cheapside.*  London: Guildhall Museum.

Overbeck, J.  1884.  *Pompeii in seinen Gebauden, Alterthumern und Kunstwerken.*  Leipzig: Verlag von Wilhelm Engelmann.

Rea, J.  1676.  *Flora, Ceres, et Pomona.*  London: Folio.

----.  1987.  *Preliminary analysis of vertebrate remains from the Calvert site in Annapolis, Maryland, and a comparison with vertebrate remains from sites in South Carolina, Georgia, and Jamaica.*  Calvert Interim Report No. 6.  Annapolis: Historic Annapolis, Inc.

Reitz, E. J.  1988.  *Vertebrate fauna from eighteenth-century Annapolis, the Calvert house site.*  Calvert Interim Report No. 8.  Annapolis: Historic Annapolis, Inc.

Rook T.  1978.  The development and operation of Roman hypocausted baths.  *Journal of Archaeological Science* 5:269-82.

Sahlins, M.  1981.  *Historical metaphors and mythical realities.*  ASAO Publication No. 1.  Ann Arbor: University of Michigan Press.

Switzer, S.  1724.  *The practical fruit gardener, & etc. being the best and newest method of raising, planting, and pruning all sorts of trees.*  London.

Taylor, C. 1979. Interpretation and the sciences of man. In *Interpretive social science*, ed. P. Rabinow and W. M. Sullivan, pp. 33-81. 2d ed. Berkeley: University of California Press.

Thompson, E. P. 1966. *The making of the English working class.* New York: Random House.

Tillyard, E. M. W. 1943. *The Elizabethan world picture.* New York: Random House.

Trostel, M. F. 1980. Letter to Mrs. J. M. P. Wright, 15 May. On file at Historic Annapolis, Inc.

Van den Muijzenberg, E. W. B. 1980. *A history of greenhouses.* The Netherlands: Wageningen.

Van Oosten, H. 1703. *The Dutch gardener, or the compleat florist* . . . Written in Dutch, trans. to English. London: D. Midwinter and T. Leigh.

Volckamer, J. 1714. *Neurenbergische Hesperiden.* Neuremberg.

Wilson, B. 1974. The orangery at Hampton. Manuscript. Towson: Hampton National Historic Site, Maryland.

Winckelmann, J. J. 1762. *Anmerkungen uber die Baakunst der Atlen.* Leipzig: Dyck.

Worlidge, J. 1669. *Systema agriculturae, the mystery of husbandry discovered . . . to which is added Kalendarium Rusticum.* London: T. Johnson for Samuel Speed.

Wright, H. T. 1952. Report on the hypocaust at Dr. Alexander Hamilton's house. Manuscript. Annapolis: Historic Annapolis, Inc.

Wright, R. 1934. *The story of gardening from the hanging gardens of Babylon to the hanging gardens of New York.* London: George Routledge.

Yentsch, A. 1989. *Contrary to nature: The Calvert orangery and its hypocaust.* Calvert Interim Report No. 9. Annapolis: Historic Annapolis, Inc.

# 12

# ARCHAEOLOGY AND THE LANDSCAPE OF CORPORATE IDEOLOGY

## Stephen A. Mrozowski and Mary C. Beaudry

"Landscape is a way of seeing that has its own history."

(Cosgrove 1984:1)

The archaeological record of past landscapes readily yields up quotidian technical details of how people have shaped and ordered the world around them: postholes indicating the courses of vanished fence lines; planting holes, root casts, seeds, pollen, and phytoliths representing flowers, grasses, and trees that once served as elements of gardens, lawns, and vistas; walks, retaining walls, and so forth. At the same time, this record is evidence of the social organization of space at different scales and at different times in history (Cosgrove 1984) and contributes to broader interpretations of space and how people use it, think about it, and are affected by it. The knowledge that "the relationship between societies and their environment as it is lived is as much a product of consciousness as of material realities" (Cosgrove 1984:6) is a recurrent theme in landscape studies and increasingly has gained a foothold in archaeological interpretations of past landscapes (e.g., Leone 1984; Praetzellis and Praetzellis 1989; Rubertone 1984; Yentsch, above).

It is thus possible to gain insight into the workings of culture in terms of consciously and unconsciously shared notions of order and causality, of reason and sense in human relations, through archaeology by attending to the affective power of the built environment--the total material expression of landscape and land use (see Rapaport 1982:11-34). "Virginia's plantation estates, like their British models, were a complete environment, house and setting, culture and nature usually playing complementary architectural roles" (Kelso 1984:159). As is true for entities such as plantations, the landscape and the built environment of nineteenth-century Lowell, Massachusetts, were part of a whole. The differences have to do with time and with scale as well as with the deliberate and self-conscious transition to industrial capitalism that found expression at Lowell.

The Boott Mills complex was no exception to this pattern. In fact, the study of the Boott Mills complex and its housing described here serves as a case study not just for the Lowell Mills but for urban industrial centers in general. The intent of the Boott Mills study is to provide a series of highly detailed descriptions of a specific manifestation of industrial capitalism as a framework both "for understanding the particular case as well as more general social and cultural processes" (Beaudry and Mrozowski 1987b:145; see also Beaudry and

Mrozowski 1987a).  The underlying premise is that "historical explanation . . . involves an attempt at particular and total description, and it does not oppose such description to explanation and general theory.  Rather, our generalizing anthropological concerns can progress only through an adequate description, and hence understanding, in our terms, of the particular" (Hodder 1987:2).  The changing landscape and much-altered built environment of the Boott Mills industrial complex and workers' housing reveal both conscious and unconscious ideologies governing the shaping and use of space in an urban industrial context.

When the Boston Associates began to survey the New England landscape for a suitable site to establish New England's first planned industrial city in 1820, they carried with them a vision, a mental blueprint of the community.  Little imagination is needed to envision these early industrialists seeing the outline of their city rising from the fields of the small hamlet of East Chelmsford, located at the confluence of the Merrimack and Concord rivers.  While not unique, Lowell does represent the genus of landscape that is clearly the expression of mind.  Unlike other landscapes that are the product of less conscious human behavior, the built environment of a planned city embodies both a purpose and an ideal.  In the case of Lowell, its purpose not only shaped the ideal, it determined its health over the course of the nineteenth century.

For archaeologists interested in examining and reconstructing past landscapes, Lowell provides the perfect opportunity to investigate how ideology is expressed materially.  Because so much has been written concerning Lowell, both during the nineteenth century and by historians today, there is no need to prove that ideology played a role in the generation of this city's distinct urban landscape.  Instead, we have attempted to trace the trajectory of that landscape in order to determine how well the experiment embodied by Lowell as a city weathered the changes wrought by the nineteenth century.  In order to do this, we have employed an interdisciplinary research strategy that matches our concerns for historical context with those for issues of environment and urban ecology.  Such an approach has been necessary for two reasons.  The first has to do with the appropriate methods for the task.  Even in a city, the landscape is a mosaic of buildings, streets, trees, weeds, and other plants.  Without some method of empirical investigation, one cannot reconstruct changing conditions over time.  This is true whether the intent is to reconstruct physical context alone (e.g., Jones and Dimbleby 1981; Schoenwetter 1981) or to recover the interface of thought and its expression through the landscape.

The second reason is an outgrowth of the first.  While the urban landscape is overwhelmingly the product of human endeavor, ecological processes continue to play a role in its texture and evolution.  Very often human action can be the mechanism that sets in motion ecological processes, such as succession, in an environment like the urban garden-- processes generated and controlled by people (Mrozowski 1987).  Detection of possible successional changes in plant communities can, as demonstrated here, help in determining the character and timing of shifts in the urban landscape.

Not only was the Lowell experiment poorly maintained as far as living conditions for workers are concerned; there is clear evidence of the corporation's differentiation in the treatment of its properties.  The evidence to support this contention comes from investigations at the Boott Mills boardinghouses (Beaudry and Mrozowski 1987a), which are continuing, and those at the Kirk Street Agents' House (Beaudry and Mrozowski 1987b), the home of the Boott and Massachusetts corporations' agents.  Much of the landscape data presented herein are drawn from the contextual analyses conducted at both sites to date (Kelso, Mrozowski, and Fisher 1987; Mrozowski and Kelso 1987). Analysis of samples collected during the second phase of investigation at the boardinghouses is in progress; therefore, the observations and conclusions offered here should be viewed as tentative.

## The Boott Cotton Mills Corporation

The Boott Cotton Mills, incorporated for the manufacture of cotton and woolen goods on 27 March 1835, were located on a 5.7-acre parcel on the Merrimack River near its confluence with the Concord River (Shepley et al. 1980:1). The company was named after Kirk Boott, "a pioneer of industrial feudalism," who, as executive manager (agent) for both the Merrimack Manufacturing Company and the Proprietors of Locks and Canals, was one of early Lowell's most powerful and prominent figures (*Dictionary of American Biography* 1932:43; Beaudry 1987a:73-76; Parker 1985). The industrial complex was located between the river and the Eastern Canal, to the south of which lay the corporation boardinghouses and tenements (fig. 12.1). The canal served as the boundary between the mill and the workers' housing as well as the power source for the mills.

The Boott Corporation at first distributed stock totaling $1 million. By 1837 an additional $200,000 in stock had been issued in reaction to unforeseen rises in the costs of machinery and construction. The corporation's capital remained at $1.2 million for the remainder of the century (Shepley et al. 1980:1). The Boott had been authorized to acquire real estate of up to $150,000 in value; the parcel the company purchased included Kirk Boott's estate. His mansion was moved to another location in Lowell, and the land where it had once stood became the site of blocks of mill housing (fig. 12.2).

John A. Lowell, one of the Boott's incorporators, was its first treasurer; he served from 1827 to 1844. It was the company's agents, however, who were the driving forces behind mill expansion and profitability. Benjamin French (1836-45) and Linus Child (1845-62) were the agents during the early years of the company. When French became agent, Mills Nos. 1 and 2 were in operation, using machinery provided by the Lowell Machine Shop. By 1842, with four mills operating, the Boott employed 950 females and 120 males who produced over 9 million yards of coarse cloth (Shepley et al. 1980:1-2).

The output of the Boott Mills increased steadily until the Civil War. Poor management in the years before the war and the cotton shortages brought on by the conflict combined in contributing to deterioration of machinery and the company's failure to pay a dividend to shareholders in 1863 (Shepley et al. 1980:1-2). Complaints that the business had been manipulated to the benefit of the directors were widespread among the shareholders.

William Burke, former head of the Lowell Machine Shop, was hired as agent in 1862. Between 1862 and 1863 the mills were closed and major repairs, rebuilding, and improvements took place. By 1868, when Alexander Cumnock took over as agent, employees numbered 1,020 females and 310 males. The quantity of spindles and looms had been more than doubled from the original numbers, and more than 14,000,000 yards of cloth were produced annually (Shepley et al. 1980:2-3).

Continued expansion characterized Cumnock's tenure as agent (1868-96), with most of the corporation's growth occurring in the 1870s and early 1880s. The mills doubled in size; between 1870 and 1874, a dividend of from 12.5 to 20 percent was paid to the shareholders. New products such as flannels, piqués, and drills were introduced, and the work force grew to 1,300 female and 500 male operatives (Shepley et al. 1980:3). In the 1880s the company

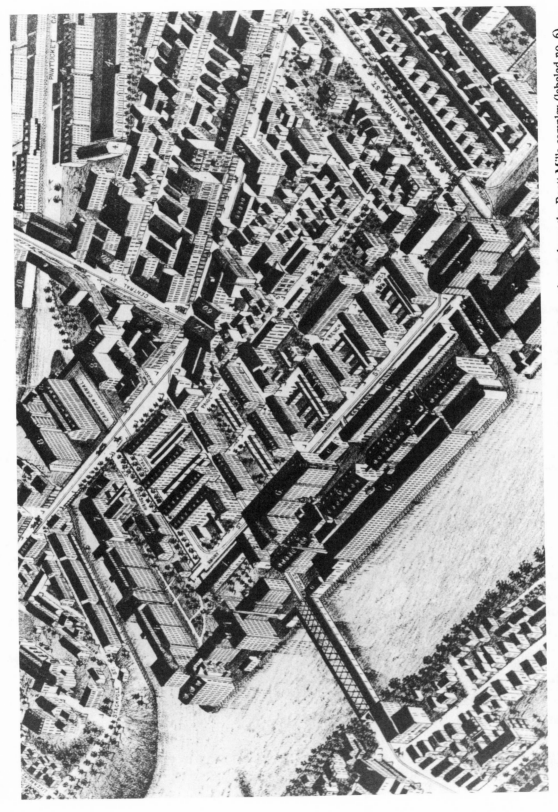

Figure 12.1. This detail from the 1876 Bailey and Hazah bird's eye view of Lowell from the northwest shows the Boott Mills complex (labeled no. 6) below the bridge along the Merrimack River. View is looking south.

was able to expand without hiring new workers. The increased efficiency of machinery, in combination with management policies such as the speedup (running the machines faster) and stretch-out (assigning each operative responsibility for additional machines) provided the means for this expansion (Gross and Wright 1985:17). Production rose steadily until 1891, after which a slowed growth of the company and changes in products in response to the market (e.g., cambrics, linens, lawns, ducks, corduroys, seamless bags, twills, and moleskins were all introduced between 1890 and 1915) insured continued profitability into the early twentieth century. There was a brief drop in employment in 1902 and 1903, and later the Great Depression caused severe drops in employment and production. By 1940 the Boott had recovered slightly, but the effects of the Depression, rising labor unrest, and the movement of the textile industry to the southern United States precluded a complete recovery. Between 1956 and 1957 the Boott Cotton Mills became an industrial real estate/management firm (Shepley et al. 1980:3-4).

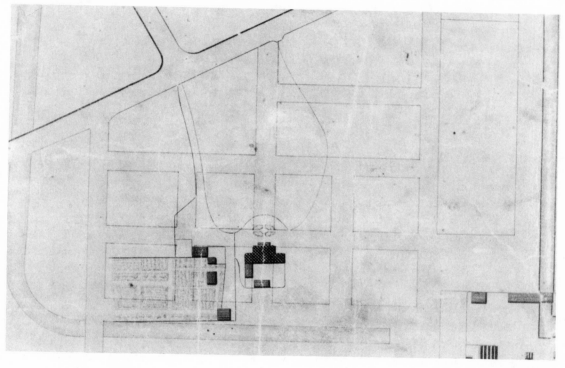

Figure 12.2. A detail of the 1825 map of "Sundry Farms at Pawtucket" showing canals and streets planned for the Boott Mills sketched in over the original content which depicted the plan of Kirk Boott's estate with its U-shaped drive, outbuildings, and gardens. (Courtesy of Lowell National Historical Park)

## Lowell's Built Environment:
## Corporate Ideology in Brick and Stone

The built environment of Lowell was "the totality of physical structures--houses, roads, factories, offices, sewage systems, parks, cultural institutions, educational facilities, and so on" as well as the landscape in which these structures were situated. Lowell's founding fathers attempted to create and control "the total living environment for labor" (Harvey

1976:265, 267; see also Beaudry 1987a, 1987b; Greenwood 1986). As such, the factory system was a conscious statement of the goals of industrial capitalists, who were candid in discussing their motives. Lowell, according to Nathan Appleton (1858; quoted in Bender 1975:99), was itself to be a large machine for making profit. Intended as a business enterprise, Lowell developed along two distinct trajectories. The industrial sector "was carefully planned according to functional principles," while the rest of town, the bourgeois sector, "was allowed to grow up in the area left over. Here functionalism was abandoned; land use decisions were made primarily on the basis of the speculative profits to be earned" (Bender 1975:100).

Planning and lack of planning went hand in hand, it seems. Bender (1975:100) notes that nineteenth-century Americans tended to view cities not as complex urban communities like those in Europe but as special-purpose locales. European cities, with their admixture of squalor and luxury, were models to be avoided. Lowell's founders sought especially to avoid the ills of industrial cities such as Manchester, England, which, with its crowded, unsanitary conditions and working-class slums, bred both disease and labor unrest. The design for Lowell aimed to circumvent such developments.

> A revealing similarity between the founders of Lowell and Thomas Jefferson, a major contributor to the plan of Washington, D.C., emerges in this context. Jefferson and Francis Cabot Lowell were both disturbed by the poverty and degradation they found in Europe's political capitals and manufacturing cities. Consequently, when Jefferson planned America's political capital and Lowell planned the nation's industrial center neither wished to duplicate their respective European counterparts, Paris and Manchester, in all their complexity. Believing the urban rabble characteristic of Paris and Manchester to be an unwelcome addition to American society, they simply blotted these aspects of city life out of their plans. Jefferson's plan for Washington made provision only for the political activities to be undertaken there. His plans reserved very little space for the general economic activities ordinarily present in a city the size of Washington. Further, Jefferson apparently gave little consideration in his original plans to the housing needs of the cartmen, bakers, artisans, and day laborers who made up the typical eighteenth-century urban scene, since he intended that every house built in the national capital be constructed of stone. A regulation that "all Houses in the said City, shall be of Brick or Stone" was promulgated in 1791. Similarly, the founders of Lowell, who did not want any urban proletariat in their manufacturing center, made their plans as if there would be none. Although Boott made ample provision for those employed in the actual production process in the mills, he never made any preparations for housing the essential day laborers who dug the canals and constructed the mills. . . . One cannot help thinking that the founder of Lowell planned the city in terms of the organizational chart--to use an anachronistic term--of their manufacturing corporation. (Bender 1975:100-101)

Lowell at first was designed to complement industrializing America's self-image as an agrarian republic as well as to provide a reassuring link with the traditional values associated with rural life (Bender 1975:73-93; Candee 1982, 1985; Marx 1964). Early views depict the manufacturing center in a pastoral setting (fig. 12.3). Lucy Larcom, a mill operative in early Lowell, and her friends, fellow mill girls, often had picnics on the banks of the Merrimack; "a walk of a mile or so took us into charmingly picturesque scenery" (Larcom 1889:209). Appleton's machine in the garden was to be its finest flower. Within the town, the monotony of row upon row of brick factories and boardinghouses was softened by careful landscaping juxtaposing industrial streetscapes and mill complexes with parklike green spaces. Larcom wrote in her autobiography that when she first began to work in the Lowell mills:

Nature came very close to the mill-gates, too, in those days. There was green grass all around them; violets and wild geraniums grew by the canals; and long stretches of open land between the corporation buildings and the street made the town seem country-like.

The slope behind our mills (the "Lawrence" Mills) was a green lawn; and in front of some of them the overseers had gay flower-gardens; we passed in to our work through a splendor of dahlias and hollyhocks (Larcom 1889:163-64).

Figure 12.3. An 1849 view of Lowell. The first to show the city's famous "mile of mills" along the Merrimack River, it nevertheless places the industrial center in a pastoral setting. (Courtesy of the Lowell Historical Society)

Neither the landscape nor industrial capitalism was to remain static, however, and change was inevitable. In many ways the initial attention paid by the corporations to the physical setting of the mills was integral to their policy of corporate paternalism. The formal paternalism of Lowell's early years was a broadly conceived strategy for controlling workers' lives under the guise of close concern for their welfare (Scranton 1984:244-45). This "strict system of moral police" (Miles 1846:128) was promoted more or less as a form of in loco parentis for the mill girls who were the core of Lowell's work force. It was characterized by the development of the boardinghouse system with its attendant rules and curfews as well as the introduction of industrial discipline into the workplace (cf. Bender 1975:65; Gross and Wright 1985:13-14).

Historical and archaeological evidence provides a wealth of information that graphically illustrates the erosion of corporate paternalism over the course of the century following Lowell's founding. Harriet Robinson, a mill girl in Lowell's heyday, wrote in 1898 of her dismay at the appearance of the mill housing, explaining that the houses were no longer "kept clean and in repair as they used to be. In Lowell, when I last walked among the blocks where I lived as a child, I found them in a most dilapidated condition--houses going to decay, broken sidewalks and filthy streets; and contrasting their appearance with that of the corporation as I remember it, I felt as if I were visiting the ruins of an industry once clean and prosperous" (Robinson 1898:209).

## The Mill Complex

The construction of each of Lowell's mill complexes involved enormous earth-moving projects in which the landscape was altered dramatically to make way for the factories and their power systems as well as for housing. Archaeological testing at the Merrimack Mills complex to the north of the Boott Mills produced evidence of extensive land filling during mill construction. Like the Boott complex, the Merrimack was built on a "poorly drained flood terrace" (Gorman et al. 1985:12) which had to be modified for mill and canal construction. The Merrimack property was extensively filled to level the land surface; mill-period features were constructed through the fill and, in some cases, through both the fill and the original buried land surface. Advance planning that incorporated construction of the mill complex, mill housing, and attendant facilities with large-scale landscape alteration is indicated by the fact that in some cases features such as foundations, drains, and privies were laid down before the deposition of fill (Gorman et al. 1985:44, 46, 48).

Lowell's landscape planners made a concerted effort to incorporate trees and grasses into the community. Figure 12.4, an 1850 illustration of the Boott mill yard, shows it covered with grass. In a later photograph the presence of trees, swaths of grass, and, curiously, what appears to be an urn is documented for 1870. This section of the mill yard was developed later than the portion illustrated in the 1850 engraving. This use of natural elements in the mill yard was, it appears, an attempt on the part of the owners to temper the urban landscape. There seems little question that this kind of landscaping was in part a response to those in the United States who preferred small-scale mill villages in the countryside, the so-called Rhode Island plan, to large, urban industrial communities (the Waltham plan) like Lowell (e.g., Parks and Folsom 1982:xxiii-xxxiii).

Corporate building campaigns altered the landscape on a grand scale indeed. Construction of the mills in their carefully planned settings created the backdrop for the workings of industrial capitalism, a setting which was viewed as a mere facade by detractors who deplored what they saw as the exploitative greed and insincerity of Lowell's founding fathers. A contemporary observer described with cynicism the artful combination of orderly factories and housing with expanses of greenery. Thayer wrote: "This external appearance reminds me again, of a costly temple, the designer of which, after having completed the external gilding and beauty, at the expense of others, fortunately died; leaving the beautiful covering a fit shelter for wild beasts, and birds of prey, who there secured a home (Thayer 1845:15, quoted in Zonderman 1986:12).

The changing configuration of the Boott mill yard reflected changes in corporate policy as well as technological innovations. The four original mills, completed in 1842, were identical in design and were laid out around a spacious courtyard on a parcel of land between the Merrimack River and the Eastern Canal (Shepley et al. 1980:1-2, 6). The company's boardinghouses, south of the canal, were oriented at a right angle to the mills along Kirk, James, John, George, and Bridge streets (see figs. 12.1 and 12.5). Across French Street, a

BOOT CORPORATION.

Figure 12.4. An inset from the 1850 Sidney and Neff map of Lowell depicts the Boott Mill yard as an open court with grassy parade. (Courtesy of the Lowell Historical Society and the University of Lowell Special Collections)

block of tenements for overseers faced past the houses toward the mills. Despite the artificial creation of a community, however, workers "were purposefully divided by sex, by nationality, and by status" (Gross and Wright 1985:21; Stilgoe 1982:331-33). As data collected by Kathleen Bond demonstrate (Bond 1986, 1987), this segregation went beyond the external arrangement of workers' and supervisors' housing, extending to the residential makeup of individual boardinghouses and tenements. And here was a strange community indeed--an artificial neighborhood whose focal point was not the church or the town square but the industrial complex that was the reason for its existence.

The expansion of the mills over the course of the nineteenth century changed the original character and layout of the industrial complex. The mill yard became crowded as new mills were built and existing structures were joined by connectors. The view of the mills in the 1852 *Gleason's Pictorial* shows well-clad ladies and gentlemen strolling around the perimeter of carefully trimmed oval lawns circled by trees (fig. 12.6), while the Sidney and Neff 1850 view of the mill yard, facing west, shows a far less elaborate and stylish setting (see fig. 12.4). Despite an 1870s photograph showing vestiges of formal plantings in the mill yard, the parklike image of the industrial complex did not survive into the twentieth century, however, because the addition of new buildings continually encroached upon the open space of the mill yard (Langenbach 1981).

Figure 12.5. Looking northwest along the Eastern Canal in the 1920s. (Courtesy of the Lowell Historical Society and the University of Lowell Special Collections)

The original mill yard was an enclosed compound, bounded on three sides by water and on the fourth side by a wall or fence. Pedestrian access to the yard was across a bridge leading from John Street; two railroad bridges, one in Mill No. 6 and the other at the west end of the yard, were the only other openings. The first mill buildings formed two parallel rows with broad open spaces permitting views to the river, neighboring mills, and the company housing (Shepley et al. 1980:19-20). By the late 1840s, the yard began to take on the form of two enclosed courtyards as more mills were added; between the 1860s and 1880s, the mill yard was fully enclosed, and numerous subsidiary structures, such as hose houses and ramps, took up what had formerly been open space.

Technological innovations such as new forms of motive power contributed to the mill yard's changing character. The addition of steam engines to the power system between 1859 and 1873 prompted the need for boiler rooms with their attendant smokestacks and for coal storage buildings (Shepley et al. 1980:14, 17-18). The evolution of the transport system for moving cotton and coal into the mills and finished products out of them increasingly affected the appearance of the complex.

By 1850 two railroad spurs were brought in from the track running along Amory Street on the south side of the Eastern Canal. Introduction of new boxcars in the late nineteenth century resulted in enlargement of the coal pocket in Mill No. 6 so that it could house the

Figure 12.6. An illustration from an 1852 edition of *Gleason's Pictorial*. At this time the famed clock tower with its shuttle weathervane had not been built. (Courtesy of the Museum of American Textile History)

greater quantities of fuel needed for the larger cars and service them.  In the mid-twentieth century the mill yard, which for some time had been an unprepossessing expanse of bare dirt with unused machinery scattered about (cf. Shepley et al. 1980:fig. 22), was paved to permit truck access.

## The Boott Boardinghouses

The Boott property lay on a ledge which sloped steeply upward from the Eastern Canal to French Street, and seven of the eight Boott boardinghouses therefore were built in a stepped plan which gave them a tripartite appearance emphasized by their stepped rooflines (Clancey 1987a:17).  Archaeological testing and excavation at the site of the Boott Mills boardinghouses revealed a pattern of extensive landfilling similar to that found at the Merrimack Mills site by Gorman et al. (1985).  The evidence for this is at the boardinghouse site; the substratum into which boardinghouse-related features were placed is not sterile subsoil (Beaudry 1987b:104).

The architecture of the Boott boardinghouses, apart from their stepped construction, was in most respects quite similar to that of the mills (Clancey 1987a).  Each of the eight blocks erected contained four boardinghouses flanked at either end by two tenements; the tenements were intended to house skilled workers and supervisory personnel and their families.  Mill workers, many of them single women, lived in the boardinghouses. Although concerns for naturalizing the urban environment were incorporated into the setting for the Boott Mills workers' housing--for instance, company boardinghouses were situated on tree-lined streets, and in some cases, ivy softened the starkness of their brick exteriors--the large courtyards afforded the mills were not present among the housing. Yards that Miles (1846:23) described as suitable were quite small considering the number of individuals who resided in each boardinghouse unit. Precise use of the yards remains problematic.

Each boardinghouse and each rear tenement had an enclosed yard or backlot with a woodshed for storage of wood, coal, and garbage awaiting collection (Bond 1987:43); the woodshed also served to enclose the privy. The small yards, two of which were fully exposed and sampled during the archaeological project (fig. 12.7), were used chiefly for service purposes such as laundering and drying clothes. Excavations revealed a variety of drainage features as well. There is little evidence that these spaces were in any way intended for worker recreation.

Figure 12.7. An overhead view of the excavations behind Boott unit 48, which was an end unit for supervisory personnel. View is to the south. (Photograph by Paul Giblin)

The archaeological and archaeobotanical evidence suggests that the yards may also have served in some measure as food preparation areas. Palynological evidence of European cereal grains, for example, indicates their presence during the occupation as either food waste or in night soil (Mrozowski and Kelso 1987:147). Seeds of both blackberry (*Rubus* spp.) and grape (*Vitis* spp.) also indicate that local fruits were incorporated into the diet, at least on a seasonal basis. It is also possible that some form of *Rubus* was actively growing in the boardinghouse yards, although their tenacity as a colonizer would have made them a difficult plant to eliminate once established, so that if this were the case, more seeds should have been found.

The Boott Corporation's changing priorities are revealed by conversion of the mill housing block along Kirk Street, beginning between 1879 and 1881, for construction of a cotton storehouse. This permitted the rebuilding of the southwest corner of the mill yard with new productive facilities (Shepley et al. 1980:16). By 1900 two more cotton storehouses were added, one of which was made possible through the remodeling of a second boardinghouse block (see Clancey 1987a; Shepley et al. 1980:18); this warehouse was recently restored to its original appearance as a boardinghouse by the Lowell Historic Preservation Commission.

The archaeobotanical analyses of samples collected during the first phase of boardinghouse investigations were exploratory in nature. However, they have produced some results that are relevant to the question of landscape changes over time. Kelso's palynological analysis, for example, suggests that the boardinghouse yards may well have contained primarily grasses at the start (Mrozowski and Kelso 1987). A general trend from grasses to weeds shows up in the pollen record. The loss of grasses to Chenopodiaceae and Compositae indicates that the yards were heavily trafficked and often disturbed. Seeds of both families were also recovered, although in very small numbers.

One plant well represented by macrofossil remains is *Solanum* spp. (nightshade). Sixty-two *Solanum* seeds were recovered from a water-management feature (a terminal box for a downspout or drain collecting roof runoff). The presence of these seeds is strong evidence that some form of nightshade, either bittersweet (*Solanum dulcamara*) or black nightshade (*S. nigrum*), was growing. The former is commonly found as a creeper on fences and exterior building walls. Thus it would seem that members of the nightshade family were a common element of the urban landscape in Lowell.

Although the boardinghouse facades were symmetrical in design, both documentary sources and archaeological evidence reveal a degree of variability among units. The exposed yards of the two units investigated archaeologically presented different pictures of land use. The end unit (a supervisor's tenement), for example, contained a planting hole abutting the rear wall of the boardinghouse. Large post holes were also discovered; presumably these held the posts for the gate that permitted access into the rear yard from the street. The yard of this end unit also appeared to be less disturbed than that of the central unit, indicating less intensive land use. To date, these differences are based on field observations; once the contextual analyses are completed, it should be possible to address these issues in greater detail.

By 1906 the Boott had divested itself of its remaining housing. This was in response to a number of factors, including decreases in employment in the early twentieth century. The growth of the family labor system may have had an effect upon the millowners' willingness to provide housing for its workers, although the preponderance of people living in Boott housing well into the twentieth century were single individuals. The employment figures for the Boott indicate that the work force remained overwhelmingly female throughout its history, a factor shown in the demographic profile of the boardinghouses even after they ceased to house Yankee mill girls in large numbers. Families for the most part chose to live elsewhere, for instance, in the neighborhoods that grew up as immigrants of various ethnic backgrounds elected to find their own housing among others of their kind

(Kenngott 1912). Understandably, the boardinghouses did not appeal to families; Blanche Pelletier Graham, a Boott boardinghouse resident as a child, revealed in interviews with Kathleen Bond her lack of playmates and the fact that very few children lived in these houses (Bond 1986, 1987).

## The Kirk Street Agents' House

The duplex built under the direction of the Massachusetts Corporation by 1845 as the home for the agents of both the Boott and the Massachusetts was in striking contrast to the simple, industrially inspired style of the rest of the mill housing (fig. 12.8). Facing on Kirk Street with its back to the overseers' block, the Agents' House was constructed in the urban vernacular style typical of upper-middle-class town houses then being built in Boston's South End and possessed impressive wood-paneled double doors. It was raised above the other structures and above the street on an artificial terrace faced with cut granite blocks. The yard was completely enclosed, the front area by an imposing wrought-iron fence set into the top course of revetment stones. Thus while the corporations achieved their goal of integrating supervisory personnel and the workers in a planned neighborhood in the vicinity of the mill, the Agents' House stood as a material symbol of the stratification of the mill work force (Coolidge 1942; Robbins 1979; see also Beaudry and Mrozowski 1987b).

Figure 12.8. The Kirk Street Agents' House. Excavations were conducted in the rear yard of the right-hand portion of the duplex. View is to the east. (Photograph by Edward L. Bell)

The contrast between agents' and workers' housing extended beyond structures to the landscape. The elevation of the Agents' House on an artificially raised terrace above street level was a conscious effort which served as a symbolic expression of the agents' position in the mill operation's hierarchy. What the archaeological investigations revealed was that these efforts did not extend to the entire yard area. There was a striking difference in the way the rear yard was utilized as compared with use of the front and side yards. This contrast is significant for two reasons. First, it represents an attempt to distance the Agents' House materially from the houses of the workers only a few feet away. Second, the difference between the front and side and rear yards at the Agents' House itself is indicative of a household in transition; it was captured between an era in which urban yards served utilitarian needs and one when they functioned solely as an ornamental extension of the dwelling.

The initial focus of the investigations at the Agents' House was the rear yard. Extensive subsurface excavation revealed a rich archaeological record comprised of relatively thin cultural layers, some of which contained extensive deposits of cultural material. The assemblage consists primarily of domestic refuse including ceramics, glassware, cutlery, and faunal remains along with other nonfood items. These include artifacts such as a thimble, a woman's circular compact, beads, comb fragments, toys, buttons, and oil lamp chimney fragments (Rodenhiser and Dutton 1987:73-95). The faunal assemblage contains some head and foot elements, which Landon (1987:139) suggests indicate that "some level of on-site preparation of larger portions of the carcass was taking place."

Initially, it was thought that the presence of such extensive deposits of domestic refuse might represent debris associated with a garden. This interpretation was not supported by the contextual analysis, however, which was based in part on comparisons with known gardens that had been examined ethnographically (Mrozowski 1987). Although the seeds of known garden weeds were discovered, no such evidence of cultigens was found (Kelso, Mrozowski, and Fisher 1987:121). With this possibility eliminated or at least unsupported, the analysis focused more heavily on taphonomic issues and the reconstruction of the landscape over time.

The contextual analysis provided a chronicle of the changing face of the Agents' House yard. It traced the development of the landscape from the period before construction, when the area was still agricultural land, apparently pasture, to the most recent twentieth-century activities (Kelso, Mrozowski, and Fisher 1987). Although the results generated from the analysis of pollen, opal phytoliths, and plant macrofossils fail to mirror one another in every instance, some general trends were observed. During the period when the dwelling served as a household for the mill agents, the yard alternated between times when it was dominated by grasses and those when weeds predominated. There also seems to be some correlation between depositional processes and periods of household transition. This correlation serves to clarify the link between archaeological formation processes and landscape development (Kelso, Mrozowski, and Fisher 1987:127). Periods of more gradual deposition were followed by events of more rapid accumulation that seem to be associated with punctuated human actions (Beaudry and Mrozowski 1987b:148-49).

Although weedy intervals are discernible in the rear yard of the Agents' House, the evidence indicates a general trend in the direction of grasses. The periods when weeds were most prominent appear to be associated with the earliest households, a time when the evidence suggests the yard was heavily trafficked and employed for utilitarian purposes

(Kelso, Mrozowski, and Fisher 1987:122, 129; Rodenhiser and Dutton 1987:95). In time, however, this space was sodded with grasses and conformed much more closely with the adjoining side and front yards. The precise dating of this change is difficult to determine, but the direction of the trend from weeds to grasses is clearly visible and is a trend opposite to that tentatively identified for the boardinghouse backlots.

The picture of the rear yard's development gleaned from the contextual analysis suggests an image quite different from that of either the front or the side yards of the Agents' House. Documents relating to the construction of the building note the use of loam in the specifications (Robbins 1979). Just how much was used is unknown; it was possible, however, to determine where the loam was placed on the site. Investigations of the side and front yards using a soil auger made it possible to determine the extent of landscaping carried out at the Agents' House (Beaudry and Mrozowski 1987b:66–71). The stratigraphy of the side and front yards was virtually identical. In both areas a thick, 25- to 40-centimeter layer of dark brown sandy loam was found overlying a bed of white sand possibly glacial in origin. This layer of loam was used to raise the level of the Agents' House while at the same time it provided a rich bed for the grasses that were always present in these yard areas.

The front and side yards, then, functioned in a very different manner from the rear yard of the Agents' House for at least part of its history. Unlike the utilitarian rear yard, the front and side yards served only as ornamental extensions of the facade of the building. As such, the landscape was a conscious expression of social status and middle-class ideals. The home was not a work area. In fact, the separation of domestic and work space was one of the hallmarks of the emerging middle-class suburbs of cities like Boston (Mrozowski 1985:57–58). In the case of the Agents' House, however, it would appear that the household was still in transition. Despite the latest in domestic technology, including indoor plumbing and running water in the kitchen (Clancey 1987b), the rear yard still functioned as a work area. Although the front and side yards reflected a modern use of space, the rear yard, like a privy in the city, was a "relic of a by-gone age" (Bell 1987:62).

An interesting sidelight to the issue of yard treatment at the Agents' House involves the fencing mentioned in the original construction accounts. In his discussion of the Agents' House, Robbins (1979) notes that a total of 594 feet of wooden fencing was listed in the Massachusetts Corporation's record of construction. If fencing was used along the side yards and at the back of the rear yards, this would account for approximately 450 feet of the total. If an additional fence was employed to divide the two rear yards of the duplex, this would account for an additional 100 feet. This leaves approximately 44 feet of fencing unaccounted for. Robbins (1979) suggests that this may have been used to enclose a garden or a stable. Either of these seems plausible, although there is no evidence of a stable being constructed at the outset. Another possibility is that the fencing was used to separate the side and rear yards. If gates were included, the 44 feet of fencing would have been enough for this purpose.

The segregation of the two spaces could have had symbolic significance. Given the transitional nature of the household, it is possible that a conscious effort was made to separate public and private space. In this case, a private rear yard used for service purposes would have been shielded from view and physically separated from the public facade that included the ornamental front and side yards. Even if we discount the possibility of fencing, the weight of the evidence suggests that some sort of boundary, either physical or conceptual, existed between the two spaces.

## Conclusions

Archaeologists interested in landscape studies are involved in a fairly unique pursuit because they seek the interface between society and nature. Often the connection between ideology and the landscape is elusive; in nineteenth-century Lowell, however, it was clear and undeniable. The urban landscape of Lowell was not a mere reflection of the ideology it embodied, it was its direct expression. Class differences between workers and overseers were not masked; rather, they were accentuated by the spatial dynamics of the built environment. It is equally important to understand the ideology governing the creation of communities like Lowell as it is to understand the ideology that the resulting landscape helped to perpetuate. Lowell was meant to make a statement and, as Nathan Appleton said in 1858, to serve as a machine into which workers fit neatly and unquestioningly as gears or cogs; the setting impressed and often cowed them just as it impressed uninvolved observers. Leone notes: "Ideology takes social relations and makes them appear to be resident in nature or history, which makes them apparently inevitable. So that the way space is divided and described, including the way architecture, alignments, and street plans are made to abide by astronomical rules, or the way gardens, paths, rows of trees, and vistas make a part of the earth's surface appear to be trained and under the management of individuals or classes with certain ability or learning, is ideology" (1984:26).

Besides their ideological content, landscapes are often the result of human actions that are important for us to decipher in terms of site formation processes and household subsistence, for example. Very often there is a direct link between the formation of the archaeological record and the shaping or neglect of the landscape. In Lowell, the landscape chronicles an experiment whose health can be measured by how carefully that landscape was maintained. In this case, the record reveals a short life for the experiment. The decay of the boardinghouses and of the entire boardinghouse system mirrored the decline of Lowell as an industrial center. The Agents' House was better maintained than the workers' housing from the outset and even into the decline, but in the end even it was subject to the ravages of urban blight and economic demise. The deterioration of the experiment is clearly visible in the archaeological record of the landscape.

## Acknowledgments

The interdisciplinary study of the Lowell Boott Mills is being performed under a cooperative agreement between the North Atlantic Regional Office of the National Park Service and Boston University's Center for Archaeological Studies. Principals for the project are Dr. Stephen A. Mrozowski of the University of Massachusetts at Boston, Supervisory Archaeologist for NPS, and Dr. Mary C. Beaudry, who serve as Research Directors for the project; Dr. Ricardo J. Elia, Boston University Co-Principal Investigator with Beaudry, is Project Manager. Other project personnel include Dr. Richard Candee of Boston University, Coordinator for Architectural Research, Thomas Mahlstedt, Consultant on Boott mill yard archaeology, Dr. Gerald K. Kelso (NPS), Palynologist, Donald G. Jones, Edward L. Bell, and Nancy S. Seasholes (Boston University), Project Archaeologists, and Research Assistants Edward L. Bell, Kathleen H. Bond, David Dutton, William Fisher, Grace Ziesing, Lauren

Cook, and Gregory K. Clancey, all of Boston University. David B. Landon is Project Zooarchaeologist, and Mrozowski, in addition to his role as Supervisory Archaeologist, is serving as Project Archaeobotanist. The authors wish to thank Dr. William Kelso for encouraging them to prepare a chapter for inclusion in this volume.

This report was accomplished with assistance from the National Park Service, U.S. Department of the Interior. The statements, findings, conclusions, recommendations, and other data in this report are solely those of the authors and do not necessarily reflect the views of the U.S. Department of the Interior, National Park Service.

## References Cited

Appleton, N. 1858. *Introduction of the power loom and the origin of Lowell.* Lowell: B. H. Penhallow.

Beaudry, M. C. 1987a. The Boott Mills Corporation mill yard and housing: Material expressions of industrial capitalism. In Beaudry and Mrozowski 1987a, pp. 9-14.

----. 1987b. Archeological testing at the proposed Lowell Boarding House Park site. In Beaudry and S.A. Mrozowski 1987a, pp. 69-114.

----. and S. A. Mrozowski (editors). 1987a. *Life at the boardinghouses: A preliminary report.* In Interdisciplinary investigations of the Boott Mills, Lowell, Massachusetts. Vol. 1. Cultural Resources Management Series 18. Boston: National Park Service, North Atlantic Regional Office.

----. and ----. 1987b. *The Kirk Street Agents' House.* In Interdisciplinary investigations of the Boott Mills, Lowell, Massachusetts. Vol 2. Cultural Resources Management Series 19. Boston: National Park Service, North Atlantic Regional Office.

Bell, E. L. 1987. A preliminary report on health, hygiene, and sanitation at the Boott Mills boardinghouses: An historical and archeological perspective. In Beaudry and Mrozowski 1987a, pp. 57-68.

Bender, T. 1975. *Toward an urban vision: Ideas and institutions in nineteenth-century America.* Baltimore: Johns Hopkins University Press.

Bond, K. H. 1986. Transcripts of interviews with Blanche P. Graham. Manuscript. Boston: Center for Archaeological Studies, Boston University.

----. 1987. A preliminary report on the demography of the Boott Mills housing units #33-48, 1838-1942. In Beaudry and Mrozowski 1987a, pp. 35-56.

Candee, R. M. 1982. New towns of the early New England textile industry. In *Perspectives in vernacular architecture*, ed. C. Wells, pp. 31-50. Annapolis: Vernacular Architecture Forum.

----. 1985. Architecture and corporate planning in the early Waltham system. In *Essays from the Lowell Conference on Industrial History 1982 and 1983*, ed. R. Weible, pp. 17-43. North Andover: Museum of American Textile History.

Clancey, G. K. 1987a. The Boott Mills boardinghouses and adjacent structures: The evidence of maps and photographs. In Beaudry and Mrozowski 1987a, pp. 15-34.

----. 1987b. An architectural study of the Kirk Street Agents' House. In Beaudry and Mrozowski 1987b, pp. 29-42.

Coolidge, J. 1942. *Mill and mansion: A study of architecture and society in Lowell, Massachusetts, 1820-1865*. New York: Columbia University Press.

Cosgrove, D. E. 1984. *Social formation and symbolic landscape*. Totowa, N.J.: Barnes and Noble Books.

Gorman, F. J. E., J. Cheney, M. B. Folsom, and G. T. Laden. 1985. Intensive archaeological survey of Post Office Square Garage, Lowell, Massachusetts. Manuscript. Boston: Environmental Archaeology Group.

Greenwood, R. E. 1986. Zachariah Allen and the architecture of industrial paternalism. Manuscript. Providence: Rhode Island Historical Society.

Gross, L. F., and R. Wright. 1985. Historic structure report--history portion: Building 6; the Counting House; the adjacent courtyard; and the facades of buildings 1 and 2. Boott Mill Complex, Lowell National Historical Park, Lowell, Massachusetts. Manuscript. Denver: National Park Service, Denver Service Center.

Harvey, D. 1976. Labor, capital, and class struggle around the built environment in advanced capitalist societies. *Politics and Society* 6(3):265-95.

Hodder, I. 1987. The contribution of the long term. In *Archaeology as long-term history*, ed. I. Hodder, pp. 1-8. Cambridge: Cambridge University Press.

Jones, M., and G. Dimbleby (editors). 1981. *The environment of man: The Iron Age to the Anglo-Saxon period*. British Archaeological Reports British Series 87. Oxford.

Kelso, G. K., S. A. Mrozowski, and W. F. Fisher. 1987. Contextual archeology at the Kirk Street Agents' House. In Beaudry and Mrozowski 1987b, pp. 97-130.

Kelso, W. M.. 1984. Landscape archaeology: A key to Virginia's cultivated past. In *British and American gardens in the eighteenth century: Eighteen illustrated essays on garden history*, ed. R. P. Maccubbin and P. Martin, pp. 159-69. Williamsburg: Colonial Williamsburg Foundation.

Kenngott, G. F. 1912. *The record of a city: A social survey of Lowell, Massachusetts*. New York: MacMillan and Company.

Landon, D. B. 1987. Zooarchaeological remains from the Kirk Street Agents' House. In Beaudry and Mrozowski 1987b, pp. 131-42.

Langenbach, R. 1981. From building to architecture: The emergence of Victorian Lowell. *Harvard Architectural Review* 2:90-105.

Larcom, L. 1889. *A New England girlhood: Outlined from memory*. Rept. 1986. Boston: Northeastern University Press.

Leone, M. P. 1984. Interpreting ideology in historical archaeology: Using the rules of perspective in the William Paca Garden in Annapolis, Maryland. In *Ideology, power, and prehistory*, ed. D. Miller and G. Tilley, pp. 25-35. New York: Cambridge University Press.

Marx, L. 1964. *The machine in the garden: Technology and the pastoral ideal in America*. New York: Oxford University Press.

Miles, H. A. 1846. *Lowell, as it was, and as it is*. Rept. 1972. New York: Arno Press.

Mrozowski, S. A. 1985. Boston's archaeological legacy: The city's planning and policy document. Boston: Boston Landmarks Commission.

----. 1987. The ethnoarchaeology of urban gardening. Ph.D. dissertation, Department of Anthropology, Brown University.

----., and G. K. Kelso. 1987. Palynology and archaeobotany of the proposed Lowell Boarding House Park site. In Beaudry and Mrozowski 1987a, pp. 139-52.

Parker, B. 1985. *Kirk Boott: Master spirit of early Lowell.* Lowell: Landmark Printing Company.

Parks, R., and M. Folsom. 1982. Introduction. In *The New England mill village, 1790-1860*, ed. G. Kulik, pp. xxiii-xxxiii. Cambridge: MIT Press.

Praetzellis, M., and A. Praetzellis. 1989. "Utility and beauty should be one": The landscape of Jack London's ranch of good intentions. *Historical Archaeology* 23(1):33-44.

Rapaport, A. 1982. *The meaning of the built environment: A nonverbal communication approach.* Beverly Hills, Calif.: Sage Publications.

Robbins, J. 1979. Historic structure report, architectural data: Boott Cotton Mills and Massachusetts Cotton Mills Agents Houses, 67 and 63 Kirk Street, Lowell National Historical Park, Lowell, Massachusetts (draft). Manuscript. Denver: National Park Service, Denver Service Center.

Robinson, H. H. 1898. *Loom and spindle.* Boston: Thomas V. Cromwell & Company.

Rodenhiser, L. B., and D. H. Dutton. 1987. Material culture from the Kirk Street Agents' House. In Beaudry and Mrozowski 1987b, pp. 73-96.

Rubertone, P. E. 1984. Historical landscapes: Archaeology of place and space. *Man in the Northeast* 31:123-38.

Schoenwetter, J. 1981. Prologue to a contextual archaeology. *Journal of Archaeological Research* 8:367-79.

Scranton, P. 1984. Varieties of paternalism: Industrial structures and the social relations of production in American textiles. *American Quarterly* 36(2):235-257.

Shepley, Bulfinch, Richardson, and Abbott. 1980. Lowell National Historical Park and Preservation District cultural resources inventory: Inventory forms and research reports. Manuscript. Denver: National Park Service, Denver Service Center.

Stilgoe, J. R. 1982. *Common landscape of America, 1580 to 1845.* New Haven: Yale University Press.

Thayer, J. Q. A. 1845. *Review of the report of the special committee of the legislature of the Commonwealth of Massachusetts on the petition relating to hours of labor.* Boston: J. N. Bang.

Zonderman, D. A. 1986. The quest for the middle ground: Factory operatives and the concept of community in antebellum New England. Paper presented at the annual meeting of the American Historical Association, Chicago.

*III. Ancient Gardens and Landscapes*

# 13

# TOWN AND COUNTRY GARDENS AT POMPEII AND OTHER VESUVIAN SITES

## Wilhelmina F. Jashemski

The eruption of Vesuvius in A.D. 79, which tragically destroyed the prosperous Campanian towns of Pompeii and Herculaneum and the many villas in the surrounding countryside, preserved detailed information about ancient Roman gardens and cultivated land that can be known from no other sites. Elsewhere in the Roman Empire fragmentary remains have survived by chance, but in the area destroyed by Vesuvius living cities and thriving country villas are preserved just as they were at the moment of destruction. It is true that all Italy was justly famous for its gardens. The ancient poet Lucretius (*De rerum natura* 5.1278) extolled the beauty of the whole land and praised the way men had decked it out by planting it here and there. Varro, in his agricultural manual (*De re rustica* 1.2.6), described Italy as a place where every useful product not only grows but grows to perfection. But the gardens of the Vesuvian area were especially renowned. Campania, in which the sites destroyed by Vesuvius were located, was particularly blessed. The ancient writers waxed eloquently in describing this plain. The elder Pliny, who knew the area well (he lost his life while trying to rescue friends during the A.D. 79 eruption), said that Campania surpasses all the lands of the world (*Naturalis historia* 18.111), a sentiment echoed by Florus (*Epitome* 1.16.3) who called it "the fairest of all regions, not only in Italy, but the whole world." Campania, which owes its fertility to Vesuvius, is so fertile that in antiquity it bore four crops a year, and it still does today.

When Vesuvius erupted, Pompeii was covered with lapilli (pumice about the size of peach pits) and ashes to a depth of 4 to 6 meters. Villas that were more distant from Vesuvius did not have so deep a covering. Herculaneum, however, was covered to a depth of 12 to 20 or more meters; the nature of the fill makes it extremely difficult to excavate, and only four city blocks, along with parts of four or five others, have been uncovered. But at Pompeii, which is much easier to excavate, approximately three-quarters of the city has been uncovered, and it is possible to get the feel of the entire city, to study its land use, the distribution and character of its places of business and homes, and to experience the prominent role of the garden in the life of the people (fig. 13.1). The garden was intimately related to almost every aspect of life--to architecture, both public and private, to city planning, horticulture, religion, sculpture, painting, aesthetic expression, economics, work, and recreation (Jashemski 1979, in press).

Pompeii was a city of gardens. Gardens were connected with public places, such as temples, theaters, palaestras, and baths, and in restaurants, inns and hotels, and schools

(Jashemski 1979, in press).  But it is the gardens connected with homes that are discussed in this chapter.  The garden was the heart of the house, whether large or small (Jashemski 1979). An elegant house might have as many as three or four large peristyle gardens.  The Pompeians placed their gardens in the middle of their house, instead of putting their house in the middle of their gardens as we do.  Even the poor, if at all possible, made space in their modest homes for tiny gardens, some no larger than a professor's desk.  The desire for a bit of green, a few herbs, and flowers appears to have been an intrinsic part of the Roman character.  It was the same instinct that prompted shopkeepers who lived in rooms above their shops to grow a few vines on their balconies to provide an arbor of shade; vine-covered pergolas were not a monopoly of the wealthy.  A few of the more fortunate ones were able to cut windows in their crowded quarters in order to enjoy the view to a neighbor's spacious garden.

Figure 13.1.  Vesuvius dominates the Campanian plain, the ancient walled city of Pompeii in the foreground, and the modern cities of Boscoreale and Boscotrecase on the lower slopes of Vesuvius.  (Photograph courtesy of Pompeii Tourist Bureau)

We find that these ancient inhabitants frequently painted the picture of a garden on their garden walls to make a small garden appear larger (Jashemski, 1979, in press).  Behind a painted fence, which separated the actual garden from the painted garden, could be pictured fountains, statues, and many birds for which there might not have been room in the actual garden.  These paintings are a valuable source of information about ancient plants and birds.

Through the years my husband photographed all the plant material in these paintings. Dr. Frederick G. Meyer, research botanist in charge of the Herbarium at the United States National Arboretum, Washington, D.C., has been working with me for years to identify these plants and compare them with the plants that grow in the area today. Dr. George Watson, formerly chairman of the Department of Zoology at the Smithsonian Institution, has been identifying the birds in the paintings. Every plant and bird is one that would have been known in the ancient gardens.

Many gardens had huge paintings of almost life-size animals that are rather startling if come upon unaware. Great estates on which wild animals roamed were owned by wealthy Romans in both Italy and the provinces. What great personal wealth made possible for a citizen in the countryside, the modest inhabitant of a town such as Herculaneum or Pompeii could suggest through the illusion of the painter's brush.

Hundreds of houses and gardens have been excavated at Pompeii and Herculaneum (Jashemski, in press). The gardens in some of the better-known houses have been replanted, and the visitor unconsciously assumes that these are accurate replicas of the ancient gardens. Unfortunately, however, there is little evidence for the way in which these gardens were planted originally. Only careful excavation will yield this information.

If an undisturbed site is carefully excavated, ancient soil contours can be found perfectly preserved, and the planting pattern is clearly visible. When the trees and plants growing at the time of the eruption died, their roots decayed and left cavities that were gradually filled with the volcanic material that covered the site. The first step in excavation is the removal of the lapilli until the level of the soil in A.D. 79 is reached and the lapilli-filled cavities are visible. The cavities are emptied with special long-handled tools, reinforced with heavy wire, and filled with cement. After three or more days the soil is removed from around the cast, and the shape of the root is revealed (Jashemski 1979:23, fig. 31). We sometimes find carbonized or partially preserved plant material and ancient pollen. Unfortunately, few excavators have been interested in such contours, root cavities, and plant remains. Precious evidence that could have been recovered only at the time of excavation has been irretrievably lost.

It was therefore unexpected good fortune when, during the excavation of the House of Polybius (IX.xiii.1-3),[1] which was the chief archaeological work at Pompeii of the Superintendency of Naples and Caserta, it became apparent that the house had a peristyle garden. The first peristyle garden to be discovered in over fifteen years, it afforded a rare opportunity to apply for the first time in such a garden the techniques that we had developed for recovering evidence about ancient plantings. Garden archaeology is a very complex discipline and requires the close cooperation of many specialists, such as soil experts, palynologists, botanists, microbiologists, bacteriologists, fungi specialists, charcoal experts, ornithologists, mammalogists, ichthyologists, and geologists. All of these specialists, and many more, have cooperated closely with me in my work. This venerable Samnite house on the Via dell' Abbondanza is one of the oldest and most interesting in the city. The garden was enclosed by a portico on the north, east, and south. Under the east portico is a large cistern, which stored the water collected carefully from the roof during the rainy season. When water from the cistern was needed, a bucket on a rope was lowered through a hole in the floor. For protection a puteal (a hollow stone or terra-cotta cylinder about 60 centimeters high) was placed over the hole. This cistern furnished the entire water supply for the house and garden until the time of the eruption. The owners had not availed themselves of the more plentiful water made possible by the introduction of the aqueduct during the time of Augustus (27 B.C. to A.D. 14).

It was with great interest that I began the excavation of this garden in 1973 (Jashemski 1979:25-30, figs. 33-43). Excitement grew as we removed the lapilli down to the A.D. 79 level and found a large tree-root cavity, then another and another until there were five large trees in all (fig. 13.2). This was completely unexpected, for the replanted gardens in the excavations had all been restored with low, formal, Renaissance-style plantings, and it was commonly assumed that this was the typical peristyle garden in antiquity. But there were still other trees in this small garden. As we removed the lapilli from near the west wall of the garden, we found strange soil formations that had the appearance of a large sombrero. When I examined them, I found a small root cavity in the center of the heaped-up soil; this was surrounded by a water channel (the brim of the sombrero). It was obvious that plants in these formations were small and that provision had been made for them to get considerable water. When we emptied the lapilli from the eight root cavities in these formations, we found in two of them terra-cotta fragments which I recognized as coming from the unusual pots with four holes (one in the bottom and three on the sides) which we had found the previous year along the walls in the large garden of the House of the Ship *Europa* (I.xv.3) (Jashemski 1979:238-41, figs. 350-51). In 1978 when we removed the soil surrounding the casts that we had made of these root cavities, we found most of the pieces of a complete pot in the soil around one cast, as well as a few fragments in the soil around two other casts.

As we removed the final layer of lapilli in the center part of the garden, lying in a southeast-northeast position were two strange marks that, when completely exposed, were clearly the outline of a ladder, with faintly visible rungs. The ladder was exceptionally long and narrow (8 meters long, .5 meters wide at the bottom, .3 meters at the top). The ladder was shaped so as to fit into fruit trees that were tall and full of dense branches, and exactly the same size as the light wooden ladders used today in the area to pick cherries and pears.

Would it be possible to identify the plantings in this garden? Dr. Carlo Fideghelli, of the Istituto Sperimentale per la Frutticoltura, Ministerio dell' Agricoltura at Rome, who has made a study of the shape of modern tree roots in the area, examined the tree-root cavities and casts. He believed that the large tree root in the northwest corner of the garden with shallow spreading lateral roots (the longest one at ground level visible for almost 1 meter) and a taproot 38 centimeters deep had the appearance of that of a fig tree. It was only much later that Dr. Frederick Meyer reported that he had identified the misshapen chunks of charcoal that we had found around this cavity; when he examined a cross section under magnification the many tiny seeds of a fig were clearly visible. The tree-root cavity in the southeast corner of the garden also had the appearance of that of a fig. These trees would have been thirty to thirty-five years old. It is perhaps significant that neither had their branches propped. Fig trees are never propped. The tree-root cavity in the northeast corner of the garden had a very different shape, with a taproot at least 52 centimeters deep and deep lateral roots. It appeared to be the cavity of the root of a fruit tree, perhaps of a cherry or a pear. The tree-root cavity on the middle of the west side also appeared to be that of a cherry or a pear tree. The presence of either of these trees would explain the presence of the tall, slender ladder. The cavity on the south side of the garden had the appearance of an olive tree. When Professor G. W. Dimbleby, of the Institute of Archaeology of the University of London, analyzed soil samples taken from this garden, he found olive pollen present and also a small amount of filbert pollen. Earlier when we had found evidence of the olive in the gardens

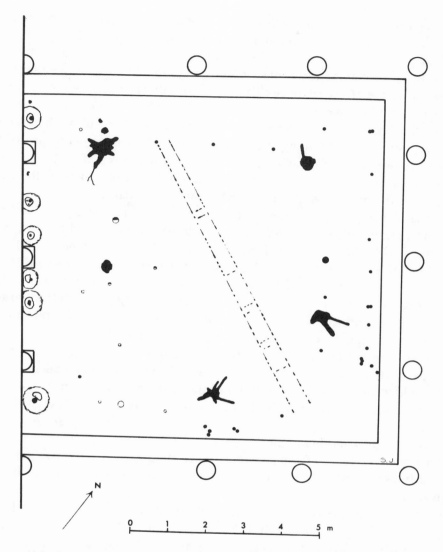

Figure 13.2. Plan of the peristyle garden in the House of Polybius; roots are indicated in black, stakes by circles. (Courtesy of Soprintendenza alle Antichità della Campania-Napoli; garden details by Stanley Jashemski)

that we were excavating we were greatly surprised, for the olive is rarely found at Pompeii today. We had by this time, however, become accustomed to finding both the carbonized fruit and plentiful olive pollen.

When Dr. Fideghelli examined the cavities and casts of the small tree roots along the west wall, he believed that they had the appearance of lemon tree roots. Pliny speaks of the citron trees that were imported in "earthenware pots provided with breathing holes for the roots" (*Naturalis historia* 12.16). This is a good description of our pots. The many nail holes in the wall above the roots indicated that the trees had been espaliered. Professor Frank Brown, then director of the American Academy in Rome when he visited our excavations, suggested that the trees could well have been lemons, a relative of the citron. Lemons fascinated the ancient Pompeians and are portrayed in numerous wall paintings. Lemons are espaliered on garden walls in the Mediterranean today; in the Pompeii area they are started in pots, and if possible, they are planted along the walls for protection.

The five large trees in this garden would have almost completely shaded the small garden. The trees were evidently pruned high enough to allow planting underneath, at least along the edges. Some of the small cavities in the middle of the garden were probably those of young trees and others were clearly those of stakes, which would have been used to prop limbs heavy with fruit or nuts. The small root cavities in a row along the east edge of the garden and scattered cavities along the south edge of the garden were probably those of shrubs. We were reminded of the myrtle bushes and ivy mounds pictured so often at the base of garden walls, as if to suggest a continuation of the actual plantings of the garden. This would have been the only aspect of this garden that was ornamental.

The dense planting found in the small garden of Polybius suggested that the soil must have been exceptionally fertile, and the soil studies made by John Foss, professor of agronomy at the University of Maryland (now head of the Department of Plant and Soil Science at the University of Tennessee), showed that this was indeed so. His tests showed that in addition to the great fertility and the well-drained condition of the soil, which the ancients had observed, the soil had another important quality. It contained large quantities of minute pieces of pumice, which because of its porous nature was able to retain large amounts of moisture and make it available (see Jashemski 1979:254-56).

Our discoveries in the garden of Polybius raised certain questions concerning the planting of peristyle gardens and the extent to which trees may have been used, especially because of the low formal plantings in the restored gardens. A thorough search through all of the reports showed that root cavities had been mentioned in only a few gardens, and some of these were not peristyle gardens. Trees were mentioned in four peristyles gardens, informal plantings in several (Jashemski 1979:30). It became important to see if additional information could be salvaged from previously excavated gardens. Even in gardens that have been previously excavated I have been able to find evidence of ancient roots, if modern roots have not been too destructive.

I examined all the peristyle gardens that had been uncovered in Regions I and II during the last period of extensive excavation (1951-61), for these had been exposed for a shorter time to the ravages of weeds and weather. In seven of these we were able to find root cavities (Jashemski 1979:31-32). In all but one the plantings were of a very informal nature. In a small house (I.xii.11) we found a little garden enclosed by a portico on three sides, with a huge animal painting on the rear wall, and a formal planting pattern. It had obviously been planted with small shrubs laid out in a very formal design. In the center of the garden was a small statue base framed by the plantings, which were undoubtedly evergreen, most probably clipped box (fig. 13.3). It was by now quite certain that many old houses at Pompeii continued their informal, old-fashioned plantings until the city was destroyed in A.D. 79. But there were also the more formal gardens.

The more generous use of water made possible by the introduction of the aqueduct greatly altered the appearance of the Pompeian garden. Before this time, plantings requiring a minimum amount of water had been used. Trees were a natural choice, for they needed water only until they had become well established. After the aqueduct was built, pools and fountains were introduced, adding great charm and variety to many gardens. The garden in the House of the Wedding of Alexander (VI. *insula occidentalis* 39-41), which I excavated some years later in 1983, was such a garden (fig. 13.4).

Figure 13.3.  Formal planting in small peristyle garden, House I.xii.11.  (Drawing by Luc Herbots)

The beautiful three-storied House of the Wedding of Alexander was one of the houses built over the city walls when they were no longer needed for protection after Pompeii was conquered by the Romans and became a Roman city in 80 B.C.  The small formal garden, stretched out at the rear of the lower level of this house, is of considerable importance, for it is the first formal garden to be scientifically excavated in an elegant house.  An impressive high, vaulted *diaeta* (garden room) decorated with the most beautiful garden paintings yet found in the Vesuvian area (Jashemski, in press) and with a strikingly patterned marble floor, opened out at the north end on the east side of the garden.  Most of the adjacent exedra, also decorated with garden paintings (poorly preserved), was occupied by a marble water triclinium, dominated by an apsed mosaic fountain, with water steps over which water fell and then rose in a jet in the middle of the couches; it eventually emptied into a pool, painted blue inside, at the east end of the garden.  Water rose from a jet from the low column in the middle of the pool and from the twenty-eight jets around the rim of the pool.  A column at each of the front corners of the pool apparently formed a pergola framing the pool.

The garden was laid out formally with passageways along the south, west, and north walls, leaving a rectangular area with slightly raised borders.  Within this rectangle, soil contours outlined an oval bed with mounded borders, which left triangular beds at each corner of the garden.  The largest root cavity in the garden (.40 by .44 meters at ground level, with a tap root .38 meters deep), apparently that of a small tree, was in the southwest

Figure 13.4.  Formal planting in the House of the Wedding of Alexander.  (Photograph by Sarah Gladden)

triangular bed.  The other three triangular beds each had a mounded area in the center, surrounded by a depression for water, which would suggest that something special had been planted there.

A total of 111 root cavities were found in the garden.  With the exception of the 28 root cavities found in the narrow, slightly raised bed at the rear of the garden on the west and another row of 16 along the north garden wall (probably those of vines), most were in the contoured borders of the oval within the rectangular beds.  These cavities were for the most part small.  This suggests a formal hedge, probably box.

The Pompeian garden was essentially a green garden.  The major plants were evergreen (e.g., box, myrtle, laurel, oleander, and ivy) and produced a beautiful garden the year around.  Amid the greenery would be a few flowers in season.  The rose, the lily, and the violet are the ones most often mentioned in the ancient authors.  Pictured in the garden painting in the *diaeta* are the rose, the flower of Venus, the tutelary goddess of Pompeii; madonna lilies; the opium poppy; the large white morning glory (*Calystegia sepium*); flowering oleanders and viburnum; the small white chamomile; the corn marigold (*Chrysanthemum segetum*); and small plants with four-petaled flowers that are difficult to identify.  Also pictured is the strawberry tree (*Arbutus unedo*) with its striking red-ribbed fruit.

Through the years as I have excavated at Pompeii, I have discovered that there were sizable plots within the city devoted to agriculture.  For over 200 years the large city block to the north of the amphitheater was known as the *Foro Boario*, or Cattle Market, a name given to it by the early excavators, who had uncovered only a small part of it and then partially recovered it. I believed that the area had been planted. After considerable initial discouragement we began to find root cavities almost exactly 4 Roman feet apart, in rows that were almost exactly 4 Roman feet apart. It became obvious that the Cattle Market was a vineyard. At each location there were two cavities, but they had been so badly damaged by modern roots that it was impossible to tell if both were those of vine roots or if one was that of a stake. It was only by excavating a part of the vineyard still covered by original lapilli that this could be determined. When this was done in the northeast part of the vineyard, we found that one cavity was always that of a root, the other that of stake. At the end of our last season in the vineyard, we had found 2,014 vine-root cavities, 2,014 stake cavities, and fifty-eight trees planted at intervals in the vineyard and at the edges. There were also two intersecting paths as recommended by the ancient authors (fig. 13.5). The large cavities along the paths were those of posts, clearly cut in half or quarter rounds, and of two vines. It was clear that the posts supported an arbored passageway similar to those in the Pompeii area today. The carefully cut posts in our vineyard were probably chestnut, recommended by Pliny because of its obstinate durability; the modern vintners also use them because, as they tell me, they are slow to decay. The ancient writers recommended planting both the willow and the poplar to furnish withes. Today the vines are still tied by the willow and the poplar.

We can be sure that our vintner did a thriving business serving guests from the amphitheater at the two masonry triclinia in the vineyard. These couches, on which the Romans reclined to eat, were made comfortable with pillows. Wine would be served. But we were to discover that more substantial food was on the menu. In the vineyard we found many bones, which we carefully collected. These were identified by Dr. Henry Setzer, formerly curator of mammals at the Smithsonian Institution. He pointed out that cleaver marks on the bones showed that they had been split for marrow, which was considered a food delicacy. The bones were debris from meals served at the triclinia. At last we know why the early excavators had labeled this site the Cattle Market. They had found bones and jumped to conclusions (Jashemski 1979:201-18, Figures 293-317).

Some years later (1980-84) we excavated a vineyard outside the city walls at the Villa Rustica found at Boscoreale in the locality of Villa Regina on the lower slopes of Vesuvius just 1 kilometer north of Pompeii. In the course of building a new apartment complex, eighty large cement pillars were put in the ground. In so doing they found evidence of an ancient country villa. Fortunately, the villa and the land surrounding it were declared a permanent archaeological zone. This is an especially important site, for it is the first time in the entire Vesuvian area that there has been an opportunity to excavate farmland attached to a villa. Our excavations showed that most of the area surrounding the villa was planted in a vineyard. We found approximately 300 cavities that appeared to be those of vines, 195 of stakes, and 46 that were too badly damaged to be identifiable. We also found 34 tree-root cavities. Most of these were in the vineyard. The carbonized olives and almonds that we found in the vineyard help to identify some of these trees; there were also carbonized grape seeds. This vineyard was very different from the formally planted one at Pompeii. The vines at Boscoreale were staked and supported by both stakes and trees, as is true in many vineyards in the area today (Jashemski 1987).

An ancient country lane running through the vineyard led directly to the main entrance of the villa. The ruts left by the wheels traveling over this lane were the same distance apart (1.32 meters) as the wheels of a cart found within the villa. The wheel ruts also continued to an unplanted area to the left of the main entrance. This area was perhaps a place to park wagons when they were not in use. A footpath led through the vineyard to the entrance to the north portico.

The villa building contained two rooms in which the grapes were pressed. After the juice was extracted, it was fermented in the eighteen dolia imbedded in the peristyle courtyard. Dionysus, god of the vine, appropriately was worshiped in the small niche *lararium* (household shrine) in the portico of the peristyle.

Figure 13.5. Plan of large commercial vineyard at Pompeii: (c) entrance, (d, e) triclinia, (x) intersection of paths; small dots indicate grapevine roots, circles indicate tree roots. (Courtesy of Soprintendenza alle Antichità della Campania-Napoli; garden details by Stanley Jashemski)

To the right of the main entrance of the villa we uncovered a small vegetable garden with a cistern to provide the necessary water (fig. 13.6). Here, no doubt, were raised the choice cabbages and onions for which the Pompeii area was famous in antiquity (Columella, *De re rustica* 10.135, 12.10.1; Pliny, *Naturalis historia* 19.140). The garden was divided into small plots separated by irrigation channels that also served as paths. The soil contours are the same as those in modern vegetable gardens in the area today.

Figure 13.6. Country road in front of Villa Rustica at Boscoreale showing casts of tree roots along the road; vegetable garden and cistern in upper right. (Photograph by Francis Hueber)

One of the most exciting discoveries was the country road that passed in front of the villa, defining the limit of the property on this side, which was marked by two boundary stones. A roadway led from the main entrance of the villa to the country road. This road was unusually deep, but the same width as the lane that ran through the vineyard. Along the country road, at the edge of the villa property we found the root cavities of a row of huge trees (see fig. 13.6), which were quite unlike those of the small fruit and nut trees that were planted throughout the vineyard. Analyses of the woody material found in the root cavities made it possible for Dr. Francis Hueber, paleobotanist at the Smithsonian Institution, to identify the huge tree on each side of the roadway leading to the villa as the beautiful umbrella pine (*Pinus pinea*). The two other large trees were definitely angiosperms (broad-leafed deciduous trees). The woody material from these roots was too badly preserved to identify the species, but both the shape and size of the root cavities suggested that these were probably plane trees.

Professor Eberhard Grüger, of the Institut für Palynologie und Quartärwissenschaften at the University of Göttingen, in his preliminary report on the examination of the soil samples taken from this site, has identified *Pinus* (pine), *Olea* (olive)-type, *Triticum* (wheat), and *Arbutus unedo* pollens among many others, including many weeds. But the analyses of these samples has only begun, and it is too soon to interpret the results.

Other evidence tells us about life on this country villa. Cement poured into a cavity in the volcanic ash preserved the appearance of a pig raised on the villa. Among the bones found in the vineyard were those of pig, sheep or goat, cow, a toad or frog, and a dog. The bones of a coot (*Fulica atra*), a water bird, were found in the trash pile that included debris from meals, located in the area around the tree near the main entrance of the villa.

Debris from meals and other refuse were found at the edge of the neighboring property on the south side of the country road. Here we found the bones of a rail (*Rallus aquaticus*), another water bird. Only the bill of a chaffinch (*Fringilla coelebs*) was found, but songbirds were considered a table delicacy. Various bones of a dormouse (*Muscardinus avellanarius*), also a table delicacy, were found in this debris. More difficult to explain are the bones of the little ermine or weasel (*Mustela erminea*) and the bones of a marten (*Martes martes*). There was also the partial skeleton of a small rodent, the pine vole (*Pitymys savii*), and an almost complete skeleton of a rat snake. This neighboring property was also planted in vines. We found six vine-root cavities, five stake cavities, and two small tree-root cavities in the area excavated.

A very different type of villa was the luxurious one at Oplontis (modern Torre Annunziata), believed to have belonged to Poppaea, the wife of the emperor Nero. Thus far the villa has thirteen spectacular gardens, which I have excavated (see plan, fig. 13.7) (Jashemski 1979:290–314, in press). The gardens inside the villa were like those in the city houses. Some were peristyle gardens, some courtyard gardens; some were informally planted, most were formally planted. The walls of five were decorated with garden paintings to make a small garden appear larger. But it is only in the villa that we find the great formally planted exterior, porticoed gardens that beckoned the visitor from both land and sea.

Only three of these exterior gardens will be discussed here. At the rear of the villa, the complex portico looked out on a large garden of architectural design. The landscaped passageway along the rear of the villa, as well as the one leading from it on the axis of the villa (which had a magnificent view looking through the villa to the sea), was edged in shrubs, probably box, of which we found many charred bits. At the edge of the garden were two parallel passageways separated by a row of huge trees. To the east of the central passageway was a diagonal one, obviously balanced by a similar one on the opposite side, the two probably meeting at the passageway on the central axis of the villa in the still unexcavated lapilli.

At the edge of the diagonal passageway four masonry bases were found. On these the marble shafts that supported the four marble heads found nearby had been mounted. Dr. Stefano De Caro, former director of the excavations at Pompeii, has identified one of the heads as a portrait of a woman of the Julian-Claudian period, the second as the portrait of a boy of the Tiberio-Claudian period, the third as the head of the child of Dionysus, and the fourth as the head of Aphrodite (De Caro 1987). These herms were set in the midst of clumps of plants, which were probably oleanders, evocative of the garden paintings that show sculpture set amid masses of oleanders. Flanking the central passageway, we found three statue bases, in which three of the centaur fountains that had been found stored in the rear portico fit perfectly.

The rooms in the east wing of the villa, which were built later in the period from A.D. 50 to 60, looked out on an Olympic-size swimming pool (17 meters wide and 60 meters long) and two handsome gardens. To the south of the pool was a formal garden which could be enjoyed through the open windows of a beautiful *diaeta*. A unique garden painting, in which flowering shrubs and birds could be seen beyond a lattice fence, decorated the lower part of the exterior wall of the *diaeta*, extending the actual plantings of the garden. In the center of the garden, and on the longitudinal axis of the swimming pool, there was a shallow square marble pool in which stood a large crater fountain of white Pentellic marble, similar to those pictured in the garden paintings decorating the walls of the small courtyard garden on each side of the large central hall in the east wing (fig. 13.8). At the south edge of the swimming pool was a sculptured marble group of a hermaphrodite and a satyr.

Along the east side of the swimming pool and on a slightly lower level than the preceding garden was a large and impressive sculpture garden in which an avenue of thirteen trees have been found thus far. In front of each tree was a statue base. Six of the almost life-size marble statues and herms that stood on them have been found. Beginning at the south, there was a head of Hercules on the marble shaft in front of the third root cavity from the south, next a statue of an ephebe in front of the fourth root cavity, and then a large white marble female figure identified as Nike, in front of the fifth root cavity. Balancing these in corresponding positions along the north end of the pool was another Nike, of the same size, in front of the tenth root cavity, then a statue of Artemis, or an Amazon, lacking the head still standing on the base in front of root cavity 11, and next a head of Hercules on the marble shaft in front of root cavity 12.

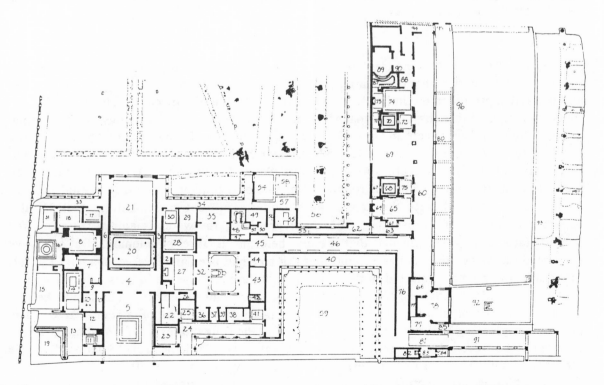

Figure 13.7. Plan of the Villa of Poppaea at Oplontis. (Courtesy of Soprintendenza alle Antichità della Campania-Napoli; garden details by Stanley Jashemski)

Figure 13.8. Detail of garden painting in north courtyard garden (no. 70 in fig. 13.7) in the Villa of Poppaea at Oplontis. (Photograph by Stanley Jashemski)

We carefully emptied the tree-root and other cavities of lapilli, studied the cavities, and then filled them with cement, making casts of the roots. The sizes and shapes of the cavities and the soil contours of the individual beds, along with the identification of the carbonized roots, branches, and pollen, now make it possible to identify the plantings of this formal garden, the first formal garden for which we have such plentiful evidence. The four statue bases VI to IX were directly opposite the large open hall in the middle of the east wing, and the plantings behind these statues were carefully planned to provide a splendid picture when viewed across the water from this room. Remnants of a branch of the tree behind base VI made it possible to identify this tree as an oleander. The root cavity behind base IX also appeared to be that of an oleander. SEM photographs of the woody material from the tree behind statue base VIII indicated that it could be either a laurel or a lemon. But when we excavated the cast of this root, we found that this tree had been air-layered in a pot. Laurels root easily and are never started in this way. Lemons are air-layered in pots. At last we had confirming evidence that the trees started in pots were indeed lemons. The cavity behind statue base VII was similar in size and also appeared to be that of a lemon tree. The picturesque planting of lemons and oleanders behind the four statues was framed on each side by large plane trees. Further excavation will reveal more of this beautiful villa garden. We can only speculate concerning its relation to the nearby bay to the south.

At Oplontis, architecture, gardens, and natural scenery united to give an effect only known imperfectly from literary and archaeological sources. Here the intimate gardens within the villa, the great formal gardens that immediately surrounded it, and the striking beauty of the natural scenery were all integrated and combined into one harmonious whole that was indescribably satisfying and beautiful.

## Acknowledgments

Support for my excavations has been provided by the National Endowment for the Humanities, the University of Maryland, Dumbarton Oaks, and the Superintendency of Pompeii. My work was greatly facilitated by the generous cooperation and gracious hospitality of Dr. Giuseppina Cerulli Irelli Superintendent of Pompeii, Dr. Stefano De Caro, Director of the Excavations at Pompeii, Dr. Antonio D'Ambrosio, in charge of the deposito at Pompeii, Ferdinando Balzano, assistant at Torre Annunziato, and Vincenzo Matrone, assistant at Boscoreale. Nicola Sicignano was our able foreman.

## Note

1. When Giuseppe Fiorelli became director of the excavations in 1870 he divided the city into nine regions. Each region was subdivided into numbered *insulae*, or blocks, and each entrance in each block was assigned a number. Thus, each door has an address of three numbers.

## References Cited

De Caro, S. 1987. The sculptures of the Villa of Poppaea at Oplontis. In *Ancient Roman villa gardens*, ed. E. B. MacDougall, pp. 79-133. Dumbarton Oaks Colloquium on the History of Landscape Architecture No. 10. Washington, D.C.: Dumbarton Oaks.

Jashemski, W. F. 1979. *The gardens of Pompeii, Herculaneum, and the villas destroyed by Vesuvius.* Vol. 1. New Rochelle, N.Y.: Caratzas Brothers Publishers.

----. 1987. Recently excavated gardens and cultivated land of the villas at Boscoreale and Oplontis. In *Ancient Roman villa gardens*, ed. E. B. MacDougall, pp. 33-75. Dumbarton Oaks Colloquium on the History of Landscape Architecture No. 10. Washington, D.C.: Dumbarton Oaks.

----. in press. *The gardens of Pompeii, Herculaneum, and the villas destroyed by Vesuvius.* Vol. 2. New Rochelle, N.Y.: Aristide D. Caratzas.

## Ancient References Cited

Florus. *Epitome of Roman History.* Latin text with translation by E. S. Forster. Cambridge: Harvard University Press, 1929.

Lucretius. *De rerum natura.* Latin text with translation by W. H. D. Rouse. Cambridge: Harvard University Press, 1975.

Pliny the Elder. *Naturalis historia.* Latin text with translation by H. Rackham and others. 10 vols. Cambridge: Harvard University Press, 1938-62.

Varro. *De re rustica.* Latin text with translation by W. D. Hooper, revised by H. B. Ash. Cambridge: Harvard University Press, 1954.

# 14

## BETWEEN THE BRADANO AND BASENTO: ARCHAEOLOGY OF AN ANCIENT LANDSCAPE

### Joseph Coleman Carter

The classical landscape of a Greek colony in southern Italy and that of an eighteenth-century Virginia plantation seem topics remote in time and space. Yet, no one might have been more interested in the former than Thomas Jefferson. He knew the ancient agricultural writers intimately (without the aid of translation) and considered them useful guides to farm management. When he finally was able to visit Italy, what impressed him most was not the monuments but the products of the land, and in particular the olive, "of all the gifts of heaven," he wrote to George Wythe in 1787 (Dumbauld 1946), "next to the most precious after bread--if not the most precious." These together with the vine, which he unfairly and erroneously identified as a prime source of financial ruin, Jefferson knew from his reading to be the principal crops of the Greek and Roman countryside.

Only in recent years have archaeologists working in the Mediterranean begun to expand their bases for knowledge of the classical landscape beyond the written sources known to Jefferson. In Italy the survey work of the British School in Rome around the Etruscan center of Veii in the 1950s and the contemporaneous exploration of the territories and hinterlands of Gela in Sicily and Metaponto in southern Italy by Professor Dinu Adamesteanu and his colleagues signaled a new direction for classical archaeology (Adamesteanu 1957; Potter 1979). Despite the extraordinarily successful results of these early endeavors, few chose to heed the call. This is all the more regrettable because the evidence for widespread rural settlement, abundant thirty years ago, is fast disappearing. Deep plowing, massive earth-moving schemes funded by the government, and urban sprawl have transformed the coastal areas in less than a generation.

Since 1974 the University of Texas at Austin has been involved in the exploration of the *Chora*, or territory, of Metaponto. We have picked up where Adamesteanu left off and extended the scope to include special studies of ancient organic remains as well as more systematic surface survey and an expanded program of excavation of rural sites. This survey of the rural landscape of Metaponto focuses on the last thirteen years, really on the last five years of work by our team. Frequent reference, however, is made to earlier results as well as to recent discoveries by other teams working in the city, *Chora*, and hinterland (Carter 1983; Carter et al. 1985).

## The Changing Population of the Territory

The *Chora* of Metaponto, as Professor Adamesteanu's work had already revealed, was densely populated. An accurate estimate of the size of the rural population is now possible, based on the results of the blanket survey of forty-two square kilometers carried out by Cesare D'Annibale and the survey team between 1981 and 1984. The transect (indicated on figure 14.1 by the rectangle) includes all of the characteristic topography of the *Chora*: the river bottom, *macchia*-covered slopes, and the high plains (see fig. 14.1). Every accessible field was covered (a total area of 31.5 square kilometers), and 488 were sites recorded on a 1:10,000-scale topographical map. The density of ancient sites (all sites and all periods) is 15.5 sites per square kilometer. So far the only comparable situation in the *chora* of a western Greek city is that currently being revealed by D'Annibale and his crew at Croton (Carter, in press; Carter and D'Annibale 1985).

What is the nature of these sites? This has been a matter of heated controversy between archaeologists and historians who are skeptical about the methods and results of survey. The majority of the sites, as Adamesteanu maintained, are isolated farmhouses. Of the sites in our transect, 267 (55%) are farm sites, 133 (29%) are tombs belonging with farm sites, and the rest consist of kilns, quarries, sanctuaries, or scatters of pottery and tiles without any clear reference to a structure (Carter et al. 1985).

How is it decided that a site is a farm, tomb, or scatter? The principal evidence is, of course, the material on the surface. A standardized method of collection insures that the full range of activities on the sites will be recorded. A site in the transect will produce, on the average, 100 artifacts. When these include a combination of building stones, roof tiles, storage vessels, cooking vessels, finewares, and fragments of millstones or mortars, it is reasonably certain that there was once a farmhouse on the site. In many cases a small burying ground, indicated by tomb tiles and fragments of fine, decorated pottery, will appear in close proximity--a good indication of the independent nature and permanent status of these rural establishments.

Nothing can take the place of the survey in defining the broad patterns of settlement, but a survey has its limitations. Excavation can shed a much sharper light on the economic and social level of the occupants, and it should remove any doubt that surface finds are a fair indicator of subsurface reality. From 1966 to date, about two dozen sites identified through surveys of the *Chora* of Metaponto have been fully or partially excavated. Typical of the second half of the fourth century B.C. is the farmhouse excavated by the university team at Ponte Fabrizio along the valley of the Venella (Carter 1981). Its seven to nine rooms arranged in rows without a courtyard were well furnished with pottery and artifacts including a remarkable votive plaque. The farm, which had a late sixth-century phase, was abandoned without signs of violence about 350 B.C. and never reinhabited. After a number of excavations of farmhouses, the probability of recovering important new information diminishes. To date seven farmhouses have been investigated; they range in date from the second half of the sixth century B.C. to the early fourth century A.D (fig. 14.2). Though some, like the large fourth-century structure known as Fattoria Stefan (after its excavator) are more elaborate in plan, with a courtyard and probable second story (Carter 1979), there is a remarkable sameness in the overall arrangements which persists for many centuries.

It is possible that a percentage of the 267 sites identified as farmhouses were not farmhouses at all, and it is likely that some of the farmhouses which once existed in the area

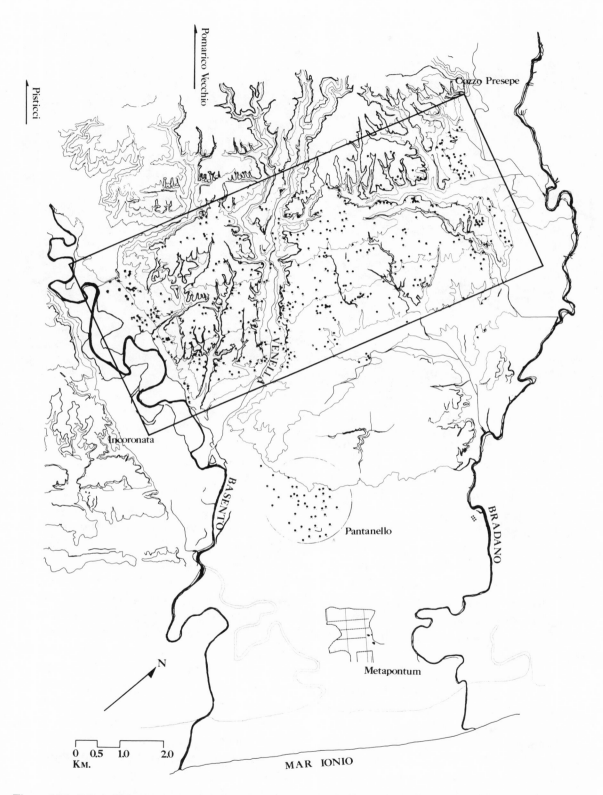

Figure 14.1. Map of the *Chora* of Metaponto with the area of the survey indicated by the rectangle (and the area around Pantanello by the circle). The dots indicate the ancient sites including farm sites, tombs, and scatters.

Figure 14.2.  Excavation of an ancient farm site, in progress.  Located along the banks of the Basento near the northwest corner of the survey area, this farmhouse had substantial remains of a fourth-century B.C. phase and one of the early imperial period (10 B.C. to A.D. 50).

of the transect have left little or no trace on the surface; 267 farms is an approximate and a minimum figure.  If, however, it is to be used to make even order-of-magnitude calculations of the entire Metapontine farm population, an estimate must first be made of the total area of the *Chora*.  It clearly began just outside the city walls and included not only the area between the Bradano and Basento but also that from the Basento to the Cavone.  It is assumed to have stretched inland a distance of 14 kilometers from the coast, corresponding to the maximum penetration of the division lines of the territory discovered in the aerial photographic research of Schmiedt and Chevallier (1959).  These boundaries encompass an area of 18,500 hectares. There are farm sites up to this point, but some are also found farther inland. Was the land beyond the lines, *eschatia*, held in common by Metapontine farmers, or was it already Lucanian territory?  What was the relation of this area to the fortified centers of Pisticci, Pomarico, and Cozzo Presepe, identified by Adamesteanu as *phrouria*?  Further survey and excavation will be required to resolve these issues, but 18,500 hectares is a fairly safe figure for the calculations of minimum farm population (Carter et al. 1985).

If the 4,200 hectares of the transect are typical of the *Chora* as a whole, as more limited surveys elsewhere indicate, there would have been 1,568 farmhouses scattered throughout the territory.  That is a very large number, but of course, not all these sites were occupied at the same time.  In the fall of 1985 the ceramic material from the sites in the transect was studied. Making use of the typology and chronology of black-glazed pottery developed by Maria

Christensen (University of Stockholm), it has been possible to place a large percentage of the sites in the transect within precise chronological limits. The sites with black-glazed pottery range in date from about 550 B.C. to the early third century B.C. Christensen's conclusions are based on a thorough analysis of tomb groups from the extensive necropolis at Pantanello and from stratified deposits in the nearby sanctuary (Carter 1989). Although there can be legitimate doubts about the absolute dates of individual sites, it is likely that the overall picture of the development of the *Chora* which has emerged from this study accurately reflects its main currents.

The percentages of sites occupied in successive half-century intervals from 600 to 250 B.C. provide a clearer and more accurate idea of the population density and its fluctuation than was previously possible. It was evident that the late archaic period was a major period of expansion in the territory, but that the farm population was nearly as high then as in the second half of the fourth century B.C. came as a surprise. The experience of excavation had taught us to expect a decline in rural population in the century from 450 to 350 B.C., but the results of the survey of the transect gave that phenomenon a quantitative definition. A consideration of not just the numbers but also the changing surface pattern of the settlement may make the survey useful in pinpointing a cause for these drastic fluctuations.

The sites of farms established during the first permanent settlement of the territory in the sixth century B.C. line up, in the area of the transect, along the bank of the Basento (fig. 14.3). They are regularly spaced about 600 meters apart. Sites also line the major tributaries, like the Venella, but here they lie in irregular intervals along the slopes of the valleys. On the high plains between the rivers there are, in the first phase, a few scattered sites and a small cluster in the area known as Pantano, which has an important all-weather spring. Aerial photographs and surface reconnaissance have located the major evidence for the division lines of the *Chora* in the high plains area known as Lago del Lupo. There is little indication of a relationship in the sixth century B.C. between farm sites and the much-discussed division lines.

Practically every site occupied in the sixth century continued to be occupied into the fifth century B.C. The big change took place in the high plains areas, like Lago del Lupo or Giamperduto, where there was nothing in the sixth century. The cluster of sites at Pantano became a small village, and there are similar ones at Sant'Angelo Grieco and on the Bradano side, which was opened to settlement at this time, at Giardinetto and San Marco. Though there was a great increase in density in the high plains, once again, few sites seem to line up along the division lines.

In the second half of the fifth century and first half of the fourth century B.C., the century of decline, there was a general large-scale thinning out of settlements. For example, there are no settlements in Giamperduto. It looks as if all the advances of the first half of the fifth century were canceled out. The lower region of the Venella, which was so dense in the archaic period, was now practically deserted, but settlements in the upper Venella were relatively denser. However, when the sixth-century map and that for the period 450 to 400 B.C. are compared, the overall distribution is similar, but few sites that were occupied in the sixth century continued into this later period. In the first half of the fourth century the thinning out reached the point that there was only one site left in the village at Pantano. It is worth noting that a relatively high percentage of the sites occupied in this period in the high plains were new sites, not occupied in the previous half century, though several had been in the archaic period.

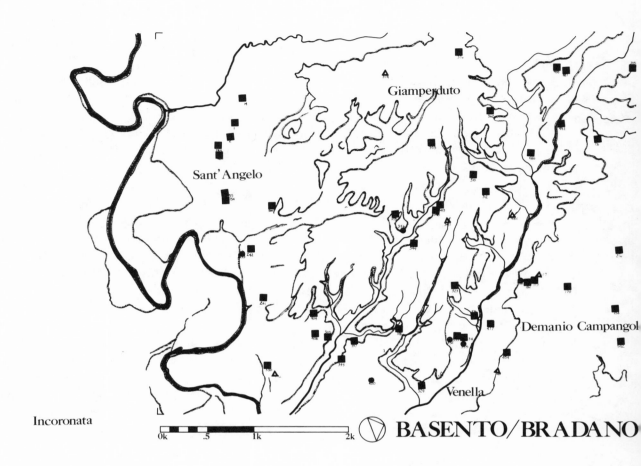

A general theory developed by geographers (Birch 1976) is useful in interpreting these fluctuations. It sees the best land (i.e., the bottomland) going to the early settlers of the sixth century B.C. This was followed in the early fifth century by an infilling, and then in the later fifth and early fourth centuries by a thinning out due to competitive forces and excessive pressure on the land. Thus, the rapid changes up to this point could have a largely economic explanation. Some facts, however, do not fit this theory.

A great and general revival of rural settlement was achieved in the period from 350 to 300 B.C. It must have been related to a general economic upsurge in the western Greek world at this time (Heichelheim 1964; Talbert 1974), but it must also have required an enormous effort. It is enough to compare the map for this period with one immediately before it. The village at Pantano returned to the flourishing state of the early fifth century B.C. The sites in general avoided the lower ground, the river bottoms, and the lower reaches of the

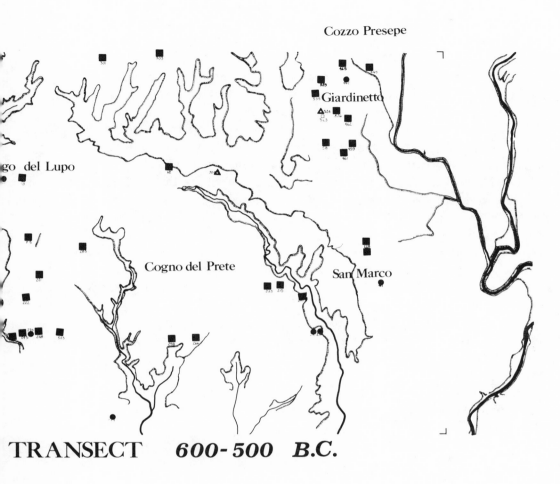

Figure 14.3. An enlargement of the rectangular area shown in fig. 14.1. Farm sites in existence in the period from 600 to 500 B.C. are indicated here by solid squares, tombs of the same period by open triangles, and scatters by solid circles.

tributaries. The tendency to move inland, and to stick to higher ground, continued into the third century, when rural settlement was finally decimated and all but disappeared.

The avoidance of low ground, from the second half of the fifth century onward, suggests that poor drainage and unhealthy conditions may have become serious problems and major factors affecting the settlement pattern. This hypothesis is supported by evidence from a variety of sources. Excavations in a number of low-lying sites in the territory and in the city itself make it clear that the level of the water table rose about one-half meter between the second half of the sixth century and the second half of the fourth century. (An even more drastic shift took place at Sybaris.) Giovanni Uggeri, in an important early study, pointed out that the sudden appearance of the river god Acheloos on Metapontine coinage about 460 B.C. heralded a major project of *bonifica*, or land reclamation and drainage (Uggeri 1969). By the second half of the fifth century, as the work of the Superintendency and the German

Archaeological Institute have shown, the principal temples had begun to sink into the mud (Mertens 1985). A major *bonifica* of the city, massive drains constructed using pieces of fallen monuments, stabilized the situation at least temporarily and permitted the ambitious construction of the theater. It is likely the *bonifica* of the city was accompanied by one in the countryside, which made possible a half century of renewed vitality and prosperity. Finally, there is the indirect evidence of malaria in the territory, in the frequent occurrence of the disease known as thalassemia in the rural necropolis at Pantanello (Carter, in press).

Metaponto's rapid decline in the early third century was the result of a combination of many factors (incessant warfare, Roman expansion), not the least of which were environmental conditions. For the moment, however, the question of population--the numbers--should be examined. In the second half of the fourth century B.C., 63 percent of the total of known farm sites in the transect were occupied. Assuming that the transect is a representative sample, the total number of farm sites in the *Chora*, in the period of its fullest flowering, would have been 987. If the entire *Chora* was divided among these 987 farm families, the average size of a farm would have been 18.6 hectares, of which about 78 percent on the average was arable land. A farm of this size was probably too large for a single family to cultivate, which raises the question of the source of the additional laborers: were they tenant farmers or slaves?

It is natural to wonder, too, what happened to the population of the territory during the periods of contraction and decline? Did it die out, emigrate elsewhere, or simply swell the urban population? (The city seems to have been practically abandoned at these times.) This problem serves to remind us that our knowledge of western Greek history is spotty at best, and that archaeology is of limited usefulness in filling the gaps in the historical record. Limited it is, but it can provide types of evidence that even the fullest contemporary accounts may well have overlooked.

## The Products of the Fields

While the population of the *Chora* fluctuated dramatically in the centuries between 600 and 250 B.C., other important changes were quietly taking place. The evidence for these is such that an excavation intent only on defining structures and chronological phases might have missed it altogether. First there is the evidence for the basic activity of the Metapontine farmer, agriculture. What did he raise? Thanks to the study that paleobotanist Lorenzo Costantini has made of the deposits of ancient seeds and organic material from the Greek sanctuary at Pantanello, the principal crops are known (Carter 1983). The circumstances that made the low-lying areas of the *Chora* uninhabitable during the fourth century created a bog within the sanctuary which was both a blessing and an obstacle. Systematic excavation would have been impossible had it not been for the well-point pumping system that was employed for the first time in 1977 and 1978 and again in 1982, when at last the main lines of the development of the sanctuary became clear.

In the earliest phase, the focus of the cult, the spring, was enclosed by a massive pair of walls in local stone. It was frequented in the late seventh century B.C., as the pottery and votives, all representing females, show. In the next century a simple shelter was erected, and the carefully cut channels of the spring began to silt up. From the mid-fifth century to the mid-fourth century the area was abandoned. It came to life again with the rest of the countryside about 350 B.C. The votives reflect a shift of emphasis in the revived cult, toward a male figure identified as Dionysos-Hades. A large reservoir was constructed to collect the springwater for the surrounding farm population. The collecting basin in turn silted up in a few years and was abandoned in the early third century B.C.

From the hillside above the spring some 2 meters of additional soil were gradually deposited over the site, and water continued to flow from the spring without interruption down to the time of excavation (and afterwards), creating conditions ideal for the preservation not only of seeds, wood, and leaves but even entire fruit (fig. 14.4). This is an exceptional and, for now, a uniquely detailed source of information on Greek agriculture and its development in the classical period (Carter 1987). Even though the deposits of seeds were below the level of the water table, the use of a well-point pumping system to dry out the ground made regular stratigraphical excavation possible. Thus it is also possible to study the development in time of Metapontine agriculture.

Figure 14.4. The area of the collecting basin in the rural sanctuary at Pantanello. Measuring some dozen meters on a side, this acted as a reservoir supplying fresh springwater to the surrounding farms. A female divinity was first venerated here, and offerings of agricultural crops were deposited along with votive figurines.

The first substantial results from this research were announced in 1982, but the work goes on with some unexpected advances. One example is the recent spectacular discovery that the uncarbonized seeds of blackberry, an aquatic plant known as coontail, and now grapes from the Pantanello sanctuary had conserved almost intact their genetic code, their DNA. Though the main impact of this discovery will be in the field of plant genetics, it has opened new possibilities for archaeologists (Rensberger 1985). In the future some may be involved in the search for new sources of plant stock to improve and guarantee sources of nutrition for future living populations.

The important results of the research, as far as the history of Metaponto is concerned, can be easily summarized. Fourteen cultivated plants have been identified and a dozen wild plants or weeds. There are the seeds of barley and wheat in about equal proportion. There are olive, fig, and grape, all mentioned in that remarkable contemporary fourth-century B.C. document the Heraklea Tablets. But besides those known from the tablets, there are five varieties of legumes and three forage crops.

A wide range of cultivated plants formed the basis of Metapontine agriculture in the fourth century B.C. However, of greater relevance to the problem of interpreting the changing settlement pattern in the *Chora* are indications of major shifts in the relative importance of basic crops. In the stratified deposit at Pantanello, the seeds of olive and grape are more numerous than the grains in the middle of the fourth century B.C. By the end of the century the proportions were precisely reversed (table 14.1).

While caution should be exercised in drawing quantitative conclusions from a limited sample at a single site, this evidence indicates that the *Chora* may have been undergoing a rapid transformation from a diversified agriculture to a monoculture of grain with all the risks, including exhaustion of the soil, that such a course entails. Though one would need similar deposits from other sites in the *Chora* to feel confident in the hypothesis of widespread change, a study of the pollen from the same stratified deposit confirms that such a change was taking place at least locally. From the pollen profile it can be seen that olive reached a peak in the mid-fourth century. Grains reached theirs at the end of the fourth century B.C. It is noteworthy, too, that legumes, which could have been used to revitalize the soil in rotation with grains, declined with olive.

It is suggestive that the evidence for a concentration on grain, a crop which requires a lower investment of capital and a smaller work force than cultivation of the olive and the grape, can be dated at the very end of the last great flowering of the *Chora*. Archaeologists confronted with the raw data of decline or destruction usually have sought to correlate them with the facts of political and social history. The study of the material evidence for ancient agriculture compels us to examine, also, the historic relationship of man and his environment.

Agriculture in the *Chora* in the periods of expansion was not subsistence farming. The wealth it produced, symbolized in Metaponto's coinage, was renowned in the ancient world. This necessitates an examination of the structure of Metapontine society, and specifically the problems of how much surplus the fields produced and how it was distributed (Carter et al. 1985).

## The Structure of Metapontine Rural Society

Basic to any calculation of surplus are accurate estimates of the population. In ancient demographic studies the productive capacity of the fields often has been used to estimate the population. A basic assumption is that all food produced would have been consumed by the local population. This was clearly not the case at Metaponto. Fortunately, the excavations of the city are advanced to the point where they can offer the basis for a convincing estimate of the size of the urban populace, to complement that which the survey has provided for the *Chora*.

Table 14.1. The principal plants discovered in the stratified deposit of the collecting basin at Pantanello (see fig. 14.4).

| Type | Level I Base level (mid-fourth century B.C.) | Level II Compacted organic material | Level III Carbonized organic material (early third century B.C.) |
|---|---|---|---|
| **Cereals** | | | |
| *Triticum dicoccum*/emmer | x | | xx |
| *Triticum compactum*/wheat | x | x | xxx |
| *Hordeum vulgare*/barley | x | x | xxx |
| **Legumes** | | | |
| *Cicer arietinum*/chick-pea | | | x |
| *Lens culinaris*/lentil | | | x |
| *Pisum sativum*/field pea | x | | x |
| *Vicia faba*/broad bean | | x | xx |
| *Vicia ervilia*/bitter vetch | | | x |
| **Forage crops** | | | |
| *Medicago* sp./alfalfa | | xx | x |
| *Avena sativa*/oats | | | x |
| *Lolium temulentum*/ryegrass | x | x | x |
| **Wild and Spontaneous Plants** | | | |
| *Carex* sp./sedge family | x | x | |
| *Euphorbia elioscopica*/spurge | x | x | x |
| *Galium* sp./bedstraw | | x | x |
| *Lathyrus* sp./vetchling | | x | x |
| *Poligonum* sp./knotweed | | x | x |
| *Ranunculus* sp./buttercup family | x | | |
| *Rubus* sp./blackberry | x | x | x |
| *Sonchus* sp./sow thistle | xxx | x | |
| *Cerotaphyllium demersum*/coontail | x | xxx | |
| *Zannichellia* sp./horned pond weed | x | xxx | |
| **Fruits** | | | |
| *Ficus carica*/fig | xxx | xx | x |
| *Olea europaea*/olive | xxx | xx | x |
| *Vitis vinifera*/grape | xxx | xx | x |

The productivity of the fields has been calculated in cereal equivalent and the requirements of a family in calories, using Food and Agricultural Organization (FAO) of the United Nations figures adjusted for prehistoric populations. Ancient figures for both productivity and consumption are fraught with problems of interpretation. The modern figures give only a rough approximation, but they do have the advantage of making calculations a great deal simpler.

Two variables that greatly affect these calculations are the average return of seed grain and family size. Reasonable upper and lower values have been assumed for both, and a maximum surplus (which is maximum productivity minus minimum family need) and a minimum surplus (minimum productivity minus maximum family need) have been calculated both for the average family farm and for the *Chora* as a whole. A farm of 14 arable hectares (78 percent of the land is arable; the average farm is 18.75 hectares) would have produced between 3 and 12 tons of surplus grain a year. A minimum surplus from the *Chora* in the second half of the fourth century B.C. would not have fed the urban population, but the maximum would have done that and left over for sale abroad 12,000 tons, or in ancient measures 170,000 (169,000) *medimnoi* worth approximately 200 (197) talents at then current prices. The wealth of Metaponto was truly in its field.

How would this enormous abundance have been divided? How well founded are references to a landed aristocracy? Is there a basis for such a theory in the archaeological data? For the *Chora* of Metaponto sufficient evidence now exists to begin to formulate an answer to this fundamental question of social structure. It is best to begin with the question of the distribution of land, the essential measure of wealth in an agrarian society. The fundamental data for this reconstruction are twofold.

First, there are the traces of ancient land divisions--a series of parallel lines that appeared first in aerial photographs (Schmiedt and Chevallier 1959) and were later confirmed on the ground. Their existence, it is fair to say, has not been universally accepted. The lines, according to the subsequent investigations of Adamesteanu and his collaborators (Adamesteanu 1973), divide the territory between the Bradano and Basento rivers into long strips, about 210 meters wide. They are oriented north-northwest 50°. One of the lines, which proved to be a buried road flanked by a drainage ditch, was partially excavated in 1986 (Carter 1989). Its position corresponds perfectly with the grid of division lines deduced from the indications on the aerial photographs. This would tend to corroborate the existence of the grid as a whole.

The second source of information for the reconstruction is the actual position of farm sites in the survey area. Only the high plains area has been considered, where all of the surface is arable (i.e., there are no slopes). Several important assumptions have been made: namely, that every farmhouse corresponded to a piece of land and, further, that the size of the lots would be multiples of measures which were widely used throughout the Greek world (Favory 1983). With these data and assumptions, a series of land plats have been developed for the major periods of the occupation of the *Chora*. There is surprisingly little variation among the various solutions. The smallest lot varies from 4.8 to 6.6 hectares (depending on whether a basic unit of 210 by 210 or 210 by 315 is used); the largest is 53 hectares; but the lots measuring 13.8 hectares are by far the most common--50 percent of the total are in this category, and 90 percent of the lots are 26 hectares or smaller (fig. 14.5). The picture that emerges from this analysis of the distribution of land is of a well-to-do but also remarkably egalitarian society.

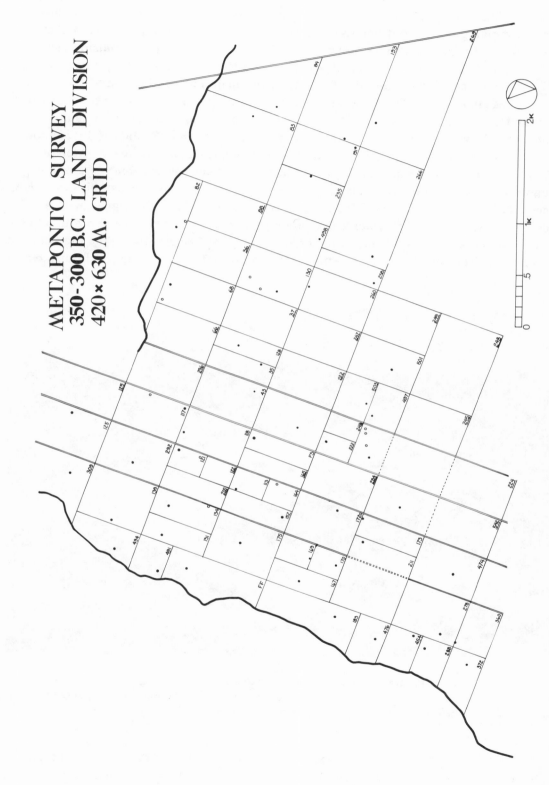

Figure 14.5. Hypothetical division of an area of the *Chora* of Metaponto into farm plots. It makes use of the actual density of farm plots in Lago del Lupo, Cogno del Prete, and Campagnolo (see fig. 14.3) in the period from 350 to 300 B.C.

Certain lots, however, are clearly larger than others, and there is no way to be sure that a farmer occupying one lot did not also control others at the same time scattered about the territory, or for that matter also pasture or woods in the presumed *eschatia* outside the *Chora* divided by the lines. In the absence of written records there can be no certainty about a division of property. The hypothesis of a society of small and medium-sized landowners, however, does find support from another source of information about the rural population.

In the fall of 1982 the university team undertook the salvage of an area of tombs which had come to light with the removal of an olive grove at Pantanello. By July 1986, 359 tombs had been systematically excavated. To date it is the largest intact area of Metapontine necropolis to have been documented (Carter, in press). Many of the tombs flank a major thoroughfare by which the city, some 3.5 kilometers distant, communicated with the *Chora* and the interior along the valley of the Basento (fig. 14.6). Others are aligned with a strip, defined by excavation in 1986, which corresponds perfectly in orientation and position to the sixth division line to the west of the central one bisecting the *Chora* between the Bradano and Basento rivers. The tombs cluster together into groups that strongly suggest family burial plots.

Figure 14.6. General view of the area of the Pantanello where tombs cluster into large family groupings. This is the point where the main ancient road from Metaponto along the valley of the Basento (seen here flanked by tombs) intersected with a smaller road corresponding to one of the division lines of the *Chora*.

There is wide variety of tomb types such as stone cist tombs and sarcophagi, *a cappucina* and Laconian tile tombs, simple earthen graves (sometimes lined with painted plaster), and cremations, all of the types familiar from Greek necropoleis of the archaic, classical, and Hellenistic periods. Grave goods include a surprisingly large number of objects in metal such as mirrors, strigils, coins, and the occasional cosmetic box or inkwell, in addition to the pottery, which, though predominantly black-glazed, also includes a high percentage of decorated wares from late Corinthian, to Attic black and red figured, to early Lucanian, Apulian, and Gnathian wares.

The chronological range is that of the two dozen or so farm sites recorded by the survey team within a 1-kilometer radius of the Pantanello sanctuary. There is a decline in the total number of tombs between 450 and 350 B.C. which corresponds to the decline in the number of occupied farm sites in the transect in the same period. Considering their distance from the city and relation to farm sites and division lines, it is natural to infer that their occupants were the inhabitants of the *Chora*.

Just as the paleobotanic analysis of the organic remains of plants from the sanctuary provided essential data for understanding the economic history of the territory of Metaponto, so the detailed study of the human skeletal remains from the necropolis has added vital information about the physical state and population dynamics of the inhabitants of the *Chora*. Discussed here are just two examples of particular relevance.

In his analysis of the human skeletal material, Professor R. M. Henneberg (of the Department of Anatomy at the University of Capetown) has dealt with the full range of questions that it normally poses: determination of stature, pathologies, nutrition, and medical and dental care; and he has added another. Using techniques developed by scientists in Hungary, Henneberg and his wife Renata, a biochemist, have succeeded in determining the blood types of over 150 of the occupants of the necropolis. The procedure, which makes use of small samples of bone marrow, was carried out in the field and in the laboratory of a local physician, Dr. G. B. Viggiani of Policoro. The preliminary results reinforce the interpretation of the tomb clusters or nuclei as family groups.

Professor Henneberg's principal concern, however, has been with the structure of this population. Determinations of sex and age at death of 240 skeletons, a statistically significant sample, reveal an abnormally high proportion of females to males. The ratio is more than 2:1. The situation, moreover, was not static. There was a progressive feminization of the necropolis. In the last half of the fourth century the ratio was nearly 4:1. Whatever the explanation, perhaps the result of warfare or very particular funerary customs, it is hard to avoid seeing a relationship between a shortage of men and a crisis in agriculture at the end of fourth century B.C.

The necropolis also casts light on the problem of the economic level of the population of the *Chora* and of the distribution of wealth. It is clear, even from a casual study, that certain individuals at Pantanello were accorded very special treatment at death; others were simply put away. Between these two extremes there is a full range of tomb types and grave goods. The most expensive tombs, were they to be isolated in the *Chora*, might very well be taken for those of landed aristocrats, while the earthen graves without goods were for those of slaves, or at least the very poor. At Pantanello, however, the very costly and very inexpensive tombs are scattered generally throughout the necropolis and its nuclei.

To understand better how burials of greater and less expense were distributed throughout the various nuclei of the necropolis and to discover if the age and sex of the occupants were a factor, we developed a system to quantify the cost of every burial. The value assigned to a burial is not assumed to reflect the real wealth of the individual but rather the financial sacrifice that the group was willing to make to dispose of one of its members. Its calculation makes use of the known contemporary costs for stone, tile, and the various objects found in the tombs. Quarried stone was very expensive and a red-figured vase incredibly cheap by today's standards.

The results of this analysis show that there was a high degree of homogeneity among the family groups that used Pantanello. In every nucleus there was a full range of burial costs, and the ranges of the individual nuclei, with minor variations, closely approximate the average for the necropolis as a whole. At this point in our study it is clear that there was indeed a favored class; it consisted of those individuals, male or female, over fifty years of age (Carter, in press).

Some ancient historians have been quick to assume, in the absence of concrete evidence, that the inhabitants of the *Chora* in the heyday of Metapontine wealth were perforce landed aristocrats (e.g., Lepore 1973). The present study, based on the ample archaeological evidence of this ancient Greek landscape, the best documented to date, points not to an aristocracy but to a community of small to medium-sized landholders. Both the size distribution of lots and the homogeneity in burial practice among family groups are indications that this society was indeed egalitarian--a worthy, classical forerunner of the Jeffersonian ideal.

Historians have been equally quick and nearly unanimous in attributing Metaponto's decline in the third century B.C. to military or political causes. The analysis of the landscape and of Metapontine agricultural practices, as outlined here, suggests that environmental conditions, both those created by man's intervention and those beyond his control, were important factors. The history of the ancient landscape has yet to be written. The present study is a first contribution for the area of the Greek colonies of Magna Grecia. If it does nothing else, I hope that it will serve to demonstrate that important clues to larger issues lie buried in the ancient landscape.

## References Cited

Adamesteanu, D. 1957. Nouvelles fouilles et recherches archéologiques à Gela et dans l'arrière-pays. *Révue Archéologique* 59:20-46.

Birch, B.P. 1976. The frontier farm settlement: A pattern-process framework. In *Geographical dimensions of rural settlements*, ed. R. I. Singh et al., pp. 30-40. Varanasi: National Geographical Society of India.

Carter, J. C. 1979. *University of Texas excavations at Metaponto, 1978*. Austin: University Publications.

----. 1981. *Excavation in the territory, Metaponto 1980*. Austin: University Publications.

----. 1983. *The territory of Metaponto, 1981-1982*. Austin: University Publications.

----. 1987. Agricoltura e pastorizia nella Magna Grecia. In *Magna Grecia*, ed. G. Carratelli, pp. 173-212. Milan: Electra.

----. 1989. *The Pantanello necropolis, 1982-1988*. Austin: University Publications.

----. In press. Metaponto and Croton--Land, wealth, and population. In *Greek colonists and native populations*, ed. J. P. Descoerdres. Oxford: Oxford University Press.

----. and C. D'Annibale. 1985. Metaponto and Croton. In *Archaeological field survey in Britain and abroad*, ed. S. Macready and F. H. Thompson, pp. 146-57. Society of Antiquaries of London Occasional Paper No. 6. London: Society of Antiquaries.

----., et al. 1985. Population and agriculture in Magna Grecia in the fourth century B.C. In *Papers in Italian archaeology IV: The human landscape*, ed. C. Malone and S. Stoddart, pp. 281-312. Oxford: International Series No. 243, British Archaeological Reports.

Dumbauld, E. 1946. *Thomas Jefferson, American tourist*. Norman: University of Oklahoma Press.

Favory, F. 1983. Propositions pour une modelisation des cadastres ruraux antiques. In *Cadastres et éspace rural*, ed. M. Clavel-Levêque, pp. 51-135. Paris: University of Besançon, Belles Lettres.

Heichelheim, F. 1964. *An ancient economic history*. Vol. 2. Leyden: Sijthoff.

Mertens, D. 1985. Metaponto: Ein neuer plan des Stadtzentrums. *Archäologischer Anzeiger*.

Potter, T. W. 1979. *The changing landscape of South Etruria*. London: Paul Elek.

Rensberger, B. 1985. "2,300 year-old seeds may yield information on ancient agriculture." *Washington Post*, 26 Dec. 1985, A3.

Schmiedt, G., and R. Chevallier. 1959. *Metaponto e Caulonia*. Milan: l'Universo.

Talbert, R. J. 1974. *Timoleon and the revival of Greek Sicily*. Cambridge: Cambridge University Press.

Uggeri, G. 1969. *Kleroi* arcaici e bonifica classica nella *Chora* di Metaponto. *Parola del Passato* 118:51-71.

# 15

# RECONSTRUCTING THE LANDSCAPE OF RURAL ITALY

## Stephen L. Dyson

In both myth and reality the ancient Romans placed much emphasis on farming, rural life, and man's involvement with the land. Those religious festivals that can be associated with the earliest phases of the city's existence had strong associations with agrarian and pastoral life (Bloch 1960:111-48). Formative historical myths glorified heroes like Cincinnatus, a man who left his plow to save the Roman state and then returned to his small, self-sufficient farm (Wills 1984). Writers throughout the later republic and the empire looked wistfully back toward the simpler, more old-fashioned world of the Italian countryside even as they fled farms and small towns for the more sophisticated life of the city of Rome. The major ancient historians such as Sallust and Plutarch depicted crises in the agricultural sector such as the perceived decline of small farms during the second century B.C. as total cultural crises, affecting the moral as well as the social and economic structure of Roman society. In the history of the agrarian myths of Western civilization, Rome was one of the great formative experiences.

An important reality lay behind this historical mythmaking. Rome built a massive empire on an essentially agrarian base. Industry, in our sense of the word, was limited to highly complex craft organizations (Peacock 1982). A few megacities such as Rome and Alexandria grew to the size and complexity of major modern urban centers. However, the vast majority of the hundreds of cities and towns that existed during the period of the Roman Empire were much smaller in size and served mainly as market and services centers for rural hinterlands. Although population estimates for the Roman countryside are and will probably always remain very uncertain, recent archaeological and historical research shows that both during the republic and the empire the vast majority of Romans lived in the countryside or in small cities and villages that were closely linked to the countryside. The course of Roman history was closely tied to the fate of its rural world.

The countryside of each part of the Roman Empire had its special historical, ecological, and geographical characteristics, and it is impossible to talk about a common Roman rural experience even for the western empire. In this chapter, the focus is on Roman Italy, its landscape archaeology, and some of the historical reconstructions that can be made from this archaeological evidence. Two major reasons lie behind this concentration on the Italian area. The first is that Italy was the homeland of the Roman people. Their culture emerged there, and the development of their agriculture and rural settlements in Italy was central to the Roman historical experience. The second is the more advanced state of research relating to the rural archaeology in Italy. Some of the best recent projects in Roman rural archaeology have centered on Italy. As a result, in spite of great gaps in our knowledge about the countryside of the Roman heartland, the development of its rural world is better known than that of other areas of the Roman Mediterranean and most of the Roman provinces in Europe with the possible exception of Roman Britain (Percival 1976; Potter 1987:94-124).

For an understanding of the present state of research on Roman rural life, a certain amount of historical and historiographical background is necessary. For a long time, study of the countryside of Roman Italy was rather sharply divided between document-based historians who concentrated on the reconstruction of Roman rural life on the basis of literary texts and inscriptions and antiquarian-oriented archaeologists who recorded major ruins in the countryside and tried to relate those archaeological remains and contemporary topographic features to a reconstruction of Roman rural history that had been developed largely from the texts. While even modern historians of ancient Rome have tended to have an urban, elite-oriented view of that culture's history, they by no means have neglected its agricultural and rural development. However, they generally let the ancient written sources define the nature of the issues to be studied as well as provide most of the evidence on which their conclusions and reconstructions have been based. This tendency can be seen in nineteenth- and twentieth-century interpretations of the so-called agrarian crisis of the second century B.C. This was a period when Rome's conquest of the wealthy Hellenistic kingdoms of the eastern Mediterranean and the importation of new wealth and masses of new slaves supposedly destroyed the small soldier-farmers who had been the basis of Roman political and military success and replaced them with large estates or plantations based on slave labor (Toynbee 1965). These economic changes were seen as leading to major social and political crises that ultimately undermined the Roman Republic. Central to this crisis were the efforts of the Roman tribunes Tiberius and Caius Gracchus to reverse this process by schemes of land redistribution and the violent end they met at the hand of senatorial oligarchs (Bernstein 1978; Riddle 1970).

Most modern reconstructions of the process of Roman rural change during this key period have been based almost totally on information provided by such Greek and Roman authors as Sallust and Plutarch with only limited attention paid to the distance in time that separated them from the events that they described, their own special biases, and the very real historiographical limitations that ancient writers faced when they attempted this type of socioeconomic history (Veyne 1984). Modern historians have tended most often to try to escape from the limits of the ancient sources by using contemporary theoretical approaches, many of which were derived from Marxist modes of analysis (Konstan 1975). Because even with their very different perspectives and approaches, both ancient moralists and modern Marxists agreed on the class-oriented basis of these second-century B.C. Roman crises, the two schools tended to reinforce each other and free the historians from any great impulse to seek out new sources and reconstructions. While the document-based historians were engaged in these debates, the topographers and antiquarians were continuing their rural researches but with a very special and limited perspective. Here again the ancient authors and their descriptions of the Roman rural world set the agenda. Much effort was expended on such tasks as the location and description of Horace's Sabine farm or the reconstruction of the country villas described in Pliny the Younger's letters (Highet 1959). Some researchers took a more systematic approach to landscape archaeology. They attempted to record all of the major archaeological monuments in a particular territory or region and integrate their evidence into a synthetic picture of a particular portion of Roman landscape and its historical evolution.  A classic example of this type of investigation is the research undertaken early in this century by Thomas Ashby of the British School at Rome in the region just outside of Rome known as the Campagna.  Ashby described and recorded in photographs a landscape and its monuments which has now largely disappeared under the sprawling suburbs of post-World War II Rome (Ashby 1927; Barker and Ferrari 1986).  This type of very significant research project which aims to record major ruins and archaeological sites that often are being altered or destroyed in the rapidly changing countryside of modern Italy is best represented by the series of local reports published in the Forma Italiae series (Castagnoli 1974).

Important as this type of investigation has been, it does not represent the type of landscape or settlement archaeology that is practiced by most theoretically and methodologically updated archaeologists in either the New or the Old World.  The Forma Italiae archaeologists have concentrated on sites that have left significant features above the surface or have produced major finds.  These tend to be official monuments or structures left behind by the elite members of society.  In most instances, no effort has been made to conduct systematic, modern surveys in the territory under investigation, which would reveal a greater quantity and range of sites and allow the reconstruction of the total settlement history of a particular portion of Italian landscape.  This older approach has not provided the more complete range of archaeological information needed by historians who wish to question the picture of rural development that has been derived from the Roman period written sources.

However, this picture is slowly beginning to change.  The first modern archaeological survey in Italy was developed just after World War II by John Ward Perkins, a successor of Thomas Ashby at the British School at Rome.  Perkins saw the rapid changes that were taking place around Rome in the aftermath of the war.  Country districts that had long been largely deserted due to a combination of malaria and concentrated, unproductive landholdings were now being transformed by a combination of land reform, more intensive, mechanized agriculture, and the suburban development spreading out from Rome.  Every year large numbers of archaeological sites were being exposed and very rapidly destroyed by tractor plowing and construction.  The moment seemed ripe to launch a long-term survey project which would use the resources and personnel of the British School to record information on the rural sites before they were destroyed and weave the data into an archaeologically based history of one portion of the Italian countryside (Potter 1979:1-18).  The region selected centered around the very important Etruscan site of Veii located some twelve kilometers north of Rome.  Veii had been an early rival of Rome, and its destruction in the early fourth century B.C. marked an important stage of Rome's expansion into an Italian power (Scullard 1967:104-10).  Even though the main center at Veii was destroyed, the countryside remained inhabited into the Middle Ages.

Season after season, British School archaeologists returned to the territory of Veii, building a survey data base on the area which is still unparalleled for any other region of Italy.  An attempt was made to collect evidence for all periods from the earliest prehistoric settlements to the Middle Ages.  Methods of collection, recording, and analysis were standardized.  The approach was extended to neighboring territories, with the result that it is now possible to write a settlement history of this area of Italy for long periods of time which is unique for the peninsula (Kahane, Threipland, and Ward-Perkins 1968; Ward-Perkins 1962, 1972).

The British School survey project around Veii can be compared in many respects with the settlement research that was being conducted by Gordon Willey at almost the same time in the Viru Valley in Peru (Willey 1953; Willey and Sabloff 1980:146-49). Both showed how survey archaeology could be used to reconstruct the settlement history of complex cultures. In the case of the Veii survey, the massive data that it provided allowed the first convincing challenge to the pattern of Roman rural development that had been derived from the classical authors. Especially striking was the fact that the Veii survey evidence showed that small farms did not disappear in that part of central Italy during the second and first centuries B.C. The number of settlers seemed to hold steady in the later second and first centuries A.D and actually increased around the start of the Christian era.

Unlike the Viru Valley survey project, which stimulated a range of survey-oriented research projects in Mesoamerican and South American settlement history, the British Veii survey did not produce a major change in the way that ancient historians and classical archaeologists did archaeology and looked at settlement history. Ancient historians remained (and still remain) largely unfamiliar and uncomfortable with the use of archaeological material, especially of the type provided by the British School surveys, and were slow to appreciate and use this new evidence. Some scholars such as Brendon Nagle of the University of Southern California did see the potential usefulness that the Veii research had for a rethinking of the traditional historical reconstructions (Nagle 1979). However, he remained for a long time an isolated voice. His colleagues remained satisfied with their written sources and traditional explanations. The classical archaeologists, especially in the United States where most of the research money was concentrated during the 1950s and 1960s, showed even less interest. With the exception of McDonald and Hope-Simpson working on Mycenaean survey and settlement research in the western Peloponessus, the classical archaeologists concentrated their efforts on the excavation of major urban sites like Sardis and the Athenian Agora which would yield beautiful art objects and high culture monuments associated with the elite of antiquity (McDonald and Hope-Simpson 1961). Although excavation techniques were improved during this period, the American branch of classical archaeology remained isolated from currents in other areas of archaeology, hostile to new theory, and uninterested in the social science approach which an emphasis on survey archaeology required (Dyson 1981a).

The disinterest of ancient historians and classical archaeologists in the new rural archaeology emerging from the British School studies can be explained by a study of the sociology of the disciplines but cannot be totally excused. Roman historians should have realized much earlier the severe limitations of the ancient texts for the types of social and economic research that modern historical studies demand. New archival sources for ancient Rome are not going to be found except in very exceptional areas like Egypt whose historical development was very different from that of the rest of the Roman Empire (Lewis 1983). However, the organization of Roman agriculture made it an ideal subject for archaeologically based historical reconstructions that employ the survey data. Roman farmers, especially in Italy, lived in individual farmsteads scattered throughout the rural areas (Percival 1976; White 1970). Most areas farmed in the Roman period either are cultivated today or have been until quite recently. Roman rural sites, even those of quite small size, produce abundant surface remains including such highly visible artifacts as roof tile fragments and such readily datable objects as glazed and molded pottery.

The changes in land use and agricultural technology, especially mechanization, that were noted for the Veii area have now spread to most parts of the peninsula. Thousands of archaeological sites have been exposed and await systematic investigation. There is a certain urgency to these developments because a few years of tractor plowing can largely destroy the smaller rural sites and thus quickly bias the sample. Moreover, in many marginal areas, farmland is being abandoned, pastureland and scrub growth are returning, and the archaeological visibility is being sharply reduced.

However, the period of the 1970s and the 1980s have seen a growing interest in survey and landscape archaeology on the part of non-British archaeologists. A number of projects have been started in different regions, and the results are beginning to be published in systematic fashion. One example is the survey conducted by Wesleyan University in the area of the Roman town of Cosa during the early 1970s (Dyson 1978, 1981b). Cosa was a Roman colony founded in 273 B.C. on the west coast of Italy about 100 miles north of Rome (Brown 1980). The colony was selected as a survey area for several reasons. Like all Roman colonies, Cosa consisted of a fortified central place and a large area of attached farmland. This land was allocated in regular units to the farmer-soldiers who formed the basis of the colony. The territory of Cosa thus provides the opportunity to study the organizational and historical development of a particularly Roman rural landscape. Moreover, the territory around Cosa was supposed to have played a significant role in the articulation of the Roman agrarian crisis of the later second century B.C. The future tribune-reformer Tiberius Gracchus passed through the area on his way back and forth to service in Spain, and the sight of the landscape devoid of small farmers and dominated by slave shepherds and the large estates helped inspire his plans for reform (Nagle 1976). Finally, both the city and port of Cosa had been investigated through a long series of excavations conducted under the auspices of the American Academy in Rome, and this allowed our research in the countryside to be coordinated with the results of the urban and port excavations (Brown 1980; McCann 1987).

The Wesleyan survey was conducted over two seasons using methods and approaches very similar to the British School surveys. The data derived from our survey showed a pattern of Roman rural change different from both the rural history of the area developed from the literary sources and the picture of Roman rural change reconstructed for the Veii area. Our evidence suggested that the territory of Cosa had a large rural population during the later second and early first centuries B.C., a period when, supposedly, its small farms were being deserted and the zone was coming under the domination of a few large estates. Our picture of rural prosperity during this period matched well the evidence from the town of Cosa itself. There the excavations showed considerable public and private rebuilding and a generally high level of prosperity (Brown 1980:47-75). However, unlike the countryside of Veii, that of Cosa did not see its fortunes improve during the later first century B.C. and the early first century A.D. Instead, there was a modest decrease in the number of sites occupied. This trend continued in the second and early third century A.D., and by the middle years of the third century A.D. the area seems to have been largely deserted. Affected were not only the small farmers but also the great estate owners. Excavations at two major villas in the Cosa area showed decline and abandonment during the later decades of the second century A.D. (Carandini 1985; Dyson 1981b). At Cosa, the Wesleyan research team also attempted to classify sites according to size and importance using a system based on the standing remains, the extent of the surface scatter, and the presence of certain materials in the surface scatter such as mosaic and floor fragments. This evidence showed that most of the really large villas were located in a very small area on the coast. They directly controlled a limited hinterland, although they were certainly engaged in profit-making agricultural activity. The one large villa site that has been extensively excavated produced the remains of olive presses located not far from the residential quarters. These large coastal villas belonged to a type known as the *villa maritima*, whose owners were as much interested in accessibility from Rome and residential comfort as they were in farm production (D'Arms 1970; McKay 1975). In contrast with these coastal palaces, the interior farmsteads ranged from those with modest comforts to very small structures with few remains other than roof tiles and the traces of mudbrick walls. These medium and small establishments were scattered relatively evenly throughout the areas of good agricultural land in the interior.

The Wesleyan Cosa survey, like those around Veii, demonstrated the limitations of facile historical reconstructions of Roman rural development based solely on the literary texts and a limited range of standing archaeological monuments. The pattern of rural development at Cosa, which was very different from that at Veii, demonstrated the importance of regional and local variations in creation of a modern history of the Roman landscape. Even within the general areas of Cosa and Veii other detailed surveys conducted by British, Italian and American groups have shown considerable microvariation, the product of such factors as earlier settlement history, natural resources, and access to larger markets. At Cosa the contrast lay between the coastal areas where the producers had access to major outside markets such as the city of Rome and could specialize in such products as wine and the interior farmers who had to be more self-sufficient (Carandini 1985).

The general conclusions derived from the Veii and Cosa surveys, especially as they related to local and regional variation in Roman rural history, are being supported by other investigations of the Roman countryside. Two recent publications provide a summary of this type of research through the mid-1980s (Dyson 1982; Keller and Rupp 1983). Survey archaeology has grown in popularity, and the importance of its results have been appreciated, even though the financial resources available for archaeology, especially for foreign projects in Italy, have become more limited. An especially encouraging development is the growing interest shown by Italian archaeological groups, both amateur and professional, in this type of research. The need for local involvement in survey archaeology is especially important because all the research continues to make clear the great variety and local quality manifest in Roman rural development. The settlement history reconstructed for the hinterland behind the decaying Etruscan-Roman center of Vulci is very different from that of the Liri valley on the main route between Rome and Naples (Carandini 1985; Wightman 1979, 1981). Communities located in southeast Italy, a region which prospered in late antiquity, had a very different rural history from those in the central mountain regions of the peninsula (Barker and Lloyd 1978; Lloyd and Barker 1981).

It is also clear that future research will have to move beyond survey-settlement archaeology to a true landscape archaeology which investigates a greater range of man-land relationships during the Roman period. During the years immediately after World War II, study of combat air photographs stimulated large-scale landscape research in Italy (Bradford 1957). This approach was especially useful for the investigation of land use organization during the Roman period because the Romans employed professional surveyors to divide the land for new colonies (Dilke 1971). Traces of these Roman divisions still survive in the landscape of many parts of the Roman world but generally can be detected only through the use of air photographs. The Italian scholar Ferdinando Castagnoli has undertaken pioneering research on Roman land organization in Italy (Castagnoli 1958). The systematic use of air photography in Italy has lagged behind similar research in France and Britain (Schmiedt 1964-70), but recently some very promising research has been conducted by French scholars on centuriation and land use systems in Roman Italy (Chouquer et al. 1987).

The ecological background to Roman rural history has been even less well researched. Some attention has been paid to geomorphological changes, especially in the river valleys, and these changes tell about climatic variation and land use alteration during different periods of Roman history (Alvarez 1972; Judson 1963; Vita-Finzi 1969, 1978). There appears to be convincing evidence of increased erosion in the period between late antiquity and the early Middle Ages. This may relate to climate deterioration and may provide a partial explanation for the decline of the Roman rural system during that period (Hodges and Whitehouse 1983:57-59).

Very little work has been done on the vegetation history of Italy during the Roman period. A pioneering study undertaken in the Veii area by an ecological research team led by Professor Evelyn Hutchinson of Yale did find evidence for changes in pollen that may relate to increased Roman farming in the area (Hutchinson 1970). However, this has not been followed up by similar research in other areas. Little has been done with questions of deforestation, although Italy from the prehistoric period onward faced a major conflict between the need for forest resources and the demands of a heavily pastoral economy (Meiggs 1982). Little research has been done on marginal lands such as swamps and marshes, even though they probably played a larger role in Roman rural life than historians and archaeologists have suspected (Traina 1986). The role of pastoralism in shaping land use and the land has received some attention, but there has been relatively little coordination between historical and archaeological research, especially for the Roman period (Barker 1981; Frayn 1984).

In spite of a long history of interest in certain aspects of Roman rural Italy, a true landscape archaeology of Roman Italy is still in its pioneering phase. Studies of large-scale land reorganization such as centuriation impress upon us the impact that the spread of Roman control had on the land. However, the survey archaeology conducted since World War II has shown how local forces shaped in many different ways this initially rather uniform pattern of Roman territorial, social, and economic organization. The great contemporary interest in ecology is only just now beginning to be felt in Roman rural studies. What is clear is our ignorance of what went on at the base of Roman society. However, the archaeological and archaeologically related studies of the last three decades have provided scholars with the tools to dispel much of this ignorance. By the end of the century, students of Roman history will have a picture of rural history very different from what we have today, one that better reflects the complex history of the Romans and the land upon which they lived.

252    *Stephen L. Dyson*

## References Cited

Alvarez, W. 1972. The Treia valley north of Rome: Volcanic stratigraphy, topographical evolution, and geological influence on human settlement. *Geologia Romana* 11:153-76.

Ashby, T. 1927. *The Roman Campagna in classical times.* London: E. Benn.

Barker, G. 1981. *Landscape and society: Prehistoric central Italy.* London: Academic Press.

----, and J. Lloyd. 1978. *A classical landscape in Molise.* Papers of the British School at Rome 46:35-51.

----, and Oreste Ferrari (editors). 1986. *Thomas Ashby: Un archeologo fotografa la campagna romana tra '800 e '900.* Rome: British School at Rome.

Bernstein, A. H. 1978. *Tiberius Sempronius Gracchus: Tradition and apostacy.* Ithaca, N.Y.: Cornell University Press.

Bloch, R. 1960. *The origins of Rome.* London: Thames and Hudson.

Bradford, J. 1957. *Ancient landscapes.* London: Bell and Sons.

Brown, F. E. 1980. *Cosa: The making of a Roman town.* Ann Arbor: University of Michigan Press.

Carandini, A. 1985. *La romanizzazione dell' Etruria: il territorio di Vulci.* Milan: Electa.

----. and Salvatore Settis. 1979. *Schiavi e padroni nell' Etruria romana.* Bari: D. Donato.

Castagnoli, F. 1958. *Le ricerche sui resti della centuriazione.* Rome: Edizioni d'storiae letteratura.

----. 1974. La carta archeologica d'Italia e gli studi di topografia antica. *Quaderni dell'Istitutu di topografia antica della Universita di Roma* 6:7-17.

Chouquer, G., M. Clavel-Leveque, F. Favory, and Jean-Pierre Vallat. 1987. *Structures agraires en Italie centro-méridionale.* Rome: Ecole Française de Rome.

D'Arms, J. 1970. *Romans on the Bay of Naples.* Cambridge: Harvard University Press.

Dilke, O. A. W. 1971. *The Roman land surveyors.* New York: Newton Abbot, David and Charles.

Dyson, S. L. 1978. Settlement pattern in the Ager Cosanus: The Wesleyan University survey, 1974-1976. *Journal of Field Archaeology* 5:251-68.

----. 1981a. A classical archaeologist's response to the "new archaeology." *Bulletin of the American School of Oriental Research* 242:7-13.

----. 1981b. Survey archaeology: Exploring the Roman countryside. *Archaeology* 34:31-38.

----. 1982. Archaeological survey in the Mediterranean Basin: A review of recent research. *American Antiquity* 47:87-98.

Frayn, J. M. 1984. *Sheep raising and the wool trade in Italy during the Roman period.* Liverpool: A. Cairns.

Highet, G. 1959. *Poets in a landscape.* Harmondsworth: Greenwood.

Hodges, R., and D. Whitehouse. 1983. *Mohammed, Charlemagne, and the origins of Europe.* Ithaca, N.Y.: Cornell University Press.

Hutchinson, G. E. 1970. Ianula: An account of the history and development of the Lago di Monterosi, Latium, Italy. *Transactions of the American Philosophical Society* 60(4).

Judson, S. 1963. Erosion and deposition of Italian stream valleys during historic time. *Science* 140:898-99.

Kahane, A. M., L. M. Threipland, and J. Ward-Perkins. 1968. The Ager Veiantanus, north and east of Rome. *Papers of the British School at Rome* No. 36.

Keller, D. R., and D. W. Rupp. 1983. *Archaeological survey in the Mediterranean area.* British Archaeological Reports. Oxford.

Konstan, D. 1975. Marxism and Roman slavery. *Arethusa* 8:145-69.

Lewis, N. 1983. *Life in Egypt under Roman rule.* Oxford: Oxford University Press.

Lloyd, J., and G. Barker. 1981. Rural settlement in Molise: Problems of archaeological survey. In *Archaeology and Italian society*, ed. G. Barker and R. Hodges, pp. 289-304. British Archaeological Reports. Oxford.

McCann, A. M. 1987. *The Roman port and fishery of Cosa.* Princeton, N.J.: Princeton University Press.

McDonald, W. A., and R. Hope-Simpson. 1961. Prehistoric habitation in southwestern Peloponnese. *American Journal of Archaeology* 65:221-60.

McKay, A. G. 1975. *Houses, villas, and palaces in the Roman world.* Ithaca, N.Y.: Cornell University Press.

Meiggs, R. 1982. *Trees and timber in the ancient Mediterranean.* Oxford: Clarendon Press.

Nagle, R. 1976. The Etruscan journey of Tiberius Gracchus. *Historia* 25:487-89.

----. 1979. Towards a sociology of southern Etruria. *Athenaeum* 57:411-41.

Peacock, D. P. S. 1982. *Pottery in the Roman world.* New York: Longman.

Percival, J. 1976. *The Roman villa.* Berkeley: University of California Press.

Potter, T. W. 1979. *The changing landscape of South Etruria.* New York: St. Martin's Press.

----. 1987. *Roman Italy.* Berkeley: University of California Press.

Riddle, J. M. 1970. *Tiberius Gracchus: Destroyer or reformer of the republic.* Lexington, Mass.: Heath.

Schmiedt, G. 1964-70. *Atlanta aerofotografico della sedo umanein Italia.* Firenze, Istituto Geografic. Militare.

Scullard, H. H. 1967. *The Etruscan cities and Rome.* Ithaca, N.Y.: Cornell University Press.

Toynbee, A. 1965. *Hannibal's legacy.* Oxford: Oxford University Press.

Traina, G. 1986. Paesaggio e 'decadenza: La palude nella transformazione del mondo antico. In *Società romana e impero tardoantico*, ed. A. Giardina, pp. 711-30. Rome-Bari: Laterza.

Veyne, P. 1984. *Writing history.* Middletown, Conn.: Wesleyan University Press.

Vita-Finzi, C. 1969. *The Mediterranean valleys.* Cambridge: Cambridge University Press.

----. 1978. *Archaeological sites in their setting.* London: Thames and Hudson.

Ward-Perkins, J. B. 1962. Etruscan towns, Roman roads, and medieval villages: The historical geography of the southern Etruria. *Geographical Journal* 128:389-405.

----. 1972. Central authority and patterns of rural settlement. In *Man, settlement, and urbanism*, ed. R. J. Ucko, R. Tringham, and G. W. Dimbleby, pp. 867-82. London: London University Press.

White, K. D. 1970. *Roman farming.* Ithaca, N.Y.: Cornell University Press.

Wightman, E. M. 1979. McMaster surface survey in the lower Liri valley. *Classical News and Views* 23:26-29.

----. 1981. The lower Liri valley: Problems, trends, and peculiarities. In *Archaeology and Italian society*, ed. G. Barker and R. Hodges, pp. 275-87. British Archaeological Reports. Oxford.

Willey, G. R. 1953. *Prehistoric settlement patterns in the Viru Valley.* Washington, D.C.: U.S. Government Printing Office.

----, and J. Sabloff. 1980. *A history of American archaeology.* San Francisco: W. H. Freeman.

Wills, G. 1984. *Cincinnatus.* Garden City, N.Y.: Doubleday.

*IV. Landscape Science*

# 16

# TWO CENTURIES OF LANDSCAPE CHANGE AT MORVEN, PRINCETON, NEW JERSEY

Naomi F. Miller, Anne Yentsch,
Dolores Piperno, and Barbara Paca

Few would question that between the eighteenth and nineteenth centuries America was transformed from a colonial outpost of England to an independent and increasingly differentiated agricultural, commercial, and industrial nation. It is less clear when and how attitudes toward the land also changed. Information from archaeological, documentary, and botanical sources does, however, make it possible to infer landscapes long gone; and so by examining the eighteenth-century cultural landscape and its subsequent evolution at Morven, Landscape Archaeology at Morven is beginning to identify how material remains in the landscape itself, at least in one part of the northeastern United States, reflect these changes.

Morven stands on property acquired in the late seventeenth century by the grandfather of Richard Stockton, a signer of the Declaration of Independence for New Jersey. Stockton was living on the property by 1760. The building one sees today at Morven is a house of seeming Georgian design, consisting of a central block and two symmetrically placed wings, all facing south (fig. 16.1). Although only the walls of the original west wing have survived numerous rebuildings, the mansion was occupied for almost 175 years by the Stockton family. The property was then leased by Robert W. Johnson of Johnson and Johnson, and subsequently, for about 40 years, it was the formal residence for the governors of the state of New Jersey. Governor and Mrs. Walter Edge gave Morven to the state in 1951. It is now administered by the New Jersey State Museum, a division of the New Jersey Department of State, and is being made into a museum of cultural history and decorative arts. Change in the house and its landscape is central to the museum's focus on material culture.

As part of the process of making Morven a museum, we are tracing the effects that the households of five generations of Stocktons had on Morven. Our goal is to find archaeological, botanical, and documentary evidence of how they used and shaped their property, especially the grounds surrounding the house where the ornamental and kitchen gardens would have been. It should be possible to distinguish lawn from shrubbery, tree holes from planting beds, and, by analyzing traces of earlier landscapes, to reconstruct the changing vistas. As our research progresses, we are beginning to identify some of the ideas that probably guided the Stocktons' landscaping decisions. Because research at Morven is in its initial stages, our knowledge is still sketchy. This chapter illustrates the range of information available for landscape and ethnobotanical analysis and discusses how it will be integrated into the museum's interpretation of Morven's history.

Figure 16.1. Morven. (Photograph by Marty O'Grady)

Any garden is complex, and reconstructing a vanished garden requires special techniques. Extant vegetation, natural terrain, and local environment determine the baseline for historical and archaeological reconstructions. In the case of a relatively recent garden, one may even discover possible descendants of the original plantings (Miller and Yentsch 1988). Cultural elements that have been imposed on the land must be located and dated. These include physical structures (e.g., roads, paths, parterres, and buildings), conceptual structures (e.g., vistas, access routes, and boundaries), and other traces of former human activities (e.g., old ground surfaces, ground covers, trees, and other plantings). In reconstructing past landscapes, one looks at archaeological evidence, historical data, and the present-day environment to guide research. At Morven, we began with a topographic study and a search for archaeological features that would yield archaeobotanical evidence for plants and trees that no longer exist. Additionally, a vegetation survey was conducted to identify plants growing on the house lot.

## Topography and the Eighteenth-Century Vista

The Stocktons' gardens were a New World adaptation of an Old World practice. English gardens of the Middle Ages and Renaissance were enclosed spaces where new plants could be introduced and developed (Thacker 1979:83, 121). Gardens were alternatively viewed as "collections of plants and as artistic compositions" (Brookes 1984:29). In the early eighteenth century, intellectuals suggested a "Man might make a pretty Landskip of his own Possessions" (Addison 1712), and the bounds of the garden were visually expanded to include the surrounding land. Not only were vistas of the nearby cultivated and natural countryside incorporated into the garden landscape, but by mid-century the surrounding countryside itself was transformed to satisfy the aesthetic requirements of picturesque landscaping (cf. Jacques 1983:105; Thacker 1979:182 ff.).

Although American colonists did not adopt the radical advice of English gardening philosophers such as Capability Brown or Horace Walpole,[1] they were aware of the English theories and put some of them into practice. Some improvement programs had primarily economic aims; treatises advocating new and better agricultural techniques were particularly popular in the colonies during the eighteenth century (Isaac 1982). But other attempts to mold the landscape were driven by social and aesthetic aims.

Documentation and local tradition state that the garden plan of Morven, dating to approximately 1770, was based on the design of Alexander Pope's villa at Twickenham. While in England during the late 1760s, Richard Stockton wrote to his wife that he planned to ride out to Pope's villa with a draftsman who would assist in drawing up a plan of the Twickenham garden (Bill et al. 1978:29). Because that garden had been partially obliterated soon after Pope died in 1744 (Martin 1984:61), it is not at all clear to what extent the Stocktons' garden actually followed Pope's design. According to tradition, however, the area south of the house corresponds to Pope's greensward, which ran from the river elevation of his villa down to the Thames River, and Stockton Street itself corresponds to the Thames River (Bill et al. 1978:31).

Although the present property is much smaller than the original Stockton estate, the most obvious features on the original lot is the house and its placement vis-à-vis the surrounding land (fig. 16.2). The house is sited on a slight rise in the natural terrain. The land around it was originally shaped, quite literally, by the construction of terraces.

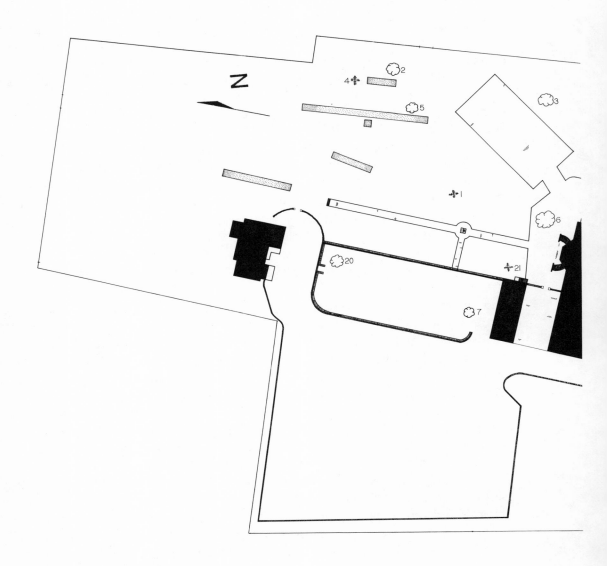

Figure 16.2. Map of Morven showing 1987 excavation trenches and trees cored by Lockwood Associates. Eastern hemlock (4); Norway spruce (1, 21); white pine (8, 9); black locust (5); catalpa (13); English walnut (19); horse chestnut (7, 15); magnolia (6); mulberry (20); Ohio buckeye (17); pin oak (11); princess tree (18); sugar maple (14); sycamore (3, 10, 23); tulip tree (2, 12, 16, 22, 24).

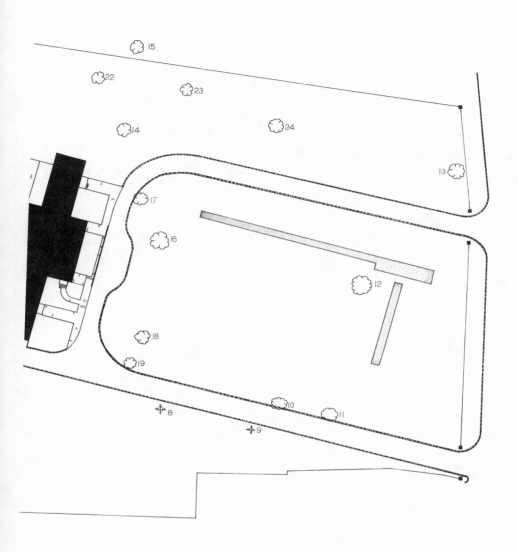

## Analogies with Other Colonial Estates

The architectural practice that used spatial dominance to represent social dominance was present from the onset of colonial settlement 100 to 150 years earlier. The house metaphorically revealed the rank of its household by the view it controlled and by its visibility in the community. For example, the Charles Calvert house in Annapolis, Maryland, was located on top of an artificially terraced hill. Not only did it provide a vista for its occupants, it was also a highly visible element in the townscape of Annapolis. The location of the house with respect to the community expressed the position of leadership the Calvert family possessed as representatives of Lord Baltimore's family in the province of Maryland (Yentsch 1989). Visibility was of equal importance to families living in the rural countryside, as witnessed by the careful placement of houses, outbuildings, and terraces in the many plantations along the shores of the James River in Virginia. High land was culturally valued (cf. Smolek and Clark 1982), and implicit in its value was the concept of a vista.

The William Paca Garden, located in Annapolis, also commanded a pleasing view. It is contemporary with Richard Stockton's garden at Morven, and the two sites have much in common. William Paca, who also signed the Declaration of Independence, built his gardens in approximately 1763. As far as we know, the Paca Garden contained the first wilderness garden built in America, yet it too had formal elements, such as terraces. This pattern is typical of the Tidewater region and can be seen in many documented sites such as the Carroll garden in Annapolis, Wye Hall on Wye Island, Maryland, Tulip Hill in Harwood, Maryland, and Sabine Hall in Virginia, to name but a few examples. It is therefore quite possible that like other eighteenth-century garden designers, Richard Stockton introduced naturalistic elements into the formal pleasure garden at Morven.

The design of the Paca Garden serves as a model against which the Morven garden plan can be assessed. Paca and Wright (Paca and Wright 1983; Paca-Steele and Wright 1985, 1987) observed that the apparent loss of order introduced into the garden plan by its wilderness features was compensated for by an overall proportional grid based on a simple geometric shape, the rectangle formed by two 3-4-5 triangles. These dimensions are identical to that of the main block of the Paca House and were derived from the basic units of measure used by surveyors in the eighteenth century. These units of measure are based on the 66-foot Gunter's chain and its basic division, the 16.5-foot rod or pole. The geometric grid at the Paca Garden determines the location of the garden wall, garden buildings (including a two-story octagonal pavilion, a bathhouse, and a springhouse), terrace edges, and the main axis of the garden. The wilderness style, then fashionable in Great Britain, was integrated into the garden in a highly controlled manner. The apparent contradiction (by today's standards) inherent in a formal wilderness becomes less jarring if one bears in mind that the American colonists were trying to tame the American landscape and therefore may have wished to formalize the underlying structure of their wilderness gardens.

## The Eighteenth-Century Garden at Morven

Richard Stockton undoubtedly knew of the geometric basis of early Georgian garden design. He might have used it at Morven. Ideas on the ideal forms for garden layouts were discussed in a range of readily available garden books that were often revised and reissued on a regular basis (see entries on John Evelyn [*Sylva*] and Philip Miller [*Garden Dictionary*] in Jellicoe and

Jellicoe 1986). Archaeological excavation and survey at Morven have already shown that the garden plan used perspective and illusion. It is likely that Richard Stockton would have used a proportional system for situating the major garden features.

The eighteenth-century topography of the garden seems to have consisted of a long, relatively flat expanse on the south side of the house, with a series of terraces and falls descending from the north side of the house. Anne Yentsch's analysis of topographic maps, provided by Constance Grieff of Heritage Research Studies, Inc., suggests that both the second and third terraces were narrower than their respective upper neighbor. If analogy with similar gardens of the time holds, this north yard would have contained a formal garden on the uppermost terraces adjacent to the house. The more utilitarian elements of the garden design would have been constructed farther out in the landscape, either on the lower terraces or along the eastern and western edges of the formal garden.

At Morven, it was not initially apparent whether the earlier ornamental garden had been in the north, east, or south yards. Two long trenches were laid out to obtain a subsurface profile across the entire lot perpendicular to the house. In the south yard the trench revealed little, but in the north yard it picked up the edge of a fieldstone feature (see fig 16.2, no. 12) that parallels a sharp drop in an earlier yard surface (fig. 16.3). Further excavation revealed the steplike arrangement of the fieldstone slabs (fig. 16.4). The steps appear to have been rapidly buried sometime in the mid-nineteenth century, although there was some evidence of gradual accumulation of eroded soil and household debris at their base.

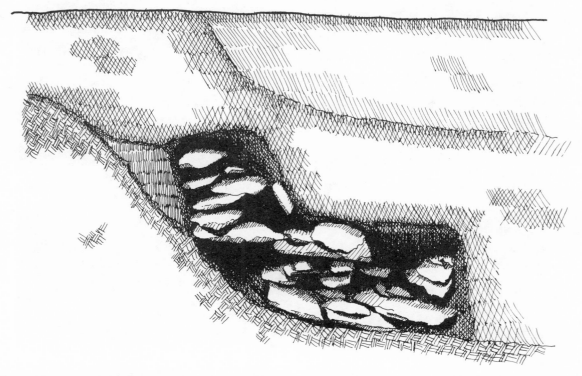

Figure 16.3. Section of upper terrace at Morven showing stones of feature 12. (Drawn by David Vandenberg)

Figure 16.4. Fieldstone steps connecting upper and second terraces (feature 12), Morven. (Photograph by Marty O'Grady)

Another subsurface feature, revealed by a ground-penetrating radar survey (Bevan 1987), lies 90 to 100 feet due west of feature 12. It is aligned with the original west wing of the house. A massive century-old mulberry tree (see fig. 16.2, no. 20) overgrown with poison ivy has hindered its excavation. Excavation in 1988 should determine whether that feature is the remains of the western steps, paired and matched to the eastern steps, thereby delimiting the garden's east and west boundaries.

The location of the steps and other subsurface features suggests that the lines of sight from the house into the vista used converging perspective, for they gradually narrowed as they extended into the landscape. Furthermore, the decreasing width of each terrace as one moved away from the house gave the illusion of greater distance as one faced north from the house. This type of perspective planning is typical of eighteenth-century landscaping practice, which uses optical illusions to make a garden appear larger to the viewer. The vista from the house and garden, with its artificial terracing, was one of immense scale, overlooking a valley, at least two streams, and perhaps ending at the southern slope of the Sourland Mountains, fifteen miles away.

Such a sophisticated approach to garden planning suggests that the designers of the garden carefully considered the proportions of the terraces. The garden at Morven may have been more naturalistic than formal in character, yet a proportional system still seems to form the basis of the garden plan. This in turn suggests that the arithmetic structure of gardens was of greater importance to the colonial gentleman architect than is usually recognized.

The upkeep of a formal terraced garden was expensive. In the nineteenth century the lower garden terraces were filled, creating the gradual slope one sees today. Excavation has shown that at or about this time the area of the leveled terrace became a plowed field.

## Evidence for Nineteenth-Century Changes: Vegetation

The proposed reconstruction of the topography, design, and vista of the garden landscape around Morven is in accord with what colleagues in Annapolis have found at the Paca Garden (Paca and Wright 1983; Paca-Steele and Wright 1985, 1987), the Ridout garden (Hopkins 1986), Tulip Hill (Paca-Steele n.d.), and the Carroll house (Shackel 1987). This is not surprising as wealthy families formed a distinctive set in colonial society, one in which there was much written communication, social contact, and discourse among members (Bushman 1984).

But what is a garden without plants? Ideally, accurate records of the plantings at Morven would have been passed down through the generations. There is, however, very limited documentary evidence for Morven, so one must rely on the physical evidence of the plants themselves, both past and present. Unfortunately, the conditions in garden sites are inherently inimical to the preservation of plant remains, because continual disturbance is one of the defining features of the garden environment.

### The Present: Extant Plants

The first stage of ethnobotanical research at Morven involved identifying, mapping, and dating the extant garden components. The plant survey had two major purposes. First, we wanted to determine if sequences of major plantings that could be associated with the various households that lived on the site were still discernible on the grounds (Miller 1988a; fig. 16.5). Second, the inventory of all types of plants (trees, shrubs, ornamentals, weeds, and lawn plants) provided a baseline useful for interpreting the plant materials recovered during excavation. Although the survey and coring are time-consuming processes, both have proved extremely useful. They do not destroy archaeological resources, and they provide information useful for evaluating archaeobotanical remains.

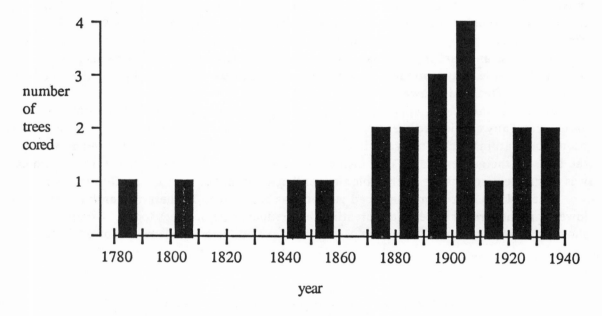

Figure 16.5.  Estimated planting years of cored trees at Morven

Today's visitor to Morven sees large tree-covered lawns at the front and back of the mansion. Groupings of trees, whether in clumps or lines, clearly represent phases in the development of the garden. We therefore thought it would be useful to find out how old the trees are. Even if one knows the exact age of a tree, one cannot tell when or if it was transplanted to its current location, but knowing even approximate ages, especially of the older trees, can help in the historical reconstruction. The base map of trees was especially useful for selecting trees to core.

Oral tradition states that two French Huguenot emigrés, Samuel and Lewis Pintard, "brought with them chestnuts from a famous tree in the courtyard of the old fortress chateau of Loche-sur-Inde, Touraine," and gave them to the Stocktons while the brothers were courting Richard Stockton's younger sisters, Abigail and Susannah (Lathrop 1928:367). Marriage records indicate that the Pintards would have been courting the two sisters in 1769 or 1770 (Stockton 1911:48). Supposedly, the gift of the seeds provided the stock for a horse chestnut walk planted by Richard and Annis Stockton. Horse chestnuts would have been an exotic species in Princeton at that time. One of the New Jersey State Museum's archaeological goals at Morven was to find traces of this walk.

As early as the seventeenth century, long avenues of trees such as limes, elms, or horse chestnuts leading to a great house were one means of creating and controlling a vista, which had "become a recognized aristocratic symbol" (Thomas 1983:207). Throughout the eighteenth-century trees were used to disguise lot boundaries or to display the extent of one's landholdings. They were an essential part of the architectural setting for a home. The Stockton house faced the King's Highway (now known as Stockton Street) on the west side of the town of Princeton, and its lands were bounded on the east by Patterson Street (now known as Bayard Lane). A reasonably accurate 1852 town map and an 1881 sketch map of the garden show that the main access road to the house was a "Horse Chestnut Walk," supposedly copied from a major garden walk in Alexander Pope's English garden at Twickenham (Bill et al. 1978; fig. 16.6). This walk stretched from Bayard Street to the front door of the house, a distance of 600 feet, whereas the distance from the house to Stockton Street used by the modern access route is only 250 feet. The walk might be said to have been designed with the intent to enhance social distance by extending the length of the Stockton property that one traversed before reaching the front door and by marking the distance with gracious trees. Excavations in 1988 revealed a late walk that may be a remnant of the horse chestnut walk known from oral tradition.

In her plant survey, Miller noted that two horse chestnuts on the adjacent property were aligned with the front of the house (see fig. 16.2, no. 15). Furthermore, they appear to be in line with the trees depicted on the nineteenth-century maps. A third horse chestnut, behind the laundry, appears to be similar in age (see fig. 16.2, no. 7). Although we wanted to find out how old these trees are, the most accurate way to age a tree is to cut it down and count its rings. We thought it would be more appropriate and aesthetic to have the trees cored. In this phase of the study, Laurence Lockwood of Lockwood Associates cored twenty-five of our largest, and presumed oldest, trees (Lockwood 1988). One or two trees were cored in each clump, as we assumed that the other trees of the group, having similar height and girth, were planted around the same time. Lockwood estimated the age of the trees by inserting a 12-inch coring device as far into the tree as possible. For many trees, the tool only reached the outer rings. He counted the number of rings per inch of these outer core segments and calculated an estimated age based on the radius of the tree. Because most of the trees that were cored are species that tend to have wider rings when they are young, the age estimates are, if anything, too high, perhaps by as much as ten to fifty years (Henry Michael, personal communication, 1988). Clearly this technique has drawbacks, yet it is the preferable way to date trees one wished to preserve.

The information obtained demonstrates that even the largest trees at Morven postdate the colonial period, despite their venerable look. One can distinguish four periods of tree planting. The first began more than 150 years ago (see fig. 16.5). The oldest trees include the horse chestnut in the west yard behind the laundry (see fig. 16.2, no. 7), and the two in the east yard within the original property bounds but now located on land belonging to the state and to the borough of Princeton (see fig. 16.2, no. 15). It is surprising that the horse chestnuts still alive at Morven may be as much as 200 years old. John Custis, in correspondence with English botanist Peter Collinson, noted that imported horse chestnuts (native to the Old World and introduced to the New World in the 1740s) took a long time to grow: "A man had need to have the patience of Job and the life of Methusala to wait upon them" (Swem 1957:61). The Morven trees (perhaps planted as early as the 1780s) are not as old as the reputed horse chestnut walk, but neither are they as young as they appear. Their slow

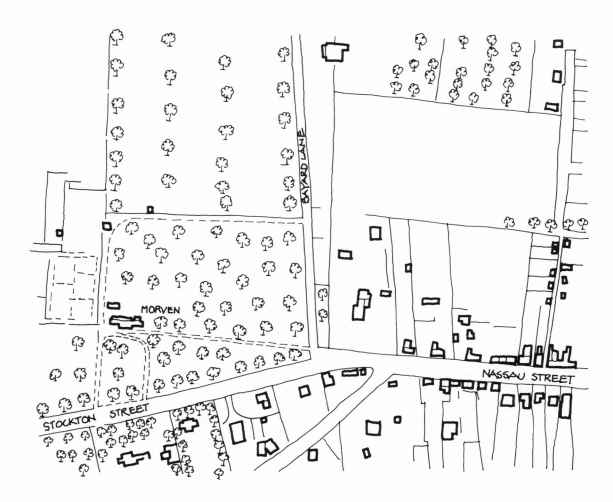

Figure 16.6. Horse chestnut walk. Redrawn from an 1852 lithograph of Princeton by Saront and Majors, surveyed and published by John Bevan. (Map on file in Princeton University Library)

growth is testimony to Custis's observation. Yet even 200-year-old trees would not have been alive when the Pintard brothers married the Stockton sisters. They are evidence, instead, of landscape elements associated with a subsequent generation of Stocktons.

The early nineteenth-century Stocktons planted other nonindigenous species in their ornamental garden at Morven, importing some from Europe and obtaining others in this country. In addition to the horse chestnuts, a sweet buckeye in front of the mansion could be between 150 to 200 years old (see fig. 16.2, no. 17). This species, native to southwestern Pennsylvania and similar regions, was first brought to the attention of the settlers in 1785 by an explorer in the Allegheny Mountains (Hedrick 1950:92). Its natural range does not extend to southeastern New Jersey. Perhaps Richard Stockton's son introduced it to the community in the early nineteenth century.

The horse chestnuts and sweet buckeye are the oldest trees on the property. There are many others that, though impressive, date to the mid-nineteenth-century phase of garden development (1840-60). This group includes two tulip poplars and a princess tree in the front (see fig. 16.2, nos. 12, 16, 18). The oldest-looking tree on the property, that is, the largest one, is one of the tulip trees in the south yard close to the street. According to tradition, Richard Stockton and his wife Annis planted the tulip tree at the entrance to their lot when they were married in 1758 (Bill et al. 1978). This is consistent with oral traditions dating to colonial times common in the mid-Atlantic and New England regions--many newlyweds planted tulip trees in their yards near entranceways to the home. Yet although the Morven tulip tree is old, it was planted no earlier than the mid-nineteenth century. Its direct tie is therefore with the third generation rather than the first generation of the house's occupants.

There are other old-looking trees on the property, including a group of three 80- to 100-foot-tall Norway spruces (see fig. 16.2, no. 1). They are relatively young, however, and belong to the late nineteenth century. A devotee of the Colonial Revival style, Helen Hamilton Shields Stockton planted them around the turn of this century when she attempted to bring the old garden back to life through artful planting, anachronistically old brickwork, and landscape alteration. What she hoped to hide was the use of the yard as farmland by Colonel Samuel W. Stockton, a direct descendant of Richard and Annis Stockton and a nephew of Commodore Robert Stockton, who obtained the property from his cousins. The Norway spruces did not belong to the eighteenth-century garden; they bear no relation to the early garden features found below the surface, such as the slope of the first terrace, and they intrude upon a nineteenth-century access road. They also cut off the house from its vista and in doing so represent more recent attitudes that link high status with seclusion rather than visibility. Finally, there is a group of trees planted after World War I.

The Past: Excavated Evidence

Archaeobotany is the technical study of plant remains from archaeological sites. At Morven, we are collecting sediment samples for recovering three types of archaeobotanical remains (macroplant remains, pollen, and phytoliths), because different types of remains can be used to answer different questions about vegetation and plant use. An archaeological garden site presents special problems to the archaeologist; plant materials that are found in a garden may not have been deliberately planted there and hence may not be associated with the people who created the garden. Postdepositional disturbance by people and animals can also confuse interpretations.

Macroremains--large items such as seeds and charcoal--are most likely to be found in trashy deposits. Macroremains are large enough to see without a microscope but frequently are too small to see during excavation. Therefore, they are extracted from sediment samples by flotation. We used a SMAP-like system (Watson 1976) designed by William Sandy of New Brunswick, New Jersey, to retrieve them. On ordinary habitation sites, one would seek macroremains as evidence of what people ate and what they burned for fuel. In a garden, original sources of seeds include intentionally planted ones, naturally dispersed ones (whether from local weeds and ornamentals or by wind or animals), and fertilizer (dung or garbage). Unfortunately, the older the garden deposit, the less likely original seeds are to remain. Uncharred seeds decay rapidly, so one cannot assume uncharred seeds are old (Minnis 1981). The vast majority of seeds Miller recovered by flotation are not charred. Tiny, thin-walled weed seeds from chickweed and carpetweed dominate the flotation samples. These weeds now grow on the property, and there is little doubt that their remains in the samples are recent. The samples contain the seeds of several other plants that grow between the bricks of the pathways (including goosefoot, dandelion, copperleaf, goose grass, crabgrass, yellow wood sorrel, and common nightshade). Types that occur in the flotation samples and that also grow today in the lawn and garden beds include Indian strawberry, yellow wood sorrel, and pokeweed. Nearly all the seeds come from plants that grow adjacent to or over the excavation units at the site (Miller 1988b).

In contrast, there are no peach trees on the property today, yet one peach pit was recovered from a stratum above the lower terrace ground surface. It is more likely to be a true archaeological find, and in future seasons sealed deposits, especially from areas that might have been dump sites, should produce others (Miller 1988b).

Archaeological pollen is the second type of plant material we sought. Windblown pollen can provide information about plants growing around the site, and other types of pollen might make it possible to pinpoint more local vegetation. Because garden soil by its nature is disturbed, it is particularly poor for pollen preservation. Mechanical abrasion and oxidation are both detrimental to pollen. Following the advice of Gerald Kelso, we took a column of pollen samples from an excavation area that had relatively deep, relatively quickly deposited sediments, namely, the leveled terrace over feature 12. Unfortunately, pollen was present in insufficient quantities to allow identification (Kelso 1988).

A third set of sediment samples was taken for phytolith analysis (Piperno 1988). Phytoliths are silica bodies (also known as plant opal) that are incorporated into many plant tissues. Although not universally formed in all higher plants, many families and genera of plants produce phytoliths in distinctive morphologies (Piperno 1987). Because phytoliths tend to persist in the soil after the decay of the contributing plants and have a narrow dispersal range, the research team expects to identify specific trees and other plants that grew in the garden. This information should help to distinguish different uses of space. For example, phytoliths may enable us to differentiate former lawns from nonlawn areas, ornamental from kitchen gardens, orchard from vineyard, and service from display areas.

Phytolith analysis comes as a recent addition to the paleoethnobotanical arsenal in historical archaeology. Over the last decade such analysis has been established as an integral part of prehistoric reconstructions, although much basic research on phytolith production, taxonomy, and interpretation needs to be carried out (see Piperno 1987). To date, work at historical sites has concentrated on the identification of fodder crops at Monticello (Rovner 1988) and on weedy grasses in urban Lowell at the Boott Mills (Fisher 1987). As far as we know, the only other garden site where phytoliths have been analyzed is Bacon's Castle on the lower James River in Tidewater Virginia (see Luccketti, above). Like Morven, the samples from Bacon's Castle contained heavy concentrations of phytoliths, but until a modern collection is made and species-specific phytoliths are identified for Tidewater Virginia (a study presently underway by Irwin Rovner and the Garden Clubs of Virginia), no identifications can be made.

At Morven sediment samples for the phytolith study were taken in and around excavated planting holes and garden beds. In addition, a series of samples was taken from the balk of the excavated terrace. Finally, a few handfuls of dirt were routinely removed from the flotation samples to provide control samples and overall coverage for the site. Preliminary results indicate that phytoliths are present in abundance in many samples. Taxa identified include the Gramineae (grasses), Cyperaceae (sedges), Compositae, ferns, squash (*Cucurbita* sp.), and a large number of arboreal and herbaceous forms that at present cannot be identified more precisely. Piperno's enlargement of the modern phytolith collection, funded by Landscape Archaeology at Morven and housed at the University Museum at the University of Pennsylvania, will facilitate identification of many of these unknown types.

The patterns of phytolith distribution indicate primary deposition of most plants rather than intrusive occurrences. For example, samples from garden beds and planting holes are phytolith rich, while soils taken adjacent to such contexts are phytolith poor or devoid of phytoliths.

The vast majority (over 90 percent) of the grass phytoliths were from the festucoid subfamily, which includes such genera as *Poa* and *Festuca*. These, of course, are common cultivated lawn grasses in the New Jersey region. Other Gramineae phytoliths belong to the chloridoid and panicoid subfamilies, which include genera like *Panicum* and *Chloris* and are likely to have been weedy as opposed to planted grasses. Festucoid phytoliths occurred in abundance both in planting holes and garden beds, and Piperno believes these eventually will be identified to the genus level.

There were fewer lawn grasses in the assemblage from the kitchen courtyard work area, an area of the site peripheral to the ornamental garden. At the same time, the plant remains from the feature samples in the courtyard area included many microscopic remains of plants and animals known as diatoms and sponge spicules, respectively. These are characteristically found where the soil is well watered and poorly drained. Since the feature was located less than 10 feet east of the well and 5 to 7 feet south of the icehouse doorway, there was ample opportunity for water to accumulate, for drainage was inhibited by the presence of subsurface brick walls and by the heavy clay concentration of the soil.

Squash phytoliths were recovered from a garden bed near the north central entrance to the house. Since the central garden path, installed by Helen Hamilton Shields Stockton around 1900–1910, lay above this planting bed, it has been tentatively dated to the late nineteenth century and the occupation of Samuel W. Stockton, the Princeton farmer. Comments about the estate by visitors during his era suggest that he did not maintain the formal or decorative gardens (Constance Greiff, personal communication, 1988), although evidence from the 1987 excavation indicates that it was his uncle, Commodore Robert Stockton, who buried the terraces. Commodore Stockton removed the work areas from the south yard, turned portions of the north yard into work areas, and emphasized the yard fronting Stockton Street. The change is also suggested by the presence of phytoliths of food plants recovered in archaeological strata dating to the nineteenth century from the present kitchen courtyard area.

Arboreal phytoliths occurred almost exclusively in planting holes whose depth and placement suggest they once contained trees. It should be possible to make precise identifications of many of these with the expanded, modern comparative collection and to provide a clear picture of the kinds of trees that were planted and their locations in the yard. These data, combined with the inventory of extant trees and their ages, will help us chart additional changes to the yard over time.

## Conclusions

The first phase of the New Jersey State Museum's historic archaeology program at Morven was designed to see whether excavation would reveal earlier landscapes. Historical information, botanical, and archaeobotanical research methods were integrated within an ethnobotanical framework from the outset of the project. Miller, in her dual role as assistant director and archaeobotanist, developed the ethnobotanical aspects of the research program. In addition, by working on site on a daily basis, she ensured that the ethnobotanical research design would be fully integrated with the other archaeological work. The results thus far are promising and suggest that intensive study of plant remains from historic sites has the potential to further refine understanding of the different ways, technological and ideological, in which the natural world was utilized by people of the past.

The changing garden vistas have been inferred from excavated features and collateral information; U.S.G.S. topographic maps suggest the terrain in a widespread area surrounding the site. Present-day vistas of or toward the Sourland Mountains suggest the depth of view that once existed. Modern growth obscures much of this from the vantage of present-day Princeton, for forests cover at least 15 percent more of the county's land than in 1899 (1970 map in Robichaud and Buell 1983:76). But eighteenth-century pictorial information on rural countrysides (Harris 1979; Nygren and Robertson 1986; Rosenthal 1982), when combined with information on eighteenth-century agricultural tillage and grazing, allows one to infer to a reasonable degree earlier appearance of the land.

As research progresses, we will integrate the botanical data with information on the garden's design obtained from plotting and dating the different garden features. As of 1987, these features include one set of terrace steps, the terrace fall line, a garden walk, a brick carriageway, several tree holes, and a planting bed. Alone, none of these landscape elements is particularly informative. Each must be related to the others in time and in space before the garden plan will emerge. Still, there is direct evidence of these features below ground.

Correspondence between nineteenth-century maps and subsurface and aboveground features direct interpretations of garden development. Garden views of the past century can be discerned, in part, amid the extant vegetation. Archaeobotanical studies, especially phytolith analysis, should help corroborate the limited documentary evidence as well as yield new information about the plants and layout of the garden.

In a mature garden landscape, the observer notices the cyclical, seasonal changes within an artificial, yet apparently stable, environment. The underlying structure is not, however, immutable. At a continuously occupied site like Morven, the most accurate garden reconstructions will acknowledge the ever-changing aspects of the evolving landscape.

## Acknowledgments

The Morven garden archaeology project was designed and funded by the New Jersey State Museum, a division of the New Jersey Department of State. The project emphasized ethnobotanical research on the advice of St. Clair Wright of Historic Annapolis, Inc., who knew, based on the restoration of the Paca Garden, how much information could be read about a past landscape from archaeology with a botanical focus. Additional funding was provided by the National Trust for Historic Preservation and the Geraldine R. Dodge Foundation.

This chapter is a substantially modified version of one that will appear in the *Journal of the Council for Northeastern Historic Archaeology*. The authors would like to acknowledge the thoughtful comments and suggestions provided by St. Clair Wright and Suzanne Crilley on the original manuscript. Henry Michael of the University Museum, Museum Applied Science Center for Archaeology, helped with the interpretation of the tree-ring data.

## Notes

1. In his 1771 essay on gardening, Horace Walpole (1827) urged landowners to graze flocks and herds on their estates to create a pleasing bucolic view. But he did not reveal that in his own pastures he grazed miniature sheep; their small size increased the perception of depth in the vista from his garden (Stuart 1979:51).

## References Cited

Addison, J. 1712. *The Spectator*, no. 414, 25 June 1712.

Bevan, B. 1987. Remote sensing survey of Morven gardens. Manuscript. Trenton: New Jersey State Museum, Trenton.

Bill, A. H., W. E. Edge, C. M. Grieff, and B. F. Schwartz. 1978. *A house called Morven: Its role in American history*. Princeton, N.J.: Princeton University Press.

Brookes, J. 1984. *A place in the country*. London: Thames and Hudson.

Bushman, R. 1984. American high-style and vernacular cultures. In *Colonial British America: Essays in the new history of early modern era*, ed. J. P. Green and J. R. Pole, pp. 345-83. Baltimore: Johns Hopkins University Press.

Fisher, W. F. 1987. Report on the analysis of opal phytoliths from excavations at the Kirk Street Agents' House, Lowell, Massachusetts. In *Interdisciplinary investigations of the Boott Mills, Lowell, Massachusetts*. Vol. 2. *The Kirk Street Agents' House*, ed. M. C. Beaudry and S. A. Mrozowski, pp. 122-27. Boston: North Atlantic Regional Office, National Park Service.

Harris, J. 1979. *The artist and the country house: A history of the country house and garden view painting in Britain, 1540-1870*. London: Sotheby.

Hedrick, U. P. 1950. *A history of horticulture in America to 1860*. New York: Oxford University Press.

Hopkins, J. W., III. 1986. A map of the Ridout garden, Annapolis, Maryland. Manuscript. Annapolis: Historic Annapolis, Inc.

Isaac, R. 1982. *The transformation of Virginia, 1740-1790*. Chapel Hill: University of North Carolina Press.

Jacques, D. 1983. *Georgian gardens: The reign of nature*. London: Batsford.

Jellicoe, G., and S. Jellicoe (editors). 1986. *The Oxford companion to gardens*. New York: Oxford University Press.

Kelso, G. K. 1988. Exploratory pollen analysis at Morven, Princeton, New Jersey. In Miller and Yentsch 1988, pp. 56-63.

Lathrop, E. 1927. *Historic houses of early America*. New York: Tudor Publishing Company.

Lockwood, L. R. 1988. Estimates of tree ages at Morven. In Miller and Yentsch 1988, pp. 46-49.

Martin, P. 1984. *Pursuing innocent pleasures: The gardening world of Alexander Pope.* Hamden, Conn.: Archon Books.

Miller, N. F. 1988a. Report on archaeobotanical remains at the Calvert site. Calvert Interim Report No. 7. Annapolis: Historic Annapolis, Inc.

----. 1988b. Report on 1987 ethnobotanical research at Morven. In Miller and Yentsch 1988, pp. 27-45.

----, and A. Yentsch (editors). 1988. *Archaeobotanical results from the 1987 excavation at Morven (Princeton, New Jersey).* Historic Morven Interim Report 2. Trenton: New Jersey State Museum.

Minnis, P. 1981. Seeds in archaeological sites: Sources and some interpretive problems. *American Antiquity* 46:143-151.

Nygren, E. J., and B. Robertson. 1986. *Views and visions: American landscape before 1830.* Washington, D.C.: Corcoran Gallery of Art.

Paca-Steele, B. n.d. The design of the garden at Tulip Hill. Manuscript. Annapolis: Historic Annapolis, Inc.

Paca[-Steele], B., and St. C. Wright. 1983. The geometry of the William Paca Garden. Paper presented at a Special Symposium on Geometric Planning in House and Garden Design, Annapolis.

----, and ----. 1985. The use of geometric principles in the design of the William Paca Garden. Paper presented at the Garden History Society Meeting, Annapolis.

----, and ----. 1987. The mathematics of an eighteenth-century wilderness garden. *Journal of Garden History* 6(4):299-320.

Piperno, D. 1987. *Phytolith analysis: An archaeological and geological perspective.* New York: Academic Press.

----. 1988. Phytoliths at Morven. In Miller and Yentsch 1988, pp. 50-55.

Robichaud, B., and M. F. Buell. 1983. *Vegetation of New Jersey, a study of landscape diversity.* New Brunswick, N.J.: Rutgers University Press.

Rosenthal, M. 1982. *British landscape painting.* Oxford: Oxford University Press.

Rovner, I. 1988. Macro and micro-ecological reconstruction using plant opal phytolith data from archaeological sediments. *Geoarchaeology* 3:155-63.

Shackel, P. 1987. The garden at the Carroll house, Annapolis, Md. In *Perspectives on an eighteenth-century garden*, ed. P. B. Potter, Jr. Tourist Brochure at the Carroll House for the 250th anniversary of the birth of Charles Carroll of Carrollton. Annapolis: Historic Annapolis, Inc.

Smolek, M., and W. Clark. 1982. Spatial patterning of seventeenth-century plantations in the Chesapeake. Paper presented at the annual meeting of the Society for Historical Archaeology, Philadelphia.

Stockton, T. C. 1911. *The Stockton family of New Jersey and other Stocktons.* Washington, D.C.: Carnahan Press.

Stuart, D. C. 1979. *Georgian gardens.* London: Robert Hale.

Swem, E. G. (editor). 1947. *Brothers of the spade: Correspondence of Peter Collinson of London and of John Custis of Williamsburg, Virginia 1734-1746.* Barre, Mass.: Barre Gazette.

Thacker, C. 1979. *The history of gardens.* Berkeley: University of California Press.

Thomas, K. 1983. *Man and the natural world.* London: Allen Lane.

Walpole, H. 1827. *The history of the modern taste in gardening, with considerable additions by the Rev. James Dallaway, 1827.* Rept. 1982. New York: Garland Publications.

Watson, P. J. 1976. In pursuit of prehistoric subsistence: A comparative account of some contemporary flotation techniques. *Mid-Continental Journal of Archaeology* 1:77–100.

Yentsch, A. 1989. The use of land and space on lot 83, Annapolis, Maryland. In *New perspectives of Maryland archaeology*, ed. R. J. Dent and B. J. Little. Special Publication of the Maryland Archaeological Society. Baltimore.

17

# A METHOD FOR THE APPLICATION OF POLLEN ANALYSIS IN LANDSCAPE ARCHAEOLOGY

## James Schoenwetter

There is obvious commonsense justice to the expectation that techniques of pollen analysis are applicable to landscape archaeology. After all, pollen analysis is a research tool which students of the Quaternary period have used successfully for over fifty years to reconstruct changes in vegetation patterns and ecology and thereby to infer climatic modifications and cultural impacts. One would expect that the recovery and study of the pollen produced by the vegetation of an earlier landscape would provide a wealth of descriptive detail on the variety, abundance, and distribution of its floral elements. Further, the landscape archaeologist's direct examination of the ancient surfaces of earlier landscapes would provide an opportunity to collect sediment samples that contain the pollen of such vegetation, so that palynology could play a major role in landscape reconstruction research.

These expectations, however, fail to recognize certain very significant features of the use of pollen analysis in Quaternary studies. Such research focuses on much broader geographical and temporal scales than those which concern the landscape archaeologist, and the sediment samples examined are normally recovered from lake beds, peat bogs, or alluvium. These foci influence both the theory and the methodology of Quaternary pollen analysis. For example, the bulk of experimental evidence that supports existing comprehension of how pollen is produced, dispersed, deposited, and preserved in samples acts to explain the sorts of palynological data that are encountered in lacustrine samples. Also, the methods of pollen analysis that are familiar to geologically and botanically trained palynologists have been designed to produce information relevant to vegetation pattern reconstruction at those temporal and geographical scales. Normal pollen analysis therefore is arguably inappropriate for the purposes of archaeological research in many situations.

One successful resolution of this problem has been to apply the normal theory, methodology, and standards of Quaternary research pollen analysis to those archaeological situations in which it is appropriate. This approach, initiated in northwest Europe soon after World War II (e.g., Walker and Goodwin 1954) is today incorporated into the multidisciplinary subfield of environmental archaeology (Shackley 1981). Another approach has been to adapt traditional pollen study to such data as may be recovered from samples of archaeological relevance with attendant caveats about the quality of the resulting inferences (e.g., Bryant and Holloway 1983; Hevly 1981). A different approach is suggested here: the creation of a method of pollen analysis which is designed specifically to accommodate differences between the interests and sampling parameters of normal pollen analysis and those of the landscape archaeologist. Many features of the method proposed here are not very distinct from those which are traditionally employed. Thus some of the skills required are those palynologists would expect to use to extract pollen from mineral soils or alluvial deposits, to identify the pollen and spores recovered, to organize data arrays in the form of pollen diagrams, or to recognize ecologically or vegetatively significant pollen groups (e.g., arboreal pollen [AP], riparian flora, or disturbed-ground weeds). But the method requires a great deal of archaeological judgment and a fair measure of awareness of the bases and quality of a wide variety of archaeological inferences. Thus it cannot be implemented properly by someone whose archaeological expertise is minimal or limited to field experience. Archaeologists without the required palynological expertise should not assume that a traditionally trained palynologist will be prepared to use this method. Indeed, the palynologist soon would recognize that this method demands extraordinary investments and is very likely not to achieve adequate results. These objections are significant, but they fail to recognize that the method is not palynological in its basic design but rather archaeological. Because the intent of this chapter is to illustrate the operation of the method, rather than to argue its epistemology, I present here only minimal discussions of its rationales. Instead, the text concentrates on the presentation of two case examples of its application. A preliminary statement of the purposes and organization of the method, however, is in order.

The method has been designed to allow recognition of sequential variations in two types of landscape conditions: land use changes and ecosystem changes. Also, it has been designed to apply to historical archaeology site situations rather than prehistoric ones. Because of these design features, landscape archaeologists should not expect this method of pollen analysis to fulfill other objectives. For example, it will not identify the floristic elements of a garden area with the sort of precision an analysis of seeds or other types of plant fossil remains from samples of the garden's soil would produce. But it will reveal more precisely the ecosystem distinctions reflected by vegetation on the local landscape before, during, and after the garden use episode. Also, the method is not designed to be a means of generating independent evidence about landscape conditions. It is designed to produce interpretations of the character of landscape conditions. It can be used effectively to test hypotheses of ecosystem change or land use change that are generated from other sources of information, but it has been designed as a means of obtaining kinds of information that are not normally otherwise available.

The method consists of six operations, or steps: (1) sampling, (2) palynological data recovery, (3) arraying information appropriately, (4) identifying temporal divisions, (5) pooling, and (6) developing inferences. As the case studies should make clear, each of these steps is strongly informed by and progresses on the basis of archaeological information and judgment.

The two case studies involve applications of the method for different purposes and also are distinctive because one application utilizes a deductive approach and the other an inductive one. Selection of objective and approach in each instance was justified by the nature of the archaeological research being conducted. It is therefore pertinent to discuss the character of the archaeological sites and the research situations involved.

## The Case Study Situations

The Ontiveros adobe was a three-room dwelling constructed of adobe brick on a cobble foundation in approximately 1815, on land that today lies within the city of Santa Fe Springs in Los Angeles County, California. The Ontiveros family abandoned the residence about 1835 in response to various legal problems concerning titles. After the parcel of land on which the dwelling stood had passed through the hands of a series of legal owners, including John G. Downey, an early governor of the state of California, it was developed as a sanitarium and spa at the end of the nineteenth century. Subsequently, it became part of a residential estate consisting of elaborately landscaped grounds and a number of buildings (Greenwood and Associates 1979). Testing operations undertaken to evaluate the possible cultural significance of the ruins and to define a data recovery plan (Bente 1980) suggested that the site consisted of three principal architectural features: the remains of the dwelling itself and two substantial pits that had been excavated and filled in during the twenty years the building had been used as a residence. Each of the pits contained a large amount of cattle bone, and so they were dubbed bone pits by the excavators.

Palynological study of the Ontiveros adobe was the first attempt to study the pollen of a demonstrably historic archaeological context in California, so it was designed to explore a variety of archaeological interests (Schoenwetter and Limon 1982:182). Because one of these was the reconstruction of the sequence of vegetational or ecological changes that had occurred at the site, the study was designed deductively to accommodate that concern.

In France, palynological study was conducted in the villages of Entrevernes, d'Here, and Chevaline, in the communes of Entrevernes, Duingt, and Chevaline in the province of Haute-Savoie, specifically to determine land use variations through time (Ayres 1987; Schoenwetter 1986a, in prep.). Maps prepared roughly 250 years ago identify the distributions of fields and buildings in and surrounding all of the villages of the province, providing a baseline of comparison with the present-day distributions (Guichonnet 1955). Our intention was to excavate tests in and near ruined constructions in these villages with the object of recovering an archaeological record spanning the past quarter millennium. The sediments and strata associated with that record presumably would produce a pollen sequence which might reveal changes in land use that were historically documented for the present century, and that information would serve as the basis for interpretations of earlier land use. Test pit excavations undertaken during two field seasons, however, yielded a historical archaeological record that is little more than a century in duration. Though palynological data has been recovered from deeper deposits, the land use reconstructions presented here are evidenced only by the pollen spectra associated with artifacts that are dated to the 1870-1985 period or are of the stratum immediately preceding those associations.

## Step 1: Sampling

There are two basic forms of palynological sampling strategy appropriate to archaeological context deposits. Specialized sampling strategies are highly oriented toward the research problem at hand, the characteristics of the site or logistic parameters imposed upon the investigation, or some combination of those factors. Basically, a specialized sampling strategy yields only those samples which it is abundantly clear will be relevant to research efforts fully planned out before excavation is begun. Specialized sampling strategies are not infrequently designed after the completion of pilot or test studies that establish the parameters of research orientation and site structure (e.g., Bohrer and Adams 1977). Generalized sampling strategies are designed to yield sample sets that are related to as much of the variability of site structure, material culture, and geomorphology encountered as possible (e.g., Dittert and Wendorf 1963:32-36). The assumption is that only a fraction of the recovered samples actually will actually be analyzed for any given research purpose but the breadth of sampling will allow opportunities to investigate many different sorts of problems.

A combination of generalized and specialized sampling strategies was employed in both the California and French case studies. In order to provide an abundance of pollen samples directly associated with all manifestations of variability in material culture, one pollen sample was collected from every provenience unit established for purposes of archaeological control. If, for example, a feature or an area of the site was excavated by a grid of 1-by-1-meter squares in arbitrary 10-centimeter levels, a sample was collected from each level in each square. In order to provide sequentially arranged samples whose positions could be related to natural and cultural strata, additional samples were collected at standardized intervals from mapped profile exposures as a specialized sampling strategy. In the French case, yet other specialized samples were collected to test research questions about the lateral and horizontal movement of pollen grains in temperate climate soil horizons and to test for possible contrasts between samples representing part of a provenience unit and samples representing the whole volume of that same unit. In the California case, specialized microstratigraphic sampling opportunities were provided by the occurrence of superimposed layers of sediment that had been brought into the Ontiveros home to fill and patch areas of the earthen floor when it became worn through traffic.

The selection of samples to be analyzed is a second aspect of the sampling step of this method. In both of the case studies, sample selection was a staged process. Small (16-sample) sets of stratigraphically superimposed samples were processed to determine what pollen extraction procedure was appropriate, to estimate what varieties and amounts of pollen the samples contained, if any, and to assess variation in the pollen sequence over time. Information obtained from these pilot studies guided subsequent sample selection. Sample selection was a particularly significant aspect of the method in these cases because the generalized sampling strategy produces many more samples than are needed to resolve prioritized research questions. When sample selection must be undertaken, the importance of archaeological expertise and familiarity with the characteristics of the site and the material culture associated with given samples cannot be overestimated. Only 63 of the 169 archaeological context samples recovered from the Ontiveros adobe site were analyzed, and only 88 of the 190 samples recovered from the French villages were selected for analysis. Many more or many fewer analyses would have been performed if such knowledge had not been applied.

## Step 2: Data Recovery

The technical procedures of extraction and identification of pollen and spores from the sediment samples are, of course, critical to implementation of the method. But they are not as significant as determining how much pollen to observe from each sample in order to form a data base appropriate to problem resolution. It is generally understood that because pollen analysis involves application of statistical test procedures, each sample's pollen spectrum should be large enough to minimize the effect of sampling error on interpretation. Early in the history of palynological studies it was recognized that pollen sums smaller than 150 grains are inadequate for this purpose (Booberg 1930; Bowman 1931), and most workers accept the minimal standard of 150 to 200 pollen grain sums (Bryant and Holloway 1983:205; Faegri and Iverson 1975:186).

The pollen sums of individual samples, however, need not be this large if the samples are not required individually to represent a particular pollen rain population. As long as the pooled pollen sum of a set of samples taken to represent such a population meets the accepted standard, the effect of sampling error on estimations of the true statistical properties of the pollen rain involved will still be minimized. In this method, sets of samples, rather than individual samples, produce the data that are to be interpreted, so the size of each sample's pollen sum may be varied to accommodate the number of samples that make up a set, the character of the statistical tests that will be used in the analysis, the prioritized research problem(s), and the logistical constraints imposed on research. Pollen sums of 100 grains per sample were chosen in these two cases because pilot studies suggested this choice would allow statistical adequacy for even the smallest probable data set that would be identified as relevant to interpretation.

In the French case, the pollen sum of 100 grains was reserved for arboreal pollen. This is traditional practice in European pollen analyses and was relevant to the sorts of interpretations we wanted to make. It may be useful here to point out that a sample's pollen sum and its pollen spectrum need not be identical. The pollen spectrum is the complete set of pollen taxa observed and the observed proportions of those taxa. The pollen sum is the number upon which those proportions are calculated. In the French case, then, the proportions of individual pollen types were calculated only on the basis of the number of grains of arboreal pollen that had been observed.

In the California case the pollen sum was identical to the whole pollen spectrum. Though we began the study with a clear set of research interests, the rarity of palynological studies of California archaeological contexts meant that we had no a priori basis for judgment of the appropriate size or character of a pollen sum suitable to the project's needs. A set of thirteen samples of the modern pollen rain was therefore analyzed. These samples had been collected to express a variety of modern vegetation patterns and ecosystem conditions, including extremes of landscape disturbance induced by humans and nature. Extraction and study of the pollen of these samples documented that pollen sums of 100 grains, in fact, were sufficient to allow adequate evaluation of the potential effect of sampling error and that calculating the proportions of pollen types on the basis of the entire pollen spectrum is relevant. The results obtained from these surface samples constitute the empirical controls for the deductive approach implemented in the California case study. Such controls are more likely to be required for studies designed to yield reconstructions of ecosystem change than those investigating land use change because there is much less supported theory about the ways ecosystem factors and relationships are expressed palynologically than about the palynological expression of vegetation patterns reflecting land use practices.

The data recovery step of the method, like the sampling step, utilizes palynological technology but is essentially informed by archaeology. Decisions about which alternative approaches or procedures to use for data recovery depend upon the character of the research problems and the sorts of opportunities that are presented by the site(s) situation(s) encountered. Decisions that are not technically feasible must be rejected in favor of others which are feasible, of course. But the rationales for the decision-making process that are normally relevant in pollen analysis may have little or no significance in this method.

A good example is the standard for deciding what level of pollen concentration is relevant to interpretation. The sediments traditionally subjected to pollen analysis in Quaternary research often yield more than 50,000 pollen grains per gram of dry weight of sample, so samples in which pollen concentrations are orders of magnitude smaller are considered suspiciously likely to produce biased pollen spectra. Sediment samples of alluvium and the mineral zones of soil profiles often yield no more than a few thousand pollen grains per gram or per cubic centimeter, but they are considered analyzable if pollen concentration is not obviously much less than 1,500 grains. In the case studies, the pollen concentration standard employed was not the number of pollen grains that occurred in a unit weight or unit volume of the sample but the number that occurred in a volume of extract convenient to microscopy. If so few pollen grains occurred that more than three hours of microscopy would be required to observe the pollen sum, the pollen concentration was considered inadequate to justify the expenditure of energy and time necessary for data recovery. This standard was rationalized by the logistical constraints of the research programs of which these pollen studies were a part. In the California case, contractual obligations required the research to be completed by a certain date. In the French case, the archaeological significance of the palynological data was not so great that extraordinary investments could be justified. In traditional Quaternary research pollen analysis, acceptance of the high pollen concentration standard obviates certain kinds of biases induced by differential pollen preservation. In the normal pollen analysis of alluvium and mineral soils the standard is smaller, but it is justified theoretically by the distinctions in the depositional processes that invested the samples with pollen grains. In the case studies, such biases were dealt with through assessment of control and replication data, so use of the pollen concentration standard was not relevant. The decision-making process involved in identifying which samples contain an adequate amount of pollen for analysis, then, was informed by knowledge of the sites and the types of deposits encountered and sampled, rather than by traditional palynological practice or the theory and methodology upon which it depends.

### Step 3: Information Array

The traditional form for information array in pollen analysis is called a pollen diagram. The individual samples that have been observed are arranged sequentially according to their stratigraphic positions along the vertical axis, and the proportions (either percentage frequencies or absolute frequencies) of the pollen taxa observed in each sample are arranged along the horizontal axis. The resulting display provides a visual basis for recognizing successive horizons (pollen zones) of variation in the palynological record.

In this method, palynological information is arrayed in a similar way, but the rationale of the array is not closely related to the geological theory that justifies the arrangement of a traditional pollen diagram. Individual samples are arranged along the vertical axis in respect to their relative antiquity. Stratigraphic position is one of the bases for identifying relative antiquity, but it is not the only one, and it may not be the best-supported one, because reversed and horizontal stratigraphy are not uncommon in archaeological sites. The dates independently applied to the archaeological context of the sample by any chronometric or relative dating technique are assumed to be intimately, directly, or indirectly associated with the pollen spectrum involved. Any or all of such dates may also be bases for such arguments. This assumption is an operational assumption common to archaeological research. A typical conclusion regarding the sequential arrangement of all of the features and provenience units of a site integrates both chronometric and relative dating techniques of various sorts, evaluates the degree of association of the dates so produced and the features or units involved, and assesses the credibility of portions of the apparent sequence in relation to archaeological information obtained elsewhere and to aspects of cultural theory (Gasche and Tunca 1983). This assumption is not often operational in geology, and its application is relatively unfamiliar to most pollen analysts. In this method, identification of the relative antiquity of the analyzed samples, therefore, is applied by an investigator with archaeological expertise.

The information arranged along the horizontal axis of the diagram may be exactly the same as would be so arrayed in a traditional pollen analysis. Normally, however, it will be an arrangement not of the frequencies of pollen taxa so much as a combination of the frequencies of individual pollen taxa and the pooled frequencies of ecologically or culturally equivalent taxa. A typical culturally defined pool, for example, might be the set of observed pollen taxa of cultivated plants.

Figure 17.1 illustrates the information array presented for the Ontiveros adobe analysis. Note that the relative stratigraphic relationship of older and younger samples from the Ontiveros adobe has been retained, but a set of samples from the bone pits has been identified as younger than some samples from the dwelling yet older than others. Also, as the original report makes clear (Schoenwetter and Limon 1982:187-92), a quasi-biostratigraphic argument was employed to identify the relative antiquity of all analyzed samples from the bone pits. Actually, identification of this sample sequence involved arguments based on vertical stratigraphic position, archaeological context-based assessment of horizontal stratigraphy, dating of directly and indirectly associated artifacts, and methodological principles that are employed in seriational analysis.

The horizontally arranged information of figure 17.1 illustrates use of a combination of pollen taxon units, culturally defined pollen units, and ecologically defined pollen units. It may also be noted that a significant number of the observed pollen taxa (Schoenwetter and Limon 1982:212) were not included for this information array at all. That is because the purpose of the information arrays of this method is very specific, as will be clarified in the discussion of the next step of the method. The information array is not presented as a summary of recovered palynological data, as is the case for traditional pollen diagrams.

Identification of the pollen units that are arranged horizontally on the information array may follow a deductive or an inductive approach. In the Ontiveros case, the pollen spectra of the surface samples provided empirical support for the conclusion that frequency variations in these particular pollen units were the ones that expressed vegetation/ecological patterns (Schoenwetter and Limon 1982:199-205). They are thus deductively identified as the units pertinent to the information array of a landscape reconstruction analysis which seeks to determine changes that have occurred through time in ecosystem conditions. In the Ontiveros case, the exotic AP (i.e., pollen of nonnative tree species) and the native AP units are both pooled sets of individual pollen taxa. The former represents arboreal taxa (e.g., elm, pecan, citrus, eucalyptus) that have been introduced to the area within the past 200 years. Though it is composed of pollen types that are produced, distributed, deposited, and preserved as a result of natural processes, it is recognizably a culturally defined pollen unit

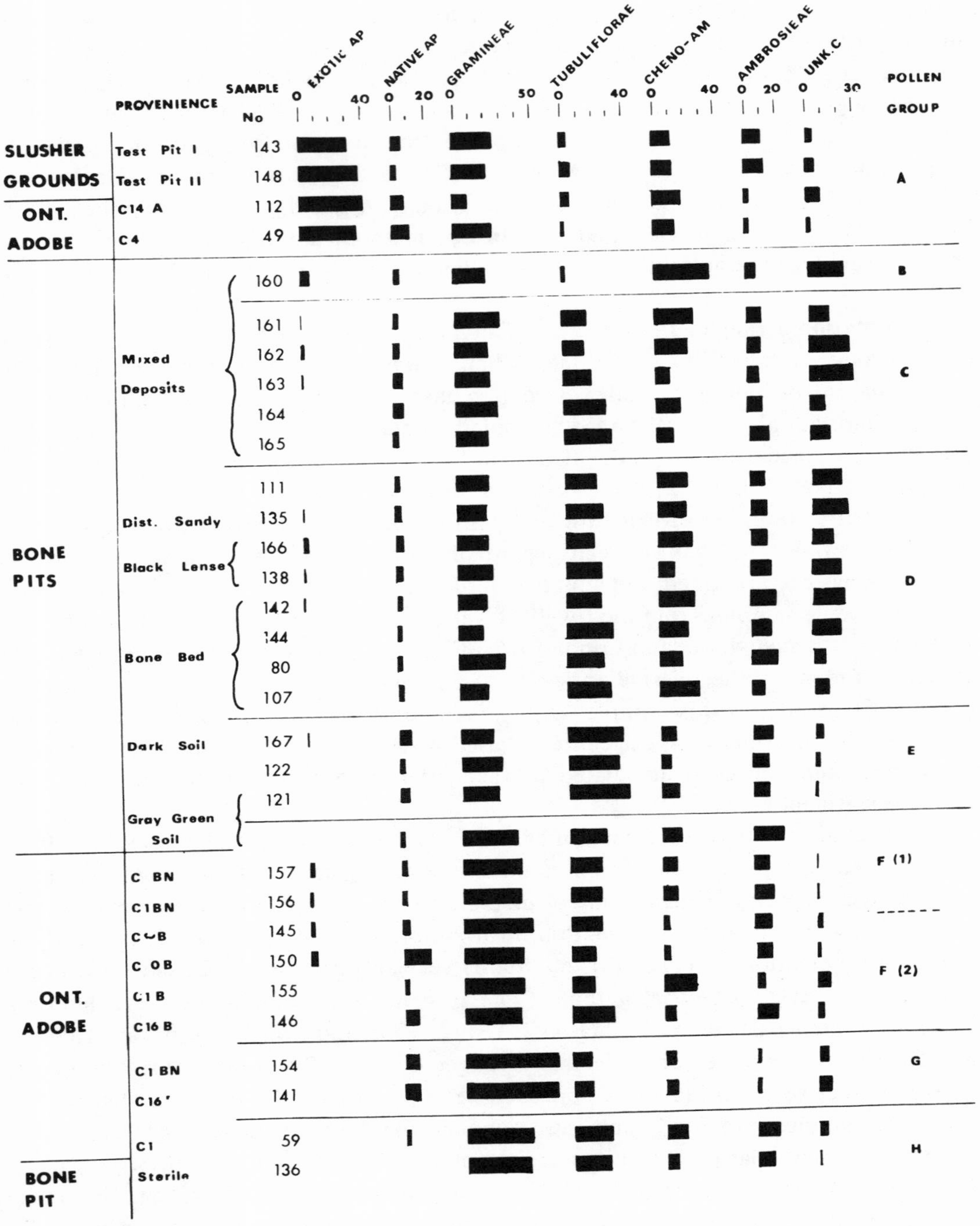

Figure 17.1. Information array for the Ontiveros adobe samples

because the existence of pollen of those types in these samples is culture-dependent. The latter represents arboreal taxa (e.g., walnut, willow, pine, oak) that were native to the area before the historic period. However, it is quite possible that the numbers and distributions of the plants that produce native AP grains were culture-dependent at the time the pollen became incorporated in the samples.

In a traditional pollen analysis, one makes the assumption that the information units arranged on the horizontal axis (which are usually pollen taxa) are not culture-dependent unless evidence exists to the contrary. The taxon Ceralia is usually considered culture-dependent because the pollen is produced as a result of agricultural activity; the pollen of disturbed-ground weeds may be so considered if it occurs in abundance or in the same samples as Ceralia pollen. Traditional pollen analyses, however, study the pollen of samples that are not recovered from archaeological site contexts, and there is no reason to assume that behavioral patterns have influenced the pollen spectra of such samples. This method is designed for study of the pollen of samples recovered from locations that are defined by the occurrence of evidence of culturally patterned human behavior. The logical way to approach the study of such samples is to assume that the pollen units identified for them are culturally dependent unless evidence exists to the contrary. Bryant and Holloway (1983:19) recognize the significance of a related assumption which justifies special concern for control pollen spectra and replications of pollen spectra in archaeological situations.

The deductive approach is a means one may employ to generate such evidence. In the Ontiveros case, the data of the surface samples provide support for an argument that the native AP unit is not, in fact, culture-dependent, because a relationship discovered to exist between the exotic and the native AP categories seems unlikely to be culturally influenced.

> The surface pollen rain data . . . suggest that the [total] arboreal pollen frequency value monitors immediate tree density, though background values of 4-15% can occur far from any trees. Today, the proportion of exotic to native arboreal pollen seems to monitor human horticulture intensity. Highly managed landscapes yield exotic:native AP ratios in excess of 1:1; minimally managed ones yield ratios below 1:1 even though exotic AP producers may be conspicuously present. (Schoenwetter and Limon 1982:205)

Figure 17.2 illustrates the information array for the palynological data recovered in the French case. This array integrates information from multiple pollen columns collected from individual test pit excavations, multiple tests within a given village, and multiple villages, so the arguments supporting the displayed sequencing of individual samples are complex and have a number of different bases (Schoenwetter, in prep.). Most of the pollen units arranged on the horizontal axis of this diagram are ecologically defined. The ecological basis of the diagram's pollen unit identification is an application of the inductive approach used in the study. The French case study illustrates that the decision making required for pollen unit identification need not be wholly based upon archaeological expertise. Indeed, it shows that sole reliance upon such expertise is probably injudicious in the majority of instances, because botanical appreciation of the biological qualities of the taxa that produce the pollen grains, scientific appreciation of the ecological relations normal to those taxa, and geological appreciation of processes that affect the character of the depositional environments in which the pollen grains are embedded are likely to be relevant to such decisions.

What is necessary for implementation of this step of the method is the capacity to weigh the relative significance of potentially relevant archaeological, historical, botanical, and geological information, and perhaps information suggested through such other disciplines as

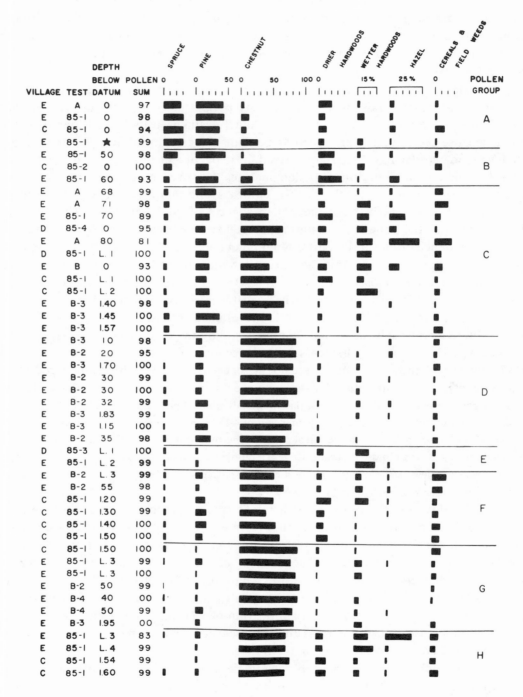

Figure 17.2. Information array for the Haute-Savoie samples: (E) Entrevernes, (C) Chevaline, (D) d'Here, (*) modern rodent burrow fill

statistics and geography as well. The investigator begins with the assumption that the pollen taxa observed during data recovery, the numbers of those taxa, and the proportional relationships of those taxa are all products of human behavior unless evidence is presented to the contrary. The task of recognizing potential evidence to the contrary, however, demands consideration of matters that are scientifically investigated in a wide variety of disciplines. The wider the information base an investigator may gain access to in order to support such considerations, the better. This conclusion will seem self-evident to archaeologists, because their training prepares them to consider the relative values of multiple forms of evidence during decision-making processes. It may seem much less self-evident to the traditionally trained pollen analyst. In contrast to the social sciences, decision making in natural science tends to be based more on documented effectiveness than on a broad base of information. In essence, the natural scientist more often expects that a decision which produced a successful result in one case will, unless the situation is quite different, likely produce a similarly successful result in another. Social scientists are taught that cultural situations which seem alike most often actually are not homologous and decision making should not be based primarily on the presumption that they are.

## Step 4: Temporal Discrimination

The purpose of Step 3 is to provide a pertinent information base for the succeeding step, temporal discrimination. This is a significantly different purpose than that of the information array procedures in traditional pollen analysis, so it requires some extended discussion.

The traditional purpose of pollen diagrams is to provide a visual display of recovered data. Inductive or deductive analyses of sequential variations in the frequency values of the pollen taxa support interpretation of vegetation pattern changes that occurred at the sampled locality. Once this interpretation has been established, assessment of the represented changes in the adaptive relationships among the plants that produced the pollen often leads to a secondary interpretation of the climatic or cultural conditions that occurred at different times. Another sort of secondary interpretation involves application of principles of biostratigraphic analysis to support identification of temporal divisions of the pollen sequence (pollen zones and zonules). Because the boundaries of pollen zones are understood to identify changes in adaptive relationships among the producer plants, those boundaries are normally positioned at points in the pollen sequence where some attribute characteristics of the earlier zone are observed to occur in the same samples that contain diagnostic attribute characteristics of the succeeding zone.

In this method, the information array created in Step 3 does not serve the purpose of providing a data base to support interpretation of vegetation change. The inherent assumption that the pollen units arranged on the horizontal axis of the diagram are culture-dependent obviates such an interpretation. Rather, the purpose is to allow identification of portions of the pollen sequence represented on the vertical axis of the diagram that are distinct from other portions. The concern here is to divide the pollen sequence into temporally organized sets of information arrays, called pollen groups. As is true of pollen zones, each pollen group is more likely than not to be identified by particular diagnostic characteristics. But it is quite possible for two pollen groups to have identical characteristics and be separable as a result of their distinctive positions in the pollen sequence. This is an expectable result of a recurrence of the cultural conditions responsible for patterning in the palynological data.

A very important feature of such a temporal division of the pollen sequence is that its boundaries tend to be sharp, rather than transitional as is the case for most boundaries of pollen zones. This is also a predictable effect of the assumption that the information array is culture-dependent. One expects that a change in whatever cultural conditions are responsible for an information array with specific characteristics would occur at a shorter-interval time scale than is expectably represented by most pollen samples. Thus, a culture-dependent pollen sequence would appear as a sequential series of episodes, each representing the operation of a somewhat different systemically organized cultural entity.

The temporal divisions are called pollen groups, in distinction to pollen zones, because though they resemble pollen zones in form, they are not related to them in theory. The extreme right-hand column of figure 17.1 illustrates how the information array for that site was divided into pollen groups. The oldest group (H) is distinguished by lower frequency values for Gramineae and higher frequency values for Tubuliflorae pollen than occur in the samples of the succeeding group (G). Members of the next youngest set of pollen samples (group F) have pollen unit frequency values essentially identical to those of pollen group H but a different temporal position. Some members of this group also contain small amounts of exotic AP; those tend to be younger, and this difference supports discrimination of two pollen group F subzones (F1 and F2). The assumption that the characteristics of a pollen group reflect the existence of a particular cultural condition operating at the site at a particular time allows one to generate a number of chronological hypotheses from the information array. (Samples of pollen group C illustrated in figure 17.2 were recovered from the occupation strata of buildings of different villages. One may suggest that these occupations date to the same interval. Archaeologists will quickly recognize the potential advantages of palynological means for generating independently testable hypotheses of intersite and intrasite temporal correlations [Schoenwetter 1986b].)

## Step 5: Information Pooling

Step 5 of the method, information pooling, has two aspects. The first pools the recovered data provided by all the samples of a pollen group; the second evaluates that pooling and presents a new information array. The first aspect produces a body of palynological information about the temporal interval represented by a pollen group which is large enough to be statistically adequate to the task of interpretation. The second aspect evaluates it in reference to the landscape reconstruction interest of the investigation and identifies the information array pattern that will effectively serve that interest.

The pooled data of the set of samples of a pollen group present the investigator with the largest possible number of pollen information units useful for interpretation, and they also constitute a set of pollen data for a specific time interval which allows a statistically more credible characterization of the episode's pollen rain than any individual sample can provide. Also, because the number of pollen spectra that have been pooled together is known, the variability of any of the pollen units within the pool can be calculated. Compared to traditional pollen analyses, in fact, one of the advantages of this method is that it requires interpretation to be based on the palynological data recovered from a set of samples (the members of a pollen group), rather than a single sample. In traditional analyses, each pollen sample has a unique stratigraphic position relative to the others, so each can only represent the pollen rain of a unique time interval. The population of samples representing each interval of the chronological scale on a traditional pollen diagram, then, is limited to one. In this method, all the samples of a pollen group represent the pollen rain of the same episode. The population of samples representing an interval, then, is not so limited, and analyses of intrapool and interpool variance may be applied that might suggest interpretations or the directions those interpretations might take.

When the data pools have been formed, the investigator reviews them as units, applying statistical tests if they seem pertinent or merely assessing their character impressionistically, to focus on those qualities of these data sets which relate to interpretive concerns. Both archaeological judgment and palynological expertise now must be applied cooperatively, for the geological and biological implications of the palynological record are neither more nor less relevant than their behavioral implications. Further consideration of this point will be reserved for the discussions of the final step of the method.

Figure 17.3 illustrates the information array resulting from the operation of Step 5 in the French case. As is true of the California case, the diagram illustrates the mean frequency value for each pollen unit of each pollen group. The number of samples and the number of observations are provided to allow some appreciation of the statistical quality of the data upon which the landscape interpretations are based. It should be noted that the pollen units of figure 17.3 are not identical to those of figure 17.2. This occurs, and is characteristic of this method, because the purpose of the information array created at Step 3 is to provide a basis for temporal division of the pollen sequence, while the purpose of the information array created at Step 5 is to provide a basis for interpretation(s) relevant to the investigator's research concerns.

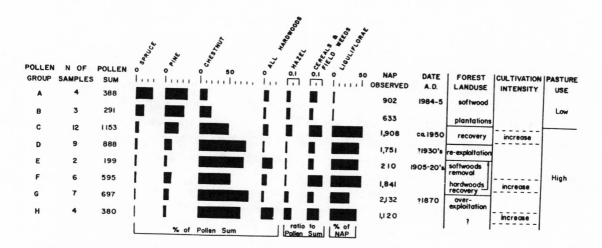

Figure 17.3. Pollen group pooled data diagram for Haute Savoie. Note use of different means for calculating pollen unit groups

The deductive approach used in the California study requires application of Step 5 to the control sample pollen data as well as to those from the site. In figure 17.4, the experimental equivalents of pollen groups were established to allow characterization of the

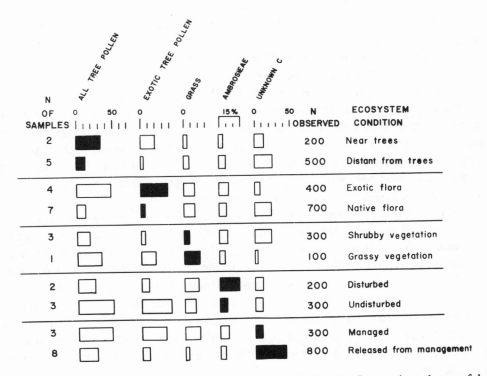

Figure 17.4.  Pooled data diagram for control samples from California.  Contrasting values useful for interpreting ecosystem conditions have been emphasized.

modern pollen rains representing ecosystem conditions affecting qualities of the landscape (e.g., disturbed versus undisturbed land, managed versus abandoned land) and vegetation patterns indicative of ecosystem conditions (exotic flora versus native flora coverage, shrubby versus grassy vegetation).  Again, it should be noted that the pollen units of the information array of figure 17.4 are distinct from those of figure 17.1.  The purpose of the array in figure 17.4 is to identify the palynological expressions of ecosystem features occurring in the region today, while the purpose of figure 17.1 is to identify palynological patterns that varied through time at the Ontiveros adobe site.

Once the analysis of the control samples represented by Figure 17.4 was completed, the same set of pollen units was used to prepare an information array for the pollen groups established for the site (fig. 17.5).  The rationale involved is that if the modern surface samples in fact allow identification of the palynological expression of ecosystem conditions today, any homologous expression in the palynological record from the site may be interpreted as an expression of homologous ecosystem conditions in the past.  This rationale may be recognized as an expression of uniformitarianism, a principle which has far more limited application in archaeological studies than in geological or biological investigations.  But it is reasonably applied here, for the interpretive concern is not the reconstruction of patterns of behavior per se but the reconstruction of patterns of ecological relationships.

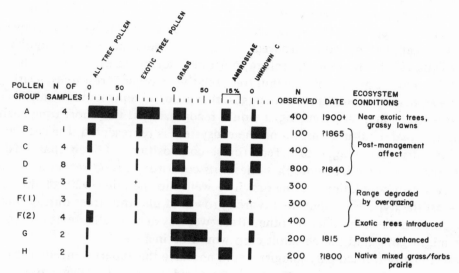

Figure 17.5. Pollen group pooled data diagram for the Ontiveros adobe site

## Step 6: Interpretation

In this method, interpretation begins with estimation of the chronometry of the pollen groups that were established in Step 4. In most cases, only a minority of the samples of any given pollen group are intimately or directly associated with chronometric dates, and it commonly is true that few or none of the samples of a pollen group are datable by chronometric associations. This situation demands concern because the duration of the temporal episode represented by a pollen group is rarely revealed by its archaeological associations and is not self-evident from its palynological characteristics. Yet the goal of accurate interpretation is clearly advanced if one knows both when the time episodes represented by the pollen groups occurred and how long they lasted.

One starts the chronometry estimation processes by considering of the chronometric dates applied to the archaeological records associated with the pollen samples. To this, one adds consideration of the relevance of historical information. An example is provided by the California case study. Historical records document the abandonment of the Ontiveros adobe in approximately 1835. Pollen group D is composed of samples that were recovered from three bone pit strata. The uppermost of these strata immediately overlies a stratum containing nineteenth-century artifacts. Pollen group D, then, may be estimated to have a duration from some point before the 1835 abandonment of the site to some point thereafter. Pollen group G contains the earliest pollen samples recovered from the dwelling floor. Historical information thus suggests that pollen groups G, Fl, F2, and E must represent episodes of very short duration because they all had to occur successively between the construction date, 1815, and that point before 1835 when the episode represented by pollen group D began.

Dating estimates provided by historical knowledge about the site may also be supplemented by consideration of historical information about landscape conditions. First, though, landscape interpretation of the results of Step 5 is required. This is the point in the method at which traditional palynological expertise is most critically significant, for sophisticated appreciation is required of the ways in which the plants that produce the pollen are adapted.

A good example of this is expressed in the French case study. As Figure 17.2 shows, during the episode represented by the samples of pollen group G, the frequency of chestnut pollen is so great that no other arboreal pollen taxa yield statistically significant pollen frequency values. This episode, therefore, must be interpreted as a period when ecological conditions favored the growth of chestnut trees relative to other forest trees. Dating estimates provided by associated material culture suggest that group G represents an episode of no more than twenty-five years. A palynologist would recognize that this short time span increases the probability that a cultural impact on the ecosystem is represented, for natural ecosystem changes normally take longer to affect forest composition. Given that information, a historical archaeologist might note that chestnuts constitute a food resource known to have been significant to populations of the province well into the mid-1920s of this century and might suggest the hypothesis that the favored growth of chestnut trees during these episodes occurred because the seedlings of other trees were systematically removed so that more chestnuts might grow and the chestnut crop would be increased.

A traditionally trained palynologist would not have the expertise needed to evaluate the credibility of this hypothesis or the skills required to test it. The palynologist might recognize, however, that an alternative cultural hypothesis could be argued on biological grounds. Relative to the other taxa of native forest trees, chestnut trees are better adapted for growth in habitats where high light levels occur in combination with soils that are less richly endowed with nitrogen and organic nutrients. If such habitat conditions were culturally generated in a forested area, weedy growth of chestnut trees would be an expectable result. However, the chestnut is not a strong competitor against other native trees under other habitat conditions. A successional phase involving proliferation of the chestnut would expectably be short-lived. Soon after the chestnut trees reached sufficient maturity to be reproductively successful (that is, soon after they began setting a mast crop), the competition of seedlings of other taxa would begin to reduce the degree of that success. Most chestnut trees established during this phase would stand, flower, and set seed for decades. But their period of favored adaptation would be completed. The palynologist might suggest the hypothesis that the episode identified by pollen group G was culturally induced by the production of such favored habitats.

This hypothesis would be very difficult to test on biological grounds. Even a cursory inspection of the history of the area, however, serves as a confirmatory test of this hypothesis. During the nineteenth century, the energy of many of the alpine streams of the region was captured by waterwheels to power the saws of a thriving lumber industry. Forested areas were heavily lumbered, with consequent creation of large canopy openings and disturbance and overturning of a significant fraction of the area previously covered by rich forest soil surfaces. The estimated antiquity of pollen group G is consistent with the date at which local village involvement in this industry may have ceased as improvements in transportation networks and technology created local access to cheaper timber products produced in other parts of France and Europe.

The point here is that landscape interpretation of the evidence arrayed as a result of the operation of Step 5 critically requires the expertise of the palynologist but also demands an appreciation of conditions of history, which are normally likely to be the province of the historical archaeologist. The method is not implementable at all without the latter's expertise, as I have tried to emphasize often in the course of this chapter. But the capacity to consider the biological implications of the pollen record may also be crucial to the final step of the method.

The basic landscape interpretations of the case studies are identified in figures 17.3 and 17.5. All the arguments supporting the interpretations are not presented here, but it is necessary to present some of them to illustrate this step of the method. For example, in the California case interpretation of the ecosystem condition represented by pollen group H is based upon the low frequency value for the all tree pollen unit, the lack of any representation in the exotic tree pollen unit, the moderate frequency value for the Ambrosieae pollen unit, and the low frequency value for the Unknown C pollen unit. The antiquity of pollen group H and comparisons with the control data of figure 17.4 support the inference that such a frequency value for unknown C pollen is consistent with an unmanaged landscape, that such a frequency value for Ambrosieae pollen is not consistent with an undisturbed ecosystem, that such a frequency value for grass pollen is not consistent with an ecosystem supporting shrubby vegetation, and that such exotic tree and all tree pollen unit frequencies are consistent with a native, treeless ecosystem. The reconstruction offered is that the pollen group information identifies a time when a native bunchgrass grassland ecosystem, involving some degree of disturbance and shrub growth, occurred at the site.

Average frequency values of the sequent pollen group (G) differ in regard to the grass and Ambrosieae pollen units. Comparison with the control data suggests the inference that an ecosystem change had occurred in which the grassland became denser, with less shrubs and less disturbed habitat. Interestingly, this is the episode during which establishment of the Ontiveros cattle ranch and construction of the dwelling occurred. The correlation may not be accidental. Schoenwetter and Limon (1982:206) suggest that the (probably unintentional) introduction of European grasses to southern California in the late eighteenth century resulted in richer early nineteenth-century pasturage for the livestock introduced shortly thereafter.

The French study was undertaken to determine the degree of correspondence between historical analysis of land use changes and the interpretations of land use change generated by this method of landscape archaeology. Today, the areas surrounding the villages selected for the study are divided into cultivated parcels that provide fodder crops for local dairy herds, parcels that are reserved for pasturage, parcels of subclimax forest that are sources of firewood and other resources, and parcels of forest that are devoted to softwood (spruce and pine) plantations of marketable timber. Though some gardening is pursued within the village, few households attempt to cultivate the bulk of the food consumed. Many households of the villages are involved in the dairy industry that is traditional for the rural segments of this part of Haute-Savoie, so they maintain milking herds and the hayfields and pastures to support them. But agribusiness conditions effectively dictate small herd sizes, and few of these households could be economically self-sufficient if members did not also engage in wage labor. During the past decade, individual household economies have become increasingly supported by activities pursued at distance from the village, and pasturage and subclimax forest use is being reduced.

Today, then, land use patterns easily fall into the classes of forested and nonforested land use. (One can note that the decision to use the pollen sum traditional to European pollen analyses, which segregates the pollen of forested and unforested lands, suits the interpretive purposes of this study for totally different reasons than it suits traditional studies.) The history of the area documents three major land use changes during the last 100 years. In the nineteenth century a flourishing village-level lumbering industry crashed, and dairy farming was the economic mainstay. The softwood plantations were established shortly after World War II. And, changing economic conditions consequent upon inclusion of France in the European Common Market in the middle of this century had the effect of reducing the sizes of dairy herds owned by individual households.

The establishment of softwood plantations seems effectively represented by the change in the spruce and pine pollen unit frequency values that occurs between the group C and the group B episodes, and the reduction of intensity in cropland and pasturage use since 1950 seems effectively reflected by the declines in frequency values for the Ceralia and field weeds and Liguliflorae pollen units in the periods represented by pollen groups B and A. As noted earlier, the character of the change in the chestnut pollen unit frequency that occurs between the group H and group G episodes may be effectively interpreted as the palynological reflection of changes in forest land use. If, as I suspect, the Liguliflorae pollen unit frequency reflects intensity of pasture use, the changes occurring between the group G and group F episodes suggest intensification of dairying when lumbering no longer was a significant factor contributing to village economy. Interestingly, some of the frequency value changes that occur in the Ceralia and field weeds pollen unit through time are statistically significant. These changes seem likely to reflect variations in the intensity of cultivation because the amount of arable land in a village district is essentially fixed.

Pollen group E is effectively interpreted as a period during which forest succession had advanced to the point that hardwoods were significantly more favored than previously. The chestnut pollen unit increase occurring in the pollen group E episode seems related to selective removal of softwoods, and it is tempting to speculate that this activity was induced by a demand for softwood lumber during World War I. Similarly, one might speculate that intensification of cultivation during the pollen group C episode reflects an increase in dairy production for local markets and home consumption during World War II. Pollen group E is followed by an episode (D) during which decline in the hardwoods pollen unit frequency and increase in the chestnut pollen unit frequency suggest hardwoods removal with consequent adaptive advantage to chestnut trees. Consideration of the estimates of antiquity provided by historical and material culture evidence suggests that the group D episode occurred between the beginning of the third and the end of the fourth decades of this century. Historical perspective on the effects the Great Depression might well have had upon household economies in this rural area lends credence to the inference that the hardwoods were selectively lumbered during the 1930s as a cash crop. That inference, in turn, suggests that the pollen group D episode began about 1930.

I noted earlier that the estimates of the antiquity and duration of the pollen group episodes provided by the evidence of association and analysis of local history were preliminary. After the landscape interpretation of the information arrays produced at Step 5 was made, a body of additional information has been generated which may be viewed from a perspective of historical knowledge and used to refine and/or modify those dating estimates. The dating estimates provided in figures 17.3 and 17.5 have been modified in this way.

## Summary

This chapter presents and illustrates a method of pollen analysis which has been created to allow landscape archaeology reconstructions when applied to historic archaeology site situations. Reconstructions of land use change and ecosystem change through time are alternative possibilities of application of the method, and the investigator(s) may choose to pursue either a deductive or an inductive approach. Most of the design features of the method bear little relation to the theory, epistemology, or operation of pollen analysis normally employed in Quaternary studies, prehistoric archaeology, or environmental archaeology. The method should therefore be properly recognized as a research tool of historic archaeology, which bears about as much relationship to normal pollen analysis as archaeology bears to geology.

Thus the method demands historic archaeology experience and expertise at each operational step. Yet, at the crucial step of inference development, appropriate application of the method also requires interpretive sophistication on the part of an investigator with biological experience and expertise. In addition, more than the technical skills required for the extraction and identification of the pollen of the samples is demanded for the palynological side of the research effort. Because few historical archaeologists combine that background with palynological expertise, it is expectable that this sort of landscape archaeology study will be implemented by a cooperating and coordinated team of scientists. This has been the situation in both of the case studies used to illustrate the method.

## Acknowledgments

The case studies research that is presented to illustrate the method could never have been performed without the support and assistance of others. Greenwood and Associates Company of Pacific Palisades, California, provided financial support for palynological studies at the Ontiveros Adobe. The Wenner-Gren Foundation and the Research and Development Committee of the Department of Anthropology, Arizona State University, provided financial support for studies of the pollen of samples from the Haute-Savoie. The Circonscription des Antiquités Historiques de la Région Rhône-Alps, as well as individual village landowners, authorized our excavations in France. Roberta S. Greenwood, John M. Foster, and Jay D. Frierman supplied historic archaeology expertise in the California case that very strongly affected my appreciation of its relevance to the method. James E. Ayres was the cooperating historic archaeologist I worked with in the Haute-Savoie. Professors David Siddle, Frank Oldfield, and Peter James, all of the Department of Geography at the University of Liverpool, and Professor Jean-Luc Borel of the Université de Grenoble, and their students, are other contributors to that effort. Finally, recognition is due those whose labor effected the excavations. Special thanks are due to the volunteer efforts of Joussard Michel of Grenoble and Lisa Greenhalge of Hull University and to Amie E. Limon and Michael M. Gregory, who were involved in technical aspects of the pollen work.

References Cited

Ayres, J. E.   1987.   Preliminary report of the Annecy project: Excavations in Entrevernes, Chevaline and d'Here near Annecy, France, summer of 1985.   Manuscript.   Lyon: Circonscription des Antiquités Historiques de la Région Rhône-Alps.

Bente, V. G. 1980. Test excavation of LAn-106aH: The Ontiveros adobe, Sante Fe Springs California. Manuscript. Santa Fe Springs, Calif.: Municipal Redevelopment Agency.

Bohrer, V. L., and K. R. Adams. 1977. *Ethnobotanical techniques and approaches at Salmon Ruin, New Mexico.* Eastern New Mexico University Contributions in Anthropology No. 8(1). Portales, N.M.

Booberg, G. 1930. Gisselasmyren. *Norrladskt Handbibliotek* 12.

Bowman, P. W. 1931. Study of a peat bog near the Matamuk River, Quebec, Canada, by the method of pollen analysis. *Ecology* 12:694–720.

Bryant, V. M. Jr., and R. G. Holloway. 1983. The role of palynology in archaeology. In *Advances in archaeological method and theory.* Ed. M. B. Schiffer. Vol. 6, pp. 191–224. New York: Academic Press.

Dittert, A. E., Jr., and F. Wendorf. 1963. *Procedural manual for archaeological field research projects of the Museum of New Mexico.* Museum of New Mexico Papers in Anthropology No. 12. Santa Fe: Museum of New Mexico.

Faegri, K., and J. Iverson. 1975. *Textbook of pollen analysis.* 3d ed. New York: Hafner Press.

Gasche, H., and O. Tunca. 1983. Guide to archaeostratigraphic classification and terminology: Definitions and principles. *Journal of Field Archaeology* 10:325–35.

Greenwood and Associates. 1979. Cultural resource evaluation and management plan for the Hawkins-Nimocks (Slusher) estate. Manuscript. Santa Fe Springs, Calif.: Municipal Redevelopment Agency.

Guichonnet, P. 1955. Le cadastre savoyard de 1738 et son utilisation pour les recherches d'histoire et de géographie sociales. *Revue de Géographie Alpine* 53:255–98.

Hevly, R. H. 1981. Pollen production, transport, and preservation: Potentials and limitations in archaeological palynology. *Journal of Ethnobiology* 1:39–54.

Schoenwetter, J. 1986a. Preliminary report on the Annecy project: June 1984–1986. Manuscript. Lyons: Circonscription des Antiquités Historiques de la Région Rhône-Alps.

————. 1986b. Palynological applications in historic archaeology. Paper presented at the 51st annual meeting of the Society for American Archaeology, New Orleans.

————. in prep. Pollen studies of historic archaeology contexts in l'Haute-Savoie, France.

————, and A. E. Limon. 1982. Appendix A: Palynological study of the Slusher estate. In *The Ontiveros adobe: Early Rancho life in Alta California*, ed. J. D. Frierman, pp. 181–212. Pacific Palisades, Calif.: Greenwood and Associates.

Shackley, M. 1981. *Environmental archaeology.* London: George Allen and Unwin Press.

Walker, D., and H. Godwin. 1954. Lake-stratigraphy, pollen-analysis, and vegetational history. In *Excavations at Star Carr*, ed. J. G. D. Clark, pp. 25–69. Cambridge: University Printing House.

# 18

# FINE-TUNING FLORAL HISTORY
# WITH PLANT OPAL PHYTOLITH ANALYSIS

## Irwin Rovner

Plant opal phytolith analysis is rapidly maturing into a robust and powerful paleobotanical data system. While the first use of phytolith analysis in archaeology occurred in 1908 and possibly earlier, the number of relevant archaeological studies before 1970, when I was introduced to phytoliths, is exceeding small. Today a small but growing group of researchers in archaeobotany and other disciplines concerned with paleoecology have contributed enormously to increased understanding of the variety and scope of archaeological contexts and problems that phytolith analysis can address.

Opal phytoliths, literally plant stones, are mineral particles of varying shape and size produced biogenetically, that is, by and within living plants as a result of normal physiological processes. Silica, the ubiquitous, fundamental component in such materials as sand, glass, flint, and just plain dirt, is the major component in opal phytoliths. They originate from silica dissolved in groundwater in the form of monosilicic acid that is carried into a plant through its roots. Eventually the silica is deposited in a mineral form identical to gemstone opal (opal A) where the water is used or lost through transpiration. When dead plant material subsequently falls to the ground and decays, phytoliths are released from the organic tissue matrix in which they were originally formed. Phytoliths, however, are entirely composed of mineral material and do not decay in the botanical sense. They can remain preserved in soil (and even rock formed from that soil) for enormous periods of time. Distinctive phytoliths have been recovered from geological deposits as far back as the Paleocene, some 60 million years ago. This is obviously far beyond the age of the earliest archaeological sites, historic or prehistoric, anywhere on the globe. The potential use of phytolith analysis in archaeology is truly global.

Most studies of phytolith assemblages in soil have provided paleobotanical data on the order of thousands to hundreds of thousands and even millions of years ago. However, as the number of soil phytolith studies increased, a pattern emerged indicating that phytolith populations are decay-in-place plant residues which remain quite stable following deposition. These studies now show that phytolith populations often reflect subtle microenvironmental, ecotonal differences and/or very specific ethnobotanical and cultural activities. As such, phytolith analysis is proving to be a superlative source of botanical information in the narrowly defined contexts and restricted time periods characteristic of historic sites and landscapes.

## Phytolith Studies in Paleoecology

Many variables of phytolith morphology, taxonomy, and frequency are the direct result of complex ecological processes. Unfortunately, these can be difficult to identify systematically. Until more is understood of the systematic nature of phytolith production and morphology, it will remain difficult to determine if variation within and/or between soil phytolith populations represents genetic (i.e., taxonomic) or edaphic (environmental) differences, or both. However, the potential is enormous.

For example, Livingstone and Clayton (1980) studied the elevation on East African hillsides where festucoid grasses, favoring cooler high altitudes, give way to a dominance of lower-altitude panicoid grasses. This point of transition will migrate vertically if mean annual temperature fluctuates as little as $\pm 1°$ C over time. Studies by the French botanist Henri Prat as early as 1934 and by German taxonomists even earlier identified distinctive phytolith forms assigned to these and other taxons in the grass family. Obviously the use of festucoid-to-panicoid phytolith ratios as a paleothermometer comes immediately to mind. The question is not really if this will work but how close to $\pm 1°$ C fluctuation will the data permit. The answer, for now at least, is not very close; but it is an interesting prospect as nothing else right now promises this kind of paleoclimatic data in fact or in theory.

Since the now-classic report by Twiss, Suess, and Smith (1969) applying grass phytolith taxonomy to soil studies, a number of investigators have produced successful paleobotanical profiles based on grass phytolith assemblages. These include the only post-Pleistocene climatic profile for south Texas (Robinson 1979a, 1979b) and a remarkable 620,000-year profile by Fredlund, Johnson, and Dort (1985) from the central Nebraska prairie. Such studies deal with time blocks of thousands and tens of thousands of years in which subtle fluctuations in mean annual temperature have little reality in the phytolith assemblages recovered. We have yet to consider, however, much less implement, what phytolith analysis can do in classical and historic sites where the parameters of context and time are much more tightly defined and precisely controlled.

## Current State of Phytolith Taxonomy

Phytolith studies also show great capacity for identification of important plant groups at very precise taxonomic levels. Phytoliths are particularly suited to the identification of grasses in archaeological contexts, providing opportunities to study grassland paleoecology and climatic change in ways impossible through pollen study. Moreover, phytolith analysis is unequivocally the best microfossil system for the study of cultivated cereals. It has been used successfully in the archaeological study of *Zea mays* (Pearsall 1978; Piperno 1983; Pearsall and Piperno 1986; Russ and Rovner 1987), rice (Watanabe 1970), millet (Netolitzky 1914; Watanabe 1968), barley (Tack 1986), wheat (Rosen 1983), and others. Particularly impressive among these studies are those by Pearsall, who pushed back the date for the introduction of maize into Ecuador by several millennia, and by Piperno for the introduction of maize (and squash, an important nongrass cultigen) into Panama using phytolith data. Most recently, Piperno (1984; personal communication, 1986) has reported a means of using phytolith data to separate domestic maize from related wild teosintes. This is paleobotanical differentiation at the subspecies level. Moreover, Russ and Rovner (1987) conducted a blind study of stereological image analysis capabilities to derive phytolith diagnostic features for closely related subspecies of maize and related wild teosintes. Although the plants used are so similar that some are difficult to distinguish without chromosome mapping or isoenzyme studies even by experts, phytolith populations from domestic maize were separated from those in the wild grasses with very high statistical confidence. It was impossible to confuse the populations even though subspecies taxa were being compared.

Phytolith taxonomy is not about to attack the entire fossil world of plants with this degree of precision. Plants that are not silica accumulators, and thus do not produce silica particles, comprise a substantial portion of the plant kingdom. Furthermore, many plants which do absorb silica produce particles that are found in identical form in unrelated plants and thus have no value for taxonomic assignment. For instance, manioc, a critical root crop in tropical regions notoriously lacking in preserved macrobotanical remains and pollen, produces a stellate hair cell phytolith also found in unrelated tropical plants. Archaeobotanic study of manioc cannot, unfortunately, be conducted with phytoliths (Piperno 1986).

Major portions of the plant kingdom beyond the grass family remain to provide an array of useful phytolith forms for archaeobotanical investigation. These include sedges, rushes, palms, and several other monocotyledonous groups. Moreover, in spite of earlier predictions to the contrary (Rovner 1971), useful phytolith forms have been identified in a wide variety of dicotyledonous plants. Piperno (1986) has found significant variation among hair cell phytoliths in a number of tropical dicotyledons, while several studies agree on the presence of characteristic forms from temperate zone deciduous trees. In addition, other studies have reported distinctive phytoliths in conifers including some which may be specific to the pines as they have not yet been found in studies of spruce, juniper, and so on.

Simply stated, the ability to identify plants and plant populations from soil phytolith data will vary substantially among and between botanical groups. Like pollen, phytoliths will provide superlative data in some taxa, be useful in others, and be totally lacking in yet other portions of the plant kingdom. Phytoliths resemble pollen in many other ways as well. Both are produced through normal life processes in living plants, are similar in size range and degree of variation, are produced in enormous quantities, and are exceedingly durable, with the advantage going to phytoliths in this last comparison.

Yet, the two systems do not provide wholly redundant information. Pollen data are derived from wind-vectored pollen rain and tend to reflect macroenvironmental conditions. A substantial portion of a soil phytolith assemblage is derived from decay-in-place residues that remain in place so long as the soil matrix itself remains stable providing considerable information pertaining to microenvironmental conditions. Because pollen is particularly useful in identifying trees but weak in grasses, phytolith data are an ideal complement. Unfortunately, interest in phytolith analysis has been inhibited by a widely held erroneous notion that phytoliths are subject to downward percolation in stable soils. It is true that further soil accumulation will depress a soil layer containing phytoliths downward, but dozens of studies show that the phytolith content in a stable soil horizon stays with that horizon, with only rare and archaeologically irrelevant exceptions (Rovner 1986). Downward percolation is perhaps no less a problem with phytoliths than with diatoms, pollen, or any other microfossil system, but it clearly presents no greater or special problems presumptively disqualifying phytolith data.

In a coordinated study using both phytoliths and pollen, Piperno and Clary (1984) derived a long paleoecological sequence in Panama. Pollen yielded data on some sixteen plant taxa, while phytoliths did likewise for more than forty taxa. However, such numerical comparisons are obviously superficial and create a false competition between pollen and phytolith analyses. The two independent data systems produced impressively consistent agreement in marking respective periods of climatic stability or change and for reconstructing the ecology in greater detail than either system alone provided. The two systems are a potent combination.

## Phytoliths as Microenvironmental Indicators

The number of phytolith studies is still so small that almost every new report deals with a unique cultural or ecological context and problem orientation. In several instances phytolith analysis provided insights, usually unanticipated, into specific microenvironments and cultural events of short duration conducted in circumscribed contexts. These reports provide some guidance in developing research designs for employing phytolith studies in historic site contexts.

One of the more convoluted examples was reported by Ralph Robinson (personal communication, 1987), who consistently found diagnostic palm phytoliths in cultural deposits of the south Texas preceramic age. Since none occurred in culturally sterile control samples, the palm residues had to be the result of a specific pattern of cultural activity. However, palm has not been part of the native Texas flora since the Paleocene, 60 million years ago. Short of absurd models such as preceramic trade in palm fronds between Texas and the Veracruz coast of Mexico or rafting palm trees home from the Caribbean islands, no reasonable explanation existed. In desperation Robinson turned to the source material for grinding stones used in plant processing. It turned out to be a metamorphosed mudstone laid down during the Paleocene. Powdered stone samples produced characteristic palm phytoliths that typically occurred in sites as the result of a specific pattern of cultural activity; namely, the grinding action that ablated the stone itself, releasing preserved 60-million-year-old phytoliths into 5,000-year-old cultural deposits.

A Paleoindian bison kill site in Wyoming produced a more germane but no less convoluted example of phytolith capabilities (Lewis 1981, 1985). Soil samples from the site yielded a high frequency of festucoid tallgrass phytoliths that probably dominated a moist, cool creekside microenvironment. By contrast, phytoliths extracted from a sample taken from beneath the rib cage of one of the animals showed a substantial increase in the frequency of chloridoid (i.e., shortgrass) phytoliths. Clearly, the bison had had a last meal on the dry shortgrass prairie before proceeding to the creek for water where they were dispatched by hunters. The thread of phytolith data stretched further to explain why no wood charcoal suitable for radiocarbon dating was recovered from fire hearths at the site. The phytolith assemblage recovered from fire hearth soil matched that from the stomach contents sample obtained from the bison remains. Undoubtedly, the early hunters had burned buffalo chips, not wood, for fuel.

Folk and Hoops (1982) found high grass phytolith content in an ash deposit adjacent to an iron foundry at the site of Tel Yin'am, Israel. They suggest that this verifies Pliny's observation that ironworkers burned wheat chaff to obtain the high-temperature fires needed for their work. Armitage (1975) extracted phytoliths embedded in the tooth tartar of domestic cattle mandibles to determine the nature of their fodder, and Holloway (personal communication, 1987) has obtained phytoliths from human coprolites, increasing dietary information. Turner and Harrison (1981) found pond lily phytoliths in the sediments of artificially raised fields created by the classic-period Maya at Pulltrouser Swamp, Belize. The Maya either harvested pond lily for use as mulch/compost on their crops or dredged the nutrient-rich swamp mud to create and enrich the raised fields, or both. Agricultural specialists are experimenting with this intensive cropping system today as a means of increasing food production in the region.

Over the years even phytolith quick-scan feasibility studies (Rovner 1983), designed to do no more than determine whether phytolith assemblages occurred in the samples, produced marvelous paleobotanical data with little or no further effort. The first of these I conducted came from the Orinoco River, Venezuela, Parmana Project (Roosevelt 1978) designed to study the introduction of maize agriculture. Ten soil samples from five sites were provided: three single samples respectively, one case of two samples, and five samples from a stratigraphic sequence at the Corozal rock-shelter site. The lowest sample from Corozal and the samples from all the other sites contained no grass phytoliths whatsoever, a fact easy to observe by quick-scan methods because the tedious task of classifying and counting individual particles is avoided when nothing appears in the sample to classify or count. In clear contrast, the next higher Corozal sample had several characteristic grass phytoliths present, and the uppermost three samples were loaded with them. Even lacking the current knowledge of diagnostic maize particles, interpretation was patently obvious without further effort: maize was introduced in level 2, and the staple food source in level 3 and thereafter. The same conclusions had already been obtained from stable isotope assessment of skeletal material from the site. Phytolith data, then, provided independent verification. With all due consideration for differences in confidence levels, information obtained through expensive, highly technical carbon isotope analysis was matched by phytolith analysis using the comparatively inexpensive human eyeball.

A similar instance of phytolith quick-scan information resulted from a study of eleven samples sent to me as part of a cultural impact assessment of three Woodland period sites in Kentucky. Grass particles were present but not very frequent, and all the diagnostic forms belonged to the festucoid class. Because maize produces panicoid phytolith types, the phytoliths provided no evidence of maize agriculture at the sites (and further suggested that no contamination from modern agriculture had occurred). Two samples produced pentagonal/hexagonal-segmented, silicified epidermal sections derived from leaves of deciduous trees, specifically oak, walnut, and butternut. Because the segment size of the archaeological specimens fell well below the range for oak, the leaves could be identified as walnut or butternut. These data supported the extant assessment that the sites were not agricultural base camps but seasonal, special-function camps. In fact, one of the two samples that produced the tree leaf segments came from a context already designated a nutting station.

A study of twelve samples from four Mississippi sites, among many tested during environmental assessments required by the Tennessee-Tombigbee Project, produced such interestingly varied assemblages that the rules of quick-scan study were violated by classifying and counting 200 individual particles per sample (table 18.1). The majority of nongrass phytoliths in all samples indicated an arboreal macroecology, while the presence of phytoliths representing all three grass subtribes suggested interesting possibilities for microecological differentiation. Because festucoid grasses prefer cool-moist environments; panicoid grasses warm-moist, and chloridoid grasses warm-dry, their relative associations occur in very precise contexts.

Table 18.1. Morphological type frequencies of phytoliths in quick-scan analysis of samples from four sites in Mississippi

| Sites | I | | | II | | | | III | | | IV | |
|---|---|---|---|---|---|---|---|---|---|---|---|---|
| Sample | 1 | 2 | 3 | 4 | 5 | 6 | 7 | 8 | 9 | 10 | 11 | 12 |
| **I. Grass** | | | | | | | | | | | | |
| A. Dumbbell | - | 3 | 6 | 2 | 1 | 1 | - | 3 | 2 | 2 | 9 | 9 |
| B. Cross-body | - | - | 1 | - | - | - | - | - | - | - | - | - |
| C. Cap/Trapezoid | - | 2 | 3 | 5 | - | - | - | - | 3 | - | - | 1 |
| D. Sinuous rect. | - | - | 1 | - | - | 1 | - | 1 | - | - | - | - |
| E. Saddle | 1 | 1 | 4 | 1 | 1 | - | - | 1 | - | 2 | 4 | 1 |
| F. Conoid/Pyram | - | - | 2 | - | - | - | - | 2 | 1 | - | - | - |
| G. Elongate | 2 | 4 | 5 | 4 | 1 | 2 | 2 | 1 | - | - | 1 | 3 |
| H. Denticulate | 1 | - | 1 | - | - | 2 | 1 | - | 1 | - | - | - |
| I. Trichome | 1 | 1 | 3 | 1 | 2 | 3 | 3 | - | - | 2 | - | - |
| J. Bulliform | 3 | 3 | - | 2 | 2 | 10 | 25 | - | 2 | 1 | - | - |
| Subtotals | 9 | 14 | 26 | 15 | 7 | 18 | 32 | 8 | 9 | 7 | 14 | 14 |
| **II. Nongrass** | | | | | | | | | | | | |
| K. Globules | 43 | 65 | 54 | 45 | 72 | 57 | 80 | 52 | 58 | 63 | 58 | 42 |
| L. Irr. aggreg. | 9 | 9 | - | 3 | 2 | 6 | 4 | 8 | 8 | 8 | - | 17 |
| M. Blk. partic. | 55 | 38 | 56 | 63 | 72 | 28 | 30 | 54 | 44 | 51 | 58 | 61 |
| N. Ang. plate | 34 | 28 | 9 | 15 | 7 | 26 | 22 | 17 | 11 | 19 | 36 | 15 |
| O. Cell/vesicle | - | 1 | 3 | 5 | 2 | - | - | - | 2 | - | - | - |
| P. Leaf epiderm | - | 2 | 7 | 2 | 2 | 7 | - | 2 | 2 | 2 | 6 | 8 |
| Q. Stoma guard | 1 | - | 5 | 1 | 2 | 1 | 2 | - | 1 | 1 | - | 1 |
| R. Jigsaw cell | 2 | - | - | - | - | 5 | 8 | 3 | 1 | 2 | - | 4 |
| S. Hair cell | - | 4 | 2 | 1 | 2 | 1 | - | - | 1 | - | 1 | - |
| T. Orng. part. | 6 | 8 | 5 | 12 | 8 | 28 | 14 | 33 | 26 | 7 | 8 | 18 |
| U. Antler | 2 | - | - | - | - | - | - | 3 | - | - | 2 | 1 |
| V. Irr. rod | 3 | 5 | 5 | 5 | 3 | 2 | 3 | 3 | 1 | 2 | 3 | 1 |
| W. Disc. | 4 | 1 | 4 | 3 | - | 2 | 1 | 2 | 5 | 3 | 2 | 1 |

| | | 1 | 2 | 3 | 4 | 5 | 6 | 7 | 8 | 9 | 10 | 11 | 12 |
|---|---|---|---|---|---|---|---|---|---|---|---|---|---|
| X. | Tracheid | 15 | 1 | 7 | 13 | 6 | 8 | 3 | 6 | 5 | 7 | 3 | 5 |
| Y. | Polyhedron | 13 | 16 | 2 | 1 | 6 | 6 | - | 6 | 17 | 21 | 8 | 8 |
| Z. | Elliptical | 2 | - | - | 1 | - | 1 | - | 1 | 2 | - | - | 1 |
| X'. | Lg. rect. | 1 | 3 | 3 | 9 | 6 | - | - | - | 2 | 4 | 1 | 1 |
| Y'. | Lg. square | 1 | 3 | 12 | 6 | 3 | 1 | 1 | 2 | 5 | 3 | - | 3 |
| Z'. | Misc. | 1 | 1 | - | - | - | 3 | - | 2 | - | - | - | - |
| | Subtotals | 191 | 186 | 174 | 185 | 193 | 182 | 168 | 192 | 191 | 193 | 186 | 186 |

Totals (n=200, all samples)

III. <u>Other Biosilicates</u>

| | | 1 | 2 | 3 | 4 | 5 | 6 | 7 | 8 | 9 | 10 | 11 | 12 |
|---|---|---|---|---|---|---|---|---|---|---|---|---|---|
| a. | Sp. spicule | 1 | - | 1 | 1 | 1 | 1 | 1 | - | - | - | - | - |
| b. | Diatom | - | - | 1 | - | - | 1 | - | - | - | - | - | - |

As anticipated, the grass phytolith distribution provided very tantalizing indications of microecological differences between and within the sites. For instance, comparison of two categories, Saddle (a chloridoid type indicating dryness; see table 18.1, part I.E) and Bulliform (not assignable to subfamily taxon but representing mesophyll water storage cells that silicify under high moisture conditions; see table 18.1, part I.J), yields interesting and consistent results. Note that the grossly disproportionate presence of water cell phytoliths in Site II samples 6 and 7 occur with no dry saddle forms. Where saddles are high in Site I sample 3 and Site IV sample 11, no bulliform types occur. The distribution of the nongrass phytolith category Jigsaw (see table 18.1, part II.R) lends further support. Interlocking epidermal leaf tissue segments, shaped like jigsaw puzzle pieces, occur in willow and soft maple trees, which favor high moisture regimes. Note that a markedly disproportionate frequency of this type occurs in both samples notable for high bulliform frequency. Jigsaw types are absent in the two samples with the highest frequency of dry saddle forms.

Clearly microecological regimes cannot be reconstructed using data derived from an average of three soil samples per site. Moisture regimes cannot be based on an analysis of categories most of whose frequency levels are 2 percent and less. Moreover, cultural activities inherently displace, combine, eliminate, mix, and otherwise bias materials from distinct microenvironments in specific site contexts. However, in such a preliminary feasibility study this is all quite irrelevant. Because the critical question in a quick-scan study asks if phytolith data can yield significant information bearing on the botanical fabric of the site and associated cultural behaviors, the answer is an unequivocal yes. Any number of further phytolith studies based on appropriate sampling and counting strategies can be implemented within an overall multidisciplinary research design.

In my most recent study, quick-scan phytolith analysis provided insights into a range of cultural activities within the microenvironmental mosaic of the Alta Toquima village site in Nevada. The site is located on a mountaintop plateau above 3,000 meters elevation. It is a cold, treeless, windswept site used today as an overgrazed summer meadow for sheep. Until approximately A.D. 1000 the area had supported a long sequence of hunters who established small, temporary seasonal hunting camps. Alta Toquima village, representing a completely different cultural pattern, consists of three clusters of circular stone house foundations and a number of scattered structures. These are situated on a low ridge overlooking a small plateau.

Significant associations of grinding stones and other household artifacts indicated seasonal use by whole families or related family groups engaged in significant amounts of plant processing. Neither pollen nor flotation yielded adequate information on the ethnobotany of the site. Soil samples were then provided for quick-scan phytolith study as a possible source of paleobotanical data, specifically to determine if detection of grass phytoliths could support a late summer grass seed harvesting model for the site.

Ultimately forty-eight samples were studied, including fourteen from features, thirteen from interior house floors, seven from cultural middens, nine from exterior locations, and five from the peripheral zones adjacent to the site. The diversity of contexts proved critical because it provided the comparisons, contrasts, and consistencies needed to interpret the phytolith data for the site as a whole.

Given the grass hypothesis and the contemporary ecology of the site, the presence of pine phytoliths in 100 percent of the samples was quite a surprise. Moreover, in terms of relative frequencies, pine phytoliths were consistently frequent in exterior samples, moderate to rare in interior floor samples, and typically rare in feature samples. Grass phytoliths, overwhelming assignable to high-altitude festucoid grasses, were distributed in an almost completely reverse pattern; that is, mostly absent or rare in exterior samples, absent to rare in house floors, but moderate to frequent in the majority of feature samples.

With lots of pine outside the houses, but grasses found only in garbage pits, the inescapable conclusion is that the site was located in a pine grove. Given the strong, prevailing winds in the area, even in summer, such a microecological selection is obvious. It also indicates the extent to which a sawmill which began operating in 1876 impacted the local ecology.

Five peripheral samples to the north, northeast, east, and west of the site were particularly instructive. The north and east samples, in the direction of the plateau area of the peak, contained substantial amounts of both pine and grass phytoliths, as did an exterior sample from the northeast house cluster. This suggests that open grass meadow existed to the east and north of the site, interfingering with the margins of the pine grove.

A peripheral sample to the west was the only one of the total tested to include a small number of chloridoid class phytoliths among a much higher frequency of festucoid forms. Because chloridoid grasses prefer warm, dry biomes, there is simply no chance that chloridoid grasses grew anywhere near the altitude of the site. Most probably the prevailing winds, from the west, scoured dust and soil of lower elevations, lifting it to the western edge of the pine grove where the dust was dropped, including phytolith particles of lower-elevation grasses. With the right kind of sampling strategy, it seems likely that the edge of the pine grove could be traced around the site circumference within an error factor measured in meters.

Even the distribution of diatoms, although very rare, added supporting information. Although diatoms are not phytoliths in the sense used here, they are biogenetic silica particles of microscopic size that respond in the same way to phytolith extraction methods. In all cases where diatoms were observed, grass phytoliths were heavy. The diatom types are those which often occur as sessile forms on the basal stalks of grasses and other plants growing at creekside locations. This supports the model that grasses were brought into the site for whatever cultural purposes and deposited selectively in trash pits. The absence of grass phytoliths in house floor and interior samples indicates that Alta Toquima residents kept their houses tidy and swept and did not use thatch in walls or roofs or for bedding, although here again, insufficient sampling is a major note of caution. The grass seed harvesting hypothesis clearly is supported by the phytolith data. Pine nuts of the limber pine, which grows in the area, may also have provided a major food source, but this is not specifically evident in the phytolith data. An initial test of limber pine nut shells and cone tissue yielded unsatisfactory results.

At this point a concluding statement is usually offered, but phytolith analysis is too young and still maturing to offer conclusions. However, phytolith data are powerful by themselves, and often more so in combination with other data systems. They do lend themselves to the study of microecological differences, to the identification of many botanical taxons with a high degree of precision, and to the intensive investigation of narrowly circumscribed contexts in tightly defined time periods. From my prehistorian's perspective, this is what classical and historic archaeology deal with.

## Postscript

Since the presentation of the original version of this chapter at the Landscape Conference, quick-scan phytolith analysis has been conducted on soil samples from three eastern colonial-period historic sites, two of which are discussed in this volume. William Kelso provided soil samples from Monticello, Virginia, Nicholas Luccketti provided samples from Bacon's Castle in Virginia, and J. Clauser provided samples from Bethabara, North Carolina.

Phytoliths were well preserved and abundant at all three sites. Both grass and nongrass taxa (e.g., conifers and deciduous trees) were observed. Importantly, the phytolith content in specific samples and contexts within each site respectively varied enormously. Although specific interpretation is not yet possible, microecological and/or distributional differences in plant populations and locations are clearly indicated.

Taxonomically, festucoid grass phytoliths dominated the assemblages at all three sites, to the near exclusion of panicoid phytoliths, for instance, at Monticello. Panicoid grasses are a major part of the natural assemblages for this region as a whole; indeed, they are often the dominant grass group. Thus, even at this preliminary stage, phytolith analysis is almost certainly elucidating cultural patterns that modified the landscape at each of these sites. The most obvious explanation is a deliberate and common pattern of the introduction of European festucoid grasses for use in lawns and meadows at American colonial-period sites. Further study, especially a systematic inventory of phytolith populations from reference species of relevant European and American grasses, should provide verification.

The preliminary results from these three sites were clear, consistent, and significant. This testing strongly supports the contention that phytolith analysis is a uniquely powerful system for the archaeobotanical study of tightly defined contexts in historic-period landscapes.

## References Cited

Armitage, P. L. 1975. The extraction and identification of opal phytoliths from the teeth of ungulates. *Journal of Archaeological Science* 2(3):187-97.

Folk, R. L. and G. K. Hoops. 1982. An early Iron-Age layer of glass made from plants at Tel Yin'am, Israel. *Journal of Field Archaeology* 9(4):455-66.

Fredlund, G. G., W. C. Johnson, and W. Dort, Jr. 1985. A preliminary analysis of opal phytoliths from the Eustis ash pit, Frontier County, Nebraska. *TER-QUA Symposium Series, Nebraska Academy of Sciences* 1:147-62.

Lewis, R. O. 1981. Use of opal phytoliths in paleoenvironmental reconstruction. *Journal of Ethnobiology* 1(1):175-181.

----. 1985. Phytolith analysis from the McKean site, Wyoming. In *McKean/Middle Plains Archaic: Current Research*, ed. M. Kornfeld and L. C. Todd, pp. 45-51. Occasional Papers on Wyoming Archaeology No. 4.

Livingstone, D. A., and W. D. Clayton. 1980. An altitudinal cline in tropical African grass floras and its paleoecological significance. *Quaternary Research* 13(3):392-402.

Netolitzky, N. 1914. Die Hirse aus antiken Funden. *Sitzungsberichte der Keisliche Akademie der Wissenschaften Mathematish-Naturwissenschaftliche Klasse* 123(6):725-59.

Pearsall, D. M. 1978. Phytolith analysis of archaeological soils: Evidence for maize cultivation in formative Ecuador. *Science* 199(4325):177-78.

----. and D. R. Piperno. 1986. Antiquity of maize cultivation in Ecuador: Summary and re-evaluation of the evidence. Paper presented at the 51st annual meeting of the Society for American Archaeology, New Orleans.

Piperno, D. R. 1983. A comparison and differentiation of phytoliths from maize (Zea mays L.) and wild grasses: Use of morphological criteria. Paper presented at the 48th annual meeting of the Society for American Archaeology.

----. 1984. A comparison and differentiation of phytoliths from maize (Zea mays L.) and wild grasses: Use of morphological criteria. *American Antiquity* 49(2):361-83.

----. 1986. A survey of phytolith production and taxonomy in nongraminaceous plants: Implications for paleoecological reconstructions. In *Plant opal phytolith analysis in archaeology and paleoecology*, ed. I. Rovner, pp. 35-40. Proceedings of the 1984 Phytolith Research Workshop, North Carolina State University, Occasional Papers No. 1 of the Phytolitharien. Raleigh.

----. and K. H. Clary. 1984. Early plant use and cultivation in the Santa Marta Basin, Panama: Data from phytoliths and pollen. In *Recent advances in Isthmian archaeology*, ed. F. Lange, pp. 85-121. British Archaeological Reports. Oxford.

Robinson, R. L. 1979a. Biosilica analysis: paleoenvironmental reconstruction of 41LL254. In *An intensive archaeological survey of Enchanted Rock state natural area*, Appendix III, by C. Assad and D. R. Potter, pp. 125-44. Center for Archaeological Research Survey Report 84. San Antonio.

----. 1979b. Biosilica and climatic change at 41GD21 and 41GD21A. In *Archaeological investigations of two prehistoric sites on the Coleto Creek drainage, Goliad County, Texas, Appendix IV*, by G. L. Evans, Murray and H. G. Uecker, pp. 102-13. Center for Archaeological Research Survey Report 69. San Antonio.

Roosevelt, A. 1978. La Gruta: An early tropical forest community of the middle Orinoco Basin. In *Unidad y Variedades Ensayos en Homenaje a José M. Cruxent*. IVIC Publication, Centro de Estudios Avanzados. Caracas.

Rosen, A. M. 1983. Phytoliths and marginal agriculture in the Chalcolithic period of the Negev Desert, Israel. Paper presented at the 48th annual meeting of the Society for American Archaeology, Pittsburgh.

Rovner, I. 1971. Potential of opal phytoliths for use in paleoecological reconstruction. *Quaternary Research* 1(3):345-59.

----. 1983. Applications of phytolith analysis in cultural resource management, site survey, testing, and significance. Paper presented at the 48th annual meeting of the Society for American Archaeology, Pittsburgh.

----. 1986. Vertical movement of phytoliths in stable soil: A non-issue. In *Plant opal phytolith analysis in archaeology and paleoecology*, ed. I. Rovner, pp. 23-30. Proceedings of the 1984 Phytolith Research Workshop, North Carolina State University, Occasional Papers No. 1 of the Phytolitharien. Raleigh.

Russ, J. C., and I. Rovner. 1987. Stereological verification of *Zea* phytolith taxonomy. *Phytolitharien Newsletter* 4(3):10-18.

Tack, M. 1986. Phytolith analysis as corroborative physical evidence. In *Plant opal phytolith analysis in archaeology and paleoecology*, ed. I. Rovner, pp. 129-32. Proceedings of the 1984 Phytolith Research Workshop, North Carolina State University, Occasional Papers No. 1 of the Phytolitharien. Raleigh.

Turner, B. L., and P. D. Harrison. 1981. Prehistoric raised-field agriculture in the Maya lowlands. *Science* 213(4506):399-405.

Twiss, P. C., E. Suess, and R. M. Smith. 1969. Morphological classification of grass phytoliths. *Soil Science Society of American Proceedings* 33(1):109-15.

Watanabe, N. 1968. Spodographic evidence of rice from prehistoric Japan. *Journal of the Faculty of Science of the University of Tokyo* 3(3):217-35.

----. 1970. A spodographic analysis of millet from prehistoric Japan. *Journal of the Faculty of Science, University of Tokyo* 3(5):357-84.

# EPILOGUE

## Thad W. Tate

This volume of essays strikes one who is not a trained archaeologist as a compelling illustration of both the promise of garden and landscape archaeology and the unusual problems that its practitioners face in the recovery of evidence. The promise is fulfilled in a series of reports on specific sites, predominantly from the early American period and from the Chesapeake region, which are set against work by classical archaeologists on ancient sites. The individual authors provide informative accounts of work that in almost every instance is still in progress. The essays incorporate a great deal of new information, much of it not obtainable from surviving documentary sources alone--a point particularly well illustrated by Kelso's recovery of Thomas Jefferson's garden at Monticello. But the chapters open up larger social and cultural themes as well.

Virtually all the archaeologists involved in these investigations are quick to recognize the unusual difficulties they encounter in finding sufficient evidence about land use in the past and in interpreting it adequately--a consequence not only of the subsequent human interference with the landscape that plagues all archaeologists but also in this instance of the acute effects of the operation of natural processes themselves in highly impermanent plant life. The final group of essays in the volume, devoted to a discussion of landscape science, addresses the resultant problems of technique and methodology with great success, one by recounting the practical experience of recovering two centuries of landscape change at Morven in New Jersey and the other two by providing a succinct account of the general application of two important techniques, pollen analysis and plant opal phytolith analysis, respectively. In a sense, they might well constitute an introduction to the volume rather than a conclusion, but in retrospect most readers will probably gain more from reading these chapters after they have come to understand the variety of questions raised by work on many of the sites described in the earlier chapters.

The substantive essays, comprising the first three sections of the volume, derive their collective strength, too, not from a rigid analysis of a single approach to the practice of garden and landscape archaeology or from a single interpretive overview but, on the contrary, from the number of differing perspectives and examples they afford. In the end, however, there is focus and coherence in the whole body of work. Too, the juxtaposition of classical and early American archaeology proves a surprisingly useful device, through which a number of common themes emerge from two seemingly disparate areas of archaeological investigation.

Given the apparent intent to be inclusive and to record the experience gained on a variety of sites by employing a number of modes of investigation, it is not surprising that the themes that emerge most clearly from the whole group of essays might be thought of as a series of spectra rather than fixed points of reference. They serve particularly well, then, as a means of weighing a range of possibilities. The most obvious of these, the contrast between urban and rural sites, is inherent in the organization of the volume. One word of caution may be appropriate here, however; it does seem possible to view the two capital towns of the Chesapeake, Annapolis and Williamsburg, from the perspective of landscape and gardening, as more nearly an extension of the countryside into a town setting than as genuinely urban locations of the order of Philadelphia or Boston. That possibility, if anything, enhances the value of considering the rural-urban theme along a spectrum rather than as dichotomous.

Other interesting themes of this sort also emerge, if less explicitly, from the essays. Among them are a progression from the microlandscape of the individual garden to the macrolandscape of whole countrysides or larger urban settings, a somewhat related contrast between major private gardens and estates and communal spaces or common landscapes shaped by a wider variety of the population, and an interplay between utilitarian and aesthetic impulses in shaping the land.

The volume itself undoubtedly remains neutral on how the meaning of such themes might be interpreted, although individual authors do not in some cases. Those essays that, for example, examine more extended landscapes, with an interest in how their spaces were shaped and defined by various social groups from slaves to urban workers to great planters and other elites, argue in some degree from a more social view of landscape, one that provides a source of understanding of the whole culture.

While that approach may be at least implicitly critical of investigations of individual elite gardens, they too may well have their place in understanding the wider culture. Although none of the authors elaborate this point, such gardens can be seen, for example, as standing at the cutting edge of the recovery in the American colonies of an increasing aesthetic appreciation of cultivated and ornamented land, once the colonists moved from the initial conquest of raw and undeveloped land toward a cleared, tamed landscape in which European pastoral values might reassert themselves. This is not to say that late eighteenth-century and early nineteenth-century gardens and other cultivated spaces did not continue to reflect strong utilitarian purposes as well, but there was a process at work here of which the gardens of the elite are often a clear and early indicator.

But these are examples of the kinds of analyses that readers can draw for themselves from this wide-ranging collection of essays. The authors have made that possible by providing such rich and varied examples of work already accomplished that they make synthesis and broader interpretation of the results much more achievable and at the same time lay down a sounder basis for the fieldwork that remains to be done.

# INDEX

# CONTRIBUTORS

*Louise E. Akerson*, Archaeological Curator, Baltimore Center for Urban Archaeology, 802 Lombard Street, Baltimore, Maryland 21202.

*Mary C. Beaudry*, Department of Archaeology, Boston University, 675 Commonwealth Avenue, Boston, Massachusetts 02215.

*Marley R. Brown*, Director, Department of Archaeological Research, The Colonial Williamsburg Foundation, Williamsburg, Virginia 23187.

*Joseph Coleman Carter*, Department of Classics, University of Texas at Austin, Austin, Texas 78712.

*Elizabeth Anderson Comer*, Director of Domestic Tourism, Office of Tourist Development, State of Maryland, Department of Economics and Employment Development, 217 E. Redwood Street, Baltimore, Maryland 21202.

*James Deetz*, University of California, Berkeley, R. H. Lowie Museum of Anthropology, 103 Kroeber Hall, Berkeley, California 94720.

*Stephen L. Dyson*, Department of Classics, Wesleyan University, Middletown, Connecticut 06457.

*Michael Hammond*, Director, Historic Old Salem, Drawer F, Salem Station, Winston-Salem, North Carolina 27108.

*Carter L. Hudgins*, Center for Historic Preservation, Mary Washington College, Fredericksburg, Virginia 22401.

*Wilhelmina F. Jashemski*, Professor Emerita, Department of History, University of Maryland, College Park, Maryland 20742.

*William M. Kelso*, Director of Archaeology, Thomas Jefferson Memorial Foundation, P.O. Box 316, Charlottesville, Virginia 22902.

*Mark P. Leone*, Department of Anthropology, University of Maryland, College Park, Maryland 20742.

*Nicholas Luccketti*, Director, James River Institute for Archaeology, Inc., Yeardley House, Jamestown, Virginia 23081.

*James J. Miller*, State Archaeologist and Chief, Bureau of Archaeological Research, Florida Division of Historical Resources, The Capitol, Tallahassee, Florida 32399-0250.

*Naomi F. Miller*, Museum Applied Science Center for Archaeology, University Museum, University of Pennsylvania, Philadelphia, Pennsylvania 19104.

*Rachel Most*, Department of Anthropology, University of Virginia, Charlottesville, Virginia 22903.

*Stephen A. Mrozowski*, Department of Anthropology, University of Massachusetts, Boston, Massachusetts 02125.

*Gary Norman*, 933 Francis Road, Glen Allen, Virginia 23229.

*Barbara Paca*, Historic Annapolis, Inc., 194 Prince George Street, Annapolis, Maryland 21401.

*Dolores Piperno*, Museum Applied Science Center for Archaeology, University Museum, University of Pennsylvania, Philadelphia, Pennsylvania 19104.

*Irwin Rovner*, Department of Sociology, Anthropology and Social Work, North Carolina State University, Raleigh, North Carolina 27695.

*Patricia M. Samford*, Department of Archaeological Research, The Colonial Williamsburg Foundation, Williamsburg, Virginia 23187.

*Douglas Sanford*, Resident Archaeologist, Historic Gordonsville, Inc., P.O. Box 610, Locust Grove, Virginia 22508.

*James Schoenwetter*, Department of Anthropology, Arizona State University, Tempe, Arizona 85287.

*Paul A. Shackel*, Department of Anthropology, University of Maryland, College Park, Maryland 20742.

*Gary Shapiro*, Bureau of Archaeological Research, Florida Division of Historical Resources, The Capitol, Tallahassee, Florida 32399-0250 (deceased).

*Thad W. Tate*, Director, Commonwealth Center for the Study of American Culture, College of William and Mary, Williamsburg, Virginia 23185.

*Dell Upton*, Department of Architecture, University of California, Berkeley, California 94720.

*Carmen A. Weber*, Archaeologist, Philadelphia Historical Commission, 1313 City Hall Annex, Philadelphia, Pennsylvania 19107.

*Anne Yentsch*, Historic Annapolis, Inc., 194 Prince George Street, Annapolis, Maryland 21401.